MW01128994

Counting Like a State

Counting Like a State

How Intergovernmental Partnerships Shaped the 2020 US Census

Philip Rocco

University Press of Kansas

This book will be made open access within three years of publication thanks to Path to Open, a program developed in partnership between JSTOR, the American Council of Learned Societies (ACLS), University of Michigan Press, and the University of North Carolina Press to bring about equitable access and impact for the entire scholarly community, including authors, researchers, libraries, and university presses around the world. Learn more at https://about.jstor.org/path-to-open/.

Published by the University Press of Kansas (Lawrence, Kansas 66045), which was organized by the Kansas Board of Regents and is operated and funded by Emporia State University, Fort Hays State University, Kansas State University, Pittsburg State University, the University of Kansas, and Wichita State University.

Library of Congress Cataloging-in-Publication Data is available

Names: Rocco, Philip, author.
Title: Counting like a state : how intergovernmental partnerships shaped the 2020 US census / Philip Rocco.
Description: Kansas : University Press of Kansas, 2025 | Includes bibliographical references and index.
Identifiers: LCCN 2024042815 (print) | LCCN 2024042816 (ebook)
ISBN 9780700638758 (cloth)
ISBN 9780700639687 (paperback)
ISBN 9780700638765 (ebook)
Subjects: LCSH: United States—Census, 2020. | Demographic surveys—United States—Political aspects. | Intergovernmental cooperation—United States. | BISAC: POLITICAL SCIENCE / Public Affairs & Administration | POLITICAL SCIENCE / American Government / Local
Classification: LCC HA201.14 .R63 2025 (print) | LCC HA201.14 (ebook) | DDC 317.3—dc23/eng/20250117
LC record available at https://lccn.loc.gov/2024042815.
LC ebook record available at https://lccn.loc.gov/2024042816.

British Library Cataloguing-in-Publication Data is available.

For the uncounted

CONTENTS

TABLES

FIGURES

ACKNOWLEDGMENTS

While it would be impossible to give a full accounting of all those who helped me complete this book, there are several people who merit special recognition for their roles in bringing the project to fruition. David Congdon, my editor at the University Press of Kansas, was a champion of this project from the instant he heard about it and continued to offer encouragement and thoughtful advice throughout the many stages of the writing process. David also recruited two exceptional reviewers, Margo Anderson and an anonymous census researcher, who provided both penetrating insights on the entire project and comments on micro-level details that dramatically improved the quality of the final product. At several critical junctures, comments from Dan Mallinson, Deborah Stone, and an audience at the Milwaukee Area Political Science Seminar helped to push the manuscript along. Don Kettl and Scott Greer were kind enough to serve as manuscript readers, supplying me with useful comments, corrections, and questions on the draft text. Financial support for the project came from Marquette University's Way Klingler Faculty Development Program and the American Political Science Association. Thanks are also due to Oxford University Press for granting permission to use material from my article "Counting Like a State: The Politics of Intergovernmental Partnerships in the 2020 Census" (*Political Science Quarterly* 138, no. 2 (2023): 189–216).

This book has its origins in a series of interviews I conducted with dozens of brilliant yet humble people inside and outside of government whose work is vital to the production of an accurate census. While their quotations are anonymized, they deserve greater recognition and thanks than I could hope to provide here. I also met several generous census experts whose advice helped me to distinguish the signal from noise. Bill O'Hare read and commented on the entire manuscript, sharing his deep knowledge of differential undercounts and disclosure avoidance procedures. Additionally, Ditas Katague and Jan Vink provided thought-provoking comments on technical and organizational details for several chapters. In the middle of revising the manuscript, Jenny Trinitapoli and Rebecca Schut invited me to present parts of the book to the University of Chicago's Demography

Workshop, whose participants offered a wealth of useful suggestions. A debt of gratitude is also owed to the Census Bureau's Office of Congressional and Intergovernmental Affairs for allowing me to present some of my findings at a 2023 roundtable, which helped to sharpen my thinking about the policy implications of my work.

Marquette University's Political Science Department has been a lively and collegial environment for planning and conducting this research. Lowell Barrington encouraged me to pursue my teaching and research on the politics of numbers at a time when the subject appeared hopelessly niche. Rich Friman and Risa Brooks also gave me confidence that there was merit, and perhaps even real practical value, in carving out this intellectual space. As the project evolved, Sam Harshner became a brother in arms, providing me with frequent reminders about the kind of work that really matters, from which I hope I have not strayed too far in these pages. Paul Nolette, my coeditor at *Publius: The Journal of Federalism*, continues to be an incomparable partner in thinking about the study of intergovernmental politics. In countless conversations over coffee or lunch, or in the hallway, other Marquette colleagues have helped to push this research in more interesting and useful directions than it would otherwise have gone. I thank especially Julia Azari, Amber Wichowsky, Noelle Brigden, Mark Berlin, Sue Giaimo, Amanda Heideman, Karen Hoffman, Monica Unda-Gutierrez, Brian Palmer-Rubin, Jessica Rich, Barry McCormick, Mai Truong, Duane Swank, and Pat Sobkowski. Throughout the project, Sahvana Williams has provided superb administrative support. Outside the department, I have also been lucky to know—luckier still to learn from—so many kindred spirits. Among others, I thank Mike McCarthy, Sonia Barnes, Ben Pladek, Kristen Foster, Max Gray, Sergio González, Elaine Spiller, Scott Reid, Paul Gasser, Gerry Canavan, Rosemary Stuart, Astrida Kaugars, Martin St. Maurice, and Chris Stockdale.

My students at Marquette also deserve a special mention here. In the fall of 2017, I began offering an upper-level seminar on the politics of numbers. The intrepid first cohort of students in that seminar brought a level of gravity and intensity to the subject of official statistics that floored me. As my syllabus has morphed over the years, my Marquette students have continued to leave an imprint on how I think and write about numbers. Additionally, I could not have completed this project without the expert research assistance of Alex Wagner, Kaitlyn Bross, Robert Dietterick, Sarah Beck, and Will Monk.

The community of social scientists who supported this work stretches far beyond the shores of Lake Michigan. Most of all, I thank the late Dave Robertson, whose intelligence and generosity ought to serve as a model to scholars everywhere and whose kindness I will forever miss. Chris Ansell, Todd LaPorte, Eric Schickler, and Sean Farhang have left an indelible mark on my thinking about the politics of public organizations, and their influence can no doubt be felt in these pages. Over the years, I have also been fortunate enough to have sterling collaborators—including Sara Chatfield, Chloe Thurston, Andrew S. Kelly, Ann Keller, Daniel Béland, Alex Waddan, Mariely Lopez-Santana, Jake Grumbach, Laura Bucci, Mike Dichio, Zac Callen, and Amanda Kass—whose curiosity and ingenuity have made doing this work so much more pleasurable.

There is simply no way of tallying the debts I have incurred to three steadfast friends, whose ideas, provocations, and senses of adventure can be found between the lines of this book. When I write, I often feel as if I am picking up on threads of conversations David Reinecke and I have had about the politics of science for nearly twenty years now. With each page of the *Federal Register* I read, I can hear the voice of Gerard Leone, making an objection, demanding a clarification, or simply taking delight in an abstruse phrase. And when I cast my eyes upon a reference map showing a sprawling metropolis, I am transported in thought to any number of excursions with Peter Ekman, who first introduced me to the phantom cities of California.

It would have been equally impossible to write a book about the census without friends who forced me to leave my office and stop thinking about it. Weekends in Door County—with Emma, Justin, and Jonah in tow—have approximated the sublime. Walks through Milwaukee with Andrew saved me during the darkest days of the pandemic, as did hundreds of exchanges with Artie, Bea, Jake, Abby, Aubrey, and Garrett. Not a day of writing this book has passed without thoughts of Jack, who left us far too soon.

No person has done more to bring the project over the finish line than my wife, Allyson. Even during the most tedious and profitless stretches of this work, she has replenished my mind and revived my senses with her love, her art, and her singularly joyful approach to life. And while our cats, Nicos and Norm, will never appear on our household's census questionnaire, their near-constant affection has made our home the perfect place to complete this book.

The pages that follow are filled with stories of people inside and outside of government whose labors, however unsung or unappreciated, make democracy work as best it can in conditions that are best described as peril-ous. If my concern for these people and their work has a source, it is my par-ents, Bart and Val. Among much else to their credit, their lives have served as a reminder that one's willingness to fight for the needs of others is, in the end, the only thing that counts.

ABBREVIATIONS

ACO	Area Census Office
ACS	American Community Survey
APA	Administrative Procedure Act
BERT	Base Evaluation and Research Team
CBAMS	Census Barriers, Attitudes, and Motivators Study
CCC	Complete Count Committee
CNSTAT	Committee on National Statistics
CPEP	Community Partnership and Engagement Program
CQR	Count Question Resolution program
CVAP	Citizen Voting-Age Population
DAS	Disclosure Avoidance System
DOJ	US Department of Justice
FCCP	Funders' Committee for Civic Participation
FMAP	Federal Medical Assistance Percentage
FSCPE	Federal-State Cooperative for Population Estimates
GAO	Government Accountability Office
GIS	Geographic Information System
GQE	Group Quarters Enumeration
GSS–I	Geographic Support System Initiative
LUCA	Local Update of Census Addresses
MAF	Master Address File
NPP	National Partnership Program
NRFU	Nonresponse Follow-Up
PCGQR	Post Census Group Quarters Review
RCC	Regional Census Center
SCCC	State Complete Count Commission
SDC	State Data Center
SNAP	Supplemental Nutrition Assistance Program
TANF	Temporary Assistance to Needy Families
TIGER	Topologically Integrated Geographic Encoding and Referencing System

INTRODUCTION

Steven Dillingham—clad in a parka and carrying a shoulder bag emblazoned with the logo of the US Census Bureau—is riding in the back seat of a snowmobile across the frozen landscape of Toksook Bay, Alaska (population 863). It is January 21, 2020, months before most Americans will complete their 2020 Census questionnaires, and the director of the Census Bureau is participating in the ritual—now more than a century old—of conducting the first census interviews in remote Alaska. In January, the ground is still frozen there, allowing for slightly easier transportation to the most isolated villages. With an early start, enumerators can also get a more accurate count of the area's residents before they decamp to hunting and fishing grounds in the spring.

The entire affair provides a dramatic bit of public relations for the Census Bureau (see figure 0.1).[1] Enumerators arrive via bush planes and dog sleds, reinforcing an image core to the organization's public identity: the tireless census taker who will not be deterred from counting everyone "once, only once, and in the right place."

Yet if the ritual of remote Alaska enumeration is intended to focus attention on the Census Bureau, a look behind the scenes illustrates the profound influence of local communities on what is often thought to be the exclusive domain of the federal government. Soon after Dillingham arrives, residents of Toksook Bay mark the occasion with a traditional Yup'ik dancing ceremony. One of the dancers is Lizzie Chimiugak Nenguryarr, who has just celebrated her ninetieth birthday and will be the first person counted in 2020. But Alaskan communities' participation in the census goes far deeper than the celebration. One month earlier at Anchorage's Alaska Native Heritage Center, a group of twenty-five people—representing Gwich'in, Iñupiaq, Yup'ik, and Koyukon cultures—met to translate census questionnaires into seven Native Alaskan languages (see figure 0.2). This involved intensive dialogue between speakers and language experts, who worked to create language for census terms that are not easily rendered in Iñupiaq or

Figure 0.1: Census Bureau Director Steven Dillingham (rear) on a snowmobile in Toksook Bay, Alaska. Source: US Census Bureau.

Denaakk'e.[2] Actions like these, as much as any visit from Census Bureau personnel, are vital to producing an accurate count of the remote Alaska population.

While the act of census taking is often associated with what political scientist James Scott refers to as the high-modernist goal of "seeing like a state"—centralizing, standardizing, and homogenizing knowledge about a country—this book makes the case that the production of the United States Census relies critically on *partnerships* between officials at multiple levels of government.[3] Though not formally responsible for census taking, state and local officials, as well as leaders of nongovernmental organizations, are integral to the implementation of the decennial count in several ways. On the one hand, the Census Bureau deliberately involves subnational governments in the process of mapping out where to count residents, mobilizing members of historically undercounted communities to participate in the

Figure 0.2: Hishinlai' Peter (left), Amaya Shaw, and Mary Fields work on translating census education materials into Gwich'in at the Alaska Native Heritage Center, December 12, 2019. Source: Tripp Crouse, KNBA.

census, and ensuring the accuracy and usability of census data. Indeed, the evidence in this book shows that bureau officials are often highly aware of the value of effective partnerships to carry out the important work of counting a complex, far-flung, and growing population. Not all the intergovernmental interactions surrounding the census are harmonious ones, however. As we will see, state and local governments form coalitions to advocate for changes to current census operations, testifying before Congress and filing lawsuits in federal courts.

Yet whether their actions are cooperative or conflictual, state and local officials have good reasons to participate in a task more commonly associated with the image of the federal "census taker." Among other things, census population counts influence each state's seat share in the House of Representatives and therefore its share of votes for president and vice president in the Electoral College. The margins for winning or losing these seats can be quite narrow: After the 2020 Census, the state of New York lost a congressional seat by a margin of only eighty-nine people.[4] Population data also influences how trillions of dollars in federal and state aid are distributed to communities around the country. When a state's population is undercounted by even 1 percent, it jeopardizes funding for vital programs like Medicaid, which provides health insurance to one in five Americans.[5] The consequences of census undercounts are significant—especially in states with large so-called hard-to-count populations. In 2020, many state and local officials felt especially motivated to devote resources toward assuring a complete count of their populations, given unprecedented implementation challenges and controversies at the federal level. Even prior to the COVID-19 pandemic, the Census Bureau confronted a perfect storm of low public trust, numerous operational challenges, and deliberate efforts by the Trump administration to minimize census participation in communities with large numbers of undocumented residents.[6]

Over the last five decades, the set of relationships that constitute what I call *census federalism* have become increasingly important to ensuring a successful population count. Even so, those relationships vary considerably. For some important activities in the census cycle, including the construction of address lists and outreach to hard-to-count communities, the Census Bureau has developed robust partnership programs that integrate state and local officials. Yet state and local officials also engage with the federal government as legal adversaries, filing lawsuits that challenge census-taking procedures that they believe will lead to undercounts of their population.

State and local engagement also varies by degree. On one end of the spectrum, California built a parallel census infrastructure, complete with a state-level office of the census, conducting extensive statewide education and mobilization operations and organizing its own independent "neighborhoods count" to survey housing units in historically undercounted communities.[7] At the other end, the state of Texas made no dedicated resource investments in the production of the decennial count until August of 2020, in the midst of the pandemic and long after the self-response period had commenced. Hence, until the decennial year itself, the state left it to local units of government and nonprofit organizations to take on this work. In between these extremes, states have relied on a combination of modest investments to tailor census outreach efforts to hard-to-count populations. These investments have varied not only in their fiscal scale but also in their timing: Some investments were made far too late to have a significant impact on outreach. Especially in places where public funds are scarce, effective intergovernmental partnerships have also relied on assistance from nonprofit organizations and philanthropists. In an era when state and local governments' capacity is increasingly hollowed out, these intersectoral partnerships have taken on an increasing significance in numerous policy domains, and the census is no exception.[8]

My goal in this book is to show how the efforts of state and local officials, often in partnership with nongovernmental organizations, contribute to census taking in the United States. To do so, I draw primarily on an analysis of observations from the 2020 Census. In one sense, this might appear to limit the generalizability of my findings. As census experts are quick to point out—and as the Census Bureau's internal histories make clear—no two decennial counts are ever quite the same. The year 2020 was also defined by multiple crises, from a pandemic to presidential efforts at sabotaging the count. Yet it is the exceptional character of the 2020 Census that makes this decennial year worthy of study. Crises, as the political scientist Peter Gourevitch once put it, "are to countries what reagents are to compounds in chemistry."[9] They provoke a set of reactions that allow us to better see how underlying structures and relationships really work. Assuming current trends continue apace, the political and operational obstacles that defined the 2020 Census may well become more relevant in the future.

Counting a Fragmented Country: Federalism and the US Statistical System

Census data and other official statistics have historically been analytical "inputs" for political science rather than a subject of study in their own right. They appear, in the words of historian Margo Anderson, as "given, obvious, uncontroversial, part of the background information we absorb in our everyday lives."[10] In recent years, however, official statistics have attracted the attention of a growing number of social scientists and historians.[11] At one level, given the role of population data in apportioning legislatures, allocating resources, and defining public problems, they are an obvious subject for political analysis. As Andreas Georgiou—the head of the independent Greek statistical agency Elstat—put it: "Statistics is a combat sport."[12] Georgiou would know. In the midst of the Greek debt crisis in the early 2010s, his implementation of European Union (EU) reforms to correct the country's public finance statistics allowed the government to continue to qualify for loans from the EU and the International Monetary Fund—loans that required the imposition of deeply unpopular austerity measures. The statistician soon became a national scapegoat, suffering nearly a decade of baseless, politically motivated criminal charges of "violation of duty," "complicity against the state," and "slander."[13] Yet in the absence of high-profile controversies, the prospect of studying the politics of official statistics can appear daunting. The civil servants who keep national statistical systems humming tend not to think of themselves, or their work, as especially political—even if it can be subject to pressure from elected leaders. In many cases, political struggles over statistics are also encoded in highly technical language.

Still, as a growing number of scholars have recognized, politics affects the production and consumption of official statistics in profound ways. While governments are typically the only entities with the authority and capacity to count a country's population, "census making"—as Emily Klancher Merchant has called it—does not merely "reflect and facilitate" the power of government.[14] Rather, the census also provides a vehicle for important societal actors—be they professional social scientists vying for authority, political parties aiming to consolidate power, racial and ethnic minorities seeking recognition or demanding equal rights—to accomplish their goals. In short, this growing body of work holds that census taking is not a state-centered project so much as it is the result of an interaction between government and society.[15]

This is certainly true in the case of the US Census. As census taking became increasingly institutionalized in the United States, and as census figures were put to use for new purposes—perhaps especially the geographic allocation of scarce resources and the administration of regimes of civil and voting rights—a new politics of census accuracy emerged. In the decade that precedes a census, organized groups and congressional policy entrepreneurs work to reshape census categories, questionnaires, and administrative procedures. Over the last five decades, census counts have also prompted litigation regarding the nature and extent of the Census Bureau's efforts at enumeration. The participants in these disputes run the gamut from statisticians to political parties and from right-wing immigration restrictionists to groups representing historically undercounted racial and ethnic minorities.[16] As the political scientist Debra Thompson puts it, the process of census taking—however rationalized it may appear on the surface—is also the product of "an incoherent, multifaceted, tension-ridden ensemble of institutions and power relations."[17]

To the extent that official statistics are taken seriously as a subject of political analysis, the focus tends to be on *national* statistical systems. In federations, however, the reality is more complicated. The United States provides a case in point. From a distance, the federal statistical system appears to be composed of thirteen principal statistical agencies and one hundred federal statistical programs, coordinated by the office of the chief statistician of the United States.[18] But a closer look reveals how the system is knit together by an intricate web of intergovernmental relationships. In some cases, state and local governments—not federal agencies—are the primary *producers* of data that are later collated into national statistics. One example is the National Vital Statistics System, through which the fifty states (as well as New York City, the District of Columbia, and five US territories) provide information to the National Center for Health Statistics on approximately 6.8 million births and deaths each year.[19] Another is the production of data on Unemployment Insurance (UI) claims by the federal Employment and Training Administration. The intergovernmental structure of the UI system requires state governments to collect claim data and transmit it weekly to the federal agency.[20]

Even where data production does not hinge directly on intergovernmental partnerships, state and local governments can provide vital infrastructure to indirectly ensure the collection or improve the accuracy of federal statistics. As I detail in the next section, state and local officials engage in multiple activities that aim to promote census accuracy, ranging from reviewing and updating the Census Bureau's Master Address File to mobilizing their residents to participate in the count. One can also find examples of state and local infrastructural support in the National Assessment of Educational Progress (NAEP). While NAEP is a congressionally mandated project conducted by the National Center for Education Statistics, state governments typically assume responsibility for a variety of administrative functions within the program. This includes designating program coordinators to manage relationships with testing contractors, securing the cooperation of public schools, and reviewing assessment results.[21]

State and local governments can also be the *subjects*, rather than the sources, of national official statistics. Beginning with the first Census of Governments in 1850, the federal government has expanded its collection of data on state and local jurisdictions to include, among other things, information on how governments are organized and the conditions of public pensions, schools, and jails.[22] Collected every year since 1957, the Annual Survey of State and Local Government Finances provides data that influences the development of federal legislation and regulations. The Department of Housing and Urban Development, for example, uses the survey's data on property tax revenues to calculate rent adjustments in multiple federal programs.[23]

Finally, state and local governments are also active as *users* and *disseminators* of data produced by the federal statistical system. Public Law 94–171, enacted in 1975, requires the Census Bureau to supply states with population data, including for specific geographic areas identified by states, for the purposes of reapportionment and redistricting. The statute requires this information be provided within one year of census day. Yet in 2021, the delayed release of data due to operational challenges stemming from the pandemic greatly compressed states' redistricting timeline—leading some states to attempt the use of alternate data sources, such as the American Community Survey, to draw legislative districts—a move that invited litigation in federal courts.[24]

In addition to using Census Bureau data in the redistricting process, states disseminate it through clearinghouses called state data centers (SDCs). The Census Bureau began encouraging the development of SDCs in the late 1970s, when despite emerging needs for demographic, housing, and economic data in the public and private sector, census data remained costly and difficult to access, available only if the user had mainframe computer capabilities and specialized programming expertise. Currently, fifty states, four territories, and the District of Columbia have SDCs, which typically operate through executive-level agencies as well as statewide networks comprised of university research centers and regional planning associations. Feedback from SDCs also shapes the Census Bureau's understanding of users' needs as well as operational issues with federal statistical products.

Not all intergovernmental relationships in the federal statistical system are highly cooperative ones. There is conflict too. Some of this conflict takes the form of subnational government agencies refusing to provide data or invest in complementary technical infrastructure. On the one hand, state and local government agencies may, for one reason or another, prefer not to share their data, even when federal laws require it. The federal government has struggled to compel state and local law enforcement agencies to produce data on the use of force by police. Despite a twenty-six-year-old law requiring the collection of use-of-force statistics and a five-year initiative to create a national database, use-of-force reporting remains nonmandatory; as of 2022, data coverage currently extends to just over 40 percent of sworn law enforcement officers.[25] Gaps in data sharing are also common in the realm of health policy. Despite federal obligations to monitor the quality of care provided to vulnerable populations in Medicaid managed-care programs, states have routinely failed to report relevant patient-level data on long-term care facilities and the administration of prescription drugs.[26]

Conflict can also take other forms, ranging from intergovernmental lobbying to litigation. For example, the Census Bureau has long had a formal process—now known as Count Question Resolution—that allows tribal, state, and local governmental units to request that the bureau review errors that may have occurred during the previous decennial count.[27] During the last five decades, state and local governments have been frequently involved in litigation over decisions at the Census Bureau and the Commerce Department, ranging from the Census Bureau's failure to use the post-enumeration survey to correct for undercounts in the 1980 Census to Commerce Secretary Wilbur Ross's decision to include a citizenship question on the 2020 questionnaire—a move that was subsequently revealed to be part of a deliberate attempt to enhance Republican Party margins in Congress.[28]

In short, the federal statistical system is "federal" not only because it is composed of federal agencies but also because it straddles the jurisdictional boundaries of the American federal system. State and local governments are implicated in this system not merely as passive consumers of data products but as data producers, sites of complementary institutional infrastructure, and disseminators of information. Through both cooperative and conflictual relationships, they help to define the contours of official statistics in the United States.

Intergovernmental Relations and Census Taking in the United States

Studying the US Census is an ideal way to explore intergovernmental dynamics in the production of official statistics. While state and local governments do not bear the primary responsibility for census taking in the United States, both historical and contemporary evidence suggests that intergovernmental relations have long been an important component of counting the US population. State and local efforts to correct undercounts extend back to the nineteenth century, when many of these governments implemented their own census counts.[29] State and local efforts also helped to pilot new census technologies. The concept of the "census tract"—a critical unit of statistical geography—was pioneered not by employees of the Census Bureau but by a Presbyterian minister named Walter Laidlaw who aimed to create a statistical geography that would allow him to track and forecast changes in his congregation better than political geographies like wards and boroughs. By 1910, Laidlaw had persuaded census officials to create tract codes for a small number of large cities. Yet census tracts first went into wide use as part of both the New York State Census of 1915 and the efforts of the New York City Department of Health to create new sanitary districts for the city.[30]

In the early twentieth century—prior to the advent of the mail-response census—state and local politicians played an important role in the hiring of enumerators and the formation of local census committees. While this local knowledge and effort was often helpful in producing decennial counts, it also led to some prominent instances of outright fraud, in which enumerators and city "boosters" conspired to pad the numbers. Arguably the most egregious of these occurred during the 1910 census when—as bureau director Edward Dana Durand noted in his annual report to the secretary of commerce and labor—enumerators and private citizens in Tacoma, Washington, conspired to add over thirty thousand people to the city's figures. After a second enumeration, the city's population was adjusted downward from 116,000 to 84,000.[31]

Yet over a century later, long after the bureau had made significant reforms to improve procedures for hiring enumerators and had shifted from in-person enumeration to self-response, state and local governments continued to play important roles in census taking. There are two reasons for this. First, the consequences of the census for the allocation of political power and fiscal resources only grew in the latter half of the twentieth century. The so called reapportionment revolution that followed the US Supreme Court's decision in *Baker v. Carr* (1962) made it mandatory to redistrict Congress and state legislatures following each census. Additionally, the enactment of major federal programs during the New Deal and the Great Society led to massive growth in federal grants-in-aid to state and local governments. Because the formulas for allocating this aid relied on population data, census counts became even more critical to state and local government operations.[32] By the late 1970s, state governments began to play a more central role in the warehousing and dissemination of census economic, demographic, and housing data, which was increasingly used for grant applications and business analysis, culminating in the construction of the State Data Center Program in 1978, as noted previously.[33]

Second, the knowledge possessed by local and state officials continued to play a critical role in census operations. For example, as the bureau began to embrace practice of self-enumeration—in which households received and returned census questionnaires by mail—local officials' knowledge of address lists and property tax records became even more essential to carrying out a complete count. Similarly, as census officials struggled to increase self-response rates, they increasingly came to see state and local governments as critical "trusted partners" who could enhance public awareness about the importance of participating in the census.

To better understand how state and local governments shape the US census today, consider that census taking is a bit like building a house. In this analogy, there are three stages to the building process. As blueprints must be drawn before any construction can begin, the Census Bureau must first develop a plan for counting, determining where and how to count. Next, as materials must be gathered to build a house, the census count is built from individual and household completion of the census questionnaire. Gathering these responses is the second stage of the census process. Finally, the house is constructed, with periodic inspections along the way. The equivalent third step in the census process is tabulating, reviewing, and refining the received census data. At each of these stages, there are important roles for state and local governments to play.

First, state and local governments can help *draw up the blueprints of the house*. They do this through their participation in a range of programs designed to help the Census Bureau establish where to enumerate. One such program is the Local Update of Census Addresses (LUCA). Authorized by the Census Address List Improvement Act of 1994 and first implemented in the 2000 Census, LUCA is the main opportunity offered to local and state governments to review and provide feedback on the address list—known as the Master Address File—the bureau uses to determine the living quarters that will be included in the census. While state and local stakeholders frequently note the value of LUCA in ensuring the completeness of the Master Address File, participation in the program varies considerably across state and local contexts. In the run-up to the 2020 Census, some states—including Texas and South Dakota—lacked any LUCA coverage for the majority of their counties, whereas other regions of the country saw LUCA participation from multiple levels of government.[34]

Second, state and local governments can help *find construction materials* for the building project—per our analogy, the data received in response to census questionnaires. That means taking actions to motivate people to complete their census forms. As early as the 1980 Census, state and local governments have been partners in census taking—committing their own institutional resources to mobilizing census participation through Get Out the Count (GOTC) initiatives.[35] These initiatives are typically aimed at raising public awareness, building trust with local communities, and providing motivation for individuals to complete census forms. Given the diversity of the communities targeted by this outreach, the interventions are truly heterogeneous, ranging from advertising campaigns to partnerships with local libraries, churches, businesses, and community-based organizations. In recent years, two types of organizations have emerged to support GOTC work. State Complete Count Commissions (SCCCs), through formal state-level partnerships with the Census Bureau, "provide the structure and support to engage the state's stakeholders and encourage [census] participation."[36] At the local level, Complete Count Committees (CCCs)—typically composed of government officials and community leaders—aim to coordinate outreach plans that will "increase awareness and motivate residents to respond to the 2020 Census."[37] As described previously, however, the depth of state and local investments in GOTC operations varies extensively across states and communities.

Third, state and local governments help to both *build the house and inspect the quality of the construction*. Intergovernmental partnerships assist in counting the population and checking the quality of that count. This cooperation occurs at several stages. During the census, members of the Federal-State Cooperative for Population Estimates (FSCPE)—experts appointed by state governors—participate in what is known as count review. Working with the Census Bureau's Population Division, FSCPE members compare census addresses with their own address lists, document instances of missing addresses, and provide new information for "group quarters" addresses, such as college dormitories and nursing homes, that were not enumerated.[38] Following the release of census results, state and local governments also have an opportunity to participate in the Count Question Resolution (CQR) Operation, which allows officials to request that the Census Bureau review and correct geographical errors that occurred during data processing. Following the chaos resulting from the COVID-19 pandemic, forty-nine local governments used the CQR Operation to challenge their 2020 Census results. The city of Detroit estimated that its population was undercounted "by as much as 8 percent, possibly leaving out tens of thousands of people" and jeopardizing $150 million in federal funding.[39]

Even as state and local governments become engaged in the process of "building" the census, sustaining effective intergovernmental partnerships faces a variety of challenges.[40] First, when compared to activities like environmental regulation or social provision, where links between federal, state, and local governments are well established, there are fewer mechanisms to cue state and local officials' attention to the importance of census operations. While subnational governments are no doubt affected by census outcomes, they do not bear primary institutional responsibility for the quality of the census. Hence, their actions related to census taking have historically faced relatively little oversight or scrutiny. Because of this, and because the quality of the census is affected by a range of exogenous conditions, tracing the returns of state and local investments in census taking has proven difficult. In the absence of strong, ongoing reminders of the importance of the national census, and without evidence that state and local census investments have significant returns, effective state and local partnerships can be difficult to secure. Additionally, once-in-a-decade census operations occur with far less frequency than other intergovernmental activities. This infrequency not only depresses their salience, it removes them from annual or biennial state and local budget cycles and creates unique problems for preserving institutional memory across the decades.

A second problem is that state and local partnerships—while increasingly important in the Census Bureau's planning efforts—may sometimes lack a strong institutional support structure. State and local governments vary extensively in their administrative capacity for census partnerships. For example, the number of full-time-equivalent employees in state data centers ranges from less than one to over one hundred and twenty.[41] Similarly, while most metropolitan local governments have at least some city planning staff, even large cities often lack dedicated personnel to support census outreach and often rely on philanthropic investments to support this work.[42] The decennial census is also far less routine than most intergovernmental activities. While state and local agencies use Census Bureau products daily, the budget and operational machinery for the decennial census ramps up only in the final years of each decade. This increases the potential for turnover and loss of institutional memory among state and local officials engaged with the census.

At the federal level, the Census Bureau lacks major fiscal or regulatory tools to induce state and local governments to collaborate on census outreach.[43] Instead, it relies on its ability to persuade others to take voluntary action. To mobilize census participation, the Census Bureau employs over one thousand "partnership specialists"—temporary employees responsible for engaging state, local, and tribal officials to take actions to mobilize census participation. In preparing for the 2020 Census, however, the bureau's Community Partnership and Engagement Program (CPEP) faced problems. While it planned on hiring nearly twice as many partnership specialists as it had for the 2010 Census, the bureau struggled to hire and retain staff for 2020 due to a lack of congressional appropriations and a tight labor market. Furthermore, during the planning phases of the census, officials overseeing CPEP reported significant variations in how regional offices communicated job expectations for partnership specialists as well as conflict between partnership specialists and staff within the Census Bureau's area census offices (ACOs).[44]

Finally, as in other policy areas, partisan conflict can also strain intergovernmental partnerships for census taking.[45] The most obvious example of this is the Trump administration's deliberate efforts to politicize the census by including a citizenship question on the 2020 questionnaire. This move was aimed at intimidating both legal and undocumented immigrants, was projected to result in an undercount of several million persons, and was intended to shift power from urban Democratic areas to rural Republican strongholds.[46] In the face of the Trump administration's assault on census integrity, the most important intergovernmental partnerships were alliances among states and local officials, who pooled resources and expertise to challenge Trump in court. These lawsuits not only helped to halt the introduction of the citizenship question onto the 2020 questionnaire, they also helped to frustrate Trump's attempt to use administrative data to identify and remove undocumented immigrants from census apportionment counts. Yet if Trump's efforts to undermine the census ran into barriers in court, they nevertheless helped to inscribe a partisan frame on debates over investments in census mobilization in a number of states. Even where the "Trump effect" was less pronounced, supporting census activity could become a casualty of more generic interparty conflict over budgets.[47]

As the evidence in this book shows, these three challenges frustrated efforts to build multiple kinds of intergovernmental partnerships for census taking. Still, officials at all levels of government occasionally found ways of overcoming these obstacles. For example, officials in some states and cities have taken steps to make more permanent investments to support census operations. Even in states and cities with more limited resources, officials have found ways of building networks both within and outside of government to sustain attention to census operations. Additionally, in some states where partisan conflict threatened to undermine support for census mobilization efforts, census stakeholders worked to reframe the consequences of census undercounts to garner bipartisan support for these investments. Not all these initiatives ultimately succeeded in securing intergovernmental partnerships. Yet examining them in greater detail offers valuable insights for proposals to enhance state and local participation in future decennial counts.

What the US Census Teaches Us About Federalism

Studying census taking, while important in its own right, can also generate broader insights about the operation of the American federal system. Scholars of American federalism tend to direct their attention to arenas of conflict where the stakes are not only high but also highly visible and traceable. Clashes between state and federal officials over the provision of health insurance, regulation of environmental hazards, and the implementation of voting rights carry a material and political significance that pushes them to center stage, both in the public sphere and in the pages of academic journals.[48] By contrast, because census taking occurs only once every ten years, and because it is primarily the responsibility of the federal government, it is all too easy for students of federalism to ignore.

The production of official statistics, however, is not just a backdrop for "center stage" intergovernmental conflicts. Rather, the numbers are very much part of the action.[49] The policies and programs that shape official statistics can have what the political scientist Suzanne Mettler calls "lateral effects" on the relationships between federal, state, and local governments.[50] Fluctuations in the quality of census counts—even small ones—can have significant repercussions for the allocation of trillions of dollars in federal grants, the administration of voting rights, and the balance of power in both Congress and state legislatures. At the same time, changes in the American federal system—particularly the expansion of federal grants in aid and the "reapportionment revolution" in the federal courts—have also had their own lateral effects on official statistics. These changes have led state and local officials to become deeply intertwined in the census cycle—as data users, as partners in data production, as lobbyists, and as litigants. Thus without studying the politics of creating and maintaining population data, we cannot truly understand how the American federal system works.

More broadly, a careful look at the US Census also serves as a reminder that federalism is not merely a blueprint that describes the relationship between the federal government and the states. Nor is it only a set of laboratories for experimenting with new policy ideas. Rather, federalism is also an *infrastructure*—of decentralized organizations, people, resources, and local knowledge—that makes governing a large, diverse society possible.[51] Over the last century, the Census Bureau has developed increasingly sophisticated technical capabilities for collecting population data. Yet even as the bureau's capacity expanded, it has nevertheless continued to rely on state and local governments to assist in the production of the census. This is not because subnational governments are assigned any powers under the Constitution's census clause. Rather, states, cities, counties, and tribes have vital resources at their disposal that the Census Bureau needs.[52] That includes local knowledge about the location of households necessary to update the bureau's Master Address File, as well as relationships of trust with civic leaders and local constituents necessary to pull off census outreach campaigns.

That the Census Bureau and subnational governments depend on one another is not, of course, a guarantee of cooperation. The partnerships described in this book are buffeted by the forces of partisan polarization and fiscal austerity that trouble all projects of intergovernmental management, as well as challenges that are unique to the collection of official statistics. Furthermore, the pattern of "census federalism" we see today emerged not only through the development of intergovernmental partnerships but also as the result of increasingly robust legal networks populated by state attorneys general. In the 2020 Census cycle, lawsuits filed by state and local officials shaped the count in profound ways, in some cases preventing—or at least hobbling—the implementation of procedures that would have harmed census data quality. Importantly, the governments involved in these lawsuits were often simultaneously cooperating with the bureau in other arenas to accomplish the same goal: enhancing census accuracy. If nothing else, this suggests that—during a moment of political turbulence—the art of intergovernmental management requires public officials to draw on *multiple* repertoires of action.

Plan for the Book

To better understand how state and local governments shape the census, I employ a mix of methodologies. At the heart of my analysis is data collected from over one hundred interviews with state and local government officials, nonprofit leaders, and census experts. These interviews, conducted primarily in 2019 and 2020, focused on both the substance of state and local participation in the census as well as what facilitated and what served as barriers to census partnerships (see the appendix for a description of the interview methodology).[53] To tease out variation in the extent of state and local participation in census partnership programs, I employ quantitative analyses of decisions made at multiple levels of government. To support my analyses of interviews and quantitative data, I examine documents produced by federal, state, and local agencies, obtained through public-facing websites, personal emails, and public-records requests.

The chapters that follow are organized in a way that emphasizes how the process of census taking unfolds over time. Chapter 1 sets the stage by reviewing the political, fiscal, and organizational contexts in which the 2020 Census unfolded. Here I trace the history of census controversies back to their roots, examining the political implications of population data as well as the landscape of political institutions and organizations that manage census taking. Understanding this history, I argue, helps to explain how state and local governments became increasingly involved with census taking—not only as the Census Bureau's partners but also as its legal adversaries.

Chapter 2 examines what was arguably the most significant political controversy surrounding the 2020 Census: the Trump administration's ultimately failed plan to include a citizenship item on the 2020 questionnaire. This controversy, I argue, emerged from the conjunction of two important forces. On the one hand, the Trump administration's decision reflected the rising prominence of *executive-centered partisanship*—in which presidential appointees leveraged bureaucratic processes to achieve partisan political objectives. At the same time, the failure of the plan was the result of *intergovernmental legal mobilization*. Greater *horizontal* collaboration among state attorneys general was instrumental in developing the legal strategy that led to the demise of the administration's plan in court.

The next four chapters provide case studies of *vertical* partnerships between federal, state, and local governments in three critical areas of census operations. Chapter 3 analyzes variation in state and local governments' involvement in partnership programs that assist the Census Bureau in establishing where to enumerate, including LUCA. Even as the bureau has improved its technical capabilities for identifying addresses remotely via satellite imaging, the local knowledge it receives from its state, local, and tribal partners remains essential for establishing where to count. Yet persistent gaps in resources continue to impede local governments' participation in the program. While census officials are well aware of these resource challenges, the bureau's institutional identity as a scientific agency rather than a grantmaking organization bounds programmatic innovations. Over the last few decades, the bureau has made numerous changes that have improved governments' participation in LUCA. What it has not done, and what it cannot do, is provide local governments with resources they lack.

Chapter 4 examines efforts to mobilize household participation in the census, especially in hard-to-count communities. Over the last several decades, the Census Bureau has responded to the challenge of mobilizing census participation not merely with advertising but by enlisting state and local governments as "trusted messengers" who can tailor messaging and outreach campaigns to the unique needs of local communities. The 2020 Census represented the largest such effort in history, with unprecedented local investments in advertising campaigns, door-to-door canvassing, and public events. Yet these investments remained highly uneven across the country. As interview data and quantitative analyses show, variation in census investments can be attributed to wide gaps in officials' perceptions of census salience. In states and cities where the risk of an undercount or a lost congressional seat was high, it was easier to make the case for prioritizing census outreach. In the midst of the Trump administration's efforts to politicize the census, proposals to invest in outreach also ran into partisan obstacles, particularly at the state level. In most, though not all, states controlled by Republicans, investing in census outreach campaigns proved to be a nonstarter. These partisan patterns did not emerge at the local level, however, where the central barriers to investing in outreach were fiscal. Indeed, limited institutional capacity—both in terms of resources and expertise—impeded state and local investments in census outreach. Especially in areas where those limits were most pronounced, sustaining intergovernmental partnerships depended on *intersectoral* linkages between government, nonprofit organizations, and philanthropists.

If effective intergovernmental partnerships mattered during preparations for the census, they became even more essential during a census year defined by unprecedented levels of chaos. Chapter 5 charts how state and local governments contributed to the population count during the COVID-19 pandemic. While state and local officials helped to pivot outreach operations as the turbulent first months of the pandemic unfolded, they also faced structural barriers to playing their intended roles, stemming from both the underfunding of census operations as well as the Census Bureau's decision to cancel the full group quarters count review at the end of the enumeration period. The chapter concludes by explaining how a third group of state officials—those in charge of state motor vehicles departments—helped thwart the Trump administration's scheme to identify noncitizens in the 2020 Census by refusing to provide driver's license information to the Census Bureau.

Chapter 6 considers how intergovernmental conflict and cooperation unfolded after the end of field operations in 2020. Here, I examine how state and local governments responded to evidence of flawed census data. While there are several administrative programs that allow governments to challenge census results, none of these was ideally suited for the anomalies that emerged during the 2020 Census. The Census Bureau was open to calls for reforming these programs, yet it proceeded with caution, and far less speed, than local governments often demanded. Additionally, neither federal district courts nor Congress proved especially responsive to local governments' demands for relief and reform. Thus while intergovernmental partnerships were essential in carrying out the census, local officials had far less leverage when it came to correcting errors in the count. This chapter also examines the role that state and local officials—along with other users of census data—played in the implementation of controversial changes to the Census Bureau's Disclosure Avoidance System (DAS), which protects the confidentiality of individual census data in accordance with Title 13 of the United States Code. While the bureau did not waver in its decision to implement the technique of "differential privacy"—which protects confidentiality by injecting tabulations of census blocks with statistical noise—actions taken by state demographers, city planners, and other data users forced the bureau to reevaluate the trade-offs in the design of the system, with significant implications for the quality of 2020 Census data.

The concluding chapter summarizes the main findings of the book and considers their implications for scholarship on census taking and official statistics more broadly. I close by reflecting on several proposed reforms to census taking in the United States. Ultimately, I argue that strengthening the quality of the census will require not only better integrating state and local officials' knowledge into operations at the Census Bureau but also building up the capacity of governments around the country to support census accuracy for the long term. The building blocks of a stronger census federalism—including networks of state and local officials, nonprofits, experts, and census advocates scattered across the country—already exist. Yet some reassembly is required.

CHAPTER ONE

Census Politics and the Federal System

On a warm August morning in 2019, Dean Goldberg—a mild-mannered city council member in Circle Pines, Minnesota—puts on a blue cape and a mask to become "Census Man." As with any superhero, Goldberg says, the masked figure has an origin story: "He was actually, as a child, one of many kids who lived in a household and he was never counted, so he vowed as he grew older that no one would go uncounted."[1] By the time the 2020 Census arrives, Goldberg will enjoy a brief moment as a national celebrity when his character is featured in a segment of HBO's comedy-news show *Last Week Tonight with John Oliver*.[2]

Along with former Minneapolis Mayor Sharon Sayles Belton, who dons a shirt bearing the words "census nerd," Goldberg canvasses crowds at the state fair, reminding them to stand up and be counted. While the 2020 Census is still six months away, Goldberg and Sayles Belton have their work cut out for them. "We know there are people who are afraid when somebody from the government knocks on the door," Sayles Belton tells reporters. "We want people to know there's nothing to be afraid of."[3] Two years later, when Minnesota holds onto a seat in the House of Representatives by a margin of twenty-six people—the closest margin for avoiding the loss of a congressional seat since 1970 (see figure 1.1)—local television stations celebrate Goldberg's efforts at improving census participation.[4]

Meanwhile, nearly two thousand miles away, Ditas Katague has been hard at work leading California's census office in Sacramento. Under Katague's leadership, the state's $187 million effort is different not only in degree but in kind from those in other states. In a climate of intense distrust, states, cities, and nongovernmental organizations have increasingly relied on "trusted messengers" to educate and activate the hardest-to-count populations to participate in the census. Katague—who has over two decades of

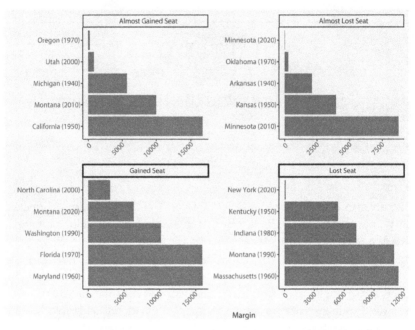

Figure 1.1: Narrowest historical margins for apportionment outcomes in the House of Representatives. Source: Tabulated by author from "Reapportionment Studies," Election Data Services, accessed March 5, 2024, https://www.electiondataservices.com/reapportionment-studies/.

experience with census outreach—expanded this idea into what she calls a "trusted ecosystem" of mutually reinforcing campaigns at the state and local level aimed at engaging marginalized, underserved communities.[5] When the results are in, nearly 70 percent of Californians will respond to the census on their own, outpacing the national self-response rate and exceeding the state's own 2010 benchmark.[6]

As the 2020 Census cycle ramps up, state and local officials like Goldberg, Sayles Belton, and Katague are working around the country to build outreach campaigns in a climate riven by political conflict and distrust. At the center of the conflict is the Trump administration's effort to include a citizenship item on the 2020 questionnaire for the first time since 1950—a move projected to have a "chilling effect" on census participation for millions of immigrants, regardless of their legal status. In response, a coalition of eighteen states, fifteen local governments, the District of Columbia, and the US Conference of Mayors—along with several major nongovernmental organizations—filed suit in federal court to stop the question from appearing on the census form. In July of 2019, the US Supreme Court issued a ruling having just that effect.

These examples illustrate two important dynamics of census taking in the United States. First, while the US census is an immense technical and scientific project, it occurs in a deeply political context. Not only do census figures have significant political effects on the quality of democratic representation and the allocation of federal resources, decisions about how those figures should be produced invite conflict and contestation. As a result, building trust in the census, especially among marginalized populations, has become a vital component of census taking and a task that begins years before the census is in the field. Second, while the US Census is, formally speaking, a task for the federal government, census taking nevertheless involves an intense amount of planning and coordination by officials at the state and local level, as well as actors outside of government. These actions run the gamut from partnerships that promote participation in the count to the preparation of lawsuits that shape the kinds of questions that appear on the census questionnaire.

To the casual observer, all of this might seem puzzling. Census taking is often depicted as nothing more and nothing less than a simple headcount. Introductory textbooks on American politics often mention the US Census only in passing, if at all.[7] At the same time, census taking is frequently depicted as a federal responsibility—one which the Constitution delegates to Congress, and which Congress delegates to the Census Bureau. Yet if the census is just a headcount, why is it also a site of significant political controversy? And if census taking is really a federal responsibility, why have state and local governments become increasingly involved, as both the federal government's partners and legal adversaries? This chapter takes up both of those questions.

The Deep Roots of Census Politics

To understand why the US Census has often invited political controversy—and why that controversy often involves officials from multiple levels of government—it is helpful to consider how census taking first emerged in the new nation. When the framers of the US Constitution met in Philadelphia

in May of 1787, they faced the daunting challenge of reconciling two competing visions of what representative democracy might look like. Under the
Articles of Confederation—the frame of government set down in the wake
of the American Revolution—there had been no need for a census. In the
Congress of the Confederation, all thirteen former colonies received only
one vote, regardless of population. Yet on the first day of the constitutional
convention, James Madison and his allies unveiled what amounted to a
radical reform. Under Madison's "Virginia Plan," seats in both houses of
a far more powerful bicameral national legislature would be apportioned
according to the populations of each state. This threatened to shift the balance of power toward highly populous states, including Virginia. Delegates
representing smaller states, most notably New Jersey's William Paterson,
launched a counteroffensive—advocating a plan that resembled the Congress of the Confederation, with an equal number of seats per state.[8]

Several months later, a committee of the delegates had hammered out a
compromise that preserved elements of both plans, thereby dividing power
between large and small states. The new Congress would contain an upper
chamber, the Senate, with two members from each state, each chosen by
state legislatures. Yet it would also contain a lower chamber—the House of
Representatives—whose directly elected members would be apportioned to
states according to the population. This arrangement would be mirrored in
the Electoral College—the group of electors formed by the states every four
years to select the president and vice president—where each state would
receive a share of electoral votes equal to the number of senators and representatives in its congressional delegation. Bringing this new government
to life demanded a census. Article I, Section 2, of the new Constitution gave
the responsibility for conducting an "actual Enumeration" to Congress once
every ten years "in such Manner as they shall by Law direct."[9]

Once the convention delegates had agreed on the new Congress's basic
bicameral structure, the need for a census itself proved relatively uncontroversial.[10] The same cannot be said for the question of who should be
counted and how. Southern delegates, in a bid to increase their power in
the House of Representatives, insisted that enslaved persons should be included in population counts used to determine representation. Northern-
ers disagreed; Massachusetts' Elbridge Gerry wondered aloud why "blacks,
who were property in the South" should count toward congressional representation "any more than the cattle and horses of the North?"[11] In the
end, the delegates agreed to apportion Congress by counting each slave as

three-fifths of a person—a rule of thumb used under the Articles of Confederation. American Indians, on the other hand, were initially excluded from the apportionment scheme entirely. In the end, Article I, Section 2, clarified that each state's apportionment population would be constructed "by adding to the whole Number of free Persons, including those bound to a Service for a Term of Years, and excluding Indians not taxed, three fifths of all other Persons." The drafters—keen not to draw attention to the "peculiar institution"—kept the word "slave" itself out of the text.[12]

The convention delegates left other questions about congressional apportionment off the table entirely, allowing them to be fought out in the first sessions of the new Congress. Most importantly, they avoided the issue of the size of the House of Representatives and the formula for translating population figures into seats for each state.[13] Thus even after an ad hoc force of US marshals had collected the data for the 1790 Census, a debate raged on about what to do with the new numbers. In early 1791, House members drafted legislation that enlarged the size of the chamber from sixty-five to one hundred and twenty, giving each state one seat for every thirty thousand persons. The Senate rejected the bill, proposing instead a House with one hundred and five seats, one for every thirty-three thousand persons. The deadlock over apportionment—which ultimately produced the first-ever presidential veto—reflected the power-distributional nature of the census. Some apportionment formulas produced better seat shares for small states like New Jersey while others were advantageous for populous ones like Virginia. The debate over the first apportionment was thus not resolved until the middle of 1792, resulting in the creation of a House of one hundred and five seats, one for every thirty-three thousand persons in the country.

This was far from the last controversy over apportionment.[14] With the rapid expansion of US territory and a growing population, delegations from the Northeast and South saw fresh challenges to their control of Congress (see figure 1.2). Each census, and each new state admitted to the Union, brought shifts in the balance of political power. Prior to the Civil War, the admission of sparsely populated western states like Wisconsin and Minnesota, where slavery was outlawed, bolstered the political strength of free states in the North, even when they experienced a decrease in population. These shifts in population could be balanced in the Senate—where each newly admitted state received two new senators—by the simultaneous admission of pairs of free and slave states. Yet the same was not true in the population-apportioned House. The fact that slaves counted as three-fifths

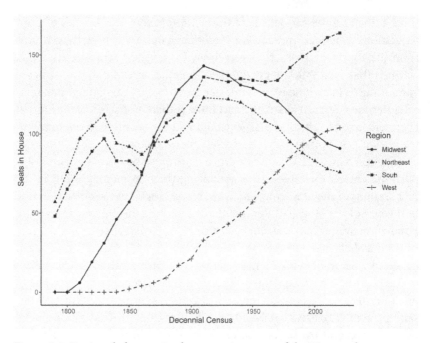

Figure 1.2: Regional changes in the apportionment of the House of Representatives, 1790–2020 Censuses. Source: Tabulated by author from Office of the Historian, "Representatives Apportioned to Each State," US House of Representatives, accessed January 13, 2022, https://history.house.gov /Institution/Apportionment/state_apportionment_pdf_2021/.

of a person for apportionment purposes, coupled with population growth outside the South, prevented Southerners from winning a majority of House seats. This dynamic pinned the future of slavery on the Senate. When the results of the 1860 elections gave Republicans control of both chambers of Congress and the presidency, the stage was set for southern secession and Civil War.[15]

Even after the Civil War and Reconstruction, population growth and territorial expansion continued to threaten the balance of political power in Congress. Congress responded to these changes by both regulating the speed at which new states were admitted to the Union and, when necessary, expanding the size of the House of Representatives to ensure large swings in population growth did not mean a loss of seats for others. Between 1880 and 1910, the size of the House increased from 293 to 433 members and no state lost a seat.[16] Yet in the second decade of the twentieth century, this dynamic broke down. Following the 1910 Census, as the House chamber became increasingly crowded, Congress decided not to increase its size again. This meant that after the admission of Arizona and New Mexico to the Union, the size of the House was fixed at 435 members, unless Congress acted to enlarge it. That decision, as historian Margo Anderson puts it, made the reapportionment of Congress after the 1920 census into a "zero-sum game," in which a gain in representation for one state required a loss for another.[17]

The 1920 Census thus ignited a war over reapportionment that lasted a full decade. A coalition made up primarily of congressional delegations from states likely to lose congressional seats successfully kept reapportionment off the agenda for a decade.[18] Year after year, this coalition repeatedly rejected all reapportionment bills brought before Congress. By 1928, the failure to reapportion Congress threatened presidential elections as well, since the apportionment of the Electoral College still relied on data from the 1910 Census. It was easy to imagine the possibility of a popular vote that favored one presidential candidate and an Electoral College vote that favored his opponent. In 1929, soon after his election to office, President Herbert Hoover called a special session of Congress to address the apportionment question. During that session, defenders of the status quo acceded to a calculated political bargain.[19] On the one hand, they agreed to create a new mechanism whereby Congress would be automatically reapportioned after each census—avoiding the chaos that had defined the 1920s. In exchange, however, they insisted on stripping language that had appeared in every reapportionment bill since 1840 that required all Congressional districts be geographically compact, contiguous, and roughly equal in population. Thus a state with a large urban population might get a larger share of seats in Congress, yet its rural-dominated state legislature could nevertheless prevent newly urbanized areas from picking up those seats. In New York, for example, one congressional district contained just over ninety thousand people while another contained close to eight hundred thousand. In short, Congress traded nonapportionment for malapportionment.[20]

In the decades that followed, rural incumbents used malapportionment to entrench their power in Congress and state legislatures. The failure to redistrict meant that a single legislator in Des Moines might represent upwards of one hundred thousand people whereas his colleague in the tiny municipality of Corning might represent just under eight thousand.[21] In malapportioned states like Iowa, the result was "minority rule by artificially created legislative majorities."[22] Despite numerous legal challenges to malapportionment, federal courts wanted no parts of the issue. As Supreme Court Justice Felix Frankfurter argued for the majority in *Colegrove v. Green* (1946), the malapportionment issue constituted a "political thicket" into which judges could not wade.[23] Rather than appealing to the courts, he suggested, interested parties should use the political process to solve malapportionment. For the next two decades, malapportionment remained a fact of life.

An ideological shift on the Supreme Court under Chief Justice Earl Warren eventually gave way to a breakthrough on the malapportionment problem. The Warren Court's landmark 1962 ruling in *Baker v. Carr* upended Frankfurter's logic, holding that malapportionment—however mired in the political thicket—was nevertheless a "justiciable" issue. In several cases that followed, the Court threw out malapportioned legislative maps in both state legislatures and Congress, enshrining a standard of "one person, one vote."[24]

The "Reapportionment Revolution," as it came to be known, only enhanced the political significance of accurate census data. If legislative districts were now required to be compact, contiguous, and equal in population, state legislatures would need population data that was not only reliable but usable for the purposes of drawing legislative district maps. In practice, that meant that population had to be tabulated at small units of census geography. This includes census tracts—small, permanent subdivisions of a county with a population that ranges from twelve hundred to eight thousand inhabitants—as well as census blocks, the smallest unit of census geography, whose boundaries are formed by both visible features (a road or a river) as well as invisible borders like city limits and property lines. In the 2020 Census, there were over eighty-five thousand tracts and over eight million blocks.[25]

Collecting and maintaining detailed data for these small geographies was essential for drawing new legislative districts. Yet even as of 1970, the Census Bureau maintained such data for only 2 percent of the country's geography. Under pressure from both the National Conference of State Legislatures and the Census Bureau, Congress eventually passed legislation remedying this situation in 1975. That statute, Public Law 94–171, required the Census Bureau to furnish population data appropriate for redistricting in the year after the census is taken.[26]

Reapportionment was not the only reason why the accuracy of census data became increasingly important in the latter decades of the twentieth century. A second factor was the passage of the landmark Voting Rights Act of 1965 (VRA).[27] Under the law, Congress required robust enforcement of the Fifteenth Amendment's prohibition on racial discrimination in voting rights. Making enforcement stick in the Jim Crow South, however, required census data. Among other things, the VRA required that legislative districts are not "racially gerrymandered"—that is, drawn to weaken the political power of racial minorities. To monitor such practices, the US Department of Justice relies on tabulations of census population data by race and ethnicity at the block level. These data, as with redistricting files delivered to state governments, have played a critical role in helping courts evaluate the legality of redistricting plans for state legislatures and congressional districts. Over the last decade, however, that role has changed to a considerable extent. In a landmark 2013 decision *Shelby County v. Holder*, the US Supreme Court struck down as unconstitutional the VRA's formula for determining which jurisdictions must have changes in their voting laws "precleared" by the US attorney general or a three-judge panel of the US District Court for the District of Columbia to ensure that they do not "deny or abridge the right to vote on account of race, color, or membership in a language minority group."[28] In the absence of preclearance, states have introduced an array of new barriers to voting, leading to a noticeable decline in ballot access for Black and Hispanic registered voters.[29]

To be sure, the *Shelby County* decision still allowed voters to bring lawsuits challenging voting-rights discrimination under Section 2 of the VRA. And while the Supreme Court further limited Section 2's scope in a 2021 decision, *Brnovich v. Democratic National Committee*, census data remain pivotal to the success of VRA lawsuits that challenge racial gerrymanders.[30] In 2023, for example, the Court held that Alabama's congressional district map likely violated the Voting Rights Act because it had been drawn to dilute the voting power of the state's Black residents—who constitute over a quarter of the state's population.[31]

A third force increasing the stakes of the census was the role of population data in allocating federal resources. Beginning in the early twentieth century and intensifying during President Franklin D. Roosevelt's New Deal (1933 to 1938), Congress initiated a rapid expansion of federal aid to state and local governments to support a vast array of goals, ranging from the construction of airports and hospitals to water pollution control. To allocate these funds, Congress employed formulas that relied on accurate population data, both at the state level and for smaller geographies, including counties and municipal governments. In the 1950s and 1960s, the grant-in-aid system expanded even further, encompassing sweeping new programs of highway construction, urban redevelopment, and aid to the impoverished. As a result, the accuracy and quality of census data became even more politically significant. Not only did inaccurate data threaten to deprive states of fair representation in Congress, it also risked the loss of resources for vital programs.[32]

As the federal grant-in-aid system grew, the link between population data and vital resources became an increasingly significant component of campaigns to encourage census participation.[33] In a television advertisement for the 2000 Census, a team of firefighters struggles to contain a roaring blaze while a narrator gravely reminds the viewer that, due to undercounts, some communities missed out on their fair share of federal funds for emergency equipment.[34] This dramatization is not far from reality. By fiscal year 2017, census data guided the allocation of over $1.5 trillion in federal dollars—well over a third of the federal budget for that year (see table 1.1). Yet this is itself an understatement of how the census shapes the allocation of resources in the United States. State governments collectively allocate nearly $600 billion in aid to local governments; census population data is frequently a key factor in the formulas that determine the state support local governments receive to support everything from public safety to schools, parks, and libraries.[35]

To understand how the accuracy of census data can affect the administration of federal aid, let's consider the largest and arguably the most significant of these programs: Medicaid.[36] Jointly administered by the federal government and the states, Medicaid provides health insurance to one in five Americans. For Medicaid as well as several other major social programs, the amount of federal funds states receive is determined by a formula that provides states with lower per capita incomes relative to the national average with higher levels of reimbursement. Based on this formula, each state is assigned an annual Federal Medical Assistance Percentage (FMAP). For example, in 2019, Mississippi's FMAP was 76.39 percent, meaning that the federal government picked up over three quarters of the costs for the state's Medicaid program. The FMAP, like other allocation formulas, is highly sensitive to the quality of census data. If the census fails to count people in a state's population, its per capita income will inevitably increase. Consequently, its FMAP rate—and the share of federal funding it receives—will decrease. For each person not counted in the 2010 Census, the median state

Table 1.1: Census-Guided Federal Expenditure in Fiscal Year 2017 ($Billions), by Department

Department ($B)	FY 2017 Expenditures
Department of Health and Human Services	$1,152.64
Department of Agriculture	$116.15
Department of Housing and Urban Development	$69.54
Department of Transportation	$54.86
Department of Education	$38.83
Small Business Administration	$37.42
Department of Labor	$7.17
Environmental Protection Agency	$4.09
Department of Justice	$2.43
Department of Homeland Security	$2.05
Department of Interior	$1.39
Department of Treasury	$0.61
Department of Veterans Affairs	$0.30
Department of Commerce	$0.28
Department of Energy	$0.26
Department of Defense	$0.11
Other Department	$1.14
Tax Expenditures	$14.92
Total	$1,504.19

Source: Tabulated by author using data from Andrew Reamer, "Counting for Dollars 2020: The Role of the Decennial Census in the Geographic Distribution of Federal Funds," GW Institute of Public Policy, April 29, 2020, https://gwipp.gwu.edu /counting-dollars-2020-role-decennial-census-geographic-distribution-federal-funds.

lost over $1,000 in FMAP-guided funds.[37] In other words, inaccurate census data is not just cells in a spreadsheet but can make a significant difference in the quality and comprehensiveness of social provision.

As the uses of census data expanded to encompass a broader range of crucial governing functions, the accuracy of these data became a potentially significant source of political controversy. Of course, no census has ever been 100 percent accurate. Yet as early as the 1910s, African American census researchers had begun to reveal evidence of a systematic differential undercount of the Black population.[38] By the middle of the twentieth century, advances in technology and statistical methods made it possible to measure inaccuracies in the census with greater precision. Thanks to the Second World War, the Census Bureau was for the first time afforded a high-quality independent source of data—selective service registrations for men of draft age—against which to compare its coverage of the population. Studies of the 1940 Census illustrated that Black men were systematically less likely to be counted than their white peers. By 1960, studies showed that Black men were undercounted at a rate of 6.6 percent, more than double that of their white peers.[39] By the 1970s, the US Commission on Civil Rights similarly charged that the bureau's procedures for counting people with Spanish-speaking backgrounds were "disastrous." Independent surveys, the Commission suggested, provided ample evidence of a Hispanic undercount. For example, a survey conducted by researchers at the City University of New York revealed that Puerto Ricans in New York City were undercounted by as much as 25 percent.[40]

Once revealed, these undercounts became difficult to ignore. On the one hand, they had significant implications for civil rights. As the final report of a high-profile 1967 conference on Social Statistics and the City put it, "Miscounting the population could unconstitutionally deny minorities political representation or protection under the Voting Rights Act."[41] On the other hand, undercounts also had geographically targeted political effects. Large cities in the Northeast and the Midwest—already losing population to states in the Sun Belt—also contained large populations at risk of being undercounted, placing at risk both their representation in Congress and their share of federal aid from programs, which were growing significantly with each passing year. As governors and mayors began to take notice of these consequences, the chorus of voices calling for the bureau to take action to correct the undercounts grew larger—and louder. Following the 1970 and 1980 Censuses, those voices had entered the federal courts—and the era of census lawsuits had begun.

By the final decades of the twentieth century, the growth of federal grants-in-aid and requirements for decennial redistricting had given state and local officials an increasing stake in shaping how census taking—an activity the Constitution delegates to federal government—worked. Over this same period, officials at the bureau were also coming to view relationships with state and local governments as increasingly important. As the US population grew larger and more diverse, the bureau now had to find more efficient ways of carrying out the decennial count. One of the most important innovations in this regard—in wide use by 1970—was self-response, in which households were encouraged to return census forms by mail, saving the labor of enumerators for following up with nonresponsive households. This innovation created challenges of its own, however. Relying on mail response only intensified the bureau's need for an accurate, up-to-date address list as well as effective methods of encouraging voluntary participation in the census. In response, the bureau now increasingly sought to create intergovernmental partnerships. States, cities, counties, and tribes possessed the kind of information—including tax and utility records—that would make a complete master address file possible. Further, governors, mayors, county executives, city council members, and tribal leaders had far stronger, and more routine, relationships with their constituents—stronger, at any rate, than a remote federal agency that contacted them only once per decade—which would position them to use the bully pulpit to mobilize census participation. But how did these relationships work? And how do they shape census taking today?

The Making of Census Federalism

The growing interdependence between the operations of the Census Bureau and the functions of state and local government has transformed census taking into a highly "intergovernmentalized" activity. Yet this interdependence alone did not dictate the shape of the intergovernmental partnerships that are described in this book.[42] Rather, the patchwork of relationships that constitute what I call *census federalism* emerged in fits and starts as the result of changes in the alignment of the *motives, means,* and *opportunities* of officials at multiple levels of government, including presidents, governors, mayors, state attorneys general, census statisticians, state demographers, city planners, and others.

To understand census federalism, we first must examine what *motivates* state and local officials to form partnerships that support a complete count. Over the last four decades, the bureau has relied on state and local officials to, among other things, support the creation of its Master Address File, mobilize participation in the census through outreach campaigns, and supply corrections to erroneous US Census tabulations. Of course, all units of government have a vested interest in helping the bureau "get it right." Yet this interest alone is hardly a sufficient condition for collective action. True, in many cases, a reminder letter from the Census Bureau or a visit from bureau staff is all the motivation state and local officials need to become partners in counting. City planners who have vivid memories of a past undercount, a lost congressional seat, or a significant drop in federal funding hardly need to be reminded of the value of census outreach or an accurate Master Address File. Similarly, prior to the 2020 Census, many states and cities with large populations of noncitizens needed little prompting to file a lawsuit to stop the Trump administration from adding a citizenship item to the census questionnaire. Yet for state and local officials, and certainly for their constituents, the effects of an accurate census are not always so obvious or traceable. For example, even as census researchers have developed an increasingly clear sense of how census undercounts affect grants in aid, it has been far more difficult for officials to establish conclusively the "return on investment" from census outreach itself.

The salience of the census is not the only factor that shapes state and local officials' motivations to take actions that shape the decennial count. The politics of census taking has also been increasingly defined by a widening ideological gap between elites in both major parties. As a number of studies have shown, this partisan polarization is asymmetric, driven largely by the Republican Party's well-documented shift to the extreme right over the last three decades.[43] A key indicator of this ideological shift is that Republicans have been increasingly willing to engage in what the legal scholar Mark Tushnet refers to as "constitutional hardball," or the violation of established norms to gain political advantage.[44] Republicans in state legislatures have, for example, led the way in passing legislation meant to disenfranchise voters who do not support them. This has included both engineering electoral advantages through both partisan gerrymandering and the introduction of administrative barriers that increase the cost of voting.[45] As the next chapter will show, it has also included efforts that manipulate the process of census taking to engineer undercounts that disadvantage Republicans' political opponents. To be sure, not all census operations have been subject to partisan polarization. As chapter 3 suggests, the Local Update of Census Addresses (LUCA) has remained fairly insulated from partisan politics. By contrast, as chapter 4 shows, for example, Republican officials in some—though not all—states were reluctant to invest in census outreach either because the census was swept up in larger partisan battles over state budgets or because they perceived that outreach campaigns would damage their reputation with conservative activists in their party. It appears that this logic held even in states that faced a significant undercount risk.

A second critical factor shaping census federalism is the *means* governments have at their disposal to engage in partnerships with one another. Building an effective outreach campaign, filing a lawsuit, and preparing an address list are all relatively costly actions. For states, cities, counties, and tribes operating under severe fiscal constraints, the costs of taking such actions may be prohibitive. And while the bureau has developed several programs to engage state and local governments as partners, it lacks the tools most federal agencies typically use to encourage intergovernmental cooperation. The bureau is not a regulatory agency, and it cannot compel states or cities to supply it with information or in-kind support. Nor is the bureau a grantmaking agency. It cannot use the "power of the purse" to support state and local governments' outreach campaigns or efforts to supply data on address lists. The bureau relies instead on a combination of technical assistance and exhortation to elicit cooperation from its subnational partners. While in some instances this has been enough, it has also forced state and local governments to find the fiscal space to support census operations. Especially given virtually all these governments operate under a balanced budget constraints and must commit significant portions of their budget to mandatory spending, support for census operations are relatively easy to deprioritize. For this reason, as chapter 4 shows, the intergovernmental relationships that support census outreach are often sustained by intersectoral partnerships between government, nonprofits, and philanthropies.

Finally, we must consider the *opportunity structure* that defines the collection of official statistics in the United States. As noted previously, the Census Bureau often explicitly attempts to create partnerships with state and local governments to support decennial operations. Over the last five decades, a growing number of census partnership programs have, for example, engaged state and local officials as users of census data, both as members of nonprofit organizations like the Association of Public Data Users and as participants of the State Data Center Program—a partnership between the bureau and state agencies to make census data available to the public through a network of state agencies, universities, libraries, and governments.[46] These partnerships have shaped the kinds of data products the Census Bureau creates.

Census officials have also engaged state and local officials as partners to improve the quality of data collection. Under the Census Address List Improvement Act of 1994, state and local governments can submit data that will enhance the accuracy of the bureau's Master Address File (see chapter 3).

Since the 1980s, the bureau has engaged state and local governments as partners in promoting census participation. These efforts expanded dramatically during and after the 2000 Census. By 2020, as chapter 4 shows, state and local governments were collectively investing billions of dollars in outreach and marketing campaigns, often directly targeting historically undercounted communities. Through the count review process—discussed in chapter 5—members of the Federal-State Cooperative for Population Estimates provide a quality check on census data collection. Finally, as chapter 6 shows, the Count Question Resolution Operation allows state and local governments to formally contest their population counts. Revisions to population counts, if accepted by the bureau, do not alter states' congressional apportionment but can nevertheless have a significant impact on the level of federal aid they receive.

Beyond these partnership activities, the bureau has also directly sought broader input from governments on planning census operations. In the years preceding the 2020 Census, for example, bureau staff held over a dozen consultation meetings with representatives from two hundred and fifty tribes, tribal governments, Alaska Native Corporations, and the National Congress of American Indians. These meetings produced a series of recommendations to improve tribal enumeration, ranging from allowing the identification of multiple heads of household to the hiring of local, bilingual enumerators.[47] The bureau also solicits feedback from state and local officials—as well as other census stakeholders—on proposed changes to the rules and procedures it uses in census taking. Prior to the 2020 Census, the bureau received over seventy-seven thousand comments calling for the end of the long-established practice of counting incarcerated persons at the correctional facility where they are held rather than at their prior home address, which "inflates the political power of the area where the prison is located, and deflates the political power in the prisoners' home communities."[48] While the bureau did not change its rules in response to this pressure, it did announce a plan to assist states that had passed legislation reallocating prisoners to their prior home addresses for redistricting purposes. These processes occur alongside regular meetings of advisory committees and experts the Census Bureau maintains to provide information and suggestions on a range of both technical and policy questions issues and major policy questions.[49]

While there are numerous venues for state and local officials to offer recommendations on changing decennial operations, their participation in Census Bureau programs does not always result in the outcomes these officials desire. As documented in chapter 6, cities challenging their 2020 Census counts did not always share the views of the bureau's career staff on the standards of evidence that should be used to adjudicate claims of an undercount. Moreover, not all debates over census taking can be effectively addressed through partnership programs, public comments, or advisory processes. On the one hand, some important decisions about census operations are not the bureau's to make. The most obvious example here is the funding of census operations. As the population grows, the Census Bureau must constantly adapt and improve its operations. Its ability to do so, however, is contingent on appropriations from Congress. When appropriators are in a cost-cutting mood, official statistics are not spared the axe. Between 2012 and 2017, Congress chronically underfunded operations for the 2020 Census—falling more than $200 billion short of the bureau's requests.[50] Bipartisan groups of officials wrote to both Congress and the president urging them to "equip the Census Bureau with the necessary funding and leadership to conduct an accurate count of the US population."[51] As the result of budget uncertainty, however, the bureau was forced to cancel several key operational tests and other projects—placing the 2020 Census on the Government Accountability Office's list of "high risk" assets.

In addition to being subject to Congress's fiscal mood swings, the bureau is constrained by its position within the executive branch itself. When Congress created a permanent Census Bureau in 1902, it placed the agency in a cabinet department. By contrast, some countries have vested responsibility for census taking in an independent statistical agency—free from direct political oversight.[52] After a year at the Department of the Interior, the bureau was moved to the new Department of Commerce and Labor. In 1913, when the department split in two, the bureau stayed within the Department of Commerce and has remained there ever since. This means that the secretary of commerce, a political appointee who serves at the pleasure of the president, has extensive—though not unlimited—authority over how the census is conducted.[53] This arrangement can place the secretary at odds with the bureau's career civil servants, and in some cases the bureau's director, who is appointed by the president, but under a statute passed by Congress in 2011, now has a fixed five-year term of office.[54]

When conflicts among federal, state, and local governments cannot be resolved through administrative processes, or through legislation, state and local officials often turn to the federal courts. Over the last five decades, the US Census has invited hundreds of lawsuits over numerous aspects of statistical operations. As the next chapter documents, there are several important reasons for this. American governing institutions—including ambiguities in census law—create numerous incentives for using litigation to resolve political disputes. Partisan gridlock, which can frustrate efforts to solve problems through the legislative process or in the executive branch, only increases the likelihood of litigation. Unsurprisingly, key features of census operations have been determined by decisions of the US Supreme Court.

In sum, while state and local governments can shape census taking in powerful ways, their participation in the politics of counting varies considerably, not only from state to state and city to city but also across the various streams of policy action that define the US Census. Indeed, "census federalism"—the pattern of intergovernmental relationships that shapes the production and consumption of population data—is not as the product of any coherent, top-down design. Rather, it is an emergent phenomenon, one that has arisen out of a growing interdependency between governments at multiple layers of the American federal system. Depending on the alignment of officials' motivations, means, and opportunities, the relationships that constitute census federalism can be more or less robust and more or less cooperative. In a state or a city where the risk of an undercount is high, where there is adequate fiscal capacity to support census engagement, and where there is minimal partisan opposition to census investments, intergovernmental partnerships are likely to be robust. By contrast, even when the undercount risk is substantial, inadequate resources and partisan opposition to census investments may impede the formation of intergovernmental partnerships. Finally, when there are few opportunities for state and local officials to influence census operations through partnerships, we might expect to see greater evidence of conflict, including conflict that takes the form of litigation. As we will see in the chapters to come, state and local governments often attempt to enhance the quality of census data as the Census Bureau's partners while simultaneously acting as the bureau's adversaries in federal courtrooms. To make sense of how these actions fit together, we now turn to a legal controversy that defined the 2020 Census more than any other: the fight over the Trump administration's proposed citizenship question.

CHAPTER TWO

Battle Royale

How State and Local Officials Stopped
the Citizenship Question

On President Donald Trump's first full day in office, his staff found themselves embroiled in a fight about numbers. In an episode that would foreshadow the duration of his four-year term, White House staff disputed estimates of the crowd size at Trump's inauguration. The new president had claimed that 1.5 million people had been at the ceremony and chastised the media reporting attendance figures that were, in his estimation, too low. For a week, the debate would continue. With no official count to rely on—the National Park Service had not produced such estimates since 1995—journalists consulted a range of crowd-size experts who put the attendance figures at anywhere from three hundred thousand to six hundred thousand people, less than half of what Trump suggested.[1]

Even as this skirmish receded into the background, Trump's war with official statistics rolled on, encompassing everything from death counts during Hurricane Maria or the COVID-19 pandemic to forecasts of how the attempted repeal of the Affordable Care Act would reduce the number of people with health insurance.[2] That war escalated on election night in 2020, when Trump—hours after the polls had closed—began insisting that Democrats in precincts around the country were going to "find . . . ballots at four o'clock in the morning and add them to the list." Trump's false allegations of massive voter fraud in the 2020 election animated what a congressional select committee would later call a "multi-part conspiracy" to overturn the results of that election, culminating in the violent January 6th attack on the US Capitol. As part of that conspiracy, Trump had—the committee found— "purposely disseminated" those false allegations, pressured state and federal officials, including members of Congress, to take actions that would overturn election results and underwrite an effort "to obtain and transmit false electoral certificates to the National Archives." Citing these same false allegations, Trump then "summoned tens of thousands of his supporters to

Washington," instructed them to "march to the Capitol" to "take back their country." Once the attack had begun, Trump sent messages to his supporters that "he knew would incite further violence," after which he "refused repeated requests" to tell his supporters to disperse.[3] While Trump's conspiracy to overturn the 2020 election failed, a large share of Republicans and Trump voters persisted in their belief that the election had been stolen.[4]

Trump's hostile relationship with facts and statistics—and his willingness to disrupt democratic processes when he did not like their results—constituted a potential threat to the integrity of the 2020 Census, too. That threat was magnified by his administration's approach to the issue of immigration. From the earliest days of his 2016 campaign, Trump promised to build a massive wall at the US–Mexico border and to deport "criminal aliens."[5] Policy rhetoric like this helped to tee up, even if it did not fully explain, Trump's most sustained effort to reshape the census, which centered on a proposal to include a new item on the 2020 questionnaire: "Is this person a citizen of the United States?" (see figure 2.1).[6] Significantly, the decision to include the citizenship item had been made not by Census Bureau experts but by Wilbur Ross, secretary of the Commerce Department, the Census Bureau's parent agency. Had Ross succeeded, it would have marked the first time the decennial census would have asked everyone living in the United States about their citizenship status.[7] Its inclusion could have placed millions of Americans at risk of being undercounted, shifting political power and resources away from states and cities with large Hispanic populations.[8] Even more troublingly, it could have underwritten an attempt to remove noncitizens from state population counts used to reapportion seats in Congress and state legislatures. Yet Ross's plan ultimately failed. As this chapter argues, it failed due to the work of a coalition led by state attorneys general (AGs), who—in partnership with major nongovernmental organizations (NGOs)—coordinated to fight the secretary all the way to the Supreme Court.

The story of the citizenship question controversy illustrates how the high-stakes politics of census taking plays out in the United States' adversarial legal system. The conflict, I argue, emerged from the conjuncture of two important forces. The first was the rise of *executive-centered partisanship*. From their earliest days in office, political appointees in the Trump administration used the state apparatus to advance the goals of the Republican Party. Despite Secretary Ross's attempts to conceal it, his plan was the brainchild of a Republican redistricting strategist who believed that a citizenship

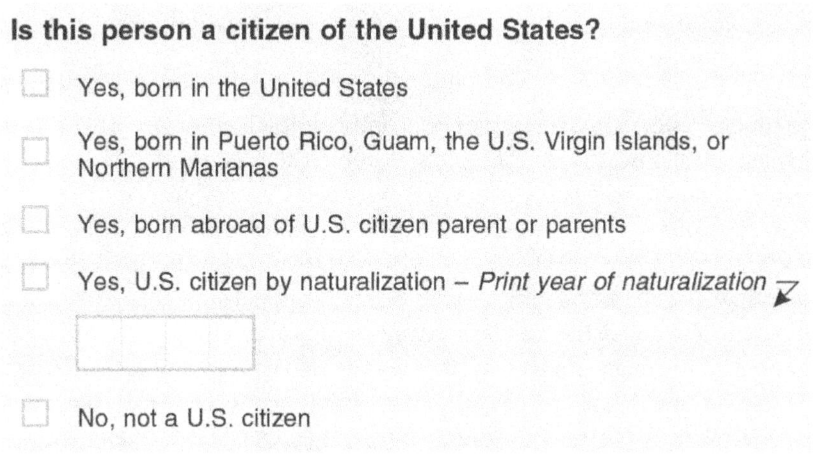

Is this person a citizen of the United States?

☐   Yes, born in the United States

☐   Yes, born in Puerto Rico, Guam, the U.S. Virgin Islands, or
      Northern Marianas

☐   Yes, born abroad of U.S. citizen parent or parents

☐   Yes, U.S. citizen by naturalization – *Print year of naturalization* ↘

```
┌──────────────┐
│              │
└──────────────┘
```

☐   No, not a U.S. citizen

Figure 2.1: Citizenship question proposed for the 2020 Census. Source: "Questions Planned for the 2020 Census and American Community Survey," US Census Bureau, March 2018, https://www2.census.gov/library /publications/decennial/2020/operations/planned-questions-2020-acs.pdf.

question would engineer a structural electoral advantage for, in his words, "Republicans and non-Hispanic Whites." Yet Ross's plan ran headlong into a second force: *intergovernmental legal mobilization*. In the several decades preceding the 2020 Census, state AGs had developed their capacity to collaborate in bringing sophisticated, multistate lawsuits against the federal government. The primary lawsuit over the citizenship question resulted in the production of thousands of pages of documents and a seven-day bench trial, both of which laid bare the extent to which Ross had gone to conceal the true reasons for his insistence on a citizenship question.[9] These revelations had a significant impact on the Supreme Court's 2019 decision in *Department of Commerce v. New York*, which put a stop to Ross's plan. This did not stop the Trump administration from attempting to accomplish their goals by other means. Yet the decision nevertheless showed the power of collective action and collaboration among state and local officials in defending the census from political sabotage.

High-Stakes Counting in an Adversarial Legal System

The US Census is no stranger to litigation. Since 1970, all but one decennial count has resulted in a significant legal and political controversy. The census invites conflict because it defines, as the political scientist Harold Lasswell famously put it, "who gets what, when, and how." Census figures have significant consequences for the political representation of millions of Americans and the allocation federal grants that flow through state and local governments, whose allocation formulas rely on census population data. Even small differences in population can have gigantic political consequences. New York lost one of its congressional seats by a margin of only eighty-nine people.[10]

As we saw in the last chapter, controversies over the census have not always taken the form of litigation. Yet in the latter half of the twentieth century, a legal conflict grew out of the Census Bureau's discovery that Black and Hispanic Americans were differentially undercounted relative to white, non-Hispanic Americans. Not only did these undercounts threaten to deprive states with highly urbanized and diverse populations of congressional seats, they also threatened to redirect billions of dollars in federal aid under major programs like Medicaid, the Elementary and Secondary Education Act, and the Community Development Block Grant program.[11] By the 1990s, the courts were awash in litigation over whether the Census Bureau could correct these differential undercounts through statistical sampling.

An important feature of these controversies is that, as with many policy conflicts in the United States, they often land in federal courtrooms and, not infrequently, before the US Supreme Court. Whereas other democracies rely primarily on experts, administrators, or multiparty negotiation to arbitrate disputes, American policymaking is defined by what Robert Kagan has called "adversarial legalism," in which disputes are resolved through legal contestation dominated by parties and lawyers.[12] Compared to their peers in other countries, American courts retain extensive authority to engage in judicial review of decisions about census taking. Understanding the politics of the US Census thus requires parsing through not only legislation, agency decisions, and press releases but also thousands of pages of lawyers' briefs, exhibit lists, trial transcripts, and judicial opinions.

The effects of the census on political power and federal funds are not the only forces animating these lawsuits. Rather, the law that undergirds the census makes it a magnet for conflict, because it both fractures authority across multiple institutions and contains important ambiguities. The Enumeration

Clause of the Constitution vests Congress with nearly unlimited discretion over census taking.[13] Yet Congress, in Title 13 of the US Code, delegates much of this authority to the executive branch.[14] Importantly, Congress located the Census Bureau within a cabinet department—since 1913 the Department of Commerce—whose secretary serves at the pleasure of the president.[15] This organizational arrangement naturally created the potential for conflict between political appointees tasked with carrying out the president's program and career experts in the civil service, bound by statutes, internal guidelines on data quality, and the norms of their respective professions. The possibility for conflict only intensified in 1976, however, when Congress amended the Census Act.[16] These amendments did two important things. First, they further consolidated the secretary of commerce's authority over census taking, giving him the power to make "rules and regulations as he deems necessary to carry out the functions and duties" of the bureau.[17] Simultaneously, the amendments imposed new constraints on the secretary's decisions. For example, Congress established limits on the use of certain statistical techniques, including sampling, in the production of census data.[18] By the 1990s, litigation had ensued over the meaning of some of these provisions, specifically whether the 1976 law allowed for the use of sampling to complement the traditional headcount.[19]

Another set of legal challenges over census taking has concerned potential violations of the Administrative Procedure Act (APA), a 1946 law that defines what federal agencies are allowed to do when they make regulations using the authority Congress has delegated to them. The APA also allows for judicial review of agency decisions to determine if they are, for example, contrary to the law or an "arbitrary and capricious" abuse of the agency's discretion. As this chapter shows, the APA has been a key tool for challenging the secretary of commerce's decisions about the census. At the same time, conservatives in the federal judiciary have pushed back to tighten the scope of APA review in recent years in ways that made a significant difference for census taking.[20]

Executive-Centered Partisanship and the Emergence of the Citizenship Question

To understand why the secretary of commerce embroiled himself in a fight over adding a citizenship question to the 2020 Census, it is helpful to look more broadly at the presidential administration in which he served. Donald Trump's presidency has been defined by what some political scientists have referred to as *executive-centered partisanship*. This is a style of governance marked by, as Nicholas Jacobs, Desmond King, and Sidney Milkis put it, "polarizing struggles about national identity that divide the nation by race, ethnicity, and religion." [21] Presidents who engage in executive-centered partisanship also strategically use the authority and resources of the administrative state to shore up the power of their party.

Beginning with his earliest days in office, with varying degrees of effectiveness, Trump deployed the administrative state to carry out key Republican Party objectives. Perhaps most significantly, he used the administrative process to pursue a crackdown on both legal and undocumented immigration, an issue he had placed at the center of his 2016 campaign. [22] Additionally, Trump engaged in an extensive attack on what he called the "deep state." This included, among other things, draining resources from federal statistical agencies, delegitimating experts in the civil service, and creating a short-lived advisory commission to propagate the myth of election fraud. [23]

The logic of executive-centered partisanship was perhaps nowhere more evident than in the Trump administration's push to include a citizenship question on the 2020 Census. This idea, after all, did not come from the bureau itself. Rather, it was the project of Secretary of Commerce Wilbur Ross. While the Census Act gives the secretary substantial, though not unlimited, authority to shape the decennial census, Ross defined his tenure by pushing boundaries. Mere weeks after his confirmation in late February 2017, Ross began asking his Deputy Chief of Staff Earl Comstock why the bureau had not proposed a citizenship item for the 2020 questionnaire. [24]

The reason for Ross's ask was not immediately apparent. The secretary claimed he was only "reinstating" a question that had been repeatedly used by the Census Bureau in the past. Yet a citizenship question has never been asked of the entire US population. Between 1890 and 1950, census forms contained a citizenship question that was asked only of the foreign-born population. Because persons born in the United States have birthright citizenship, this question was simply irrelevant for people born in the United States. [25] Starting in 1960, this question did not appear on census forms. [26] The adoption of a statutory requirement for annual alien registration, the bureau reasoned, made it unnecessary to inquire about the citizenship status of all households. By 1970, the bureau had also adopted a self-response survey—as opposed to door-to-door enumeration—as the primary mode of census administration. Asking additional questions on the short form, Bureau researchers found, increased the costs of fielding the census and took a toll on the response rate itself. The bureau also concluded that reintroducing a citizenship question on the short form could cause misunderstandings, confusion, or fear and would, in turn, generate a lower response rate.[27] Thus the citizenship question, as well as a number of other items, was moved from the census questionnaire itself to what became known as the "long form" census, sent only to a small representative sample of American households. In 2010, the long-form survey was replaced by the annual American Community Survey (ACS). Both the long-form survey and the ACS are used for statistical purposes other than a complete enumeration of the US population. Today, the short-form census is the only instrument the Census Bureau uses to obtain the complete count required by the Constitution.

These changes in bureau policy notwithstanding, the idea of reintroducing a citizenship question on the short-form census had floated in circles of conservative political activists for years. There are several potential rationales that could have animated this move. First, given increasing support within the Republican Party for reducing both legal and undocumented immigration, it is possible that the question was intended to cast a spotlight on what the Trump administration had cast as a crisis. To be sure, the addition of the question would likely reduce census participation among noncitizens and citizens alike. Yet even an artificially deflated population might allow Republicans to claim, however erroneously, that Trump's hardline policies on immigration had worked.[28]

Second, political appointees like Ross could have perceived that adding a citizenship question to the census would have advantageous partisan effects. As numerous analyses would eventually show, the citizenship question would have depressed census participation in areas with large noncitizen and Hispanic populations, shifting federal money and congressional seats away from states where those populations are concentrated. On the national level, this would have included both Democratic strongholds like California as well as Republican redoubts like Texas. Yet at a state level, the effects would have been more one-sided. Urban areas with a large Democratic voter base would experience higher differential undercounts than Republican suburbs. In New York, for example, such a shift would mean a net gain in state representation for Republican-heavy Nassau County and a net loss for the boroughs of Brooklyn and Queens.[29] This would allow Republicans to improve their margins in state legislatures, which play a powerful

role in shaping the national political arena through both congressional redistricting and the passage of election laws.[30]

A third potential rationale has less to do with differential undercounts
themselves and more to do with how President Trump and Republican state
legislators could have used data on noncitizens to make a more fundamental
change in the structure of American political representation. The argument
went as follows: if noncitizens could be identified in the census, they could
also be removed from the population figures used to redistrict Congress and
state legislatures—engineering a long-term structural advantage for Republicans. The history of this idea is a long one. Since the "reapportionment
revolution" of the 1960s, the Supreme Court has held that the Constitution
requires Congress and state legislative districts to be composed of a roughly
equal number of people, regardless of their eligibility to vote or citizenship
status. Yet for decades, Republican redistricting strategists and conservative
legal advocates have argued that the Court's protection of the "one person,
one vote" principle applies to individual *voters*, not persons.[31]

By 2015, this argument reached the Supreme Court in the case of *Evenwel v. Abbott*, in which two Texas voters claimed that the state's legislative
districts—drawn using total population rather than populations of eligible
voters—violated the Equal Protection Clause of the Fourteenth Amendment. The Court unanimously rejected this argument. Yet in separate concurring opinions, two conservatives—Justices Samuel Alito and Clarence
Thomas—argued that the Constitution gave states wide latitude to apply the
"one person, one vote" principle as they saw fit, even if that meant excluding
noncitizens from the population bases used in redistricting.[32]

Making this work legally, however, virtually required citizenship data
derived from the census. As the *Evenwel* case had made clear, the most granular data available for excluding noncitizens from redistricting population
bases came from the American Community Survey's tabulations of citizen
voting-age population (CVAP). Yet this data, used by the Department of
Justice to administer the Voting Rights Act, could not be easily used for
redistricting. For example, redistricting required population counts to be
accurate at the block level, the smallest unit of census geography. CVAP
data were often highly inaccurate at this level. Moreover, CVAP data were
not even available for Census Voting Districts, a geographical unit virtually
all states used as a building block in redistricting. Most importantly, it appeared highly unlikely that the Supreme Court would accept CVAP data as
a valid alternative to "actual enumeration" data from the census.[33]

No one understood these challenges better than Thomas B. Hofeller, a longtime Republican redistricting strategist with close ties to the Trump administration. In a 2015 analysis commissioned by the Washington Free Beacon, a conservative news outlet, Hofeller had argued that identifying and eliminating noncitizens from Texas state legislative districts—which would only be legally possible with census-derived citizenship data—"would be advantageous" for enhancing the political power of "Republicans and non-Hispanic whites."[34] As a cache of documents released following his death in 2018 would reveal, Hofeller had pushed this plan to members of President Trump's transition team as well as Ross's expert adviser on the census.[35]

Soon after his confirmation as secretary of commerce, Wilbur Ross also became an aggressive proponent of adding the citizenship question. On the advice of White House advisor Steve Bannon, Ross soon spoke with Kansas Secretary of State Kris Kobach (R) about the idea and its significant consequences for congressional apportionment.[36] Ross also contacted Attorney General Jeff Sessions about the proposal.[37] By May, 2017, the secretary was in hot pursuit of a legal rationale to justify the inclusion of the question, emailing Earl Comstock that he was "mystified" at the lack of progress on revising the questionnaire given the deadline to submit census questions to Congress in less than a year.[38]

Ross's confusion may well have been the result of his ignorance about basic Census Bureau procedures. Questions proposed for the census typically undergo a lengthy process of legal, technical, and policy review. For example, a proposal to integrate questions on race and ethnicity on the 2020 Census underwent nine years of intensive research and analysis, and received extensive stakeholder input, prior to the bureau's internal December 31, 2017, deadline for finalizing census questions. Because a final decision had not been made by this deadline, the bureau opted against making changes to the race and ethnicity question. By contrast, as of that same internal deadline, the bureau researchers had done *no* statistical analyses concerning the effects of a citizenship question on response rates or data accuracy.[39]

The secretary could not easily circumvent these processes. The Paperwork Reduction Act and other federal regulations still required Ross to provide a valid justification for adding a citizenship item to the 2020 questionnaire.[40] Ross, for reasons that will become clear momentarily, did not wish to be transparent about his motivations for including the citizenship question. So Deputy Chief of Staff Earl Comstock, well aware of the legal constraints, proceeded to find another federal agency "that would have a reason" to request the inclusion of a citizenship question.[41] The agency that seemed best capable of laundering the request was the Department of Justice (DOJ), whose Civil Rights Division used CVAP estimates from the American Community Survey in its enforcement of the Voting Rights Act.[42]

If Ross thought that the DOJ would quickly and enthusiastically support the proposal, however, he was sorely mistaken. Under intense media and congressional scrutiny following the firing of Federal Bureau of Investigations Director James Comey, DOJ leaders displayed little interest in Ross's plan. By the beginning of the summer, officials at both the DOJ's Executive Office of Immigration and the Department of Homeland Security had both turned Comstock down, much to Ross's chagrin.[43] As he would later admit in an email, the secretary knew that the issue would likely end up in the Supreme Court, which meant that the Commerce Department "should be very careful" about the kinds of documents that went into the administrative record justifying the decision.[44] It would have to look like an authentic request from the DOJ, not one cooked up in the Commerce Department.

After several months of conversations with Commerce Department lawyers, Ross had reached his breaking point and contacted Attorney General Jeff Sessions personally. He was ultimately put in touch with the acting Assistant Attorney General for Civil Rights John Gore.[45] Gore and other political appointees at the DOJ would eventually deploy the arguments developed by the Commerce Department in a letter—later signed by the Justice Management Division's Arthur E. Gary and thus dubbed the "Gary letter" in legal proceedings—suggesting that the census was the "most appropriate vehicle" for collecting reliable data on the citizen population of voting age.[46]

The Gary letter's rationale for requesting the citizenship question ran as follows. The DOJ wanted census-derived citizenship data to better enforce Section 2 of the Voting Rights Act. This part of the law prohibits racial "vote dilution," in which a racial group is "improperly deprived of a single-member district in which it could form a majority." To enforce this requirement, DOJ must evaluate "whether a racial group could constitute a majority in a single-member district." Making this determination typically required CVAP data derived from the American Community Survey. Yet, as the letter put it, ACS data was not ideal, in part because its one-year, three-year, and five-year estimates did not "align in time" with census data governments used for redistricting.[47]

After receiving the letter, Census Bureau staff naturally had questions for the DOJ. Yet the attorney general now prohibited DOJ lawyers from meeting with them.[48] The bureau's chief scientist John Abowd set about evaluating the potential effects of the citizenship question on response rates and data quality.[49] In light of extensive research on the relationship between census content and data quality, Abowd's conclusions were not surprising. Adding a citizenship question would substantially increase the costs of taking the census and would likely lead to a drop-off in self-response rates. In a series of memoranda prepared for the commerce secretary in late December and early January, Abowd analyzed several different options for obtaining citizenship information from the census. Under what Abowd labeled as "Alternative A," the bureau could leave the questionnaire as it was and prepare a separate estimate of CVAP for all Census Blocks. The secretary's preferred option, "Alternative B," involved adding a citizenship item to the 2020 questionnaire. By contrast, under "Alternative C," the bureau would leave the census questionnaire as is but "add the capability to link an accurate, edited citizenship variable from administrative records to the final 2020 Census microdata files."[50]

Based on his analysis of these alternatives—presented in a January 19, 2018, memo—Abowd recommended collecting citizenship data from administrative records only (Alternative C). As table 2.1 shows, Alternative C provided the improved CVAP data DOJ purportedly needed. True, the addition of the citizenship question (Alternative B) would also provide this data, yet this option had a significant downside. It would contribute to significant cost increases and would "harm the quality of the census count." For a fraction of the cost of Alternative B, collecting citizenship data from administrative records would produce better CVAP data without constituting the threat to self-response posed by adding a citizenship question. On March 1, following discussions with Secretary Ross, Abowd analyzed a fourth option (Alternative D), which would combine a citizenship question with the collection of administrative data. Yet as Abowd put it, this option would do little to mitigate "the negative cost and quality implications of Alternative B" and would still produce "poorer quality citizenship data than Alternative C."[51] In sum, even when evaluated according to the criteria the secretary had identified, adding the citizenship question—either alone or in combination with administrative records—was remarkably inferior to other proposed alternatives.

As Census Bureau statisticians evaluated the contrived DOJ request, Ross directed Commerce Department officials to meet with stakeholders to discuss the proposal. Most of these stakeholders—which included leaders

Table 2.1. Analysis of Alternatives from Abowd Memoranda on January 19 and March 1

Alternative	Impact on 2020 Census	Impacts on Citizen-Age Voting Age Population (CVAP) Data
Alternative A (Status Quo, Special Data Product)	*Cost Increase*: $200,000 (later revised to $350,000)	None
Alternative B (Citizenship Question)	*Cost Increase*: $27,500,000 *Quality Risks*: 154,000 fewer correct enumerations; citizenship status is misreported at a very high rate for noncitizens.	Block-level data improved but with serious quality issues remaining.
Alternative C (Administrative Data Only)	*Cost Increase*: < $2,000,000	Improved quality for block-level citizenship data.
Alternative D (Citizenship Question and Administrative Data)	*Cost Increase*: > $27,500,000 *Quality Risks*: 154,000 fewer correct enumerations; citizenship status is misreported at a very high rate for noncitizens.	Lower quality citizenship data than Alternative C due to lowered record linkage rate for persons with administrative citizenship data.

Source: *New York v. Department of Commerce*, "Technical Review of the Department of Justice Request to Add Citizenship Question to the 2020 Census," Ad. Rec. (2018), 1277–1278; *New York v. Department of Commerce*, "Preliminary Analysis of Alternative D (Combined Alternatives B and C)," Ad. Rec. (2018), 1308–1312.

of scientific societies like the American Statistical Association, former Census Bureau directors, and members of the bureau's own Scientific Advisory Committee—opposed adding the item to the 2020 questionnaire.[52] Commerce Department officials were forced to seek out "someone thoughtful who can speak to the pros of adding [a citizenship] question." Ron Jarmin, interim director of the Census Bureau, attempted to identify a researcher or policy analyst at the American Enterprise Institute, a venerable conservative think tank, to do just this. Yet he came up short. Not a single person at the institute was apparently willing to go on record in favor of the question. The only think tanks that stepped up to the plate were the Center for Immigration Studies and the Heritage Foundation, both of which had supported using citizenship data for a reason *other* than the one Ross was hoping to employ as a cover story.[53] Specifically, policy analysts at both organizations had long supported fully *removing* undocumented persons from apportionment counts used in congressional redistricting—just as Thomas Hofeller had envisioned.[54]

Yet neither Abowd's memorandum, nor the preponderance of stakeholder commentary, appeared to persuade Ross. On March 26, 2018, he issued a memorandum announcing that he would adopt Alternative D. This would add citizenship item to the 2020 questionnaire and collect additional citizenship data via administrative records. Ross summarily eliminated the status-quo option (Alternative A) because it ignored the DOJ request. On the other hand, he dismissed statisticians' concerns about including the citizenship question (Alternative B) because they had been based on response rates from the American Community Survey, whose response rates differed from the decennial census. Ignoring much of what Abowd had written, Ross concluded that he "was not able to isolate what percentage of decline was caused by the inclusion of a citizenship question rather than some other aspect of the long-form survey."[55]

Even if the citizenship question had "some impact on responses," the secretary argued, the "value" of "more complete and accurate data derived from surveying the entire population outweighs such concerns."[56] Further, even though the bureau concluded that using administrative records (Alternative C) would produce higher-quality citizenship data than either Alternatives B or D, Ross expressed doubts: "The Census Bureau is still evolving its use of administrative records, and the bureau does not yet have a complete administrative records data set for the entire population."[57]

Ross's memo would prove to be the first shot in a war that would consume census preparations over the next two years. Public officials and nongovernmental organizations around the country quickly sounded the alarm.

Putting the Citizenship Question on Trial: State and Local Governments Take Action

One week after Secretary Ross released his decision memo, a coalition of eighteen states, fifteen local governments, the District of Columbia, and the US Conference of Mayors filed suit in the Southern District of New York to stop the plan from going into effect. Several months later, a coalition of nongovernmental organizations led by the New York Immigration Coalition and the American Civil Liberties Union would file a companion suit. Even before Ross's plan was finalized, state and local officials had become aware of the potential harm the citizenship question could do to their representation in Congress and their receipt of census-derived federal funds. In early February, 2018, a coalition of twenty state AGs, led by New York's Eric Schneiderman, sent Ross a twelve-page letter warning him that adding a citizenship question would "disproportionately harm states and cities with large immigrant communities" and jeopardize the Census Bureau's ability to carry out its obligations under the Constitution.[58] Ross now had a problem on his hands: a phalanx of legal opponents, organized primarily by state AGs along with a coalition of nongovernmental organizations . Over the next year, this coalition would ultimately put his plan on ice.

A New Context for Census Litigation

State and local governments have been at the center of census litigation for the last five decades. Following the release of the 1970 Census results, the bureau experienced a flood of lawsuits filed by local officials and organizations representing ethnic and racial minorities, which claimed that census enumeration procedures had led to systematic undercounts.[59] In nearly every decade since, the US Census has been subjected to a similar onslaught of litigation.[60] Yet the political and institutional context for the 2020 Census differed from the past in several ways that both intensified and widened the scope of the conflict. First, most lawsuits on prior censuses concerned either the implementation of new technologies to improve statistical accuracy or the secretary of commerce's decision about where overseas federal employees should be enumerated. Sixty-eight of the eighty-eight lawsuits filed during the 1980, 1990, and 2000 Census cycles focused on statistical procedures (see figure 2.2). Prior to the 2020 cycle, however, federal courts had only dealt with issues of citizenship in the census three times. Two of

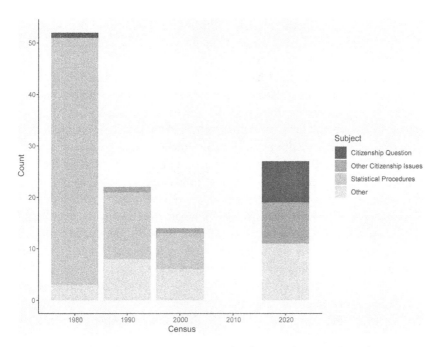

Figure 2.2: Federal litigation concerning the decennial census, by subject, 1980–2020 cycles. Source: Author's analysis of US Bureau of the Census, *1980 Census of Population and Housing: History* (Government Printing Office, 1986), appendix 10B; US Bureau of the Census, *1990 Census of Population and Housing: History* (Government Printing Office, 1995), appendix 12B; US Census Bureau, *History: 2000 Census of Population and Housing*, vol. 2 (US Census Bureau, 2009), 517–594; Jennifer D. Williams, *The 2010 Decennial Census: Background and Issues* (Congressional Research Service, 2011); Madiba Dennie and Thomas Wolf, "The State of Census Lawsuits," Brennan Center for Justice, January 12, 2021, https://www.brennancenter.org /our-work/analysis-opinion/state-census-lawsuits.

these challenges—ultimately rejected in district court—focused on the in-clusion of noncitizens in apportionment counts.[61] Only one case, dismissed by a district court in 1980, had ever addressed the possibility of including a citizenship question on the short-form census. Moreover, the 1980 case was focused on whether the secretary was *required* to include such a question, not whether he was allowed to do so if he knew it would cause significant problems for census accuracy.[62]

Thus Ross's decision to include a citizenship question on the census—and the Trump administration's subsequent actions to collect citizenship data in the absence of the question—opened up a relatively unsettled legal terrain. The decision would have significant political stakes. On the one hand, it intensified an already-fractious debate over the Trump administration's nativist immigration policy. At the same time, it had dire consequences for state and local governments that social science researchers and networks of policy advocates would soon make visible. Even under conservative projections of how the citizenship question would affect the undercount, over a dozen states would lose funds under several major federal programs and half a dozen states would lose representation in the House of Representatives.[63] The somewhat unsettled nature of census law, combined with the potentially explosive effects of Ross's decision, guaranteed that state and local governments' participation in the case would be extensive and that the case would likely reach the Supreme Court.

Over the decades preceding Ross's decisions, state and local governments had also become increasingly effective at challenging federal agencies in court. Between 1990 and 2017, the annual number of multistate legal actions brought against the federal government more than tripled.[64] In these lawsuits, state AGs leveraged an increasingly deep pool of financial resources and broad-based interstate networks made up of policy and legal experts.

Aside from bringing suits themselves, state AGs often file coordinated *amicus curiae* (friend of the court) briefs in coalition with their peers across the country.[65] Additionally, state AGs exert various forms of "soft power," including regulatory comments and formal letters to federal agencies.[66]

State and local governments exhibited a particularly high level of coordination in response to Ross's decision. As noted above, the first complaint against Ross was filed by a coalition of thirty-four units of government and the US Conference of Mayors. By the time his decision reached the Supreme Court, it would attract amicus briefs on both sides of the issue cosigned by thirty-seven additional state and local governments or organizations representing these governments (see figure 2.3). This was nearly four times higher than the average number of state and local parties and amici in all prior census cases reaching the high court.[67]

State legal actions challenging federal policies are also, increasingly, a form of partisan policy combat. Over the last twenty years, Republican and Democratic Attorneys General Associations have increasingly attracted the

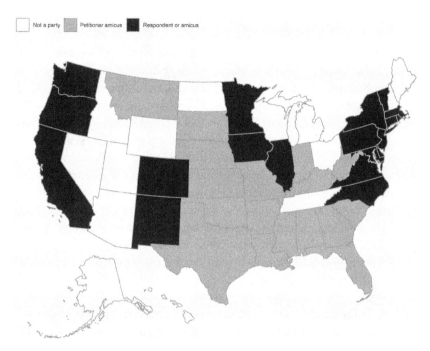

Figure 2.3: State involvement in *Department of Commerce v. New York* (2019). Source: US Supreme Court, Docket No. 18–966.

attention of political donors, as have the campaigns of individual AGs. By the first year of Donald Trump's presidency, as Paul Nolette and Colin Provost have found, amicus briefs prepared by partisan coalitions constituted over 78 percent of all those filed by AGs in the Supreme Court.[68] While partisan conflict over the census is nothing new, coordinated multistate census litigation has taken on an increasingly partisan cast. In the lawsuit concerning the citizenship question, all state government plaintiffs, as well as all amici supporting them before the Supreme Court, were Democratic state officials.[69] Similarly, all amicus briefs filed in support of the Trump administration came from Republican state officials. Thus by the time the conflict over the citizenship question reached the Supreme Court, thirty-six states and the District of Columbia were involved as parties or amici, split along partisan lines.[70]

Putting the Legal Support Structure to Use

Stopping Ross's plans required state and local governments to have a well-resourced and highly coordinated legal strategy. Lawyers challenging Ross's decision had to weave together arguments about multiple provisions of the US Constitution, the Census Act, and—perhaps most importantly—the Administrative Procedure Act (APA). Under the APA, federal courts are to set aside agency decisions that are made contrary to law. They are also required to set aside "arbitrary and capricious" decisions, or those that do not follow a logical and rational decision-making process. For example, a secretary of commerce who included a new question on the census but failed to provide a "coherent explanation" for deviating from past practices or failed to consider evidence about the effects of that decision on census data quality might fail "arbitrary and capricious" review in the courts.[71]

To effectively make these claims on the merits, plaintiffs in census lawsuits must also prove that they have standing to sue. Specifically, they must show that the actions of the federal government have injured or are highly likely to injure a legally protected interest in a concrete way.[72] State governments can sue over census procedures if they constitute a "substantial risk" of losing federal funding or a seat in the House of Representatives. Yet even after clearing this bar, plaintiffs are not done. They must still demonstrate that their injuries are traceable to the actions of the defendant. For example, there must be a causal connection between the secretary of commerce's decision to include a citizenship question and the expected loss of a seat in the House. Finally, plaintiffs must prove that the Court can redress their injury. For example, a state must be able to show that by preventing the citizenship question from going on the 2020 questionnaire, the Court will be able to reduce the net undercount, thereby stemming the loss of federal funding or congressional representation.

Thus in addition to a team of seasoned lawyers, the plaintiffs needed a great deal of evidence that supported their legal claims. Beyond factual testimony and evidence about how Secretary Ross made his decision, the government plaintiffs in the case required expert witnesses who could use social science research to testify about how including a citizenship question would increase the differential undercount and how that undercount would translate into a loss of congressional representation and federal funds. By the end of the trial, plaintiffs would introduce 688 exhibits, among them the declarations of close to a dozen expert witnesses.

Bringing a lawsuit against Ross's Commerce Department also involved unique challenges of its own. Commerce Department lawyers employed a variety of legal tactics to stop the case from proceeding. During the "discovery" phase of the case—in which plaintiffs obtain evidence from the defendants in the form of depositions and document production—the Commerce Department submitted a highly selective administrative record, which omitted key materials concerning Ross's deliberations and communications about the citizenship question from the spring and summer of 2017, the period when the secretary and his staffers were attempting to concoct a rationale that other agencies could use to request the inclusion of the question. Commerce Department lawyers also made multiple challenges to the Court's authorization of discovery *beyond* the administrative record. In over a dozen separate motions, they attempted to halt the case altogether. Responding to this aggressive defense strategy required extensive resources and legal expertise.

The Office of the New York State Attorney General led the coalition of government plaintiffs, whose suit landed before Judge Jesse M. Furman of the Southern District of New York, an appointee of President Barack Obama.[73] The plaintiffs made several key legal claims. First, they charged that Secretary Ross had violated the Enumeration Clause of the Constitution, which required "an actual Enumeration" of the "whole number of persons" in the United States. Adding a citizenship question would "deter participation in the decennial census," causing an undercount.[74]

Second, they charged that Ross's decision violated the APA because it was made contrary to two laws that govern the collection of official statistics: the Census Act and the Information Quality Act. Specifically, the secretary had violated the Census Act's mandate that he collect information from administrative records rather than questions on the census form itself to the "maximum extent possible"; he had also failed to mention his desire to include citizenship as a census item in a mandatory report to Congress. Further, the plaintiffs claimed, Ross violated the Information Quality Act's requirements to adequately test the citizenship question, minimize its burden on respondents, maximize data quality, and ensure the highest rates of response.

Third, the plaintiffs argued that Secretary Ross had violated the APA because his decision was both "arbitrary and capricious" and an "abuse of discretion." There was, they alleged, no support for the idea that the DOJ required citizenship data from the census to enforce the Voting Rights Act.

The secretary had provided no reasoned explanation for violating seven decades of "settled and well-considered practice" and contradicting factual findings made by the Census Bureau's experts. Ross had also ignored relevant aspects of the problem, including the risk of increasing the inaccuracy of census data.[75] For all these reasons, they asked the Court to enjoin the Commerce Department from including the citizenship item on the 2020 Census questionnaire.

Lawyers for the Commerce Department were eager to kill the suit before the discovery process could proceed. By late May 2018, they moved to dismiss the suit on multiple grounds.[76] Their arguments leaned heavily on the idea that the plaintiffs did not have standing to sue.[77] Among other things, the allegations that the citizenship question would result in a reduced response rate were "too speculative" and were "not fairly traceable" to the secretary's actions since it would be "impossible to isolate and quantify the number of individuals who would have responded but for the addition of the citizenship question." Another key claim was that the plaintiffs could not sue under the Enumeration Clause of the Constitution, in part because the federal government used the census for purposes beyond a "strict headcount," including the allocation of federal funds to state and local governments and the administration of the Voting Rights Act.[78]

After weighing these issues, Judge Furman issued a ruling in late July. He found only one of the defendants' arguments—the claim that Ross had not violated the Enumeration Clause—plausible. By contrast, he denied all of the defendants' remaining motions to dismiss—finding that the plaintiffs still had standing to sue and that the secretary of commerce's decision could not be insulated from judicial review. The bottom line: The case could proceed.[79]

Furman's ruling also meant that the Commerce Department's lawyers had to rely on another legal gambit: shielding as much information about Ross's decision from discovery as they could. Their legal strategy, as they likely knew, could easily crumble once it became obvious that the citizenship question resulted from the secretary's own machinations rather than a genuine request from the DOJ. If they could not stop the case from proceeding, the next best option was to prevent the admission of evidence that would undermine their defense.

Lawyers for the Commerce Department attempted to keep damaging evidence from coming to light in several ways. First, they produced an initial administrative record that was sanitized of numerous important details relating to Secretary Ross's deliberations and communications in early 2017, prior to the DOJ's issuance of the "Gary letter."[80] Whenever possible, they also slow-walked their responses to court orders compelling the production of key documents in the case. Finally, they asserted that the disclosure of numerous documents, as well as the depositions of Secretary Ross and Assistant Attorney General John Gore were protected by several legal privileges. This ranged from attorney-client privileges, Title 13's protections of personal identifying information in the census, as well as "deliberative process" privileges, which shield certain kinds of internal agency communications from disclosure.[81]

In the face of this strategy, the plaintiffs' lawyers fought to pry loose every bit of the evidence they believed would be germane to the case. Luckily, the public record clearly showed that the call to create the citizenship question came from the president and senior administration appointees and not from the DOJ. All of this suggested that the Commerce Department was acting in bad faith, which warranted the production of "extra-record evidence" such as depositions and sworn declarations. With this evidence, the plaintiffs successfully petitioned Judge Furman for an order compelling the defendants to complete the administrative record and an order authorizing discovery "outside the record," which plaintiffs hoped would ultimately include depositions from Gore and Ross.

As the trial date drew near, and as evidence about Ross's real motivations for including a citizenship question became clearer, his legal team grew increasingly desperate. In September, lawyers for the secretary petitioned the Second Circuit Court of Appeals, and ultimately the Supreme Court, to block further discovery in the case, including and especially the depositions of Ross and Gore, as well as to halt the trial itself. At every turn, plaintiffs argued forcefully that these petitions were meritless, in part because Furman had carefully applied the law and because the evidence of bad faith on the part of the Trump administration was overwhelming. In the end, only one of these challenges was successful. In late October, the Supreme Court blocked the deposition of Secretary Ross in a brief, unsigned opinion.[82] On November 5—without Ross's deposition in hand—the case proceeded to a bench trial in front of Judge Furman.

The Citizenship Question on Trial

The proceedings that unfolded in Judge Furman's courtroom could well be called "the census trial of the century." Arguing the case for the government plaintiffs was a team of over a dozen seasoned litigators led by Matthew Colangelo and Elena Goldstein of the New York attorney general's office. Alongside them were six prominent lawyers representing the coalition of nongovernmental organizations also suing the Commerce Department, including Dale Ho of the American Civil Liberties Union, as well as John Freedman, Ada Anon, and David Gersch, who together represented the New York Immigration Coalition. Collectively, plaintiffs brought decades of litigation experience to bear on the case. The Trump administration also brought in a team of nine experienced DOJ career attorneys, several of whom would later—and for unspecified reasons—request to leave the cases.[83]

The strength of the plaintiffs' litigation strategy was on full display over the course of the seven-day trial. To begin, they introduced several expert witnesses to testify about the effects of the citizenship question on the response rate. The first of these was D. Sunshine Hillygus, a Duke University political scientist who had served for six years on the Census Scientific Advisory Committee and who testified that "noncitizens and Hispanics are differentially concerned about the confidentiality of a citizenship question" and would be "less likely to participate" in a survey that includes such a question.[84] Even using the "best conservative estimate" produced by researchers at the Census Bureau, including a citizenship question would result in a 5.8 percent reduction in self-response. Yet Hillygus also gave several reasons why this number was too low. For example, while the estimate was based on data collected for the 2010 American Community Survey, the citizenship question—thanks to the efforts of the Trump administration—would be far more visible in 2020, which could further depress self-response among noncitizens and recently naturalized immigrants alike.

On cross-examination, the DOJ's Martin Tomlinson attempted to undercut the force of Hillygus's testimony.[85] His questions aimed to show that Hillygus had not conducted her own research on the effects of the citizenship question and that she had no inside knowledge of how the bureau's communications campaign might attempt to offset the effects of the citizenship question. On redirect examination by the plaintiffs' lawyers, Hillygus emphasized that any uncertainties in her analysis were further evidence that the Census Bureau had not done its due diligence in pretesting the citizenship question prior to Ross's decision to include it.[86]

Nor was Hillygus's testimony the only evidence the plaintiffs offered up to chart the potential magnitude and effects of an undercount. Throughout

the course of the trial—in both affidavits as well as testimony on the stand—
the plaintiffs' expert witnesses reinforced her argument that the scale of the
undercount could be larger than the 5.8 percent estimate initially calculated
by the bureau. Even a modest 2 percent undercount of households containing noncitizens, the political scientist Christopher Warshaw testified, would
reduce the population enumerations of jurisdictions home to large numbers of noncitizen households. More than a dozen cities or counties would
lose a substantial portion of their state's population, diluting their residents'
power in state legislatures. The inclusion of the question could also put half
a dozen states at risk of losing a seat in Congress.[87] Moreover, as an affidavit
by the social scientist Andrew Reamer confirmed, under this almost implausibly optimistic 2 percent assumption, plaintiff states like New York and
New Jersey would lose millions of dollars in federal funding under grant
programs to support education, health insurance, social services, and home
energy assistance.[88]

Beyond the analyses of expert witnesses, the plaintiffs relied on the testimony of state and local officials themselves. One local official appearing on
the witness stand was Joseph Salvo, a veteran of four censuses and director
of the population division at New York City's Department of City Planning,
which supported both the city's outreach efforts as well as its review of address lists to inform the bureau's Master Address File. Salvo's background
lent credibility to two of the key claims that he made on the stand. First, his
testimony revealed that the harms of the citizenship question extended beyond congressional representation and federal funding. By weakening the
quality of census data, the citizenship question would also impede the city's
ability to make decisions about how to allocate public services. For example,
Salvo noted that the Department of Health frequently requested population data to calculate rates of disease incidence by neighborhood. While
the Health Department collected high-quality data on the numerator for
these rates, a census undercount would mean an inaccurate denominator,
meaning that "the Health Department can't make good decisions on where
to deploy resources."[89]

Second, Salvo's testimony cut away at the Commerce Department's argument that lower self-response rates were nothing to worry about.[90] Lawyers
for the secretary had suggested that even if the citizenship question resulted
in lower self-response rates, this problem could be offset through the Non-
response Follow-up (NRFU) operation, during which census enumerators
visit unresponsive households to collect census data in person. Yet Salvo

suggested otherwise. A household unlikely to self-respond to the census due to the citizenship question would, for the same reason, be just as likely not to respond to a NRFU enumerator. Additionally, as Salvo's experience with the 2000 Census revealed, NRFU often failed to capture households with addresses that did not make it into the bureau's Master Address File or were erroneously classified as vacant. In 2010, he estimated, this problem had resulted in an undercount of sixty-five thousand residents of Brooklyn neighborhoods like Bay Ridge, Dyker Heights, and Bensonhurst. Finally, the lower self-response rate would result in an enormous increase in the workload of NRFU enumerators. In short, the administration's depiction of NRFU as a cure for all the citizenship question's ills was a fantasy.

The trial culminated in nearly three grueling days of witness testimony by the Census Bureau's chief scientist, John Abowd.[91] While Abowd served as the defendants' sole expert witness, his testimony in fact added more weight to the arguments made by the plaintiffs. As he testified, the Census Bureau had supplied Ross with the best available analysis about the consequences of adding the question, which suggested that it would conservatively result in a 5.8 percent decrease in self-response. Understandably, Abowd had strongly cautioned against adding the citizenship question. Yet as the administrative record revealed, Ross had little interest in the chief scientist's analysis or opinions. Forced to confront this fact on the witness stand, Abowd became visibly choked up and held back tears.[92]

As an expert witness, Abowd also weakened the defendants' argument that NRFU could cure the ills of the citizenship question. The bureau, he testified, had never tested how NRFU operations would work with a citizenship question on the census.[93] Yet there was, he said, little reason to believe that households declining to self-respond would be more likely to respond to an in-person enumerator.[94] Additionally, Abowd said, NRFU would simply miss some uncounted people altogether. For example, some households self-respond to the census but for one reason or another fail to identify some of their inhabitants. In this situation, which is not uncommon but would be exacerbated by the inclusion of a citizenship question, the household will never receive a visit from a NRFU enumerator. That is because, even though the household has uncounted members, returning a self-response form means that the entire household will be classified as *already having responded* to the census.[95]

In their closing statement, the government plaintiffs boiled the case down to a simple argument. Secretary Ross had concocted a phony cover story to justify including the citizenship question, ignoring the threats to data quality, in clear violation of the Administrative Procedure Act. As the lawyer Matthew Colangelo put it, this decision would cause significant harm on states, cities, and counties. Hanging in the balance, he said, was the question of "whether communities have the full weight of their actual presence represented at national, state and local representation in democracy" and the "distribution of hundreds of billions of dollars."[96]

Arguing for the defendants, the Justice Department's Brett Shumate locked in on two main claims. First, the plaintiffs did not have standing to sue in part because the injuries they alleged would be caused by the citizenship question were instead the result of the "political climate" or the "macro-environment" for the census. In other words, even if Secretary Ross had not decided to include the citizenship question, fear and distrust of the government would keep many people from responding to the census. Because there was no "definitive empirical evidence" that isolated the effects of the citizenship question from the effects of the environment, any claim about those effects was speculative at best.[97]

On the merits of the plaintiffs' case, Shumate went after the argument that Ross's decision had violated the Administrative Procedure Act. Despite ignoring the experts, Ross had made a "policy judgment" that was defensible within the bounds of the APA. Passing over the evidence that the secretary had cajoled the DOJ into making the request for the question, Shumate also argued that Ross's decision was not based on pretext: "After all, if Secretary Ross had already prejudged the issue, why would he engage in all of this process, why would he ask questions of the Census Bureau, review all of their memos?"[98]

Judge Furman was not evidently impressed by these defenses. In a lacerating, 277-page opinion, issued on January 15, 2019, he handed the plaintiffs a resounding victory. By including the citizenship question, Secretary Ross had committed a "veritable smorgasbord of classic, clear-cut APA violations."[99] The secretary had violated the Census Act's commandment to use administrative records as opposed to introducing new questions "to the maximum extent possible." He had also ignored the act's directive to report to Congress that he was considering including a citizenship question at least three years before the census date.[100]

Furman further determined that the secretary's decision was "arbitrary and capricious."[101] First, rather than considering the evidence he had before him, Ross had "alternately ignored, cherry-picked, or badly misconstrued" the administrative record. Second, he had ignored important aspects of the problem, including whether it was even necessary to respond to the DOJ's request for the citizenship question. In fact, there was no evidence in the record at all to suggest that the Justice Department actually needed this data to enforce the Voting Rights Act. Third, the secretary—with no justification whatsoever—simply disregarded past policies and practices. Adopting a question that would result in data that was "less accurate and less complete" compared to an alternative flew in the face of each of the federal government's Statistical Policy Directives and Quality Standards as well as the Census Bureau's own internal Statistical Quality Standards.

Perhaps most damningly, however, Furman found that Ross's justification for adding the citizenship question was a pretextual ruse.[102] The DOJ request was little more than a ruse that concealed the true basis for Ross's decision. The secretary had made up his mind on the question long before the DOJ letter appeared on his desk, deliberately attempted to outsource the decision, and then scrubbed the administrative record to cover his tracks.

"To let Secretary Ross's decision stand," Furman concluded, "would undermine the proposition—central to the rule of law—that ours is a 'government of laws, and not of men.'"[103] Accordingly, he vacated Ross's decision and barred him from reinstating the citizenship question unless he could cure the "legal defects" described by the opinion. With census field operations less than a year away, this was virtually impossible. Yet as Ross had long suspected—and as everyone involved with the case no doubt knew—the fate of the citizenship question would ultimately be decided not in a Manhattan courthouse but in a building known as the "marble palace" some two hundred miles south.

The Roberts Court Steps In

A little over a week after Judge Furman's decision, the Trump administration's solicitor general, Noel Francisco, had petitioned the Supreme Court for a writ of certiorari to review the case.[104] The Court was under no obligation to do so; it grants only a small fraction of such petitions each term. And this petition was an especially unusual one. In short, Francisco asked the nine justices to take up the case *before* the Second Circuit Court of Appeals even had a chance to review Judge Furman's decision. The Supreme Court's rules allow it to grant such petitions in rare cases "of such imperative public importance" as to warrant deviation from the practice of review by a court of appeals.[105] The Trump administration's argument here boiled down to time: Given that the census questionnaire had to be finalized by June 30, 2019, there was not enough time for two levels of review. Even though the governments and NGOs challenging the citizenship question urged the Court to deny the petition, they too recognized that there would be inadequate time for appellate review. The Supreme Court soon granted the petition and scheduled oral arguments for April.[106]

From one vantage point, these were not opportune times to challenge the Trump administration in front of the Supreme Court.[107] With the re-tirement of Justice Anthony Kennedy and his replacement by Justice Brett Kavanaugh, the court's balance of power had decidedly shifted to the right. When compared to his predecessor, Kavanaugh held a far more robust and expansive view of the power of the president.[108] Moreover, even before Ka-vanaugh's confirmation, Chief Justice John Roberts had authored several prominent opinions expanding the scope of presidential power. In impor-tant cases over the prior decade, including the first two years of the Trump administration, the Roberts Court had made it harder for plaintiffs to sue the federal government and limited lower courts' ability to apply "arbitrary and capricious" review—both of which were essential elements in the citi-zenship-question litigation.[109]

There was also reason to believe the Court might not accept Judge Fur-man's holding that Secretary Ross had provided a false pretext for his deci-sion. Writing for a 5–4 majority in *Trump v. Hawaii*, Roberts himself had discounted numerous pieces of "smoking gun" evidence suggesting that President Trump's decision to ban travel from majority Muslim countries had been motivated by anti-Muslim bias. Instead, Roberts concluded that the decision reflected only "the results of a worldwide review process under-taken by multiple Cabinet officials."[110] Lawyers for the Trump administra-tion would similarly argue that Judge Furman was wrong to conclude that Ross's decision on the citizenship question had been pretextual. Even if the secretary clearly favored the inclusion of a citizenship question from his first day on the job, their briefs claimed, he had not acted with an "unalter-ably closed mind" and had stated "rational contemporaneous" reasons for pursuing this goal.[111]

Adding to these challenges, the Trump administration had strong Re-publican allies in the states. Several weeks after the Court took up the case, a coalition of fourteen Republican AGs and two Republican governors filed a forty-six-page *amicus curiae* brief that both advanced the administration's

positions while undercutting those of the state and local government respondents (plaintiffs before the District Court) in the case. The brief mainly
defended Secretary Ross's purported rationale for including the question:
enhancing compliance with the Voting Rights Act. "The American Community Survey," the brief argued, "has flaws recognized by everyone, including Respondents" that made its uses for VRA enforcement "hazardous
and prone to litigation."[112] Census data on citizenship, they argued, would
be more accurate, granular, and authoritative than data from the ACS. Dis-
counting the bureau's own analyses about the question's effects, the brief
therefore concluded that the question would offer benefits to state governments that outweighed its harms.[113]

Still, there was at least one ray of hope for the governments and NGOs
suing to prevent the inclusion of the citizenship question. Chief Justice
Roberts, according to some journalistic accounts and academic analyses,
was concerned with protecting the Supreme Court's waning institutional
legitimacy. Therefore, in some high-stakes cases, Roberts could be expected
to cast a deciding vote that "split the difference" between the court's conservative and liberal wings.[114] For example, during the initial legal challenge
to the Patient Protection and Affordable Care Act (ACA), *NFIB v. Sebelius*,
Roberts had agreed with conservatives that the law's institutional mandate
to purchase insurance was an invalid use of Congress's authority under the
Constitution's commerce clause but ultimately voted with the Court's liberals to uphold the mandate as a tax. With public confidence in the Court at
record lows, and with the political motivations for the citizenship question
on full display, Roberts may not have been willing to further sacrifice legitimacy to endorse Ross's plan.

As with the legal challenges to the ACA, the citizenship-question controversy had attracted attention from influential stakeholders around the
country. With significant implications for political representation, federal
funding, and the quality of census data itself, more amicus briefs were filed
in *Department of Commerce v. New York* than any other prior piece of census litigation reaching the Supreme Court.[115] Among those organizations
filing briefs in favor of the respondents were some of the country's largest businesses, representatives from leading scientific societies—led by the
American Statistical Association—as well as five prior Census Bureau directors who had served under both Democratic and Republican presidential
administrations. The case directly implicated Congress's obligations under
the Enumeration Clause of the Constitution as well as the directives it made

to the Commerce Department under the Census Act. By early March, the US House of Representatives itself had petitioned the court to allow its general counsel to participate in oral arguments. Whatever the outcome of the case, it would have significant political reverberations.

Additionally, like *NFIB v. Sebelius*, the legal controversy over the citizenship question gave Roberts an opening to burnish his conservative reputation without placing the Court's legitimacy at greater risk. Recall that Judge Furman had ruled Secretary Ross's decision had violated the Administrative Procedure Act for three reasons: (1) it had contradicted the text of the Census Act, (2) it was arbitrary and capricious, and (3) it was based on a false pretext. Yet to prevent the citizenship question from appearing on the 2020 Census, Roberts only needed to construct a five-vote majority behind *one* of the three arguments. For example, even if Roberts and the four other conservative justices did not accept either of the first two rationales, the chief justice could nevertheless build a majority with the court's four liberals on the question of pretext. A ruling centered on pretext would also allow the Court to punt the ball back to Ross, who would then have to develop a new rationale for collecting citizenship information. Still, given the June 30th printing deadline, any plan for collecting such information would likely *not* include placing a citizenship item on the 2020 questionnaire.[116]

If Roberts hoped to build a consensus on the court, as opposed to a bare majority, the oral arguments—held on April 23rd—revealed this to be all but impossible. US Solicitor General Noel Francisco began his argument by erroneously declaring that Ross's decision merely reinstated a question that had been asked "in one form or another for nearly 200 years."[117] Before he could finish another sentence, Justice Sonia Sotomayor interrupted, noting that the citizenship question had not been on the short-form census since 1950, in part because of its effects on the response rate. When Francisco turned to his argument that the secretary had indeed considered the evidence before him when making the decision, Sotomayor was similarly relentless, arguing that Ross's decision memo had "pluck[ed] out" a single sentence from expert reports while ignoring the "wealth of statistics" that suggested that the citizenship question would lead to lower response rates.[118] Justice Elena Kagan also pushed back with equal force on Ross's rationale for including the question "You can't read this record," Kagan concluded, "without sensing that [Ross's rationale for the decision] is a contrived one."[119]

Conservatives were no less aggressive when questioning New York

Solicitor General Barbara Underwood, the ACLU's Dale Ho, and Douglas Letter, who argued on behalf of the House of Representatives. Underwood began her argument by emphasizing that Secretary Ross had added the citizenship question despite having "uncontradicted and strong evidence that it will cause a decline in the response rate of non-citizens and Hispanics, to the detriment of the states and localities where they live."[120] Chief Justice Roberts shot back, asking whether the citizenship data wouldn't improve the enforcement of the Voting Rights Act. Justices Samuel Alito and Neil Gorsuch also attempted to poke holes in Underwood's argument that the citizenship question would, by itself, cause a lower response rate. As Alito put it, "Citizens and non-citizens differ in a lot of respects other than citizenship," which suggested that there might be multiple explanations for why individuals might not complete the census, other than the citizenship question itself.[121]

Alito's view was characteristic of the conservative justices' understanding of Ross's decision. As they saw it, the decision had always been Ross's to make, and he was due significant deference when making it. The secretary was not confident in the bureau's prediction that a citizenship question would produce a 5.1 percent decline in response rates among noncitizen households, in part because these predictions could not isolate the effects of the question itself. Against this uncertainty, Ross had to consider the potential benefits of more complete and accurate citizenship data for the enforcement of the Voting Rights Act. His decision, according to this view, was therefore *not* arbitrary and capricious.[122]

The oral arguments illustrated a wide gulf between the conservative and liberal justices. While Supreme Court deliberations occur behind closed doors, sources close to the deliberations revealed to reporters that Roberts initially planned to rule in the Trump administration's favor, a full reversal of the District Court's decision. In the weeks that followed, however, Roberts changed his mind. While he maintained that Ross's decision was not arbitrary and capricious or explicitly contrary to law, he began to accept the idea that it had been based on a false pretext.[123]

What prompted Roberts's about-face is not entirely clear. From the outset, the factual record in the case showed that Ross had lied about his motivations for including a citizenship question on the census. The question for the chief justice, then, was whether this evidence was sufficient reason to pump the brakes on Ross's plan. For other conservatives, including Justice Clarence Thomas, Judge Furman's finding of pretext had essentially been motivated by a preexisting bias against the Trump administration, a bias the Court could not endorse.[124] It is possible that the circulation of opinions and memoranda among the nine justices persuaded Roberts to abandon the view that the pretext analysis was, as Thomas saw it, an "unprecedented departure" from the Court's precedents.

Yet the deliberations did not occur in a vacuum. Another potential motivation for Roberts' decision could have been a May 30th court filing by the ACLU, whose lawyers led the coalition of NGOs that had sued to stop the implementation of the citizenship question. The filing contained extensive evidence contradicting the sworn testimony of two of witnesses in the case concerning Secretary Ross's motivations for the decision. The evidence—which included a transcribed interview with John Gore, the principal deputy assistant attorney general in the Civil Rights Division—went straight to the heart of the pretext issue. It revealed, in short, that late Republican redistricting specialist Thomas Hofeller had ghostwritten a DOJ request for the citizenship question, which Ross's expert adviser A. Mark Neuman had shared with Gore in October of 2017. The DOJ adopted this rationale wholesale when it made its formal request to Ross several months later. Hofeller's interest in the citizenship question, however, had not been the enforcement of the Voting Rights Act. Instead, as his files showed, the citizenship question would—by allowing legislatures or the president to remove noncitizens from the population bases used in redistricting—would create a structural electoral advantage for "Republicans and Non-Hispanic Whites" in the redistricting of Congress and state legislatures.[125] The US solicitor general called these claims "frivolous" and an "eleventh-hour campaign to improperly derail the Supreme Court's resolution of the government's appeal."[126] Nevertheless, the revelations—which received wide media attention—clearly cut against the Trump administration's insistence that Ross's decision was genuinely motivated by a request from the DOJ.

The Chief Justice Decides

The Supreme Court announced its decision in *Department of Commerce v. New York* on June 27th, with little time to spare before the deadline for printing census forms. As he had in *NFIB v. Sebelius* seven year earlier, Roberts wrote a majority opinion for a fractured Court. And, as in that earlier case, his opinion reflected several important tensions in Roberts's own views about the relationship between judges and bureaucrats. Still, the practical effect of the decision was obvious: The Chief Justice had cast the pivotal vote to keep the citizenship question off the 2020 questionnaire.[127]

Unlike many Supreme Court decisions, *Department of Commerce v. New York* cannot be easily described with a single vote tally. In the first part of the opinion, the nine justices agreed unanimously that at least some of the respondents in the case had standing to sue. There was also unanimous agreement among the justices that asking a citizenship question was not unconstitutional. The Enumeration Clause had given Congress, and by extension the secretary, wide latitude to ask about citizenship.[128]

Yet when it came to the Court's analysis of the APA claims in the lawsuit, the consensus ended. What emerged instead was ultimately two separate 5–4 opinions. First, Chief Justice Roberts, joined by Justices Thomas, Alito, Gorsuch, and Kavanaugh, found that the secretary's decision was not arbitrary and capricious because it was "supported by the evidence before him." In interpreting the decision, the five conservative justices gave Ross a wide berth. Whereas the District Court had found that Ross ignored the citizenship question's effects on the response rate, Roberts' majority opinion argued that these data were "inconclusive" and that—in light of the uncertainties—Ross had determined that the benefits of obtaining "more complete and more accurate citizenship data" outweighed the "uncertain risk of reinstating a citizenship question."[129] Additionally, Roberts and the conservatives concluded Ross's decision was not contrary to the Census Act. For example, he had not violated the Census Act's command to avoid adding direct inquiries on the census form "to the maximum extent possible" because he believed it was necessary to add a citizenship question to obtain the "more complete and accurate data that DOJ sought."[130]

On the issue of pretext, however, Roberts parted company from his conservative brethren. In the final section of the opinion, the chief justice joined the Court's four liberals to argue that Ross's decision was grounded on a false pretext. Ross had been "determined to reinstate a citizenship question from the time he entered office . . . [and] instructed his staff to make it happen."[131] He had then lied to cover it up. This added up to a departure from what Roberts called the "reasoned explanation requirement" of administrative law: that agencies should offer "genuine justifications" for important decisions so that they can be "scrutinized by courts and the interested public."[132] In other words, while Ross was due wide deference, the Court did not have to give its blessing to a lie.

This split opinion invited strong dissents on both sides. Led by Justice

Stephen Breyer, liberals criticized Roberts's analysis of the secretary's consideration of the evidence before him and insisted that Ross's decision was a textbook "arbitrary and capricious" decision.[133] Conservatives—in separate opinions authored by Justices Thomas and Alito—blasted Roberts for taking into consideration of extra-record evidence and opening a "Pandora's box" of pretext-based challenges to agency decisions.[134]

Nevertheless, the consequences of the majority opinion were clear enough. Roberts remanded the decision about the citizenship question to Ross. In theory, this allowed the secretary to develop a new, legitimate justification for including a citizenship question. In practice, however, the Court had put a halt to Ross's scheme. With the printing deadline approaching, producing a new administrative record to justify the inclusion of the question was entirely infeasible.[135]

The War Continues

Reaction from the White House was swift. Within hours of the Court releasing its decision, President Trump tweeted: "Can anyone really believe that as a great Country, we are not able the ask whether or not someone is a Citizen? Only in America!"[136] Within a few weeks, however, Trump had regrouped. In a ceremony held in the Rose Garden on July 11th, the president—flanked by Secretary Ross and United States Attorney General William Barr—announced that the administration would abandon the citizenship question. Instead, he would sign Executive Order 13880, which directed the Census Bureau to obtain the citizenship status of everyone living in the United States using administrative records. "We have great knowledge in many of our agencies. We will leave no stone unturned."[137]

What made Trump's order particularly significant was another legal battle between state officials and the Census Bureau. One month prior to Trump's Rose Garden announcement, a federal district court in Alabama had denied a motion to dismiss a lawsuit filed by Alabama's attorney general, Steve Marshall, and a Republican member of the state's congressional delegation, Representative Mo Brooks.[138] First filed in 2018, the lawsuit argued that the federal government's policy of including all residents in census counts used to apportion Congress and the Electoral College violated multiple provisions of the Constitution that govern apportionment. Including undocumented individuals in apportionment counts, Alabama's lawsuit alleged, would deprive the state of its "rightful share of political representation."[139] Prior to the 2020 Census, Alabama was projected to lose one congressional seat and one Electoral College vote, both of which would go to states with higher shares of undocumented immigrants.[140] To solve the problem, the state's AG argued, the court should prevent the Census Bureau from producing apportionment counts covering the entire population of the United States and should declare unconstitutional any apportionments based on total population.

Alabama v. Department of Commerce was not, legal experts seemed to agree, poised to become a landmark decision reshaping congressional apportionment. "You count everybody," said Justin Levitt, a professor of election law at Loyola Law School in Los Angeles, in an interview with the *Washington Post*.[141] Not only did the plain language of the Constitution's language on apportionment fail to make a distinction based on residents' legal status, Levitt argued, prior litigation on the issue left "little room for debate."

Yet if Alabama's lawsuit had little chance of persuading judges, it gave Trump a window of opportunity following the Supreme Court's decision on the citizenship question. During the ceremony in the Rose Garden, US Attorney General William Barr cited Alabama's lawsuit as one important motivation for Trump's executive order directing the Census Bureau to collect administrative data on undocumented immigrants. "Depending on the resolution [of Alabama's lawsuit], this data may be relevant to those considerations," Barr said.[142]

The message was clear: If the citizenship question couldn't be used to remove undocumented immigrants from apportionment counts, the Trump administration would find another way to do so. Suddenly, Alabama's lawsuit had transformed from the effort of a single state into a vehicle for presidential ambition. The state and local officials who participated in the citizenship-question litigation took notice. Prior to the signing of Executive Order 13880, three local governments (King County, Washington; San Jose, California; and Santa Clara County, California) had joined the Alabama lawsuit as intervenor-defendants, claiming that removing undocumented residents from census counts would cause them to lose political representation and federal funding.[143] A month after Trump's Rose Garden appearance, New York Attorney General Letitia James announced that her state, along with fourteen others, the District of Columbia, nine cities and counties, and the US Conference of Mayors would be requesting to join them.

The week after James made her announcement, Arlington County, Virginia, and the city of Atlanta, Georgia, requested to join the intervening jurisdictions.[144] State and local governments may have won the battle over the citizenship question, but the war—as we will see in chapter 5—would continue.

Saving the Census from Sabotage

In the absence of a coordinated legal counteroffensive, the 2020 Census would have included the citizenship question. The effects of this question would have been stark. In December 2019, the Census Bureau released the results of a randomized controlled experiment "to compare response rates on questionnaires with and without a citizenship question." As expected, the citizenship question had targeted effects. In areas where noncitizens made up more than 11 percent of the population, the addition of a citizenship question led to a nearly 1 percent decrease in the self-response rate. Areas with a large Hispanic population saw an even higher drop-off (1.1 percent) in self-response when the citizenship question was added.[145] Predictably, the addition of the question did not result in an *overall* decrease in self-response—a fact that Secretary Ross celebrated as "gratifying news."[146] Yet the question was never intended to reduce self-response overall. Rather, it was meant to advantage the Republican Party by generating an undercount targeted in areas with high levels of Democratic Party support, and to create an opportunity for states and the president to remove noncitizens from redistricting population bases, full stop. In this respect, there is ample evidence to suggest the plan could have worked.

As this chapter has shown, however, state and local officials played a central role in keeping the citizenship question off the 2020 Census. They did so not as the Census Bureau's partners but as litigants in an adversarial legal system. Essential to their victory were state AGs who, over the last two decades, have developed the capacity to coordinate effective multistate lawsuits that shape the policies of the federal government. The collaboration that mattered here was not merely *intergovernmental*—composed of networks of state AGs and local officials—it was also *intersectoral*. AGs collaborated with major NGOs, who played a significant role in the litigation. These collaborative efforts placed Ross's decision on trial and produced the evidence about the false pretext for the decision that ultimately led Chief Justice John Roberts to cast the pivotal vote against the plan.

Yet *Department of Commerce v. New York* was not the last word on the citizenship question. The majority opinion left open the possibility that a future presidential administration could—with a more coherent strategy—include a citizenship question on the census. At the same time, proposals to bar the Census Bureau from asking about citizenship on future question-naires have made little headway in Congress. In short, we can expect to see further intergovernmental litigation on this issue.

Nor was the Court's decision the end of the war over the 2020 Census. As we will see in chapter 5, the ruling did not stop the Trump administra-tion from trying an alternative approach to manipulating the census for partisan advantages. It also failed to solve the more mundane problems that plague census taking, including the creation of a complete and up-to-date list of addresses and the launch of an effective outreach campaign to en-courage census participation. As the next two chapters show, both of those efforts depended critically on interactions between federal, state, and local governments—not as legal adversaries but as partners.

CHAPTER THREE

A Sense of Where You Are

Local Knowledge and the Master Address File

While the figure of the "census taker" looms large in the Census Bureau's iconography, most people who responded to the census in 2020 did not encounter any such person.[1] That is because for more than fifty years the bureau has relied largely on "self-enumeration," in which residents respond to the census questionnaire by mail and—for the first time in 2020—via internet response. The labor of the Census Bureau's army of enumerators is now mostly reserved for following up with unresponsive households.[2]

If self-enumeration, attempted for the first time in 1960, was necessary to efficiently count a growing, far-flung population, the process created operational challenges of its own.[3] The most foundational of these was the development of a complete and current list of mailing addresses. The task is far harder than it might seem. As communities evolve, residential addresses change: a family farm becomes a suburban housing development, a defunct brewery transforms into condominiums, an oil boom leaves a new colony of mobile homes in its wake. All these events produce anomalies that the bureau cannot easily resolve on its own. For a recently converted structure containing five separate households, census data may reflect only a single address.[4]

Self-enumeration produces high-quality census responses. Indeed, when compared with responses provided to enumerators, self-responses have lower rates of missing data on key variables, including age, sex, and race/ethnicity.[5] Yet eliciting these responses demands an accurate and up-to-date address list. Because missing addresses do not receive census questionnaires, an inaccurate address list increases the risk of what is known as coverage error, which arises "when persons or housing units are not represented in the census are not represented in the census results exactly once and in the right place."[6] In the 1980 Census—which produced a sizable differential undercount that invited a decade of lawsuits—fully half of the coverage error was the product of missing housing units.[7] Even after significant operational improvements, missing housing units accounted for 30.5 percent of the coverage error in the 1990 Census.[8]

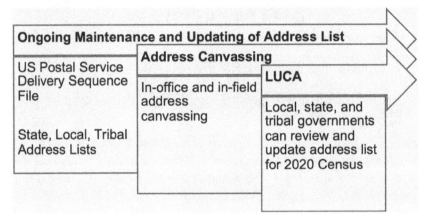

Figure 3.1: Census Bureau operations for updating the Master Address File, 2020. Source: Based on "2020 Census Operational Plan: A New Design for the 21st Century," US Census Bureau, January 2022, https://www2.census.gov /programs-surveys/decennial/2020/program-management/planning -docs/2020-oper-plan5.pdf.

Today, ensuring that all living quarters are included on the Census Bureau's address list depends on the bureau's relationships with state, local, and tribal governments (see figure 3.1). Since the 2000 Census, intergovernmental partnerships have supported the Local Update of Census Addresses Operation (LUCA), authorized by Congress in 1994, which allows governments to review and propose modifications to the Master Address File (MAF) for their area.[9] In the program's "New Construction" phase, governments can provide further information on living quarters under construction with completion expected by Census day. Following the creation of the American Community Survey, first implemented in 2005, the bureau also required more continuous updates to the MAF. Over the decade following the 2010 Census, the bureau's Geography Division undertook the development of a new partnership program, Geographical Support Systems Initiative (GSS–I), which invited state and local officials to share address information with the bureau on a continual basis.

As this chapter shows, intergovernmental partnerships play a central role in helping the bureau combat institutional drift resulting from the near constant changes in housing and address stock.[10] These partnerships are largely insulated from the kind of partisan battles we saw in chapter 2. While the political conflicts of the 1990s foreclosed some approaches to dealing with the technical challenge of counting a growing population, both LUCA and GSS-I demonstrate how the transmission of local knowledge contributes to the bureau's broader effort to improve the accuracy of its address list, which one National Research Council panel has referred to as "the most important factor in determining the overall accuracy of a decennial census."[11]

Yet, however important intergovernmental partnerships might be to the quality of the address list, they are by no means easy to maintain. Especially for smaller and medium-sized jurisdictions, the barriers to participating in LUCA can be formidable. Beyond the relatively low visibility of the program, a scarcity of resources—including technical capacity and skill—remains a perennial complaint of state, local, and tribal partners. To the extent that the bureau has been able to address these problems over the last three decades, it has been driven largely by deliberate efforts to generate feedback from state, local, and tribal partners. Nevertheless, this learning has been constrained by an adverse fiscal context. Not only does the bureau lack grantmaking authority to support state and local transmission of address lists and other geospatial data, it remains under constant pressure to keep the costs of census taking in check. Reforms to LUCA over the last twenty years have focused instead on minimizing the burdens of participation, taking advantage of existing sources of institutional capacity (namely, state governments), and reducing the pressure on the once-per-decade LUCA process by moving toward a continuous update of address lists. Thus, even as the bureau has improved its technical capabilities for identifying addresses remotely, via satellite imaging, the local knowledge it receives from its partners remains essential for establishing where to count.

The Address List and the Politics of Census Modernization

To understand why intergovernmental partnerships are now so important to the census address list requires a brief historical sketch of the technical and political entanglements that defined the US Census in the final decades of the twentieth century. As the country's population grew, the bureau's traditional in-person enumeration procedure came under increasing strain. The cost of census taking ballooned—more than doubling between 1930 and 1940. At the same time, the reality of a differential undercount was also becoming increasingly apparent.[12] Demographer Ansley Coale estimated that the 1950 Census had undercounted "nonwhites" by 12 to 13 percent.[13] Yet even as accurate census data became more significant in determining how billions of federal dollars were spent, and to the administration of a new civil rights regime, the decades that followed were nonetheless defined by sizable differential undercounts, driven in significant part by gaps in the census address list.

1960 marked the first time that the bureau employed mail response as a primary means of enumeration; by 1970, mail response was employed to enumerate approximately 60 percent of the US population.[14] In a sprawling country with a decentralized government, compiling address data was a gargantuan undertaking. Prior to the 2000 Census, the Census Bureau did not maintain the permanent MAF that it possesses today. Rather, the bureau had to compile address data from multiple sources before each census and did not maintain these records after the census was complete.[15] This meant purchasing address data from commercial providers. Because this data covered largely metropolitan areas, the bureau would improve on the list by hiring tens of thousands of local canvassers to verify addresses in the field.[16] Yet this process continued to produce coverage errors. Mail list vendors could not easily satisfy the bureau's requirements for up-to-date addresses; in areas with little demand for address data, updated lists were nonexistent. During the "pre-canvass" phase, address listers received poor quality maps that made it difficult to locate addresses. The bureau was also plagued by high staff turnover.[17]

Aware of these limitations, officials at the bureau began to revamp the address list procedure for the 1980 Census in part by calling for local officials in some thirty-nine thousand jurisdictions to "compare the bureau's working estimates of housing-unit counts in their jurisdictions with their own records before the census began, and then look at preliminary counts resulting from the enumeration."[18] These reviews would provide the bureau with a means of incorporating missed addresses, thereby reducing the heavy undercount experienced in prior decades. Yet by February of 1980, the bureau recognized significant technical problems with the pre-census phase of the program. An unusually high number of addresses contained in the bureau's tape address register lacked geocoding and, with the census only months away, maps necessary for local governments' review were not yet ready. Providing this poor quality information to local officials, the bureau explained, would only create unnecessary confusion and concern. Yet the abrupt cancellation caught local government leaders off guard.[19] As

Alan Beals, then-executive director of the National League of Cities, put it, "We are very disturbed we are going to run into the same problems of credibility as we had in 1970."[20]

The cancelation of the pre-census local review only stoked resentments in what would become a decade-long battle over the results of the 1980 Census. Even before the results of post-enumeration analyses—which would ultimately reveal a 5 percent difference in the net undercount between the Black and white populations—were published, local officials in Detroit and New York City had begun to raise serious concerns about the accuracy of the count, which resulted in a decade-long legal battle over whether the bureau was required to statistically adjust the results of the 1980 Census to correct for the undercount.[21] Yet adjustment was not the only front in the war over the undercount. Following the release of the 1980 Census results, officials in Essex County, New Jersey, and Denver, Colorado, challenged their counts, claiming that the bureau had incorrectly classified occupied housing units as vacant. As part of this challenge—which ultimately landed before the US Supreme Court—lawyers for the governments attempted to use the Freedom of Information Act to compel census officials to produce address lists to allow comparisons with local data. Yet in the case of *Baldridge v. Shapiro* (1982), the bureau's lawyers argued, and a unanimous Supreme Court decided, that census address lists were covered by Title 13's confidentiality protections, which meant that they could not be released to local governments.[22]

Even if the Census Bureau often prevailed in such disputes, the stream of litigation hardly subsided. By the end of the decade, fifty-two lawsuits would be filed challenging the bureau's 1980 procedures.[23] Nor did courtroom victories produce solutions to critical problems. The Court's decision in *Baldridge v. Shapiro* hardly made it easier for census officials to share address data with local governments to ensure an accurate master address list.

In many ways, the technical problems of building a reliable and usable database of addresses, and assigning these addresses to geographic areas, dwarfed the legal challenges the bureau faced. After reviewing the results of the 1980 count, bureau officials determined that in order to ensure consistency in the bureau's geographic data products, they needed "a single, integrated geographic support system" that would both geocode addresses and produce the reference files used for tabulating census results.[24] While census officials wanted the technology to be in place for the 1990 Census, the project was initially projected to take twenty years. Expert consultants had informed the bureau it would not be possible to develop the software and the data necessary to build the system in time for the upcoming count. Nevertheless, census officials plunged ahead, in collaboration with staff from the US Geological Survey. The work was arduous, but the result was a major technological victory. The Topologically Integrated Geographic Encoding and Referencing (TIGER) database contained all seven million census blocks in the country. Whereas prior censuses required enumerators to use maps with highly variable quality, the new national system printed maps that were consistent and this "patchwork quilt" of data sources could be used to document both physical features (e.g., rivers and lakes) as well as geographic entities the bureau uses to collect and tabulate data.[25] Thus the 1990 Census was the first count to employ both a computerized geographic information system and a computerized master address list.[26]

These technical achievements aside, the bureau faced significant challenges in preparing the address list for the 1990 Census. As with the 1980 count, census officials would again attempt to engage local governments in a pre-census "housing check" as well as a post-census local review. Yet only 16 percent of eligible governments participated in the pre-census review. This was not because local officials tacitly agreed with the bureau's figures, however. As a General Accounting Office study would later find, nearly half of the governments that did not review the bureau's counts "lacked funds, expertise, or staff to carry out the program. An additional third lacked the data necessary to validate their census counts."[27] Similarly, while the post-census review program (discussed at greater length in chapter 6) led the bureau to revisit over 20 percent of the country's census blocks, census officials viewed it as inefficient and ineffective at improving the quality of the count.[28]

In reviewing the results of the 1990 Census—evidently the first census to be less accurate than the one before it—the General Accounting Office concluded that the "American public has grown too diverse and dynamic to be accurately counted solely by the traditional 'headcount' approach and that fundamental changes must be implemented for a successful census in 2000."[29] Yet while census experts—including members of the National Academy of Sciences Panel on Census Modernization—increasingly supported the inclusion of statistical adjustment as part of a "reengineered" 2000 Census, the idea ran headlong into Republican leaders in Congress who, as the Reagan and Bush administrations had before them, opposed efforts to use a post-enumeration survey to adjust for the undercount. By 1999, the Supreme Court had ruled that Title 13, the statute that governs the census, prohibited the use of sampling to apportion the House of Representatives and the Electoral College, though it left the constitutionality of sampling for apportionment purposes an open question and permitted the adjustment of census counts for other purposes, including the bureau's planned post-enumeration survey.[30]

With the issue of statistical adjustment mired in legal and political gridlock, however, both bureau officials and members of congressional census oversight committees continued to search for other opportunities to deal with the glaring realities of the undercount. Arguably the most significant of these opportunities was the improvement of the census address list. The 1990 Census not only missed about 3.6 million existing housing units, it also included two million units improperly, including units that did not exist, counting some units twice, and placing other units in the wrong location.[31] A pre-census local review program with weak participation from local governments had done little to remedy the situation but created a potential avenue for census reform that was less likely to ignite partisan passions.

At the heart of efforts to reform the local review program was Rep. Thomas C. "Tom" Sawyer (D-OH), then the chairman of the Census and Population Subcommittee of the House Post Office and Civil Service Committee. Sawyer had made headlines in 1991 when a study prepared by his staff revealed the significant undercount of the Black population in the 1990 Census and again when the secretary of commerce refused to adjust the results in response to the undercount, a move that Sawyer called a "gerrymander on a national scale."[32] Yet while Sawyer succeeded in passing legislation to convene a national expert panel on census accuracy, his efforts to promote the statistical adjustment of the census continued to face political and legal headwinds. By 1994, Sawyer had introduced another piece of legislation—targeted on the census address list itself.[33]

To develop reform ideas, Sawyer's subcommittee staff sought out input from local officials like Joseph Salvo, New York City's long-serving chief demographer. The staffers, Salvo recalls, "actually collaborated with us—the locals—to see whether what was being proposed made sense."[34] The bill that resulted from this collaboration, dubbed the Census Address List Improvement Act, proposed three modest but meaningful reforms. First, it directed the US Postal Service to provide postal delivery sequence data to the bureau. Second, the legislation required the bureau to develop a new process allowing local governments to review address information—including confidential information—and to make recommendations for changes to the address list prior to census field operations. Third, the bill both required the bureau to respond to local requests and directed the Office of Information and Regulatory Affairs to set up a process allowing state and local governments to appeal determinations of the bureau. The most important practical implication of Sawyer's bill, however, was that it transformed a local review process that had been discretionary, and thus prey to cancelation should funds run short, into a congressional mandate.

Rather unlike efforts to promote statistical adjustment, Sawyer's bill encountered virtually no opposition and passed both House and Senate on voice votes in October of 1994. With little fanfare, LUCA was born, and the hard work of building a permanent address list began.

LUCA and the Challenges of Intergovernmental Collaboration

Like the review programs that preceded it, LUCA assumes that local governments large and small will cross-check the bureau's address lists with independent sources of information. Yet while local knowledge is evidently valuable to the bureau, governments may not always be willing or able to provide it. During the first two iterations of LUCA, in 2000 and 2010, inducing participation remained challenging. As table 3.1 shows, during the 2010 cycle, only 29 percent of eligible governments registered to participate in LUCA. Participation was especially low among governments with relatively small numbers of residential addresses, tribal governments, and minor civil divisions like townships. What accounts for these challenges?

To better understand the answer to this question, let us examine the process of responding to LUCA in Oneida County, New York. There, LUCA is the domain of Dale Miller, a principal planner for the Herkimer-Oneida Counties Comprehensive Planning Program. Known locally as "Mr. Census," he researches and disseminates census data daily for the purposes of economic development and regional policymaking.[35] For Miller and similarly situated individuals across the country, what are the ingredients of successful participation in the LUCA program?

First, and most basically, the top elected officials in governments like Oneida County, where Miller works, are expected to be responsive to the bureau's invitation to participate in the program, voluntarily delegating to

Table 3.1a. LUCA Participation in 2010 by Government Type

Government Type	N Eligible	% Eligible Registered
State	51	55
American Indian Reservation	331	34
County	3,115	51
Minor Civil Division	16,440	17
Incorporated Place	19,392	36
Total	39,329	29

Table 3.1b. LUCA Participation in 2010 by Size (Number of Residential Addresses)

Size (Number of Residential Addresses)	N Eligible	% Eligible Registered
1,000 or fewer	24,377	18
1,001–6,000	9,617	41
6,001–50,000	4,624	59
50,001–100,000	348	82
100,001–1,000,000	321	84
1,000,001 or More	42	64
Total	39,329	29

Source: Rebecca Swartz, Peter Virgile, and Brian Timko, *2010 Census Local Update of Census Addresses Assessment Report* (US Department of Commerce, 2012), https://www2.census.gov/programs-surveys/decennial/2010/program-management/5-review/cpex/2010-cpex-199.pdf.

someone like him the task of preparing a LUCA submission. Effectively communicating information about the program may seem like a simple task, but it is important to remember that the benefits of LUCA participation are, unlike intergovernmental transfer programs, not necessarily immediately evident or apparent to local officials. As a survey of LUCA 2010 participants showed, 75 percent of LUCA participants said that the bureau's advanced mailing was the single most important reason for participation in the program.[36] One of the major criticisms of the first implementation of LUCA—during Census 2000—was that the bureau had "not effectively communicated the expectations of the [program] with local governments." Especially in jurisdictions with limited resources, the bureau's key points of contact—the "highest elected officials"—had limited time or resources to devote to communicating with the bureau.[37] Small local governments often did not have regular business hours. In some cases, the bureau did not even have up-to-date contact information for their highest elected officials. In larger cities, elected officials were often inundated with work; supporting the census, easily understood as the bureau's business, was not necessarily a top priority.[38]

Second, given that the Census Bureau does not provide intergovernmental grants to support LUCA, local elected officials are expected to use their own resources to employ someone like Dale Miller or, in the case of larger jurisdictions, a unit of several people. Yet as two decades of experience with LUCA prior to 2020 have suggested, the availability of local resources to support LUCA submissions varies greatly. As table 3.2 suggests, insufficient staff or lack of funds accounted for 53 percent of the reasons given by governments for not participating in LUCA during the 2010 cycle. An additional 21 percent of the responses focused on governments' lack of time to participate in the program.

A closer look at a few participating jurisdictions helps to capture the variation in resources. On one end of the spectrum are metropolitan cities like New York, whose Department of City Planning has long been a pioneer in developing software and technical capabilities to cross-check the bureau's address list with other data local data sources. Beyond this, the department employs its own field canvassers to visit thousands of blocks across the city's five boroughs, documenting "mailboxes, doorbells, utility meters, address signage, and entry ways in order to establish the count of units in each structure." In 2020, the department's field canvassing effort involved a sophisticated approach to quality control: field canvassers fanned out in teams of two, traveling around the city to canvass housing units. Agreement from both canvassers was required to establish the count of housing units. Afterward, all properties "were checked twice by different staff members, with any differing outcomes (in terms of both number of units and street address information) resolved by a third check."[39]

At the other end of the spectrum are rural jurisdictions like Upshur County, West Virginia. In December of 2017, just as larger cities were ramping up their LUCA 2020 efforts, Terry Cutright—president of the County Commission—announced that the government would not be participating in LUCA. "Personally, I don't think we have the manpower to do it," Cutright said. Indeed, the limits on county resources were noticeable. The only person evidently available to prepare a LUCA submission was a building

Table 3.2. Reasons Given for Nonparticipation in LUCA 2010

Entity Type (N Reasons Given)	Insufficient Staff or Lack of Funds	No Time/ Too Busy	No Local Address List Available	Concerns About Address List Security/ Confidentiality	Restrictions on Address List Use	Other Reason
State (N=4)	0 (0%)	0 (0%)	2 (50%)	0 (0%)	0 (0%)	2 (50%)
American Indian Reservation (N=9)	3 (33%)	2 (22%)	0 (0%)	2 (22%)	0 (0%)	2 (22%)
County (N=574)	321 (56%)	139 (24%)	49 (9%)	26 (5%)	14 (2%)	25 (4%)
Minor Civil Division (N=5,609)	2,980 (53%)	1,209 (22%)	550 (10%)	272 (5%)	73 (1%)	525 (9%)
Incorporated Place (N=3149)	1,695 (54%)	545 (17%)	165 (5%)	141 (4%)	29 (0.9%)	574 (18%)
Total (N=9,345)	4,999 (53%)	1,985 (21%)	766 (8%)	441 (5%)	116 (1%)	1,128 (12%)

Source: Rebecca Swartz, Peter Virgile, and Brian Timko, 2010 Census Local Update of Census Addresses Assessment Report (US Department of Commerce, 2012), https://www2.census.gov/programs-surveys/decennial/2010/program-management/5-review /cpex/2010-cpex-199.pdf.

permit officer and floodplain coordinator who had once attended a Census Bureau training. At the same time, there was some doubt among commissioners as to whether the person in question even had access to the data necessary to check the address list in question, necessitating some amount of field canvassing. To Cutright, it looked like the Census Bureau was expecting the county to "knock on every door" and "do what the Census Bureau does." Strictly speaking, this was hyperbole. Yet while a LUCA submission would hardly have required knocking on every door, the commissioner's sense of frustration is entirely understandable. Around the country, resource disparities are well known to impede LUCA participation.[40]

Preparing LUCA submissions also requires that eligible jurisdictions have a sufficient level of local expertise. Because LUCA is built on the presumption that the bureau needs "local knowledge" it does not have, participating jurisdictions must have a person or organizational unit possessing not only a reservoir of technical skills but an intimate knowledge of how to obtain and use highly variable local data sources appropriate for the task at hand. In this respect, Oneida County is lucky: Dale Miller has four decades of experience working with census data. He is no stranger to address lists.

For other jurisdictions, access to both this level of formal expertise and tacit knowledge can be more difficult to come by. This is in part why the bureau's technical training workshops provide extensive information to participants on the kinds of housing units that may be included in a LUCA submission, as well as instructions on how to use the bureau's various software and submission procedures (see figure 3.2). In recent years, state agencies have increasingly provided supplemental training for local officials preparing LUCA submissions, often inviting seasoned experts like Miller to share their experiences and advice with participating governments. Still, as a 2010 report on LUCA participation concluded, "Large, well-staffed governments" could afford to send staff to conferences and training sessions, yet for small villages and towns, "even a few hours of training, preparation, and address review was a relatively large additional burden."[41] Prior to 2020, staff not conversant with commercial Geographic Information System (GIS) software required significant extra time to learn the bureau's Partnership Software, which apparently "baffled some government personnel, especially less specialized personnel of smaller government."[42]

Finally, LUCA participants must have access to, and facility with, adequate sources of information to allow for a reliable, accurate comparison with the MAF, which has been integrated with the TIGER database since the

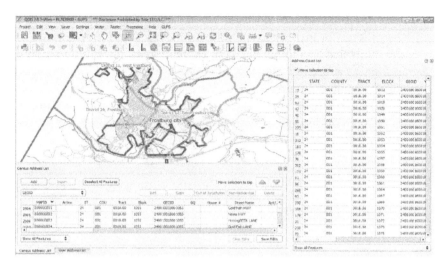

Figure 3.2: Screenshot from Geographic Update Partnership Software. Source: Dale Miller, "Preparing for Local Update of Census Addresses," webinar, State Data Center Network, November 29, 2017, author's files.

2000 Census.[43] In Miller's case, that means using not one but three databases, marrying them together to address the gaps in each. The New York State Street Address Maintenance Data, for example, covers the entirety of the state and identifies both street address and structures but does not identify individual housing units. To deal with these deficiencies, Miller uses both real property tax parcel data—which, despite some coding errors, includes property classifications that allow him to identify the existence of multiple housing units more easily—as well as 911 telephone data. Now, thanks to the existence of ubiquitous geospatial data through Google Earth, Trulia, and Zillow, the task of identifying the number of lots in remote trailer parks makes Miller's job at least somewhat easier.[44]

In sum, there are several barriers to effective intergovernmental partnerships within the LUCA program. While the program relies on "local knowledge," the production of this knowledge can be costly. For fiscally constrained local governments, especially those of small towns and villages, the resources and expertise necessary to generate a bona fide LUCA submission are hardly in great abundance. Moreover, unlike many intergovernmental interactions that attract scholarly attention, the federal government has neither fiscal nor regulatory tools in its possession to induce collaboration.

Instead, the bureau relies on exhortation—informing governments that participation is in their interest and that missing addresses may result in undercounts that lead to missing political representation or future federal grants. Because that warning alone—whether implicit or explicit—is not enough to conjure resources where they may not exist, the bureau and its potential partners have had to set up processes for intergovernmental policy learning, both during and after census operations. These processes, as the next section describes, have led to meaningful changes to LUCA since it was first implemented.

Policy Learning and Intergovernmental Partnerships, 2000–2020

While the challenges of intergovernmental collaboration endure, state and local governments' experiences have also reshaped the census address list in important ways since LUCA was first implemented. They have done so both through their participation in census tests undertaken to pilot new techniques as well as their participation in retrospective evaluations of LUCA operations. Perhaps most importantly, state and local partnerships have figured prominently in the bureau's efforts to update and improve the MAF/TIGER data on a *continuous* basis, reducing some of the pressure on the once-per-decade LUCA effort. Still, intergovernmental policy learning has occurred in the context of fiscal constraint. Not only does the bureau lack grantmaking authority, it faces intense pressure to minimize the per-household cost of census taking. Hence, the bureau has responded to local governments' resource constraints through other means, such as minimizing administrative burdens and allowing higher levels of government with greater capacity to make submissions on behalf of low-capacity local governments.

Reshaping LUCA: Tests, Pilots, and Feasibility Studies

Since roughly 1940, the Census Bureau has routinely conducted *census tests*, including full-scale "dress rehearsals" to pilot new techniques, methodologies, or operational procedures.[45] This testing generates knowledge that may result in alterations to the bureau's operational plans, and LUCA is no exception. The bureau first piloted LUCA operations in its Census Dress

Rehearsal, which took place in three specially selected sites: Columbia, South Carolina (chosen for its mix of address types); Menominee County, Wisconsin (selected because it contained the Menominee Indian Reservation); and Sacramento, California (which offered greater population diversity). For each of these sites, the bureau used the Postal Service's Delivery Sequence File to create an MAF and then provided local governments the opportunity to review local address lists and propose their own additions, corrections, or deletions.

Immediately, the 2000 Dress Rehearsal revealed several major operational problems with LUCA. Barely more than half of the sixty governmental entities in the South Carolina site participated—a fact that led to significant streamlining and simplification of the bureau's program. Local officials in areas with large numbers of non-city-style addresses had significant difficulty in verifying listed addresses such as "Route 2, Box 19" with structural information about households (e.g., "white house with green shutters"). As a result, the bureau modified its procedures to provide such governments with block counts to review rather than addresses. Additionally, while the bureau provided local officials with addresses from surrounding jurisdictions to ensure coverage accuracy, this led to "substantial confusion on the part of the local officials and they tried to delete the units outside their jurisdiction." In a second round of updates, time constraints led bureau staff to accept most MAF revisions submitted, which created erroneous addresses in the MAF—leading to wasted enumeration effort and additional coverage errors.[46]

Census testing has allowed state and local officials to communicate important information about the LUCA operation to the bureau, yet these tests are only useful to the extent that they provide an accurate representation of planned census operations. This is not always possible, however. By the time of the 2000 Dress Rehearsal, the bureau had not yet completed its reengineering of the MAF process to address known problems with address canvassing and quality assurance review. Similarly, during the 2010 Dress Rehearsal, the bureau was not yet able to test its newly developed partnership software, a central component of LUCA. Nor did the bureau initially test the new computer-based training software it had developed to supplement classroom learning—limiting opportunities for user testing prior to national implementation.[47]

What the bureau learns from census tests also hinges on both internal evaluation of their results and external oversight. In the 2000 Dress

Rehearsal, the bureau did not collect data on variables that would have allowed it to analyze how individual operations contributed to the overall address list. Similarly, during the 2010 cycle, the bureau failed to collect data on how many localities would opt out of using the MAF/TIGER Partnership Software, necessitating further instruction on address file conversion. After a review by the Government Accountability Office, however, the bureau "agreed to disseminate instructions on file conversion on its Web site and provide instructions to help desk callers."[48]

The bureau also employs demonstration programs to test out new operations for the first time. In 2006, for example, the bureau conducted a pilot program to evaluate the feasibility of allowing state governments to participate in LUCA, given resource and time constraints at the local level. After selecting five counties in Indiana and Wisconsin, the bureau coordinated with the state data center (SDC) and the Federal-State Cooperative for Population Estimates (FSCPE) agency in each state, providing these agencies with the census address list and asking them to provide additions, deletions, and corrections. Based on a validation in the field, bureau staff determined that state participation was feasible, which led to a significant change in LUCA operations.[49]

Internal and external evaluations of census testing, however important, can only occur if there is something to evaluate. Yet fiscal constraints and leadership problems can lead the bureau to cancel or scale back its testing plans. While LUCA was ultimately included in the 2008 Census Dress Rehearsal, the bureau eliminated the program from the 2004 and 2006 Census tests. By the time the 2020 Census cycle arrived, the bureau opted not to include LUCA in its scheduled census tests, as it had in the previous two decades. Rather, changes to the program were based in part on retrospective evaluations, another source of policy learning to which we now turn.[50]

Learning from Retrospective Evaluations

In addition to census testing, the bureau's modifications to the LUCA program since 2000 have relied in part on evaluations and interactions with intergovernmental stakeholders that occur after census operations have concluded. Following the 2010 Census, Brian Timko and Becky Swartz of the Geography Division organized several research teams to develop alternative designs for LUCA 2020. Among the groups Timko and Swartz organized was a "looking back" team, which would retrospectively examine all phases of the 2010 program looking for improvements that existing documentation and data appeared to require. Complementing this work, another team would conduct focus groups with LUCA participants, gathering input from tribal, state, and local governments on potential alternative designs.[51]

By early 2014, these groups had produced several valuable research findings.[52] Yet the data the bureau collects does not speak for itself. The lessons census officials glean from surveys, focus groups, and "looking back" reviews depend in part on the operational and programmatic context in which the learning is done. This is best exemplified by the bureau's treatment of resource challenges. As noted previously, inadequate resources to support LUCA submissions continue to be a predominant complaint of program participants and an important explanation for nonparticipation in the program—creating, in some cases, the impression that LUCA is yet another "unfunded mandate." At the same time, the bureau both lacks formal grantmaking authority and operates under near-constant demands to pursue solutions that are cost effective. As a result, bureau officials have responded to concerns about insufficient resources at the local level not with requests for intergovernmental grants but with proposals to further streamline participation requirements, encourage collaboration between small and large units of government, and enhance partnership software to facilitate easier use by governments with limited technical capabilities.[53]

In at least one instance, bureau officials' interpretations of retrospective evaluations concerning LUCA have been the subject of some controversy. For the 2010 Census, the bureau had expanded options governments had for participating in LUCA—allowing for the review of different types of media with different levels of security requirements. A 2010 survey revealed that less than half of responding governments were even aware that they had these choices. In the end, more than 90 percent of participants chose the standard participation option.[54] At the same time, however, four of seven focus groups conducted by the bureau voiced concerns about eliminating two less burdensome participation options. An inspector general report reviewing the bureau's decision raised further concern, after discovering that governments using options now slated to be eliminated were predominantly communities with lower levels of household income. Still, the bureau maintained that its experience in 2010, as well as recent state and local investments in geospatial technologies, would likely mitigate participation barriers in 2020.[55]

The bureau is not the only site in which retrospective evaluations of

LUCA are collectively processed, however. Drawing on the expertise of seasoned LUCA veterans like Dale Miller, the state data center network has hosted webinars to provide newcomers with insights on how to prepare program submissions.[56] Agencies within larger units of government, such as the New York City Department of City Planning, routinely evaluate their participation in LUCA, drawing lessons about the quality of their planning efforts and submissions.[57] In states like California, such evaluations led to the creation of a $7 million appropriation for grants to support local government participation in LUCA. Virtually all California counties participated in LUCA 2020.[58]

Beyond LUCA: Intergovernmental Partnerships and the Development of the Master Address File

Intergovernmental partnerships have also informed the development of the MAF outside the context of the LUCA program itself. The driver of this change was the replacement of the long-form census—whose burdensome length helped to depress overall participation—with the American Community Survey (ACS), implemented for the first time in 2005. Because the ACS was designed to be fielded in the fifth year of each decade, the bureau required address-list updates throughout the decade, not simply in the census year. Yet by 2010, census officials judged that the existing structure for making these updates was insufficient. This helped to prompt the bureau's Geography Division to develop a plan allowing local, state, and tribal governments to continuously provide up-to-date address, feature, and boundary data to the bureau, a plan that came to be known as the Geographic Support Systems Initiative (GSS-I).[59]

From the beginning, Geography Division officials—led by then-division chief Tim Trainor—were keen to leverage insights from intergovernmental partnerships to structure GSS-I. In the fall of 2011, the division kicked things off with a three-day Census Address Summit, bringing bureau staff together with over thirty state and local officials working routinely with geospatial data. Held at the picturesque National Conservation Training Center in West Virginia's Shenandoah Valley and led by Trainor himself, the summit aimed to inform the bureau about how state and local officials worked with address data and to begin brainstorming pilot projects that could inform the bureau's reengineered efforts to update the MAF.[60]

Discussions at the summit reinforced several important operational challenges state and local officials faced in maintaining current address lists. A GIS technical manager from Dallas reported that he knew for a fact that the city's data systems did not have full address coverage. Apartment buildings constructed prior to the development of modern address creation systems often proved difficult to track, for example. Another difficulty was identifying subaddresses "hidden" within a single parcel of land. Learning about these units could not be done remotely and instead required phoning landlords and in at least one case "driv[ing] 45 minutes into the middle of a pecan farm."[61] Because the bureau lacked grantmaking authority, Trainor emphasized, it could not respond to these challenges with intergovernmental aid but with services "in kind," in the form of technical advice and support.

Over the next three days, exchanges between bureau officials and external stakeholders led to the development of six pilot research projects aimed at testing operational ideas that would support continuous updating of the MAF. Within a year, the Geography Division had approved five of these pilots, which teams of external stakeholders and census officials conducted over the following year. The topical focus of the pilots illustrates both the scale of challenges the bureau faced in expanding its approach to continuous updating of the MAF. One team focused explicitly on the seemingly prosaic task of outreach to address state, local, and tribal address authorities. After months of research, however, the team found that the term *address authority* was poorly defined. While governments often had multiple authorities with some role in the production or management of address data, not all persons responsible for maintaining address data had the authority to share it with the federal government. In addition to better defining the concept of an address authority, the group concluded that the bureau needed to draw on the experience of its regional offices to foster relationships with state and local officials who had the authority to share address information. Another team convened with the goal of identifying how to facilitate state and local governments' adoption of a new technical standard for address data developed by the Federal Geographic Data Committee.[62] The group's discussions with officials confirmed that few tools or no-cost trainings existed to facilitate the adoption of the standard, suggesting that the bureau should quickly create a working group to develop necessary training manuals and courses.

This research had immediate practical consequences. By 2013, the Geography Division had begun to use insights gleaned from communication with state and local partners and the results of pilot projects to structure the new GSS-I partnership program.[63] Under the new program, the bureau would request information from state and local partners to supplement commercial and USPS address data, all of which would feed into the MAF/ TIGER system. Division officials soon secured partnerships to acquire data covering 7,864 governmental entities, which represented 37 percent of the housing units from the 2010 Census. This was proof that partner data could be employed to "both validate and supplement the MAF," at least in urban and suburban areas that were likely to experience population growth. A more continuous update project not only enhanced the quality of the address list but it also allowed the bureau to better target address-canvassing efforts on areas most likely to need improvement. It would also ensure that 2020 LUCA operations would begin with the most up-to-date set of addresses available.[64] Indeed, by the time LUCA was underway, the bureau had acquired high-quality address data for 38,160 governmental entities, representing 88.8 percent of the housing units included in the 2010 Census.[65] Of the 106.7 million addresses it collected, 99.5 percent matched address records already in the MAF.[66]

Intergovernmental Partnerships and the Address List in the 2020 Cycle

By 2020, the Census Bureau had increasingly come to rely on intergovernmental partners to support its efforts to develop a complete and up-to-date address list. As with prior counts, LUCA provided state, local, and tribal governments an opportunity to review address lists prior to the creation of the bureau's enumeration universe. Yet a decade of technological innovations, pilot projects, and consultation with state and local stakeholders had also constructed something that the congressional authors of LUCA's authorizing legislation did not envision: a process by which the bureau's state and local partners, along with the US Postal Service and commercial data firms, would *continuously* update the bureau's address list. If successful, this continuous update would, among other things, allow the bureau to better target its typically costly address canvassing efforts and, where LUCA was concerned, create redundancies that would minimize the likelihood of coverage gaps.

Yet if intergovernmental policy learning had reshaped the process of updating the address list, some features of the bureau's approach to these

Table 3.3a. LUCA Participation in 2020 by Government Type

Government Type	N Invited	% Invited Registered
State or State Equivalent	52	90
American Indian Area	357	41
County or County Equivalent	3,113	60
Minor Civil Division	16,315	13
Incorporated Place	19,491	37
Total	39,328	29

Table 3.3b. LUCA Participation in 2020 by Government Size

Address (Number of Residential Addresses)	N Invited	% Invited Registered
1,000 or fewer	24,009	18
1,001–6,000	9,756	37
6,001–50,000	4,791	63
50,001–100,000	375	85
100,001–1,000,000	343	89
1,000,001 or more	45	91
Total	39,328	29

Source: Shawn Hanks, Liz Lane, Lyndsey Richmond, and Nadine Huntley-Hall, *2020 Census Local Update of Census Addresses Assessment Report* (US Census Bureau, 2022), https://www2.census.gov/programs-surveys/decennial/2020/program-management /evaluate-docs/EAE-2020-LUCA-Assessment.pdf.

partnerships did not change. In the absence of grantmaking authority, and amid constant pressure to reduce costs, the bureau could not address some of the most important barriers to participation in LUCA: local governments' lack of dedicated resources. True, the bureau had attempted to find ways around this, encouraging states to submit address information on behalf of small local governments with limited capacity. Nevertheless, LUCA participation did not increase between 2010 and 2020. Of the nearly forty thousand state, local, and tribal governments invited to participate in the 2020 program, only 29 percent registered to participate in the program— roughly the same percentage as the previous decade (see table 3.3).[67]

Participation in LUCA 2020 varied substantially across the country, as figure 3.3 shows. On the one hand, most counties had at least some coverage

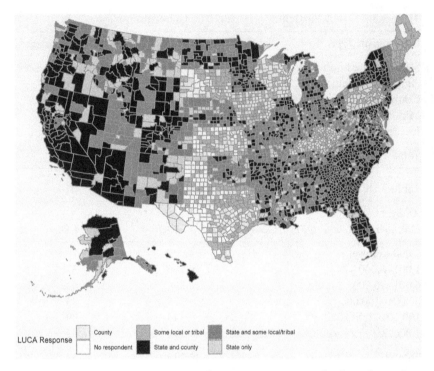

Figure 3.3: 2020 LUCA participation by county. Source: Author's analysis of LUCA respondent data. Note: Shading does not reflect contributions from multiple local units of government in a single county area. Tribal governments include Alaska Native Regional Corporations.

in the program. In 44 percent of county areas, a LUCA response was sent from the county government, either alone or in conjunction with local, tribal, or state governments. An additional 40 percent of county areas saw LUCA submissions from at least some local or tribal governments within their borders, either alone or in conjunction with state governments.[68] In 10 percent of county areas, state governments were the only unit of government to prepare a LUCA submission. Finally, only 6 percent of county areas had no coverage whatsoever.[69]

To further probe factors associated with LUCA 2020 participation, table 3.4 presents the results of a logistic regression analysis of county government LUCA submission decisions. The dependent variable here is whether the county or county-equivalent government responded to LUCA. The model

Table 3.4. Logistic Regression Analysis of County LUCA Participation in 2020

	Coef. (Robust SE)
County Population (Ln.)	0.42 (0.04)***
County Median Household Income (Ln.)	0.70 (0.18)***
County 2010 Final Self-Response (%)	−0.91 (0.45)*
Trump Vote Share 2016 (%)	−0.26 (0.30)
State Respondent	0.44 (0.09)***
Any Incorporated Place or Minor Civil Division Respondent	0.37 (0.10)***
Any Tribal Respondent	−0.09 (0.20)
Log Likelihood	−1954.07
N	3143

Note: Cell entries are logistic regression coefficients with robust standard errors in the parentheses. Source: Author's analysis.
***$p < 0.001$; **$p < 0.01$; *$p < 0.05$.

also includes four independent variables. First, to capture the basic intuition that counties with larger populations are more likely to participate in the program, the analysis includes a logged measure of county population.[70] Second, probing the Office of Inspector General's finding that a county's wealth—one indicator of government capacity—was significantly associated with more intensive 2010 LUCA participation, the regression includes a measure of median household income.[71] Third, to consider the possibility that counties with larger "hard-to-count" communities may have greater motivations to respond to LUCA, the model includes a measure of the county's 2010 Census self-response rate.[72] Given that political polarization may shape even low-salience intergovernmental interactions, the regression also includes the county's 2016 Republican presidential vote share as a proxy for the partisan alliances of county officials. The model also includes three control variables. The first is an indicator of whether the state in which the county is located prepared a LUCA submission. The latter two indicate whether at least one local or tribal government within each county prepared a LUCA submission.[73]

The results here indicate that counties with larger populations and higher levels of resources were significantly more likely to respond to LUCA. By contrast, counties with higher levels of self-response in the 2010 Census were less likely to prepare LUCA submissions. This could indicate that counties with larger hard-to-count populations may have been more motivated to respond to LUCA. On the other hand, there appeared to be no relationship between a county's partisan context and LUCA participation. This may suggest that LUCA is insulated from partisan politics to a greater extent than other census operations, including those we will explore in chapter 4.

While LUCA participation still faces at least some of the same struggles it did a decade ago, there are several important contextual factors to consider. First, LUCA 2020 did not occur in isolation. By giving state, local, and tribal governments an opportunity to submit information earlier in the decade, the bureau succeeded in taking some pressure off the once-per-decade LUCA process. Indeed, as noted previously, between 2013 and 2018, governments submitted nearly 107 million address records to the bureau through GSS–I. This is more than double the number of addresses submitted during 2010 LUCA operations. Of these, 99.5 percent matched to the MAF. Second, while there were gaps in governments' ability to participate in LUCA, allowing state governments to prepare submissions creates substantially more coverage than would have been possible were the bureau to have relied solely on local submissions.

Collectively the number of addresses submitted in LUCA was four times higher than the Census Bureau expected.[74] In the end, the MAF included 16.5 million addresses submitted by LUCA participants. Most of these addresses—13.3 million—have their origins in prior censuses or updates to the USPS Delivery Sequence File that occurred before 2020. The remaining 3.2 million addresses originated uniquely in the 2020 LUCA program. Yet only a third of these LUCA-added addresses were successfully enumerated, due in part to a large number of "fruitless investigative leads." For the members of the Committee on National Statistics' expert panel on the 2020 Census, these results suggest that the bureau "opted to place new, locally provided addresses into the census operational workload and let fieldwork sort out the results."[75] Clearly, the addition of a large number of addresses that duplicated existing entries in the MAF, as well as addresses that were not ultimately enumerated, suggests that there is room for improving LUCA's efficiency and effectiveness. Nevertheless, LUCA remains a vital source of data for updating the address list. Indeed, the 2020 LUCA operation was the origin of nearly half of the unique addresses added to the MAF in 2020 and over a third of the newly added addresses that were eventually enumerated.[76]

Making Local Knowledge Matter

From a distance, census taking might look like a textbook example of what James Scott has called the "high modernist" state, which counts and categorizes its subjects from a centralized position, detached from—sometimes unaware of—the unruly world that so often thwarts its best laid plans. Yet this chapter suggests that, over the last few decades, census officials have surely been aware of one implication of Scott's analysis: When counting a vast and heterogeneous population, local knowledge is indispensable, even to the most mundane of tasks.[77]

In the United States, accurate and up-to-date information about housing quarters is highly decentralized.[78] Even with the advent of satellite technology, which has allowed the bureau to pioneer the technique of in-office address canvassing, the task of maintaining an up-to-date census address list in the face of frequent churn in the US address and housing stock would be impossible to manage without assistance from state, local, and tribal officials who have access to property tax records and 911 data, as well as tacit knowledge about who can help to fill in missing data "on the ground."[79] At the same time, governments participating in these partnerships have also been able to derive an apparent benefit from doing so. Following LUCA 2020, officials in Hudson County, New Jersey, calculated that the addition of over fourteen thousand new addresses had the potential to generate an additional $220 million in federal funding per year.[80]

Whatever one believes about such forecasts, the apparent value of an accurate address list to state, local, and tribal officials does not necessarily translate into effective intergovernmental partnerships. Since 2000, the implementation of LUCA has demonstrated how profound gaps in resources and personnel inhibit governments' participation in the bureau's geographical partnership programs. The bureau has learned a great deal from its interactions with intergovernmental partners and has modified its approach to developing the address list in dramatic ways. Within LUCA, that has meant easing some of the administrative burdens associated with participation and allowing higher levels of governments with greater technical capacity to respond on behalf of those that lack adequate resources to prepare submissions. The bureau has also expanded its efforts to develop the address list beyond LUCA, building an infrastructure that allows governments to continuously submit address data throughout the decade.

The significance of intergovernmental partnerships in developing the census address list has no doubt grown over the last few decades. And while the bureau's Geography Division has learned a great deal during this period, at least one important aspect of the bureau's intergovernmental relations has not changed. While facing pressure to reduce costs, not to mention highly uncertain annual appropriations, it is worth recognizing that the bureau has not become a grantmaking institution, which helps to explain why resource and personnel challenges at the local level remain a barrier to participation in these programs.

The same pressure for cost control has led the Government Accountability Office to speculate that the development of a process for continuously updating the address list may make LUCA an unnecessary and duplicative operation.[81] Ending LUCA would require an act of Congress, however, a fact that might caution against early pronouncements of the program's death. Whatever their complaints about LUCA, state, local, and tribal officials value having an opportunity to review address lists and receive feedback on the quality of their address data. LUCA also helps to raise awareness about the importance of census participation at a crucial phase in the cycle of census taking. Finally, as the bureau has moved toward a system of continuous updates to the address list, LUCA provides a critical redundancy in a process where the consequences of error are significant.

In short, the address list used in the 2020 Census could not have been created in the absence of a rich network of intergovernmental partnerships. At the same time, this work has taken on an increasingly intergovernmental character without a coincidental transfer of resources. As a result, many important decisions about whether to invest in census accuracy lie not in Congress, which has the constitutional mandate for census taking, but in state capitols and city halls where—despite experiencing the effects of census quality—responsibility for census taking is far less institutionalized. This is true not only for the preparation of LUCA submissions and the transmission of geospatial data but for campaigns to motivate US residents to respond to the census. These efforts, which are the focus of chapter 4, have been subjected to far more partisan contestation than LUCA, however. Census outreach also draws in a far broader range of interests and actors at all levels of government. As we will see, coordination problems abound.

CHAPTER FOUR

Getting Out the Count

Partnerships, Politics, and Census Promotion

An accurate census is a public good whose quality depends on broad public participation. As with the creation of all public goods, mobilizing participation means overcoming barriers to collective action. Not only do many US residents find it difficult to perceive a personal benefit from being counted, public awareness of this once-per-decade collective activity is also limited. As surveys conducted by the Census Bureau in 2018 show, only 33 percent of respondents reported that they were "extremely familiar" or "very familiar" with the US Census. Only 37 percent of respondents believed that participation in the census would benefit them personally.[1]

Beyond low public awareness of the census, or of the benefits of participation, a large minority of US residents do not feel that their participation in the census will make a difference in securing fair congressional representation or a fair share of federal funds; asked whether it matters if they are personally counted in the census, 41 percent of respondents to the bureau's Census Barriers, Attitudes, and Motivators Study (CBAMS) replied that it matters "a moderate amount," "a little," or "not at all." Additionally, close to a quarter of US residents report being either "extremely" or "very" concerned that the 2020 Census results would be used against them—fears that are felt most strongly among "non-Hispanic Asians, individuals not proficient in English, and those born outside the US."[2] Some of these suspicions stem from the bureau's cooperation with the US military to support the internment of one hundred and ten thousand people with Japanese ancestry during the Second World War. Even though Congress adopted robust and effective confidentiality protections in the 1950s, the census environment today is beset by a perilously low level of trust in government.[3] Prior to the 2020 Census, trend surveys found that generalized trust in government was the lowest it had been since the measure was first developed.[4] As chapter 2 showed, the Trump administration reinforced that deficit in trust with its targeted effort to discourage census participation among immigrant communities by including a citizenship question on the 2020 questionnaire.

The Census Bureau has long relied on outreach and promotional campaigns that raise awareness about the count, inspire trust that personal information will remain safe and secure, and give residents a sense that their participation matters and will yield important benefits in terms of political representation, recognition, and support from federal programs. Arguably the first instance of census advertising came in 1910, when President William Howard Taft issued a "Census Proclamation" declaring it "the duty of every person to answer all question on the census schedules applying to him and the family to which he belongs."[5] Yet, as with the address list (see chapter 3), advertising and promotion became even more important in 1970, as the bureau shifted away from relying primarily on in-person enumeration and toward self-enumeration via mail response. This shift required recipients of census forms to know—in the absence of direct contact with an enumerator—what the census was, why it was important (and safe) to fill it out, and how to correctly provide the requested information. In 1950, the bureau first secured the assistance of the Advertising Council, a nonprofit organization that had developed a reputation for supporting wartime campaigns such as encouraging military enlistment and the purchase of war bonds.[6] Yet by 1990, the council's generic radio and television commercials, billboards, and advertising collateral appeared to have had few appreciable effects on census participation. Between 1970 and 1990, mail-response rates declined from 78 percent to 65 percent. It was not until 2000 that Congress gave the bureau the resources to pay market rates for advertising. With an advertising budget that was at the time only second in size to McDonald's and Wendy's, the bureau hired a major firm—Young and Rubicam (now called Y&R)—to do both general advertising campaigns and to contract for specialty campaigns targeted at populations with the lowest census mail-response rates.[7]

Paid advertising has not been the only tool the bureau had for conducting promotion and outreach, however. Beginning in 1980, the bureau slowly built up an infrastructure for supporting partnerships with governments at the state, local, and tribal level, as well as businesses and nonprofits. These "trusted messengers" would ideally communicate the importance of taking the census in hard-to-count communities in a way that advertisements by the bureau never could.

The 2020 Census featured the most extensive network of intergovernmental and intersectoral partnerships the bureau had ever developed. Yet the character of these partnerships remained quite uneven across the country. As this chapter shows, partnerships for census outreach were often beset by fiscal and operational problems at the bureau as well as long-term patterns of fiscal austerity, which had hollowed out the organizational capacity of many state and local governments.[8] Additionally, at the state level, funding for census outreach was often trapped by partisan political battles.

These challenges were not insurmountable. In some states where partisan conflict over census investments might have emerged, census entrepreneurs helped to reframe the importance of census investments in ways that appealed to Republican elected officials. A robust national effort by nongovernmental organizations (NGOs) helped to fill in critical gaps in outreach activity. Indeed, census outreach exemplifies what public administration scholar Robert Agranoff refers to as the "network era" of intergovernmental management, in which NGOs and public agencies develop intersectoral partnerships "to solve problems that no single agency or program alone can solve."[9] The fact remains, however, that outreach partnerships continue to be unevenly institutionalized at the state and local level. To understand why this is a problem, let us first turn to the history of the bureau's efforts to promote census taking to an increasingly large, and often wary, population.

The Emergence of Intergovernmental Partnerships for Census Promotion

The 1980 Census marked the bureau's first attempt to create formal partnerships with state and local governments in support of its outreach efforts. One reason for this is that the passage of the State and Local Fiscal Assistance Act of 1972—which marked the beginning of the federal government's decade-long experiment with sharing general revenues with subnational governments—created a network of some thirty-nine thousand local entities receiving significant federal aid, which was distributed according to a formula based in significant part on the size of the population.[10] Given elected officials' interest in ensuring that their governments received a fair allocation of revenue-sharing dollars, the bureau sent out packages to these officials encouraging them to create organizations known as Complete Count Committees (CCCs) in advance of the 1980 Census. These organizations—inspired by an effort that took place in Detroit prior to the 1970 count—would mobilize government agencies and community groups to promote the census in a variety of ways, ranging from mayoral proclamations and festivals to highway billboards and census reminders printed on utility bills, public-assistance checks, and receipts for commercial products.

The initial results of the partnership push left something to be desired. For the 1980 Census, roughly 10 percent of the local governments invited to form CCCs did so, a fact that can be attributed to the Census Bureau's decision—with limited resources at its disposal—to ration technical assistance in a way that prioritized a smaller number of metropolitan cities. Still, the 1980 results suggested the importance of continuing to engage officials at multiple levels of government to carry out census promotion. The bureau thus planned for a more extensive network of intergovernmental partnerships in the 1990 Census. On the one hand, the bureau began partnership work with local governments earlier than it had before—conducting high-visibility personal visits with mayors in "model cities" and regional meetings with elected officials two years before the census went into the field. If this alone did not generate an especially substantial increase in the number of local governments doing promotional activity for the 1990 Census, the bureau also moved beyond local governments in its establishment of partnerships in two ways. At the state level, bureau staff worked with governors to encourage the development of state-level CCCs. They also sought to leverage connections to state agencies that formed the network of state data centers (SDCs), which had been inaugurated in 1978 to facilitate easier use of census data. The hope was that the SDCs' ties to private firms, universities, and regional planning agencies would allow these agencies to serve as effective mechanisms for promoting census awareness and participation. Finally, for 1990, the bureau also formalized its relationships to tribal governments and Alaska Native villages, building on a prototype of a "tribal liaison program"—a parallel structure to CCCs—first piloted during the 1986 test census on the Choctaw Reservation in east central Mississippi. Participation in this program was strong for 1990, with over 90 percent of tribal governments and Alaska Native villages participating.[11]

Building on these results—and with the aid of a far more substantial budget appropriation—the bureau greatly expanded on the partnership program for the 2000 Census. Among other things, the bureau hired over six hundred so-called partnership specialists to establish and maintain communications with state, local, and tribal officials as well as nongovernmental organizations. This was more than double the number of partnership staff hired for 1990. The planning of the partnership program also began even earlier; the bureau hired its first regionally based partnership specialists in 1996, ramping up the intensity of its efforts during a longer "education phase" during which specialists held over 4,215 educational meetings and conducted with governmental and nongovernmental organizations as well as nearly ten thousand briefings and presentations with community groups. Finally, the bureau pushed beyond generic mobilization efforts by undertaking a variety of special initiatives focused on building partnerships in geographies where higher undercounts appeared likely, including cities and states with large populations, areas with large tribal populations, regions recently devastated by natural disasters, and unincorporated and geographically isolated colonias along the US–Mexico border.[12]

The new approach brought stunning results. Of the more than thirty-nine thousand state and local governments contacted prior to the 2000 Census, roughly 80 percent established some partnerships with the bureau.[13] Yet the extent to which partners undertook promotional activities envisioned by the program varied considerably. On the one hand, as a national survey revealed, 70 percent of partner organizations reported that they conducted one or more outreach activities. Still, over 60 percent of partners provided no financial or in-kind support, limiting the kinds of activities partner organizations could engage in. Only 14 percent of partners, for example, established CCCs to coordinate census outreach; only a quarter donated any staff time for promotional activities.[14]

With the growth of the partnership program in 2000—a trend that continued over the following decade—the bureau found it increasingly necessary to demonstrate that the strategies it adopted had a significant effect on improving participation in the census. At a relatively high level of abstraction, most evaluation studies showed that the bureau's sophisticated marketing and partnership campaign had improved census participation among historically undercounted minorities. As one study reported, African Americans who recognized four advertisements from the census marketing campaign had an 80 percent chance of mailing back their census form compared to a 31 percent chance for those who recognized no ads. When compared to the 1990 Census, the undercount of African Americans was cut in half, and the undercounts for Asians, Hispanics, and Native Americans vanished entirely.[15] Nevertheless, it remained difficult to isolate the effects of individual partnership activities on census participation. As the bureau's final report on the Partnership and Marketing Program bluntly stated, the effects of the program's activities were "confounded with one another" making it "impossible . . . to measure their effects separately."[16]

In response to these challenges, the bureau's 2010 Integrated Communications Program (ICP) contained several innovations. Among other things, the bureau contracted to improve its software for tracking and monitoring partnership activities and customer relations using the cloud-based online platform provided by Salesforce. Additionally, the 2010 program more aggressively targeted partnership activities in so-called hard-to-count (HTC) areas. To do so, census officials made use of an enhanced planning database that provided geospatial information on where census enumeration might prove most difficult, including housing variables (e.g., the percentage of multiunit structures) and economic indicators (e.g., the percentage of households in poverty), which Bureau researchers used to compute into an HTC score for every census tract in the nation. Thanks to the mid-decade American Community Survey, these scores could be updated with data more current than the last census.[17] Using these scores, staff could better direct their efforts to develop partnerships in places where the risk of a census undercount was highest.

The enhanced targeting of partnership formation evidently had its intended effects. Census tracts with the highest HTC scores also saw the greatest concentration of partnership activity whereas high HTC census tracts saw activity by an average of six organizational partners—three times higher than the average in low HTC tracts. With a more sophisticated partnership database, the bureau could also track differences in the level of material commitments—ranging from hosting events to distributing educational materials—made by partner organizations. On average, high HTC tracts saw four times the number of commitments that low HTC tracts did. Using this data on partnership activities, the bureau was able to show that, all else equal, increasing the number of partners in a high HTC census tract from one to two resulted in a 0.3 percent increase in the mail-response rate between 2000 and 2010.[18] While self-response to other government and private-sector surveys continued to decline, the final mail participation rate in the 2010 Census was 74 percent, the same as it had been in 2000. Nearly half the states and more than half of US counties increased their participation rates over the decade.[19] Nevertheless, census partnerships would continue to face challenges from all sides in the decade to come.

Census Partnerships in 2020: Innovations and Frustrations

The Census Bureau's preparatory work for the 2020 Integrated Partnership and Communications Operation (IPC) began in 2016, following the completion of a new operational plan. At the helm of the operation was an "integrated project team" composed of staff from offices across the bureau and chaired by Tasha Boone, then the deputy chief of the Decennial Census Management Division, and Kendall Johnson, executive director for the 2020 Census Integrated Communications Contract. Integrated operations are particularly important here because, unlike the construction of the census address list, the task of census promotion involves not one but multiple bureau divisions and occurs during not one but multiple phases of the census cycle. During the planning phase, for example, the project team relied not only on 2010 assessment reports and consultation with the bureau's advisory committees and external stakeholders but on a range of information produced by units across the bureau. To develop strategies for mobilizing hard-to-count populations, the team required data from the bureau's planning database. This ultimately led to the creation of a new geospatial data tool called the Response Outreach Area Mapper (ROAM), which allowed the bureau and its partners to map hard-to-count census tracts for the purpose of tailoring promotional campaigns.[20] Simultaneously, the team drew on data from the Customer Liaison Marketing Services Office call center and the Census Questionnaire Assistance Center to identify and address common barriers to census completion. For information on local organizations, events, and region-specific communication requirements, the bureau drew on input from regional census centers. As we will see, maintaining coordination across the bureau's operations and regions remained an important challenge as the 2020 cycle ramped up.[21]

Bureau officials wanted to develop partnerships that were both national and local in scope. The National Partnership Program (NPP), managed from Census Bureau Headquarters, tapped national-level organizations—ranging from business associations like the US Chamber of Commerce to advocacy organizations like the National Association of Latino Elected Officials—to do outreach and promotion work. Yet targeted local partnerships constituted a far larger focus for the bureau. Managed by the bureau's field directorate, the Community Partnership and Engagement Program (CPEP) aimed at developing partnerships with state, local, and tribal governments, community-based organizations, and local businesses.

The bureau's efforts to develop intergovernmental relationships differed in at least three respects from the prior two decades. For the first time, the bureau's partnership specialists would specifically encourage the development of State Complete Count Commissions, organizations designed to coordinate outreach activities statewide. Second, to assist with outreach, partners would now have access to a publicly accessible tool to map hard-to-count populations at the tract level. Third, when compared to the 2010 Census, the bureau planned to increase its hiring of partnership specialists—the individuals who would make and maintain contact with community partners—by 88 percent.

Equally important, the 2020 partnership program unfolded against a backdrop of congressional budget constraints and significant changes to the bureau's organizational structure (see table 4.1). Even prior to the development of the operational plan, the bureau had—as part of an initiative to "extract every efficiency" in its field processes—eliminated six of its twelve regional offices, which play a key role in supporting field staff and building local partnerships.[22] The bureau also significantly reduced the number of area census offices (ACOs), organizational units that provide a critical interface between the decennial management structure and the massive temporary workforce of partnership specialists, address listers, and enumerators. In 2010, the bureau relied on 494 ACOs. By 2020, that number shrank to 248 such offices, with each office covering a far larger geographic area.[23] Finally, despite plans to increase the number of partnership specialists for 2020, the bureau did not increase spending on the partnership program. In fact, while the bureau increased its communications campaign funding by $104 million between 2010 and 2020, it reduced funding for partnership staff in local and regional offices by $46 million.

Beyond these new organizational realities, the bureau encountered a far tighter labor market for hiring partnership specialists and other temporary personnel than it did during the 2010 cycle, which took place during the Great Recession. In January 2008, the first month of hiring for partnership staff, the headline unemployment rate was 5 percent, and by 2009, unemployment ranged from 7 to 10 percent—during which time the bureau, thanks to funds provided by the American Recovery and Reinvestment Act, hired close to three thousand partnership staff. By May of 2018, unemployment had fallen to 4 percent. This, the bureau reported, helped to explain why recruitment efforts for partnership staff experienced "smaller than expected applicant pools, declined offers, and turnover."[24]

These operational conditions, when combined with austerity-induced

Table 4.1. Organizational Context for Census Partnership Programs, 2010 and 2020

	2010 Actual	2020 Estimated
Number of Regional Offices	12	6
Number of Area Census Offices	494	248
Funding for Partnership Staff in Local and Regional Offices ($Millions, FY2017)	$334	$248

Source: Government Accountability Office, *2020 Census: Office Managers' Perspectives on Recent Operations Would Strengthen Planning for 2030* (US GAO, 2021), https://www.gao.gov/assets/gao-21-104071.pdf; Government Accountability Office, *Actions Needed to Address Challenges to Enumerating Hard-to-Count Groups* (US GAO, 2018), https://www.gao.gov/assets/gao-18-599.pdf.

organizational changes, had consequences for census partnership efforts. Most immediately, hiring partnership staff proved challenging. The bureau eliminated two thousand "partnership assistant" positions that had existed in 2010. And while the bureau had planned to increase the number of partnership specialists it hired, it missed several time-sensitive deadlines for making these hires. After failing to clear a goal of hiring 1,501 partnership specialists by June 30, 2019, the bureau pushed out its deadline to September 1, at which point it still found itself 185 specialists short of the goal. This late hiring created gaps in the bureau's efforts to recruit community-level partners, including in hard-to-count areas.[25] The downsizing of ACOs only accentuated these gaps. By 2019, some cities with large hard-to-count populations simply did not have an ACO to provide the organizational interface to recruit and retain outreach personnel. This included the city of Newburgh, New York, which joined the Center for Popular Democracy Action to unsuccessfully sue the bureau over the inadequacy of its operational plans for the count.[26] In fact, none of the bureau's six regions had at least one ACO per million people. In the states falling under the purview of the Chicago and Philadelphia Regional Census Centers (RCCs), the number of ACOs per capita was considerably lower than other regions.[27]

The strain on ACO managers, who oversee field operations at the local level before and during enumeration, was evidently mirrored in the partnership program. In March of 2019, the Census Bureau reported that it would allocate least one partnership specialist for each ACO. Yet during

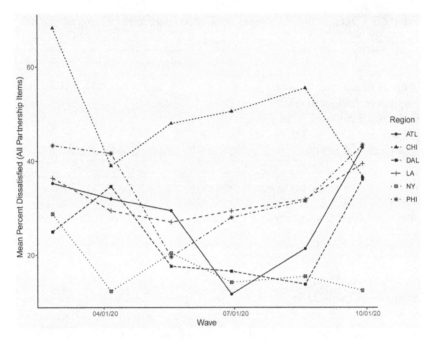

Figure 4.1: Area census office managers' dissatisfaction with communication between ACO and partnership program by regional census center and survey wave. Source: Author's analysis of "2020 Census Survey of Area Census Office Managers," Government Accountability Office, accessed November 27, 2024, https://files.gao.gov/special.pubs/gao-21-105237/censusacom2a /product/index.htm. Note: Each point represents the percentage of area census office managers in each region reporting that they are "very" or "generally" dissatisfied with "communication and coordination between the ACO and partnership program specialist." An analysis of variance shows there is a statistically significant difference between the six regions in how ACO managers responded to these items [$F(5,30) = 6.87$, $p = 0.0002$].

multiple waves of a survey conducted by the Government Accountability Office (GAO) between February and October of 2020, managers frequently reported having no or limited contact with partnership specialists. The result was that relationships between partnership specialists and ACO managers were of highly variable quality.

Figure 4.1 plots the percent of managers in each of the bureau's six regions who were "generally" or "very" dissatisfied with the quality of communication and coordination between the ACO and the partnership program in each wave of the survey. As is visible here, managers' experiences of the partnership program vary significantly across regions. Managers in the Chicago region consistently reported the most negative perceptions of the program, for example, while those in the New York region consistently reported the most positive perceptions. Indeed, coordination between partnership staff and ACOs in some regions appears to have been frustrated from the outset, given that partnership trainings were held before ACOs were scheduled to open.

By the end of 2019, the operational challenges haunting the partnership program had become increasingly well-known, the subject of multiple GAO audits, congressional hearings, and several lawsuits. To an extent, this external pressure ultimately served its purpose. By March of 2020, the bureau had met its hiring targets for partnership specialists. In turn, partnership specialists had surpassed the bureau's goal of establishing three hundred thousand community partners. Partnership staff had secured at least one community partner in 85 percent of the census tracts classified as the "hardest to count," roughly 15 percent shy of its goal. For their part, partners had also apparently held roughly two hundred and seventy thousand events related to census promotion nationwide.[28]

Nevertheless, important questions lingered. Had these partnerships been established with sufficient time to allow for census promotion, especially in historically undercounted communities? What exactly did the data on the number of partnerships and partner "commitments" mean? What would it take for these partnerships to result in meaningful resource commitments as opposed to just cells in a spreadsheet? It is to those questions we now turn.

State Governments as Census Partners: The Politics of Attention, Partisanship, and Institutional Capacity

Among the core innovations that distinguished the 2020 CPEP from partnership programs in years past was the bureau's emphasis on the creation of State Complete Count Commissions (SCCCs) as a kind of organizational intermediary, not only between the bureau and its audiences but also between the bureau and local communities. There are at least three reasons for this. First, state governments often have the fiscal resources and organizational capacity for engaging in census promotion that many small and medium-sized communities lack. Hence, persuading state officials to concentrate time and resources on census promotion could have knock-on effects at the local level, either by providing grant funding to support census outreach, educational support, or technical assistance for communities who wish to establish their own Complete Count Committees (CCCs). Second, because of their existing linkage with county and municipal governments, states have the capacity to play a unique role in *coordinating* census outreach across the state. Finally, state agencies make regular contact with residents, including through the provision of social services. Census promotion efforts can thus "hitch a ride" on these preexisting communication networks.

On the surface, persuading states to create SCCCs appeared to be an easy task. As CPEP ramped up in 2018, weekly reports to the secretary of commerce from the bureau's Field Division gave the impression of success. By early October, a memorandum prepared by Albert Fontenot Jr., associate director for Decennial Census Programs, suggested that "38 states or state-equivalents" agreed to form SCCCs while an additional eleven were "considering" forming these organizations.[29] Only a small handful of states, the memo claimed, had indicated that they were unlikely to commit resources until after upcoming gubernatorial elections.

Just what these counts meant on the ground was another story, however. Indeed, at the time the memo was sent, only thirteen states had formally created commissions via legislation, executive order, or a more informal arrangement. The number of formally established SCCCs would not reach the benchmark contained in Fontenot's October 2018 memo until September of 2019, with only months to go before the census went into the field (see figure 4.2).

What mattered for state census planning was not just the *creation* of SCCCs, however, but the amount of time these organizations had to plan their work prior to the census year. At one end of the spectrum, California's SCCC—created via executive order in April of 2018—is housed within the state's Census 2020 Office, which coordinates actions with local and tribal governments, community-based organizations, and the media. Even in states that did not have a formal census directorate, census mobilization efforts can be highly coordinated. The Montana Complete Count Committee, supported by the state's Census Economic Information Center and led by the state's lieutenant governor, held regular meetings since early 2018 and developed a comprehensive set of plans for outreach to community organizations, local governments, educational institutions, businesses, and

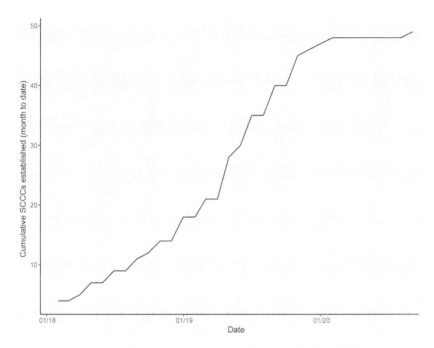

Figure 4.2: State complete count commissions by month of establishment. Source: Author's analysis of legislation and executive orders. Note: Count includes fifty states plus the District of Columbia.

the media. Multiple interviewees reported that states creating SCCCs in late 2019 or early 2020 had engaged in limited efforts to plan communication campaigns.[30] In one such state, a governor's census liaison reported not knowing that the governor had issued an executive order creating a statewide commission.[31]

Further, public records requests I made in several states revealed that commissions established earlier in the cycle had ample time to hold meetings and develop communication plans; of the twenty commissions created by the end of 2018, 80 percent had organizational websites. Those established later had less time to plan and met less frequently.[32] Of the twenty-six commissions created in 2019 or 2020, only 42 percent had formal organizational websites. In South Dakota, the SCCC was not created until August 31, 2020, several months before the end of census data collection—and well after the initially scheduled end of the self-response period.[33]

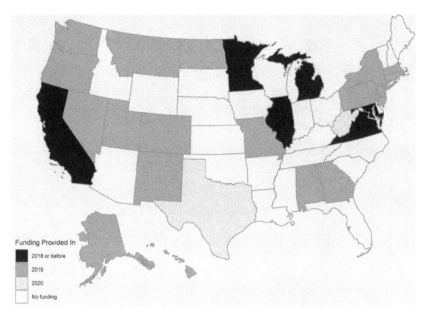

Figure 4.3: State funding for census outreach, by year. Source: Author's analysis of state legislation.

Beyond the staggered timing of SCCC creation, states varied considerably in their allocation of dedicated funding for census outreach (see figure 4.3 and table 4.2). Between 2017 and 2020, twenty-eight states provided at least some funding for census outreach. Of those that provided any funding, the average was $11 million and ranged from $100,000 (Montana) to $187 million (California). Typically, these funding packages were the result of annual budget negotiations and helped to support some combination of planning capacity (full-time employees), ad buys, educational campaigns, printed material, and outreach grants available to local governments or community-based organizations. Interviews with state and local officials revealed that the practical value of later spending—especially in the census year itself—was not necessarily equivalent to spending earlier in the cycle. In at least one state, a resource commitment that came in late 2019 left state officials and nonprofit organizations with a great deal of confusion and little lead time for planning outreach initiatives.[34]

The variation in state governments' resource and organizational commitments arguably owes less to the character of CPEP itself than it does

Table 4.2. Census Investments by State

State	Total 2020 Census Funding	State	Total 2020 Census Funding
Alabama	$1,200,000	Montana	$100,000
Alaska	$600,000	Nebraska	$0
Arizona	$0	Nevada	$5,000,000
Arkansas	$0	New Hampshire	$0
California	$187,000,000	New Jersey	$9,000,000
Colorado	$6,000,000	New Mexico	$3,500,000
Connecticut	$500,000	New York	$20,000,000
Delaware	$0	North Carolina	$0
Florida	$0	North Dakota	$100,000
Georgia	$3,750,000	Ohio	$0
Hawaii	$750,000	Oklahoma	$0
Idaho	$0	Oregon	$7,700,000
Illinois	$30,500,000	Pennsylvania	$4,000,000
Indiana	$0	Rhode Island	$500,000
Iowa	$0	South Carolina	$0
Kansas	$0	South Dakota	$0
Kentucky	$0	Tennessee	$0
Louisiana	$0	Texas	$15,000,000
Maine	$0	Utah	$1,000,000
Maryland	$5,000,000	Vermont	$0
Massachusetts	$6,650,000	Virginia	$1,500,000
Michigan	$500,000	Washington	$15,500,000
Minnesota	$2,200,000	West Virginia	$1,000,000
Mississippi	$0	Wisconsin	$0
Missouri	$500,000	Wyoming	$0

Source: Author's analysis of state legislation.

to challenges that are internal to the states. For public officials, making organizational or fiscal investments in census outreach was hardly a foregone conclusion. Indeed, numerous officials described a pervasive lack of awareness of the census. As one SCCC chair in the Southwest told me, because few state officials could recall states' investments in prior years, they questioned why the state would spend money in 2020: "Isn't that the US Census Bureau's job?"[35] Of state officials' perceptions, one SCCC member from a primarily rural western state told me: "How [the census] works, what happened 10 or 20 years ago, that is really missed."[36] Institutional ambiguity was a pervasive theme in the interviews. Even in states where the risk of an undercount was high, officials described initial organizing efforts as haphazard. "Nobody has a plan," another SCCC member told me, "Nobody has a blueprint to do this work."[37] In one state that had made virtually no investments in census outreach, a governor's census liaison explained that an outreach campaign was low on the "hierarchy of needs": "Our state can't worry about [the census] because our state is having to focus on that foundation of our mandated federal and state [responsibilities]."[38] In the face of these ambiguities, interviews revealed that officials made sense of the census environment by drawing on available memories of prior census counts, partisan identities, and technical and institutional resources.[39]

Census Salience

One factor that tended to stimulate census investments at the state level was the salience of the census itself. State officials, my interviews revealed, appeared to draw not only on projections of current undercount threats but also on available memories of past census counts when making decisions about how to invest resources.[40] One SDC official related to me how her state made significant changes to its census operations following two significant undercounts in 1990 and 2000, one of which resulted in the loss of a congressional seat and a substantial amount of federal dollars. These experiences led state legislators to vest greater capacity in the SDC, which began to hire more statisticians and economists. In 2010, the legislature also began to fund a statewide outreach campaign. Successive undercounts had also left a mark on the state's political leadership, especially the state's lieutenant governor, who made census mobilization activities a priority. The effects of these prior experiences were evident in 2020. In comparison to states with a similar population size and budget, her state had developed an elaborate set of plans for census mobilization and a durable network of relationships with local and tribal officials, as well as community-based organizations, that were poised to carry out outreach operations.[41]

In the absence of these prior experiences or clear projections of seat loss in 2020, state officials lacked strong attentional cues about the effects of an undercount or the importance of census outreach.[42] In a state that did not experience an undercount in 2010, one SDC official reported that census investments were not an easy sell: "We had a new administration start in

2018. . . . The census wasn't on the agenda. Economic development for the state was. And so [the census] got forgotten about during the legislative session when you could have appropriated money."[43] Indeed, even when states have experienced undercounts in the past, their effects are not easily traceable. As one SDC official in a state with a growing population told me: "[Our] General Assembly can look at the track record and say, well, we, we didn't really invest in 2000 and we got two [congressional seats]. And we did invest a little bit in 2010 and we didn't get [another] seat. So there's no real indication that us spending money on the census helps us or hurts us."[44]

The challenge of "remembering what happened 10 years ago" appeared to be widespread. In one state, the only available record of 2010 Census outreach activities was—as one interviewee told me—"a couple of pages" of material.[45] The absence of recorded procedures or protocols places a premium on tacit knowledge. Yet this knowledge is not always evenly distributed throughout the government agencies that engage with the Census Bureau. As one state official told me: "The people who have that institutional memory of, you know, 'we really need to invest'" tended to occupy positions in "the finance portions of the state that see the impact of [Census Bureau] data."[46] These officials, she argued, had been particularly important in shaping the state's actions because they could pose questions that shed light on the effects of undercounts: "If we don't get those federal dollars, how [is the state] going to fill those gaps?" Beyond simply making investments, state officials drew on tacit knowledge to plan their outreach strategies. Because of her experiences as county treasurer, one SCCC chair in a primarily rural Great Plains state had been acutely aware of an undercount in 2010. During her time as treasurer, she had identified major discrepancies in a city's census population and the number of sewer hookups within city limits. The knowledge she accrued during this time had given her a qualitative sense of where the undercount problem was most acute as well as a set of relationships with local officials that she continued to leverage in the SCCC's outreach efforts.[47]

Partisan Identities and Incentives

My interviews also revealed a distinctive (though not universal) partisan pattern in states' census investments. States with Democratic governors and state legislatures were significantly more likely to create SCCCs earlier and to provide funding for state census efforts. Interview data confirmed that this pattern can, at least in part, be explained by how Democratic and Republican officials perceive the returns on investment in census mobilization.

A centerpiece of appeals for state census funding is that a significant undercount will lead to a substantial loss of funds transferred to the state in federal programs whose allocation formulas rely heavily on census population data. This is the premise underlying widely cited studies from George Washington University's Andrew Reamer, studies that tabulate funds allocated using census data by both state and program.[48] Investing in a complete count thus arguably has a high rate of return, especially if a state's undercount risk is high. In states with Democratic gubernatorial administrations, officials I spoke with often described leadership on census investments coming from high-ranking officials.[49] One SCCC member noted that the state's Democratic governor "talks about the census wherever she goes and committed cabinet-level resources to the Commission."[50] One SDC official in a heavily urbanized state with a large immigrant population noted how the state's Democratic governor had prioritized census work. The governor's personal involvement, he said, facilitated cooperation with other agencies: "People know they have to respond right away."[51]

To be sure, leadership from Democratic governors varied. One SDC official described how—despite the lieutenant governor's consistent advocacy for the census—appropriations for outreach by local governments and community action agencies remained inadequate. In her estimation, the administration was good at reminding the public about "high-level details of what is going to happen." Still, because the governor had only recently taken office and had little prior experience with census operations, the administration failed to provide adequate technical assistance or material resources that would facilitate outreach.[52]

Yet whereas some Democratic governors and legislators may have lacked experiences that helped to cue the urgency or significance of the census, Republican leaders often did not employ the same situational frames when considering their responses to a potential undercount. As one SCCC chair in a rural, solidly Republican state told me:

> I wanted [the governor] to mention the census in his 'state of the state' speech and he didn't. . . . Why doesn't he tie the census to education funding? And he refused to do that too. . . . He's a moderate Republican . . . but his chief of staff is really conservative and is really worried about

him being re-elected. And so he does things that are more conservative than you would think that he would do. And this is probably one
of them.[53]

The issue here was not necessarily that the governor failed to appreciate the
negative impact of an undercount on intergovernmental revenue. Rather,
his calculation may have instead reflected the political challenge of making
an appeal for resources *directly* to support funding for federal programs
Republicans often oppose. As one local CCC member told me, Republicans
in the state legislature had been "astounded" when they heard about the
amount of census-designated federal dollars the state received because, "if
we get more federal funding then we can cut taxes in the state and not rely
so heavily on state funds."[54] Yet, perhaps because the logic of this appeal is
more circuitous, investing in the census may be less likely to top the list of
Republican gubernatorial priorities.[55] Moreover, even when the relationship
between an undercount and a loss of federal funds was apparent to Republicans, the issue of fiscal and organizational support could become a "sacri-
ficial lamb" in partisan budget battles. As one governor's census liaison told
me, funding for the census in his state had been caught up in a budget fight
that lasted most of the year, in which Republicans would be more likely to
"hold their breath until they turn blue" rather than cave to the Democratic
governor's fiscal requests.[56]

The politicization of the census at the national level, combined with the
fact that the 2020 Census coincided with a presidential election (a coinci-
dence that occurs every twenty years), did not help matters in Republican-
led states. Several interviewees I spoke with described how the Trump
administration's efforts to place a citizenship question on the census had
poisoned the bipartisan attempts to fund outreach; depoliticizing an issue
on which the president was apparently highly involved remained difficult.[57] In at least one case, a recently elected Republican governor leveraged the census as a means of attacking his partisan opponents, reversing
the efforts of his predecessor to create a SCCC and provide funding for
census outreach.[58] In other cases, Republican governors and state legislators had more general philosophical objections to investing in the census.[59] As one governor's census liaison told me, the governor was elected
"as a conservative" and that his "mentality as an individual is that [the cen-
sus] is a very grassroots community-based thing. . . . The best work on this
that will actually move the needle and have an impact is more grassroots,

community-led, with the governor's office and the State Complete Count Committee having some convening power."[60] As a consequence, he suggested, the governor did not request a significant legislative appropriation for the census.

Regardless of party or ideology, governors taking office for the first time in 2018 or 2019 also had difficulties prioritizing census outreach.[61] In describing why her state was so late to create a Complete Count Commission, one state administrator cited the prior (Republican) administration's lack of action as "the biggest problem" yet went on to note that while the incoming Democratic governor was eager to take action on the census after taking office in January of 2019, the state's budgeting process "is such that the governor essentially comes in and has three months to create their budget and present it to the legislature."[62] The creation of the SCCC fell to the bottom of the list of priorities until the budgeting season was over in the late summer.

There were also important exceptions to the partisan pattern. One SCCC member described how the commission's chair, who held a post in the Republican governor's office, effectively illustrated to the state's cabinet agencies how census data affected intergovernmental grants that supported their work.[63] Interviewees in Republican-led states often cited gubernatorial concerns with losing a congressional seat and legislators' concerns with accurate redistricting data as a source of motivation for census investments.[64] Others noted that regional planning organizations had appealed for investments because of the role census data plays in structuring firms' investment decisions.[65]

Thus while partisan identities are no doubt powerful in shaping officials' decisions about census investments, these identities are to some extent mutable. That is, it is possible to find appeals for census investments that resonate with members of both parties. In one Republican-led state, I interviewed two officials—one Republican and one Democrat—both of whom agreed that the governor's office and state legislators had identified a logic of justifying census incentives that was "collaborative and nonpolitical."[66] "We are growing the state," one official told me.[67] Thus the governor's appeal focused on the growth of the state's population, emphasizing that a fair share of "our federal tax dollars . . . should be coming back to our state and investing in . . . our community and our people."[68]

Institutional Capacity

My interviews also revealed how preexisting institutional arrangements affected how state policymakers made sense of their roles and responsibilities in mobilizing participation in the 2020 Census. State and local officials are not typically involved in census operations and the decennial census is a rare event. While a small handful of state and local interviewees were veterans, having worked in some capacity with anywhere from one to three prior counts, most individuals I spoke with described 2020 as their first experience with census work. The census "learning curve" was a steep one. Developing a strategic plan for outreach demanded some facility with the Census Bureau's dense, technical operational plans, information on the location and identity of populations that were less likely to respond, models of successful information campaigns, and strategies for securing the cooperation of local civic leaders in raising awareness about the census. In the absence of readily available routines for strategic planning and implementation, interviewees at the state and local level reported searching for information from Census Bureau partnership specialists and regional staff as well as state data center staff and, in some cases, state demographers.

The interviews also revealed variation in the availability of technical support for overcoming the learning curve. This was most visible when it came to relationships between local and state officials and Census Bureau staff. Restructuring in the regional and areawide census offices in recent years had, numerous interviewees agreed, created new barriers to coordinating with state and local census liaisons. One veteran SDC director noted how competition between Census Bureau partnership specialists and regional office staff produced conflicting meeting schedules. "I would get a call from a Partnership Specialist who says 'we're trying to organize meetings in [county]. Can you help us out?' And I'd say, 'Well we actually have a meeting scheduled there in two weeks. Would you like be a part of this meeting?' And they would say, 'Oh well that's not a good day for me.'"[69]

Beyond frequent turnover at the bureau, one potential reason for the lack of communication was that partnership specialists, in the estimation of several interviewees, had incentives to maximize the number of partnerships they created, often at the expense of aiding existing partners. Beginning in 2018, the Census Bureau used partnership tallies as key performance metrics in weekly and monthly performance management reports.[70] Yet these tallies often did not reflect the depth of the partnerships secured by the bureau. Several interviewees reported that, after establishing contact, partnership specialists were difficult to reach. Additionally, partnership specialists were frequently denied discretion from the bureau to communicate candidly with CCCs about potential approaches for engaging hard-to-count communities.[71]

Given turbulence at the federal level, state and local institutions—particularly SDCs and other public and private organizations with experience in census outreach—often provided the expertise necessary to make census investments. "These things come along only every ten years," one SDC director reported, "So you gotta kind of pick up whatever is laying around and try to make it work."[72] No state appeared to imitate California's model of employing a quasi-permanent Office of the Census to coordinate its complete count activities. Far more frequently, state efforts were supported by SCCCs and coordinated by SDCs, a single cabinet official, or a governor's liaison to the Census Bureau.

In some cases, a well-resourced SCCC helped to fill in crucial knowledge gaps at the local level about the importance of making census investments. As one SCCC lead told me:

A lot of times we'd show up to city halls and a lot of times people wouldn't know what the census is. . . . So when we sat down where we gave them a lot of literature, we talked them through about what the best steps are and really encourage them to take it as their own because they know their own community. . . . [We] talked about the money that was at stake and having people realize how much money is comes from census, from the US Census and all the programs that, that, that have paid for or not, you know, all the roads and everything else that the US Census numbers go to.[73]

Making these sorts of appeals appeared to be significantly harder in states where SDCs had been underfunded or had few ties to executive-branch agencies. One university-based SDC director reported that in the past ten years, the entire network of SDC coordinating agencies in the state had "fallen apart" due to a lack of support from the state's Department of Commerce. While the state nevertheless made significant fiscal investments in census outreach and awareness (largely due to the high potential for an undercount), the absence of a strong coordinating network meant that information about census operations rarely "filtered down" to the SDC or to local officials.[74]

Preexisting institutional networks also served as conduits of information about the importance of census outreach. As one SDC director in a primarily rural state told me, her organization had built up networks of census data users and coordinating agencies at state universities over the last twenty years, which provided a set of relationships that supported census information campaigns.[75] Similarly, in a heavily urbanized state, one SCCC member told me about state-level meetings convened to share outreach plans from large cities in other states.[76]

SDCs and SCCCs were not alone in collating existing knowledge about best practices in census outreach. Indeed, the ad hoc nature of census operations in many states, cities, and counties meant that there were few people whose full-time responsibility is developing and executing outreach plans. Thus nonprofit organizations and philanthropic foundations often stepped in not merely to "fill capacity gaps" but to serve as a primary coordinating venue for census outreach itself.[77] This action reflected a broader push toward census work among national philanthropic consortia as well as the coordinating work of entrepreneurial nonprofit leaders at the state and local level. In one Midwestern state, a large healthcare foundation took on a principal role in helping officials to finance and develop census outreach plans. The foundation provided the state's municipal league with a $500,000 grant over a two-year period to encourage local governments to create complete count committees. The municipal league's census project lead not only had strong existing relationships with officials in these communities but she was well-acquainted with the types of officials who were usually tasked with census outreach in these communities, whose workload had increased in recent years, reducing their "bandwidth" for census work. To bridge these problems, she bundled together a series of virtual census tool kits, which provided not only strategies for advertising in hard-to-count communities based on the Census Bureau's own behavioral and attitudinal research study (CBAMS) but also a guide for engaging appropriate stakeholders in the community, who were likely to be highly motivated to lead local engagement efforts.[78]

Institutional capacity also affected the range of tools for officials to evaluate the potential *effects* of their plans for census response and, if necessary, to revise these plans in light of available information. The SCCC and CCC models are ostensibly designed to make visible and usable the highly localized and tacit knowledge about how to do effective outreach. Yet these organizations are temporary and sometimes ad hoc. Indeed, states' capacity for

developing census response strategies that are adapted to on-the-ground realities often resides elsewhere. As noted previously, state data centers played
a crucial role in highlighting the effects of undercounts and encouraging
state and local investment in census operations.[79] SDCs' involvement in
partnerships with the Census Bureau's Geography Division, including the
Local Update of Census Addresses (LUCA), can create a virtuous cycle of
census effort. While legislators were sometimes less willing to commit millions of dollars for outreach work, investing in LUCA helped to generate a
more accurate address list, which improved emergency services and other
data infrastructures at a nominal cost. Census advocates could use small
wins like this one to illustrate to elected officials that accurate census data
had benefits that extended beyond securing fair representation in Congress
and a fair share of federal grants.[80]

Philanthropies and nongovernmental organizations also provided valuable expertise that enabled census investments, even in states with little internal capacity. In some states and cities, few investments in census outreach
would have been made in the absence of philanthropic engagement.[81] In one
state, members of a philanthropic organization could identify only one "cof-
fee-stained packet of papers" detailing how the state had coordinated census
outreach in 2010 and thus relied on their partnerships with community
organizations to develop a media strategy and to translate census information into the most commonly spoken languages of hard-to-count communities.[82] Organizations with extensive histories of community outreach were
particularly important in helping state and local governments to revise their
outreach strategies. This was certainly true in a rural, western state whose
SCCC relied extensively on the expertise of a member who helped to run a
voter-engagement organization focused largely on the state's Latinx population. As he told me: "Government officials, legislators, they work in sort of
like the limelight," he told me, not "with the folks who are not registered to
vote, don't turn out very often."[83] As a result, drawing on his network of contacts, he formed a statewide Latinx Complete Count Committee. "We can
see the data," he said, "We know exactly where the [undercounted] people
are. So we're doing community events there where, you know, we don't necessarily have to knock on every door. . . . I mean, that's one of the beauties
of actually creating your own complete count committee and inviting folks
who have some of this expertise."[84]

Quantitative Analyses of State Census Investments

To further explore the role of census salience, partisanship, and institutional capacity on states' census investments, I carried out two sets of quantitative analyses. In the first, I examine states' decisions to fund census outreach. Here, I use logistic regression to model states' decisions to provide census funding as a binary choice. I also use an ordinary least squares (OLS) regression to model per-capita state funding. In both models, the unit of analysis is the state year. The models include data for the years 2017 to 2020. States fall out of the analysis once they have provided initial funding for census outreach. Both models also include several independent variables. First, to capture the salience of the census for state officials, I include a variable indicating the size of the state's net undercount in the 2010 Census as well as a variable indicating the number of congressional seats the state was projected to gain or lose following the 2020 Census. Second, as an indicator of the partisan identity of state officials, I include a measure of the number of chambers of state government, including both the legislative and executive branch, controlled by the Democratic Party. Third, to capture states' institutional capacity, the models include a logged measure of the state's per capita operations budget. Finally, I include a control variable indicating the size of the state's population as well as year indicators for the first two years in the analysis. Each model is estimated with robust standard errors clustered on the state.[85]

As tables 4.3 and 4.4 show, whether we model state census funding as a binary choice or a continuous level of per-capita expenditure, there are three statistically significant findings. First, states are more likely to make investments if they experienced a larger net undercount in 2010. When funding is modeled as a binary outcome, states expecting an increase in congressional seats following the 2020 Census are also less likely to fund census outreach. The statistical significance for the seat-change coefficient disappears in the OLS model, however. Third, states with greater levels of Democratic control of government are significantly more likely to make investments in census outreach than those with greater Republican control of government. Finally, states with higher per-capita operational expenditures capacity are significantly more likely to invest in census outreach than those with lower operational expenditures.[86]

Beyond funding itself, as noted, we can also think about the timing of states' decisions to create State Complete Count Commissions as an indicator of their investment in outreach. As noted previously, my interviews

Table 4.3. Logistic Regression Analysis of State Census Funding Decisions

Variable	Coef. (SE)
2010 Net Undercount	1.56 (0.58)**
2020 Projected Seat Change	−1.38 (0.52)**
Democratic Control	1.02 (0.27)***
Per Capita Operations Budget (Ln.)	1.04 (0.42)*
Population (Ln.)	0.16 (0.49)
2017	−5.6 (0.98)***
2018	−2.77 (0.71)***
Log Likelihood	−42.93
Observations (Clusters)	167.00 (50)

Note: Cell entries are coefficients from logistic regression with clustered robust standard errors in parentheses. Source: Author's analysis.
***$p < 0.001$; **$p < 0.01$; *$p < 0.05$.

revealed that when states moved quickly to create these organizations, they improved their ability to coordinate census outreach with government, nonprofit, and private-sector partners around the state. By contrast, commissions created in later 2019 or 2020 often existed only on paper or were capable of doing little coordination of outreach efforts prior to self-response period.

Table 4.4. OLS Regression Analysis of Per Capita State Census Funding

Variable	Coef. (SE)
2010 Net Undercount	0.27 (0.13)*
2020 Projected Seat Change	−0.15 (0.10)
Democratic Control	0.21 (0.07)**
Per Capita Operations Budget (Ln.)	0.10 (0.03)**
Population (Ln.)	0.10 (0.10)
2017	−0.25 (0.11)*
2018	−0.26 (0.08)**
R^2	0.29
Observations (Clusters)	167.00 (50)

Note: Cell entries are coefficients from logistic regression with clustered robust standard errors in parentheses. Source: Author's analysis.
***$p < 0.001$; **$p < 0.01$; *$p < 0.05$.

Table 4.5. Cox Proportional-Hazards Model Estimates for State Complete Count Commission Establishment

Variable	Coef. (SE)	Hazard Ratio
2010 Net Undercount	0.46 (0.32)	1.55
2020 Projected Seat Change	−1.01 (0.27)***	0.36
Democratic Control	0.79 (0.18)***	2.19
Per Capita Operations Budget (Ln.)	1.41 (0.52)**	4.12
Population (Ln.)	−0.72 (0.49)	0.48
N, Events	1322,48	
Likelihood Ratio Test	68.76 ***	

Note: Cell entries are Cox proportional-hazards model coefficients with standard errors in parenthesis. The final column lists the associated hazard ratios for each variable. Source: Author's analysis.
***$p < 0.001$; **$p < 0.01$; *$p < 0.05$.

To examine the timing of SCCC creation at the state level between January of 2017 and August of 2020, I use a Cox proportional-hazards model. This model analyzes the likelihood that a state will create an SCCC as a function of time (measured in months). Survival analysis is appropriate here in part because the Cox model drops states from the analysis upon SCCC creation, eliminating the need to cluster standard errors. The analysis includes the same independent variables—except the year indicators—used in the models of state census funding.

The results of the Cox proportional-hazards model are presented in table 4.5. Coefficients and standard errors are presented in the middle column while hazard ratios are presented in the final column. Hazard ratios greater than 1 indicate an increase in likelihood of SCCC creation while hazard ratios below 1 indicate a decrease in likelihood. The results here suggest four statistically significant patterns. First, states expecting a gain in congressional seats following the 2020 Census were significantly more likely to delay the creation of an SCCC when compared to states that expected to lose congressional seats or experience no change. Second, unlike state census funding decisions, the size of the net undercount in 2010 did not have a statistically significant effect on the timing of SCCC creation. Third, states with greater levels of Democratic Party control created SCCCs more quickly than states largely controlled by Republicans. Finally, states with higher levels of administrative capacity—as indicated by per-capita operating budgets—were quicker to create their SCCCs when compared to states with lower levels of capacity.[87]

Local Investments in Census Outreach: The Role of Intergovernmental and Intersectoral Partnerships

While there is no comprehensive accounting of it, local governments also committed a prodigious level of resources to census promotion in the 2020 cycle. New York City led the way, spending roughly $40 million on census outreach. Yet for many cities, counties, and tribal governments, making such investments—including but not limited to the creation of CCCs—often proved an arduous undertaking. Still reeling from the fiscal effects of the Great Recession, many jurisdictions lacked adequate resources to allocate to existing public services. As one survey of American municipalities suggested, in fiscal year 2018, "total constant-dollar general fund revenue growth slowed to 0.6 percent."[88] For several decades, a growing number of state governments had adopted several policies that further crowded out fiscal space for local census investments. These included unfunded mandates on municipalities and counties, cuts to state's local revenue-sharing programs, as well as property tax limitations.[89] By 2018, local government employment had not yet recovered to its prerecession baseline.[90] Thus even in jurisdictions that were able to finance census outreach, responsibilities for planning and coordinating often fell onto officials in "catch-all" offices with large existing portfolios.

One way of understanding this variation is by examining the data the Census Bureau collected on the formation of CCCs. Figure 4.4 illustrates variation in the total number of local CCC contacts made by the Census Bureau in each US county or county equivalent. As is visible here, CCC contacts were present through much of the country, with the densest clusters in heavily urbanized counties. Sparsely populated rural counties were the least likely to have at least one CCC contact.[91] Still, we should not rely on CCC contacts alone as an indicator of local outreach effort.[92] As several interviewees told me, partnership staff had incentives to inflate the number of partnerships they made, coding both a city's well-resourced local outreach campaigns and a school district official's verbal agreement to hang census posters as equivalent to the creation of a CCC. Indeed, drilling down into the data reveals evidence that some partnership specialists counted contacts with multiple members of county commissions or city councils as their own unique CCCs.[93]

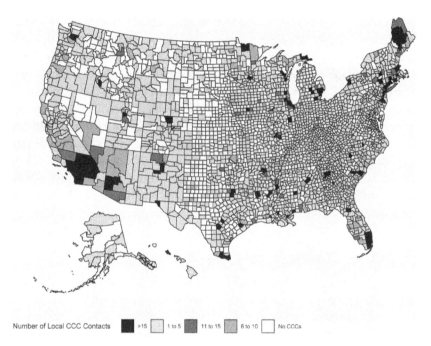

Number of Local CCC Contacts   >15   1 to 5   11 to 15   6 to 10   No CCCs

Figure 4.4: Census Complete Count Committee contacts, by county. Source: Author's analysis of "Census Complete Count Committees," US Census Bureau, March 19, 2020, https://www.census.gov/library/visualizations /interactive/2020-complete-count-committees.html.
Note: Figures reflect all contacts listed in Census Bureau database, after removal of duplicates.

Nevertheless, the spatial variation in figure 4.4 resembles the patterns found when examining the government websites of the four largest munici- palities in each state for evidence of CCC formation. While almost all large cities (those with a population of two hundred and fifty thousand or more) created a CCC in 2018 or 2019, the same cannot be said for smaller cities.[94] Only 39 percent of cities in the sample with a population of less than fifty thousand created a SCCC. Smaller cities were more likely to create a CCC in states that allocated funding for census outreach than in states that did not. Cities tended to play the role of the lead jurisdiction on CCCs, with coun- ties, city-county partnerships, and intergovernmental organizations play- ing a more limited role. Interviews with local CCC members also revealed several distinctive organizational approaches. Large cities and counties often ran census outreach through a formal, standalone census office or through a large CCC with extensive support from a public relations firm. Medium-sized cities took one of several routes to organizing. One such model was a regional CCC run from a central city's department of administration or community services or a city-county partnership, sometimes with strong support from nonprofit partners. Finally, some small and medium-sized cities relied on a more limited effort supported by members of a single city department who were not necessarily able to devote considerable hours to census outreach work.[95] These variations, as the next sections suggest, can be attributed to major differences in how local officials experience the threat of undercounts and the institutional resources they have to respond to them.

Census Salience and Local Investments

Before they can make investments in census outreach, local officials—like their counterparts at the state level—must first overcome the institutional amnesia associated with a process that occurs only once every ten years. This is one reason why creating awareness about the census and the risks associated with an undercount is arguably the first and most important task of the bureau's partnership program. It is also one reason why the experience of prior undercounts, or the looming threat of losing a congressional seat, appeared to provide a focal point for generating investments in outreach. As one CCC chair told me:

> I think that in the past the census has always been [seen as] a federal issue. But the state . . . got whacked in 2000. We lost a congressional [seat] in 2010 and we had a significant undercount. And if you look at the census map for all the counties in the country, once you get to [our state], you will see massive, massive low response rates. . . . This was sort of was the perfect storm to realize that in 2020 and especially with lack of federal investment and the politicization of the census in the past year and a half, I am going to say has probably had the most dramatic effect on what we've been doing.[96]

While the experience (or threat) of undercounts was a common driver of census salience at the local level, it was not the only one. At least one interviewee—a local official in the Southwest—mentioned the importance of a growing population in driving census investments, suggesting that as one of the fastest growing cities in the country, an accurate count was essential to maintain federal grants for city service. Added to this, the Trump administration's proposal to introduce a citizenship question raised serious concerns about the possibility of an undercount of the undocumented population. This cued the attention of both the mayor and the city council to the importance of funding census operations.[97] How these cues translated into action, however, hinged on the character of local political institutions.

The Imprint of Local Politics

While partisanship often played a defining role in structuring states' decisions to invest in census outreach, the same cannot be said for local partnerships.[98] Only one local interviewee, for example, clearly identified partisanship as a barrier to census investments. There, the issue was that a Republican-dominated board in a suburban county went overwhelmingly for Donald Trump in the 2016 presidential election. Because Trump had made the census into a "politically charged" issue, neither the board members nor the staff of any of the county's departments—including the planning department—was motivated to invest in outreach. A community foundation stepped in to fill the gap, bringing in $60,000 in total to support census outreach.[99]

This experience was not a common one, however. If local officials reported that partisanship thwarted census investments, it was because the state had underinvested in outreach or provided little guidance or support to local governments.[100] Yet when it came to the actions of local officials themselves, this kind of evidence was harder to find. Even in solidly Republican cities and counties, local CCC members and census advocates observed few partisan roadblocks. As one such person informed me, he had not "run into pushback from Republicans." There were, he believed, three reasons for this. First, he said that there were always "rumors" that the state might get back a congressional seat it had lost in recent years and it would be presumably held by a Republican. Second, Republicans at the local level realized that the census shaped federal grant funding, which helped to provide political space to lower taxes. Third, Republican elected officials were convinced that undercounts would hobble efforts to "bring commerce" into the state given long-standing barriers to workforce development. An undercount would not only translate into a smaller share of federal aid, it would only reinforce the perception that the state was not worth employers' investments.[101]

If local politics mattered, it arguably had less to do with the partisan affinities of local officials and more to do with whether elected leaders, particularly mayors and county executives, were able to use the powers of their office to direct resources toward census outreach.[102] When I asked one CCC chair about the greatest facilitators of outreach work in her city, she told me flatly: "We had the million dollars and we had the mayor."[103] Almost immediately after being elected in November of 2018, the mayor had made census outreach a top priority—securing a significant sum for census outreach in her first budget. Moreover, owing to her long tenure in public service—which included nearly a decade on city council—the mayor also had numerous relationships with community-based organizations. She was thus able to staff the city's census outreach campaign with seasoned veterans from the world of community organizing—particularly in the city's hardest-to-count census tracts.[104]

Where elected officials lacked these connections, planning for census outreach proved to be a more delicate dance. As one CCC chair in a large Southwestern city told me, both he and the city's mayor were strongly aware of the dangers of inaugurating their outreach campaign without consulting community groups first. This was especially significant given concerns about the Trump administration's proposed citizenship question among organizations representing immigrant communities. Thus prior to planning the city's outreach campaign, the CCC organized a series of eight focus groups with individuals and organizations representing historically undercounted communities. Beyond shaping the city's approach to communicating with residents about the census, these focus groups helped to inform the city's mapping of community assets—including nonprofits, schools, and libraries—which could serve as trusted brokers of information about the census. When merged with tract-level "hard-to-count" scores, this information could be used to identify gaps in census promotion.[105]

Top elected officials also used their office to advance census outreach in other ways. In regions with a dense landscape of philanthropic and non-profit partnerships, mayors and county executives found greater success by using their offices to convene stakeholders—including funders—rather than relying on legislative approval of outreach funds.[106] Additionally, several interviewees emphasized that the city's outreach efforts relied centrally on mayoral leadership to direct "public-facing" city or county agencies to use their authority to communicate about the census, on everything from library receipts to utility statements.[107]

Yet even when elected officials were highly mobilized, maintaining a strong focus on census outreach could still prove difficult. As one CCC member—a regional planner and self-described "cheerleader" for the census—told me, "Every time I go to a meeting, there's fewer and fewer people."[108] However necessary, the committee's reliance on voluntary partnerships, and the absence of dedicated staff meant it was difficult to ensure that the action plan—once developed—could be executed. This brings us to the issue of local governments' capacity.

Local Capacity for Census Outreach

Arguably the most significant barrier to local governments' investment in census promotion, including but not limited to the formation of CCCs, was the scarcity of fiscal and organizational capacity. According to a 2021 National League of Cities survey, municipal budgets accounted for the greatest share of funding (45 percent) supporting local governments' census outreach activity.[109] Yet the adequacy of those funds is another question entirely. In all but the largest metropolitan cities and counties, officials I spoke with cited a lack of internal resources to support outreach work. While a handful of large cities had one or more full-time employees whose effort was dedicated exclusively to census preparations, my local interviewees were far more likely to have the census added to their list of existing responsibilities. In one medium-sized city (with a population of roughly one hundred and twenty-five thousand), an interviewee told me, the census was "not a huge budget item." To the extent that the city's own scarce budget could be allocated to census outreach, it would be in the form of "in kind" voluntary contributions of effort and social media from various departments.[110] A census outreach coordinator in a similarly sized city in the Northeast—who was nearly out of breath when we spoke from running between meetings—reported that the city had "very few resources," including staff time, to commit to its CCC. What made things worse was that no one else seemed to have resources either. Neither the state nor local nonprofits were able to step in to fill the city's resource gaps.[111]

This example points to the importance, articulated by many of the local interviewees, of securing external resources to support census outreach. State governments played a primary role here. According to the National League of Cities, transfers from states and other local governments accounted for

17 percent of cities' census outreach funding.[112] In California, for example, grant funding was largely channeled through the state's fifty-eight counties as well as through over one hundred and fifty administrative community-based organizations (ABCOs)—usually community foundations with strong ties to historically undercounted populations.[113] Counties and ABCOs, in turn, pushed funding to municipalities to support advertising campaigns, special events, and the construction of questionnaire assistance centers.[114]

In addition to making grants to cities and nonprofits, states also subsidized local governments' census investments through the provision of information and expertise. State-level interviewees described going on exhaustive "road shows" to municipalities around their states, advertising the potential returns on census investments as well as the risks of undercounts.[115] Highlighting these effects was particularly important given that in many states, local officials charged with census outreach operations were typically burdened with a number of other responsibilities that took priority.[116] As one SDC director told me, encouraging local investments in census outreach required understanding the unique effects of undercounts on individual jurisdictions, since not all jurisdictions experience uniform losses or gains in legislative representation or federal dollars. Rather, narratives about the perils of undercounts were most likely to be effective if they were tailored to local context. One such narrative went like this:

> [One city's] boundary was represented wrong in the Census TIGER file. And when the Census Bureau did their count, they assigned the population for [the city] right on the edge of where one of these lines goes through a high density [area]. . . . [City officials] had never looked at their maps and it's a smaller community, so it's not like they have a lot of full-time staff. . . . If the bureau would've had this population counted, it probably would have been around 90 or so people and . . . that would have pushed [the city] up to [second-class] and their [state sales-tax turnback] rate would've been a lot higher. . . . [The SDC] helped them see the light and say, "If we get these boundaries right, then that helps give us a chance to get the count right."[117]

In states that did not make such investments, smaller jurisdictions often struggled to finance census promotion. As the mayor's census outreach coordinator in one large Southern metro told me, his state's failure to invest in census outreach further limited the city's ability to buy materials for census advertising, do outreach events, and install census information kiosks. While the city was able to allocate roughly $100,000 in advertising (including bus wraps, posters, buttons, and T-shirts), the reach of the organizing campaign was necessarily limited by the absence of state funds.[118]

Even when states did provide funding for census outreach, it did not always reach local governments in time to develop a solid outreach plan. As the CCC chair in a large East Coast city told me, his state had allocated over $1 million for census outreach but then proved reluctant to provide grants to local governments beyond a "very, very small amount of matching funds." Yet applying for these small grants of barely more than $2,000 was more time consuming and, in the view of some at the city, more trouble than it was worth.[119] In another state, a local CCC member informed me that her city—which had a population of roughly one hundred and fifty thousand—never received state grant funding it was promised and that, after several months of phone calls and emails with state officials administering the funds as well as state legislators, the money had still not arrived as of September 2019, forcing the CCC to downsize its outreach plans. In fact, a follow-up interview with this CCC member in December of 2020 revealed that state support for local census outreach never arrived at all.[120]

Where states were less fiscally and administratively involved—or where state involvement arrived on a delayed timeline—local governments relied more extensively on the support of nonprofit organizations and philanthropies. For its part, the philanthropic community was highly mobilized on census outreach from the beginning. As the National League of Cities survey suggests, "Philanthropies, nonprofits, and foundations" accounted for 25 percent of cities' funding for census outreach.[121] One of the largest national efforts to coordinate private funding for census outreach was that of the Funders' Committee for Civic Participation (FCCP). Founded in 1983, FCCP is a philanthropy-serving organization. Rather than making grants on its own, it convenes a national network of funders to coordinate support for democratic institutions, including the protection of voting rights and support for fair state redistricting processes.[122]

After first becoming involved in census outreach in the 2010 cycle, the FCCP developed a broader cadre of philanthropic leaders, called the Democracy Funders Collaborative, to coordinate efforts for the 2020 cycle. At the head of what came to be known the "Census Subgroup" was Gary Bass, executive director of the Bauman Foundation. After months of interviewing census experts and funders, Bass and his team developed a multipronged plan to coordinate advocacy for improvements to census infrastructure, expand philanthropic investments in census participation, and coordinate public outreach and education. By 2016, FCCP began holding quarterly meetings with census stakeholders and funders to strategize, share information, and to identify early challenges and successes with funding efforts. The effort soon expanded to include three national "funders' tables" to generate, pool, and manage resources, as well as three tables composed of "implementing organizations" centered around census advocacy, awareness, and the combatting of misinformation.[123]

By 2020, the efforts had begun to bear fruit. The initiative organized over one hundred funders to provide $118 million for a coordinated "plan of action" as well as $75 million in state philanthropic funding.[124] Recognizing the unevenness of state and local support for census outreach, the subgroup reserved funding for a specific census equity fund, which made grants to sixty-nine organizations in twenty-eight states, Washington, DC, and Puerto Rico. These organizations operated in locations with "high concentrations of historically undercounted populations and low public and private census funding."[125]

It is hard to overstate the effect of this national strategy on the activity of local philanthropies and nonprofit organizations. As the executive director of one community foundation told me, a national retreat in January of 2017 sparked his interest in the census as a "cornerstone of democracy" and he quickly recommended to his board that the organization become a regional leader on census outreach. By the fall of 2018—after months of regular meetings between foundation executives, the mayor, and the county executive—he had become the cochair of the joint city/county CCC and had helped to coordinate over $500,000 in private fundraising to complement the city's fiscal investments in outreach.[126] A robust nonprofit sector often benefitted public officials' census organizing initiatives. In rust-belt cities, rural Midwestern counties, and the low-density municipalities of the Southwest, community foundations could double or even triple governments' fiscal contributions to census outreach.[127]

Often, nonprofits' contributions came not merely in the form of fiscal support but organizational expertise. Whereas government officials often had census outreach "piled" on their other responsibilities, nonprofit organizations could more readily provide dedicated full-time employees to support project management. Perhaps more importantly, the nonprofits often most involved with census outreach at the local level already had experience in community outreach or mobilization efforts, including but not limited to targeted Get Out the Vote campaigns.[128]

To see the value of these intersectoral partnerships, consider the experience of one interviewee, the director of a democracy campaign for a statewide association of nonprofits in a city of over two million people. A full two years before the city or county established complete count committees, her organization had made the census part of its campaign to strengthen local participation in democratic processes. With over two decades of work in voter mobilization, the campaign's director was keenly aware of the challenges of engaging historically underrepresented and undercounted populations. Given the city's experience with outreach during the 2010 Census, she was also conscious of the challenges of coordinating census mobilization across multiple nonprofits and government entities. Thus by the time government entities had established their own CCCs, her organization—with links to nonprofits and grant-makers across the metropolitan area and the state—was well-positioned to play a leading role. By the final months of 2019, she and her colleagues were coordinating a review of over $1 million in city-run outreach grants to community-based organizations. As she put it, arguably the greatest value of her organization to local elected officials was its relationships to existing nonprofits, grant-makers, and governments:

> I think when you've got a complicated state like ours where the [metro area] is vastly different from [the center of the state], which is vastly different from [the southern part of the state] . . . it's hard because you are focused on where you live. . . . You're local, your locality matters. . . . So that you do believe you have the stake in the fight together. And that takes time. . . . You can't ask someone, some grantee that's in our county to say, hey, let's work collaboratively with someone in City X, then say, hey, let's work collaboratively with someone in City Y, right? That takes time to be able to make sure that everybody understands, okay, this is the best practice that works here. But it could also work here if it was tweaked a little, right? . . . You need . . . these trusted messengers to have the time and the capability to come together. . . . So I think the beauty of our [2020 Census program] is that it really does bring grant makers and nonprofits together.[129]

Her organization's connection to a statewide network of grant-makers allowed for the pooling of resources from across the state prior to the legislature's passage of census outreach funding legislation. This permitted smaller community-based organizations to receive seed money to begin planning their outreach strategies well in advance of 2020 and to provide a "model" of what other organizations could do.[130] Even where nonprofits lacked extensive connections to large pools of resources, however, their preexisting relationship to organizations with expertise at mobilizing civic participation proved essential. As the leader of a nonprofit democracy campaign in one large Midwestern city told me, most government officials he met informed him that they were "doing [outreach work] for the first time." His organization, which was central to planning the city's outreach effort, had the ability to import knowledge from other recent mobilization campaigns:

> *CCC Chair:* A big part of what we do is help and work to support our non-profit partners in building their leadership pipelines and internal capacity to do not only the work that they do every day, but the shared strategy around the Census. So, we have some goals around hiring, building the teams that will be able to knock on 116,000 doors. So, it revolves around . . . the CCC.
> *Interviewer:* Internal capacity—you mean by that . . . ?
> *CCC Chair:* Staff [who] are trained to talk about the Census, [who] can answer questions or give . . . credible and knowledgeable responses about concerns folks may have about confidentiality, citizenship concerns. . . . We've knocked on around four to five thousand doors already this fall [2019] to . . . do a test run for next spring, and we did that in hard-to-count neighborhoods. . . . So, we can test what messages are resonating with people.[131]

As this interview suggests, nonprofits often provided capacity to local governments that they would not have otherwise had. Fiscally, nonprofits often had greater flexibility to make channel funding to community-based organizations and governments, even prior to the passage of state funding legislation. To local governments with strained capacity, these organizations also provided dedicated staff who often had years of experience with civic mobilization campaigns. At the same time, none of my interviewees believed that nonprofits could have successfully mobilized census participation in the absence of support from government partners.

Perhaps the most complicated source of external capacity for local governments was the Census Bureau itself. On the one hand, a survey by the National League of Cities suggests that over 70 percent of cities identified the bureau as an "effective partner" in census outreach.[132] There is a great deal of truth to this. Through CPEP, the bureau provides local governments with both a "recipe" for census outreach based on years of research and experience from prior years, as well as advertising collateral, in the form of flyers, walk cards, and giveaway swag like pencils, lip balm, and tote bags. On the other hand, there is wide variation in city responses to this question. Whereas 73 percent of respondents from cities with a population of less than fifty thousand rated the bureau as an effective partner, only 44 percent of the largest cities in the survey—with populations greater than three hundred thousand—did the same.

As one nonprofit leader in a densely populated Southern city told me, the problems with CPEP staffing were visible almost immediately. Inadequate funding meant that by 2018, the bureau had hired only two partnership specialists for the entire state. But by the middle of the year, one of the specialists had quit. With months to go before 2020, she reported that the state had only a "handful of Partnership Specialists" to cover the entire state.[133] High turnover among partnership specialists, in turn, helped to sour local officials on census promotion. As the same nonprofit leader told me, she often found herself attempting to reenergize local partners after a bad experience: "They're like, 'No, because the [Census Bureau] already spoke to me. It gave me no resources. I tried to follow up and I couldn't get them.' . . . I think that's consistent across the board. The [partnership specialist] will make the initial contact and they'll get the buy in, but then they disappear."[134]

This experience of abandonment resonated with a local CCC chair in a large Midwestern city. Partnership specialists, in his view, were "very good at reaching out to a lot of people, but then when it comes to following through with the quality training or interacting beyond what might be on their script that they might be allowed to say or communicate, they're not empowered to actually help CCCs take meaningful action." The result was that community partners often had no clear sense of with whom they should be coordinating.[135]

In other cases, local officials reported that partnership specialists they had spoken to lacked substantive knowledge of census procedures, which helped to create confusion among partners. The census director in a Southern city with a population of nearly five hundred thousand put it in stark terms. One thing she learned was that she "couldn't rely solely on the US Census Bureau because the information they were putting out into the community was false information." Originally, she said, partnership specialists had informed her that there would be a toll-free telephone number that individuals could call to request a paper census questionnaire. In turn, the city's initial communications with residents—which included more than ten thousand pieces of literature—advertised this information. Another partnership specialist then informed her that individuals would not be able to request paper forms. Panicked, she then called yet another partnership specialist, who told her that paper forms could be requested by phone. In fact, as she later found out, the bureau's operational plan allowed individuals to complete the census on the phone via an interview with a customer service representative whereas paper questionnaires would not be sent out to most households until April of 2020, and not by telephone request. The lesson for her was that a poorly staffed partnership program meant more work for her and her staff: "The Partnership Specialists are not experts and if you're going to be an expert in this and not waste resources and put misinformation out in the community, *we* damn well better be the experts."[136]

The partnership program's resources and staffing decisions were not the only source of confusion, however. Rather, the Trump administration's policy decisions also helped to create a high level of confusion on the ground. In one census training session I attended in December of 2019—hosted by a community foundation rather than the bureau—the handouts included an out-of-date packet from the National Association of Latino Elected and Appointed Officials suggesting that the citizenship question would still be on the census questionnaire even though the Supreme Court had, five months earlier, quashed the Trump administration's plan. In the middle of the meeting, the bureau's partnership specialist—a skilled veteran of three censuses—quickly sprang up to make copies of the current sample questionnaire. At this point, the presenters nearly lost the crowd's attention.[137]

In some cases, partnership specialists lacked not formal knowledge of census procedures but local knowledge about the communities they were tasked with mobilizing. The CCC chair for a city of nearly four hundred thousand praised the bureau's regional staff but complained about one of the specialists initially sent to her. "He drove me crazy," she said. Hailing from another state, he reportedly had little awareness of key community partners and appeared unwilling to listen to her. She had far more positive experiences—as did other CCC members I spoke to—with partnership specialists hired from her own city who were more familiar with the local political and organizational context.[138] Yet in the end, as the evidence here suggests, many local CCC chairs still found it necessary to become "their own" partnership specialists, often with assistance from state governments and nonprofits.

Politics and Partnerships

Over the last several decades, the Census Bureau has come to rely more extensively on partnerships with state and local governments, as well as philanthropies and nonprofit organizations, to strengthen its communications and outreach strategies, particularly within hard-to-count communities. The reason for this is simple: However well targeted the bureau's own advertising campaigns may be, the bureau—like the federal government more generally—faces a deficit of trust that creates a demand for "trusted messengers." To support this work, the bureau has made a considerable number of institutional innovations, from well-developed organizing models like the Complete Count Committee to geospatial technologies for pinpointing hard-to-count populations.

Yet, as this chapter has shown, making meaningful investments in census outreach can be a heavy lift. First, the bureau faces its own fiscal and operational challenges in implementing an effective partnership program. As the evidence from 2020 suggests, inadequate funding and a tight labor market made it difficult for the bureau to reach its hiring targets for partnership specialists in a timely way. While the quality of the partnership program varied regionally, a common and significant problem is that specialists were incentivized to formally record a high number of "partnerships" in the bureau's database even if they did not represent serious commitments and even at the expense of following up with partners who needed more information and guidance. The challenge of communicating accurate and up-to-date information to partners was only augmented by the Trump administration's chaotic and ultimately failed attempt to introduce a citizenship question on the 2020 questionnaire.

These challenges were not the bureau's alone, however. Despite what might appear to be obvious incentives for state and local governments to invest in census outreach, this work remains under-institutionalized at the subnational level. While a few states like California and large cities like New

York and Phoenix have developed a more sophisticated administrative apparatus to manage their outreach campaigns, these jurisdictions are hardly the norm. Nevertheless, jurisdictions were more likely to make these investments when primed to do so, either by the memory of past undercounts or the threat of losing a congressional seat. States that experienced a larger net undercount in 2010 were significantly more likely to expend resources on outreach prior to the 2020 Census. States expecting to lose congressional seats following the 2020 Census were also faster to establish SCCCs to coordinate outreach work. Qualitative interviews confirm that both prior undercounts and the potential threat of an undercount in 2020 played a significant role in shaping policymakers' decisions about census investments at both the state and local level. Where these threats were less pronounced, securing agenda priority for investments in census outreach proved more difficult.

There is also strong evidence that, at the state level, partisanship plays an important part in shaping officials' decisions to invest in census outreach. Not only were states with higher levels of Democratic control more likely to invest resources in census outreach, they were generally faster to set up SCCCs. The qualitative interviews suggest several reasons for this. On the one hand, funding for outreach was swept up into the Trump administration's politicization of census administration, particularly where the citizenship question was concerned, intensifying existing partisan divides on census outreach, with Republican governors and state legislators occasionally operating under the impression that funding outreach stood in conflict with party priorities. In other cases, census outreach funding became subject to broader partisan conflicts over state budgets, with Democrats favoring greater spending and Republicans favoring less spending. Partisan attitudes toward the census were not immutable, however. Not only were partisan patterns in census investments essentially nonexistent at the local level but the data reveal several prominent cases in which overriding concerns about an undercount persuaded Republican governors to make significant investments.

State and local census investments also hinge critically on preexisting administrative capacities. States with higher per-capita operation budgets were both significantly more likely to invest in census outreach and more quickly established SCCCs. As qualitative interviews reveal, preexisting institutional structures such as state data centers played a significant role in helping to make the case for meaningful census investments both at the state and local level. By contrast, it was far more difficult to convince poli-cymakers to make significant investments when organizational networks of census data users had either fallen apart or experienced significant turn-over. In some states where government support flagged, philanthropic part-nerships also helped to stimulate investments, providing crucial expertise and resources to support census outreach.

Finally, state and local governments' tasks as partners are not merely intergovernmental but intersectoral. As evidence from 2020 suggests, a ro-bust effort by the philanthropic and nonprofit communities not only substi-tuted for state or local activity where it did not exist but also supplemented outreach efforts when government personnel lacked adequate resources, expertise, and ties to community-based organizations. This was especially important for smaller local governments, which often had difficulty devot-ing dedicated staff capacity to census outreach.

The partnership program for the 2020 Census thus represented the cul-mination of decades of policy learning and institutional change at multiple levels of government and in nongovernmental organizations. Yet even as the bureau has increasingly come to rely on state and local governments as partners in census outreach, the institutional depth of those partnerships remains uneven. If anything, the evidence here demonstrates that inter-governmental relations for census outreach are not entirely immune to the headwinds of austerity, partisan polarization, and a dependence on non-governmental sources of fiscal and organizational support. Strengthening these connections in the years to come will require greater attention not only to the adequacy of congressional appropriations to the Census Bureau itself but also to strategies for enhancing the contributions of state, local, and nongovernmental actors to the massive undertaking of ensuring census participation, especially in communities that remain the hardest to count.

CHAPTER FIVE

Between a Pandemic and a Power Grab
Federalism and the Politics of Census Integrity

It was built as a quartermaster depot during the Civil War. Later, it became a shirt factory. In the Korean War years, parachutes and refrigerated trucks were manufactured there. Today, the massive complex in Jeffersonville, Indiana, close to the Kentucky state line, serves as the Census Bureau's National Processing Center, collecting and capturing data for the decennial census and all manner of federal surveys. During a census year, the center is usually abuzz with activity. Yet in late March 2020, the entire facility went eerily quiet. The COVID-19 pandemic had begun to ravage the United States, triggering a wave of restrictions on in-person activities across the country—including census taking.[1]

The temporary closure of the Jeffersonville facility offered a powerful reminder that the collection of official statistics is a precarious and locally situated human undertaking. Because census taking and tabulating requires in-person activity on a mass scale, the pandemic constituted an unprecedented threat to operations. This not only forced the bureau to substantially alter its field operations, it also brought many of the activities I had been observing since 2019 to a halt. Plans for census festivals, door-to-door canvasses, and "census Sundays" following church services were soon cancelled. One of my interviewees—a department manager in a medium-sized western city—described the last days of his work as a surreal scramble to migrate events online. "I told my wife it felt like *Shaun of the Dead*," he said.[2] Like his peers, he was pulled away from much of his census portfolio toward responding to the public health emergency itself. The research travel I had planned for this book was quickly cancelled, and many of the virtual follow-up interviews I scheduled were delayed—some indefinitely.

This chapter shows that state and local officials responded to the chaotic 2020 Census environment with a diverse repertoire of tactics, simultaneously adapting cooperative outreach strategies to new realities while employing litigation to forestall an attempted sabotage of the count. First, as the bureau's outreach partners, state and local governments faced the challenge of adapting their work to a highly fluid operational plan. The pandemic consumed excess administrative capacity that could have been devoted to state and local census outreach. Officials cited dedicated resources and staff, strong interorganizational partnerships, and administrative flexibility as key factors enabling them to adapt to this environment. Yet in some cases, and despite the best efforts of dedicated personnel, adaptation proved virtually impossible. Pandemic restrictions canceled promotional efforts targeted at hard-to count communities. Additionally, the bureau's response to the pandemic significantly curtailed the Count Review Operation, during which state officials can compare freshly collected census information with their own data sources to identify potentially missing housing units and group quarters.

Second, state and local officials also found themselves locked in multiple conflicts with the federal government. After all, the Census Bureau's efforts to realign its operations to meet pandemic conditions did not occur in a political vacuum. Rather, they collided with the Trump administration's unprecedented effort to exclude undocumented immigrants from the apportionment count. Most directly, officials from numerous states simply refused to furnish the administrative data necessary to advance this plan. This added fuel to a fire within the bureau, where top career civil servants resisted the president's scheme on the grounds that it would violate federal standards for data quality. As litigants in federal court, state and local governments would also play a significant role in stalling the implementation of this plan.

Simultaneously, state and local officials engaged in conflict over the operational timeline itself. Because the bureau's revised COVID-19 plan created the possibility that apportionment data would not be available until after the end of Trump's term, the bureau's Trump-appointed director, Steven Dillingham, abandoned the initial operational changes in favor of a "rush plan" that cut short numerous counting operations, including those targeting the country's hardest-to-count communities. State and local officials responded both in the public sphere, raising the alarm about the potential outcomes of the Trump administration's gambit, and in federal courts, as parties in lawsuits seeking to stop the apportionment exclusion and the rushed timeline altogether. District court rulings in favor of state and local governments—while eventually stayed by the US Supreme Court—helped to extend the timeline for counting by several weeks while delaying the implementation of the apportionment exclusion plan, which never came to fruition. In this sense, state and local officials contributed to the quality of the 2020 Census as both intergovernmental partners and legal adversaries.

COVID-19 and Trump: Operational Adjustments Collide with a Power Grab

Within days of the World Health Organization's pandemic declaration, the Census Bureau received its first report of an employee—an Iowa-based canvassing supervisor—infected with COVID-19.[3] Even in a climate of scientific uncertainty, the dire situation in which the Census Bureau found itself became clear almost immediately. On the one hand, the uncontrolled community spread of the disease and the subsequent enactment of stay-at-home orders would necessitate a significant pause in field operations. Yet a pause of any length would cause the bureau to miss the December 31st statutory deadline for delivering population counts to the president. Moreover, regardless of how the bureau managed these conditions, questions lingered about the residents of "group quarters," which had either been vacated (college dormitories) or remained epicenters of viral spread (nursing homes, prisons). Further questions arose as to what would happen to densely populated places like Manhattan, where hundreds of thousands of residents either left or died during the first wave of the pandemic.[4]

On April 13th, nearly a month after Director Dillingham had announced the suspension of all 2020 decennial field operations, the bureau issued a revised operational plan with adjustments to account for the COVID-19 pandemic, which was soon approved by the Office of Management and Budget.[5] The new plan—developed through consultation with both census experts as well as census stakeholders, including state and local governments—aimed to balance the bureau's objective of ensuring a complete count with the imperatives of protecting public health and respecting state and local health regulations and contained a number of important changes (see table 5.1). Most notably, the deadlines for the largest data-collection operations were pushed back to October 31st. This would give private households ample time to self-respond and account for the pausing of in-person NRFU operations. In concert with these changes, the bureau would also push back the deadlines for other operations that required in-person enumerators.

Altering the operational plan under crisis conditions had a significant

Table 5.1: Selected Operational Adjustments to the 2020 Census

Operation	Original Schedule	COVID-19 Revisions (4/13/20)	Replan Dates (8/3/20)
Remote Alaska	Jan. 21–Apr. 30	Jan. 21–Jun. 19	Completed (8/28/20)
Self-Response	Mar. 12–Jul. 31	Mar. 12–Oct. 31	Mar. 12–Sep. 30†
Update Leave (Stateside)*	Mar. 15–Apr. 17	Jun. 13–Jul. 9	Completed (8/13/20)
Update Enumerate*	Mar. 16–Apr. 30	Jun. 14–Jul. 29	Completed (8/13/20)
Service-Based Enumeration**	Mar. 30–Apr. 1	Plan in Development	Sep. 22–24
Targeted Non-Sheltered Outdoor Locations**	Mar. 31–Apr. 1	Plan in Development	Sep. 23–24
Group Quarters Enumeration	Apr. 2–Jun. 5	Apr. 2–Sep. 3	Closed Out (8/26/20)
Transitory Locations**	Apr. 9–May 4	Sep. 3–28	Sep. 3–28
Non-Response Followup (NRFU)	May 13–Jul. 31	Aug. 11–Oct. 31	Aug. 9–Sep. 30†
Delivery of Apportionment Data	Dec. 31, 2020	Apr. 30, 2021	Dec. 31, 2020‡
Delivery of Redistricting Data	Mar. 30, 2021	Jul. 31, 2021	Plan in Development‡

Source: Adapted by author from National Academies of Sciences, Engineering, and Medicine, *Understanding the Quality of the 2020 Census: Interim Report* (National Academies Press, 2022), 16.

Note: * *Update Leave:* Census invitation packets are dropped off at doors in areas where most households do not receive mail at their home's physical location; *Update Enumerate:* In-person interviews of two thousand households in remote parts of northern Maine and southeast Alaska; ** *Service-Based Enumeration:* Engagement with service providers at soup kitchens, shelters, and regularly scheduled food vans to count the people they serve; *Targeted Non-Sheltered Outdoor Locations:* Enumerators count persons living in identifiable outdoor locations open to the elements; *Transitory Locations:* Enumerators count persons residing in campgrounds, recreational vehicle (RV) parks, marinas, hotels, motels, racetracks, circuses, or carnivals; † Later extended as a result of the District Court for the Northern District of California's preliminary injunction in *New York v. Trump*, which was subsequently upheld by the Ninth Circuit, by stayed the Supreme Court on October 13. Within hours of the stay, data collection ended; ‡ Despite the replan schedule, delivery of apportionment data did not ultimately occur until April 30, 2021, and delivery of redistricting data did not occur until September 30, 2021.

impact on the time-sensitive nature of census taking. The bureau initially decided to push back the date for delivering apportionment data to the president past the statutory deadline of December 31, 2020, to April 30, 2021. Technically, extending the deadline for the delivery of apportionment data would have required an act of Congress. Yet while the bureau made this request, it did not wait for congressional approval before implementing the new plan. As the head of field operations put it during a stakeholder meeting in late May: "We have passed the point where we could even meet the current legislative requirement of December 31st. We can't do that anymore."[6]

Praise for the bureau's new schedule was nearly universal. Former Census Bureau directors, civil rights leaders, and state and local officials all praised the new timeline as a sound response to the operational realities presented by COVID-19. Ensuring a complete and accurate census would, they reasoned, simply take more time.[7] Even President Trump appeared to support the new plan, going so far as to suggest that the bureau did not even need congressional approval to miss the statutory deadline: "I don't know that you even have to ask [Congress]. This is called an act of God. This is called a situation that has to be. They have to give it. I think 120 days isn't nearly enough."[8] And so, until the end of July 2020, the bureau proceeded with the new plan, pushing back NRFU and leaving most area census offices closed. During this time, the bureau as well as its partners repeatedly communicated elements of the new plan, most importantly the new October 31st deadline for self-response, to the public.

Yet on August 3rd the bureau abruptly, and with little public justification, changed course when it issued yet another operational plan. The revision—dubbed by its critics as the "rush plan"—now announced that all data collection for both self-response and NRFU would end on September 30th, one month earlier than the bureau had maintained throughout the spring and summer (see table 5.1). Self-responses delivered after September 30th would not be counted, even as the self-response rate hovered around 63 percent in early August. The new plan also cut the amount of time allotted for post-collection data processing by half. This abbreviated timeline meant the cancellation of a key stage of the Count Review Operation, in which members of the Federal-State Cooperative for Population Estimates (FSCPE) could check the accuracy of Group Quarters data.[9] These rapid revisions to the plan—which bureau officials reportedly had been given only hours to make, in the absence of consultation with the bureau's traditional stakeholders—were all in the service of one goal: delivering apportionment data to the president by December 31, 2020, rather than in April 2021.[10]

Understanding these abrupt changes to the operational plan requires us to look carefully at what was happening not at the Census Bureau's Suitland, Maryland, headquarters but inside the White House and the Commerce Department, where the rush plan decision was actually made.[11] In the spring, the Trump administration had maintained it was a necessity to extend the key census deadline into 2021. Yet by mid-July, the strategy had changed. Contradicting the views from within the bureau, the White House now insisted on the delivery of apportionment numbers before the end of Trump's term of office. The operational feasibility of the new timeline notwithstanding, the administration also sought an additional $1 billion in emergency congressional appropriations to support the effort.[12]

The reason for the administration's abrupt change in strategy was a July 21st presidential memorandum ordering the secretary of commerce to estimate the number of undocumented persons in each state and to exclude these persons from the population base used to reapportion Congress. This memo grew out of Executive Order 13880, which President Trump signed in July of 2019, following the Supreme Court decision that eliminated the citizenship item from the 2020 questionnaire. In that order, Trump had directed the Census Bureau to obtain administrative data from federal and state governments concerning citizenship status. As we saw in chapter 2, Alabama's Attorney General Steve Marshall and Rep. Mo Brooks (R-AL) had also filed a lawsuit that bolstered the Trump administration's efforts by arguing that undocumented persons should be removed from apportionment.[13] Now, in the midst of a pandemic, White House officials were taking matters into their own hands. Removing undocumented persons from the apportionment count would have had significant effects on the balance of political power and resources in the United States. If implemented, it could have led to a loss of congressional seats in Democratic Party strongholds like California, New Jersey, New York, and Illinois. Excluding the undocumented from census data would also have diverted federal funds away from large population centers.[14]

As Trump faced the prospect of losing a closely contested 2020 presidential election, timing was everything. The only way to guarantee that undocumented persons were excluded from the counts was to ensure that the apportionment figures were delivered before the end of his term. Were the apportionment numbers not delivered until April of 2021, there would be no way to guarantee execution of Trump's plan.

While the administration's reversal of the initial COVID-19 operational plan was intended to support his goal of excluding undocumented persons from apportionment figures, the new timeline also presented other serious risks to the quality of the census. With NRFU largely stalled until the end of July, the new plan would force the bureau to count a large universe of households that had not yet responded to the census in a fraction of the time such an operation would typically require. Further, the ongoing pandemic had placed significant strain on the bureau's efforts to recruit enumerators—increasing the number of "no shows" at training sessions and employee onboarding.[15] Given that new enumerator hires typically had to wait sixty days for a background check, a shortened timeline provided far fewer opportunities for nonresponse follow-up. Bureau employees immediately recognized the operational impossibility of the plan. As an internal email from one employee, sent only two days after Trump's memo on apportionment exclusion, noted: "We need to sound the alarm to realities on the ground—people are afraid to work for us [as enumerators] . . . any thinking person who would believe we can deliver apportionment by 12/31 has either a mental deficiency or a political motivation."[16]

Unsurprisingly, the August 3rd rush plan invited swift outcry from numerous census experts and stakeholders. Civil rights groups and large coalitions of census outreach partners urged the bureau to return to the revised plan issued in April.[17] As four prior directors of the Census Bureau put it in a press release issued the same day as the new plan: Failing to extend the deadlines "will result in seriously incomplete enumerations in many areas across our country."[18] An inspector general's evaluation confirmed some of the major threats to data quality. First, the new plan would reduce the time to recover from "possible external contingencies affecting local areas or regions" such as natural disasters and further pandemic restrictions. One of the major concerns, as a senior Census Bureau official put it, was "whether we can get out of the field by September 30th because, you know, we don't usually do field work for the census during hurricane season. And . . . you do that for a reason."[19] By September, wildfires in the west as well as tropical storms in the southeast had already begun to tax the limited amount of organizational slack the bureau had.[20]

Second, while some bureau officials remained confident they could reach their target of "resolving" or "completing" at least 99 percent of housing units in every state by the end of data collection, others expressed concern that the bureau had "no runway" of time to correct errors discovered in the process, in part because the new plan streamlined the data-processing stage of the census, eliminating important quality assurance measures. This included cancelling several internal review processes, including the second-stage of the Count Review Operation, during which state demographers were to review Group Quarters data. Other review processes were placed on a compressed timeline, which, according to an internal bureau slide deck, would "create serious risks for errors not being discovered in the data."[21] As one official reported to the inspector general, "All these changes squeeze out all of the . . . slack that was in the schedule that is there for a reason."[22] As we will see, pushing back against this timeline would ultimately require litigation.

In sum, the collision between the Census Bureau's attempt to adapt census operations for a pandemic and the White House's effort to radically revise the apportionment counts by December 31st created a chaotic environment not just within the federal bureaucracy but within the networks of intergovernmental partners involved in census taking. As the next section indicates, for state and local officials involved with the census, adapting to the chaos was a fraught endeavor.

Getting Out the Count During COVID-19: Intergovernmental Partnerships Under Stress

By the end of 2019, state and local officials around the country—along with their nonprofit and philanthropic partners—had planned an impressive array of campaigns and events to promote the census both before and during the self-response period, which was set to begin in early March of 2020. While Complete Count Committees employed a range of advertising techniques—from bus wraps to leveraging social media influencers—in-person activities were a cornerstone of their outreach strategies. Some cities, for example, planned to rely on informational canvassers who would fan out everywhere from city blocks in hard-to-count neighborhoods to music festivals, farmers markets, and college basketball games. Others worked with community groups to integrate census messaging into public festivals and block parties in historically undercounted neighborhoods. To facilitate census enumeration for the first online census, cities and counties also purchased computer kiosks for use in public libraries and schools.[23] Yet on March 11th, as the number of cases of COVID-19 outside China increased thirteen-fold, the World Health Organization issued a pandemic declaration. By early April, virtually every state had enacted at least some public health measures, ranging from social-distancing requirements and restrictions on public gatherings to the closure of schools and nonessential businesses.[24] These restrictions varied significantly in their intensity, scope, and endurance.[25] Some tribal governments—with varying degrees of success—closed their borders at the beginning of the pandemic, not allowing anyone in or out.[26] Yet even where legal restrictions were weaker, in-person activities drastically diminished as rates of COVID-19 infection, hospitalization, and death rose.

The pandemic constituted a significant threat to critical in-person outreach activities, especially many in-person activities targeted at hard-to-count communities with limited broadband internet access. Philadelphia officials' efforts to respond to the pandemic are instructive here.[27] Initially, the city's Philly Counts 2020 campaign had planned at least three major Census Action Days to take place at the beginning of the self-response period, in March and April of 2020. Integrating the Census Bureau's "hard-to-count" data with information on broadband access and the city's own asset mapping, the campaign planned for canvassers to distribute informational door hangers in designated priority blocks. Additionally, Philly Counts teams would attend several block parties each weekend and invite representatives from the Census Bureau's Mobile Questionnaire Access program, who would help people complete the census on one of the bureau's tablets or on their own devices. Yet in anticipation of the city's stay-at-home order, issued on March 22nd, Philly Counts cancelled all its in-person events.

Within a week, Philly Counts made a "pandemic pivot," launching phone-banking programs in partnership with several city agencies and nonprofits, through which six hundred volunteers would make some three hundred thousand calls to provide reminders about the census. Virtually no one on the ground believed this was enough, however. Meeting hard-to-count neighborhoods "where they were" at the beginning of the pandemic meant taking into consideration the stark new realities they faced. Not only did members of these communities face disproportionately higher rates of infection, they also faced job losses, food insecurity, and a lack of adequate personal protective equipment. Thus the campaign worked with the Department of Public Health to develop a COVID Community Response Captain program, which would inform members of the team about COVID-19 updates and build connections with over one hundred organizations across the city. These partnerships helped to fuse census awareness with the provision of goods and services, ranging from food boxes to personal protective equipment. By September, Philly Counts had distributed "9,000 masks, 11,000 bottles of hand sanitizer, and 7,000 tote bags," all of which were emblazoned with a census QR code. Working with the city's SHARE Food Program, the campaign also had placed "over 100,000 Census informational items—including palm cards, stickers, and doorhangers—into meal boxes being delivered to distribution sites."[28]

If the Philly Counts team was able to quickly pivot outreach to meet the new reality of COVID-19, it was in part because the campaign had a significant level of dedicated internal capacity. The campaign was led by five directors and a team of nearly thirty staff members and interns. Its eighteen subcommittees were chaired by a cross-cutting network of civic, religious, and political leaders. Planning for the campaign had also begun in December of 2018 and involved holding one hundred monthly meetings of the organization's eighteen subcommittees across a diverse array of neighborhoods in the city.

During the early days of the pandemic, it was hard to overstate the value of both organizational leaders and staff who were dedicated exclusively to the census.[29] "It really helped that I was just focused on the census . . . [that] it consumed, you know, 48 hours of my week for eight months," one CCC leader in a large Southwestern city told me. Because of this, she had thought deeply about how people might receive information about the census in their daily lives. Thus, soon after the pandemic hit, she was able to quickly integrate new information about the emergency into her existing cognitive scheme. During the pandemic, what mattered was using her organization's capacity to help address the most basic needs, through food-share boxes and information about how to get stimulus checks, but using those points of service as opportunities to provide reminders about the census.[30]

In communities that lacked this kind of dedicated capacity—frequently, though not exclusively, smaller cities and counties—pivoting operations proved more challenging. Because census outreach in these communities was often tasked to officials with a diverse portfolio of assignments, the onset of the pandemic meant that census work would take a backseat to other priorities.[31] As one CCC leader in the Midwest informed me, between March and April, at least half her team was pulled into managing pandemic response.[32] This was not uncommon. As another CCC leader in a medium-sized western city told me, a lot of the members of his team were from nonprofits who, when the pandemic hit, "obviously had bigger things to worry about."[33]

Yet, even when CCCs had adequate staff capacity, adapting to the pandemic environment required a level of operational flexibility that some governments simply lacked. Over half of my follow-up interviewees cited their inability to retrofit outreach plans as a barrier to adapting to pandemic conditions. As one CCC leader in a Midwestern state informed me, the state's contracts with local governments and nonprofit organizations for outreach work were drawn up with fairly rigid performance metrics, such as the number of doors to be knocked. Following the enactment of public health restrictions, these contracts had to be rewritten and then approved by multiple state agencies. "Coming up with a whole new plan last minute . . . of course it was difficult. And then if [the state] has got to process, I think it was over 300 . . . different organizations across the state. I mean, can you imagine the number of contracts?"[34] As another official involved with outreach work in the same state told me: "It was as fast as a glacier. I mean, it is just ridiculous. . . . The second round of funding started on July 1, but I didn't get approval until it was the end of August . . . so I had one business day to spend all my money."[35]

CCCs with access to more flexible grant dollars had a different experience altogether. For some philanthropic grants, foundations simply said, as one CCC staffer told me: "You have the money, just do the best that you can."[36] In the case of one state government, the flexibility proved to be the result of a happy accident. The state agency had held back on disbursing half of its legislative appropriation for outreach until 2020. "In retrospect," as one state CCC leader told me, "the fact that we hadn't put all the money out . . . [meant that] we were able to change everything when the pandemic came."[37]

If intergovernmental and intersectoral contracts determined how flexible outreach campaigns could be in responding to the pandemic, then the quality of intergovernmental relationships defined what governments *did* with the resources they had. In addition to simply sharing up-to-date and accurate information about shifting operational plans, intergovernmental partnerships were essential for adapting strategies to reach hard-to-count populations. With in-person canvassing essentially on hold, CCCs were forced to relocate outreach activities to locations that were not affected by stay-at-home orders. This included COVID-19 testing sites, social service offices, grocery stores, school homework pickup sites, and food distribution locations. CCCs, which already had strong links to social service agencies and nonprofits, could more quickly and easily pivot their outreach activities to these sites.

The state of California provides an example of how a highly coordinated census outreach campaign with well-established intergovernmental partnerships facilitated a "pandemic pivot."[38] California's investment in census outreach was noteworthy not only for the scale of its fiscal effort (the final allocation from the state legislature exceeded $187 million) but also for the extent of the California Census Office's efforts to coordinate outreach at both the state and local levels. At the heart of the coordination was the Statewide Outreach and Rapid Deployment database (SwORD). The SwORD dashboard provided state and local partners with maps and data concerning the location of the state's hardest-to-count areas, built around California's own Hard-to-Count Index. It also included tools to target and record outreach efforts and activities such as canvassing and events—allowing the Census Office to monitor outreach work in real time. Data on hard-to-count communities also informed the office's selection of thirty-five state agencies and departments as partners given their contact with these communities. When the pandemic hit, these agencies became important conduits for information about unemployment claims, stimulus checks, and housing and food assistance—which only added to their credibility as census messengers.[39]

Beyond these connections to state agencies, the state Census Office had developed a statewide structure connecting local CCCs as well as administrative community-based organizations, which coordinated outreach to hard-to-count communities across ten regions in the state. As part of this statewide structure, the Census Office held regular calls to allow for the sharing of information and best practices. These regular calls fostered relationships that allowed local communities to learn from one another in a moment of chaos. The Census Office also used these regional calls to learn about on-the-ground activities, complementing the updates they received via SwORD.[40] As a survey by the Census Office found, the word most commonly used by partners to sum up their experience in 2020 was "collaboration."[41]

When it comes to leveraging formal intergovernmental coordination during the pandemic, California may represent one of the more successful cases. But it is not alone. Over half of the state and local officials with whom I conducted follow-up interviews in late 2020 mentioned preexisting intergovernmental relationships as a factor that assisted in adapting to the pandemic. Both state and local officials routinely noted the importance of connections to social service agencies as conduits for information when in-person outreach became impossible and of statewide calls to support strategies for pivoting to the pandemic environment. Even in one Southern state that had made only modest investments in census outreach, the governor's census liaison maintained a laser focus on the census throughout the early months of the pandemic, repeatedly assembling meetings between leaders of state agencies involved with census communications.[42]

These intergovernmental linkages were hardly universal, however. Over a third of follow-up interviewees mentioned a lack of intergovernmental partnerships as a barrier to adaptation. States that had refused to fund census outreach in the years leading up to the census left local governments without an extensive capacity to coordinate with one another in 2020. As one statewide CCC chair told me, efforts to secure emergency funding for census outreach when the pandemic hit did not resonate with her state's Republican governor.[43] Even states that had provided funding for census outreach could lack coordination. As a state data center lead in the Midwest told me, her state had no central information portal to communicate rapid changes in operational plans to local grantees. As one state official told me, this required her to use her existing email listserv to provide a forum for local CCCs to exchange ideas.[44]

As in the years leading up to the 2020 Census, the quality of relationships between state and local partners to the Census Bureau varied widely as well.[45] In some regions, partnership specialists and regional staff proved to be highly responsive to local needs in the face of the pandemic. As one state official in New England informed me, his interactions with bureau officials were not only positive but essential: "If we didn't have that relationship . . . I think we would have been in deep trouble."[46] A local CCC staffer noted a similar experience: "Having someone to translate and explain what's really going on and why something is the way that it is is extremely helpful."[47] But these impressions were hardly universal. Before and during the pandemic, the Census Bureau experienced difficulties with turnover in CPEP. As one state CCC staffer told me, partnership specialists in her region "kept quitting." The specialist she engaged with most frequently "got very angry at us in the beginning, and then she basically never talked to us."[48]

Some of the tension between the bureau and its intergovernmental partners had less to do with the administration of the partnership program than it did with the confusion created by the bureau's operational adjustments to the pandemic. Two examples will suffice here. First, a key dilemma for state and local officials around the country was the Census Bureau's Group Quarters Enumeration. During the early weeks of the pandemic, students residing at colleges and universities throughout the United States were sent home prior to scheduled Group Quarters enumeration—which relies on administrative records rather than individually submitted responses. Under the Census Bureau's residence rules, students residing away from their parent or guardian's home during the school year should be enumerated at their school address. Confusion and miscommunication during the pandemic exacerbated existing confusion about this rule. For example, Census Bureau messaging frequently stressed that everyone should be counted "where they are" on April 1st, the reference date known as "Census Day." Yet for students who were sent home from college as of Census Day, following this guidance to the letter would directly contradict the bureau's residence rules.[49] And despite the best efforts of state and local officials to triage census tracts with low levels of self-response, it remained difficult if not impossible to monitor response rates in group-living facilities, in part because data from the Group Quarters Enumeration was not included in the bureau's public-facing response-tracker dashboard. The same problem prevented state and local CCCs from monitoring the enumeration of people experiencing homelessness and residing in transitory locations in 2020.[50]

A second issue over which state and local outreach partners had little direct control was the publication of President Trump's July 21st memorandum on apportionment exclusion and the subsequent introduction of a rush plan that would cut short time the allotted to self-response and NRFU by a matter of weeks. The apportionment exclusion memorandum itself, which was widely covered in Spanish-language news, had an identifiable chilling effect on census response—and forced outreach partners around the country to expend additional resources on addressing lower levels of trust in the census among immigrant communities and correcting misinformation. As Bitta Mostofi, commissioner of New York City's Office of Immigrant Affairs, noted in a court filing, the memorandum forced her census outreach teams to "devote more time and energy to combatting misinformation, fear, and confusion."[51] The director of the Massachusetts Immigrant and Refugee Advocacy Coalition, Vatsady Sivongxay, agreed. Following the publication of the memorandum, she had been forced to "divert time and resources" from organizing to promote NRFU responses to dealing with misinformation that developed because of the memorandum.[52] The abrupt introduction of the new plan on August 3rd also stirred confusion among the bureau's own employees as well as state and local partners. As one state official in the Midwest told me, having to constantly change public messaging about the deadline made it "hard to be the credible voice for the census."[53] Indeed, even the most well-organized and financed state and local outreach efforts could hardly have planned for the level of chaos occasioned by the Trump administration's attempted power grab.

Count Review: A Victim of the Rush Plan

Outreach was not the only focus of intergovernmental partnerships in 2020. State officials also played an important role in improving the accuracy and quality of census data through count review. One of several operations the Census Bureau has undertaken since 2000, count review aims to examine and remediate discrepancies and anomalies in census counts prior to data processing and publication. To do so, the bureau relies on the Federal-State Cooperative for Population Estimates (FSCPE), an intergovernmental partnership established in 1973 through which state demographers and other officials work with the Census Bureau's Population Division to generate population estimates that can be used between decennial years. Count review resembles the Local Update of Census Addresses (LUCA), described in chapter 3, in that state FSCPE organizations or agencies support census accuracy by providing the bureau with local knowledge. As of 2020, LUCA and count review submissions also employed the same Geographic Update Partnership Software. Yet count review also differs from LUCA in at least two important respects. First, whereas LUCA involves local, tribal, and state officials, count review only involves members of the FSCPE. Second, LUCA occurs several years before the census is taken, while count review begins after address canvassing and is designed to both identify housing units missing from the Master Address File (MAF) and identify large group quarters—such as college dormitories—that were either missing from the MAF or geographically misallocated. Third, in contrast to LUCA, the Census Bureau's relationship with FSCPE participants in count review is contractual, and state agencies are reimbursed to support up to one hundred hours of state employees' time in the review, in addition to travel expenses.[54]

Count review has the potential to impact census figures in significant ways. During the 2010 Census, officials from forty-two states and Puerto Rico participated in at least some aspect of count review, helping to identify 86,422 housing units missing from the MAF. Additionally, FSCPE members helped to identify 173 group quarters misallocated to the incorrect collection block and 313 missing group quarters. The total population associated with misallocated and missing group quarters was, respectively, 29,054 and 47,922.[55] Given the significant displacement of residents in group-living facilities—including nursing homes and college dormitories—during the pandemic, FSCPE members' ability to identify missing or misallocated Group Quarters enumerations took on even greater importance in 2020.[56]

Prior to the Trump administration's August 3rd rush plan, the 2020 Count Review Operation was proceeding relatively smoothly. During January and February of 2020, every state as well as the District of Columbia and Puerto Rico participated in a pre-enumeration review of housing units and group quarters addresses.[57] There were challenges, to be sure. As one FSCPE participant told me, participating in count review required staff time—to prepare paperwork, attend mandatory webinars and conference calls—that exceeded the number of hours the bureau reimbursed. Added to this, staff vacancies at the bureau meant that states often had difficulty obtaining the technical assistance they needed to address challenges in submitting data and interpreting Title 13 privacy guidelines.[58] These barriers aside, FSCPE participants helped to add over two hundred and forty thousand housing units and over sixty-five hundred group quarters to the enumeration universe.[59]

The next count review event was initially scheduled to take place between June 15th and 19th of 2020. During this event, state demographers would be able to identify whether any Group Quarters in their state went unenumerated and the reasons why. The results of this stage of the review would be incorporated into the final Group Quarters Enumeration (GQE). As the result of the Census Bureau's initial COVID-19 modification plan, however, the Post-Enumeration Group Quarters Review was pushed to late September, several weeks after the conclusion of the rescheduled GQE. With the release of the Trump administration's August 3rd rush plan, however, this review was essentially cancelled. As an email from the bureau to state officials read, meeting the December 31st deadline "precludes conducting the [count review] event."[60] As an internal Census Bureau slide deck predicted, this move was "virtually certain" to elicit objections from state demographers and governors.[61] One Virginia FSCPE participant put it bluntly: "We lined up the resources and the personnel ready to provide input. And all of a sudden, that's canceled."[62]

What replaced Group Quarters review under the newly compressed schedule was a far more limited operation. FSCPE members received Excel files containing a subset of just over seventeen hundred Group Quarters facilities on which the bureau had the least information.[63] Of this subset, state FSCPE partners proposed that the bureau revisit 569 cases, 497 of which the bureau ultimately approved for "late Group Quarters Enumeration."[64] This hardly satisfied FSCPE leaders who generally felt that—while the limited process allowed them to correct some errors—it fell far short of the mark for a post-enumeration review.[65]

State and local officials' ability to respond to these operational changes in real time was limited. In contrast to officials working on census outreach, they could not simply adapt their plans to the new realities. Nor was there an easily available legislative path. While state and local officials appealed to Congress to extend the deadline for Census completion, the glacial pace of the legislative process, not to mention the likelihood that the president would veto any emergency Census legislation that ultimately passed, made an advocacy strategy inoperable. Not even one of the deadline extension bills introduced in 2020 ever received a vote on the floor of either chamber of Congress.[66]

Two options remained. First, state and local officials could hope for the success of lawsuits filed by a coalition of NGOs and government partners in August, which sought to enjoin the Trump administration's rush plan.[67] As we will see, however, the US Supreme Court would soon put this strategy on ice. Second, following Trump's loss in the 2020 presidential election, they could appeal to the incoming Biden administration to remediate the damage caused by the gutting of the Group Quarters review. Over the months that followed the election, this is precisely what cities, states, and NGOs did. By the spring of 2022, repeated recommendations from state and local officials, FSCPE members, the American Statistical Association, and census advisory committees resulted in the creation of a new Post-Census Group Quarters Review Program. Through June 30, 2023, state, local, and tribal governments could review and suggest modifications to population counts in group-living institutions. Revisions produced through the new program could not result in changes to redistricting or congressional apportionment. Instead, they would help to inform future population estimates.[68] Had the 2020 presidential election turned out differently, however, it is doubtful that this special program would have been implemented.

Apportionment Exclusion and the Politics of
Intergovernmental Data Sharing

A third way in which state and local governments shaped the character of the census during the field period was by providing—or more importantly by failing to provide—information that would have supported the Trump administration's plan to remove undocumented immigrants from apportionment counts. This is one instance in which "uncooperative federalism," together with career civil servants' commitment to data quality, helped to preserve the integrity of the census in the face of a political power grab by the White House and the Commerce Department.[69]

Understanding how intergovernmental data sharing affected the Trump administration's ability to accomplish this plan requires briefly returning to the events of July 2019. Less than two weeks after the Supreme Court's decision in *Department of Commerce v. New York*, which effectively prevented the citizenship question from appearing on the 2020 questionnaire, President Trump took a second bite at the apple. In Executive Order 13880, he directed all federal executive agencies to supply "the maximum assistance permissible, consistent with law, in determining the number of citizens and noncitizens in the country."[70] Speaking in the Rose Garden, Trump lashed out at the Court's decision: "There used to be a time when you could proudly declare, 'I am a citizen of the United States.' Now they're trying to erase the very existence of a very important word and a very important thing: citizenship."[71] He would not, he said, be backing down.

Soon, the bureau's top career officials were meeting with political appointees to explain how they—with the support of other federal agencies—would go about collecting data on the size of the undocumented population.[72] There were essentially two approaches the bureau could take, each of which had its own statistical, administrative, and legal liabilities. First, there was the so-called aggregate residual method. This technique involved using American Community Survey data to create an estimate of the foreign-born population in each state and, from this estimate, approximating the number of illegal immigrants in each state enumerated in the 2020 Census. Administratively speaking, the aggregate residual method was the easier of the two. Methodologically, however, it created significant problems. Not only would foreign-born populations have to be adjusted based on limited data, prior research suggested that the final estimates were highly sensitive to the modeling assumptions one used. Even two very similar models could result in estimates that varied by over one million people nationally, far higher than the margins that typically determine the allocation of congressional seats. Yet the more fatal flaw here was that the aggregate residual method relied on statistical sampling, which the Supreme Court had ruled in 1998 was explicitly prohibited under the Census Act.

Alternatively, the bureau could link decennial census responses to administrative data from federal and state agencies that indicated citizenship status. Then, after identifying records of persons counted in the census for whom administrative records could not resolve citizenship status, the bureau would use a model to statistically impute residents' citizenship status. One advantage of this approach was that it was less obviously illegal, at least given the Supreme Court's holding in *Utah v. Evans* (2002), which stated that the bureau could legally use "hot-deck" imputation—a technique to infer population characteristics for nonresponsive households by replacing missing values with observed responses from similar households.[73] On the other hand, linking census records to administrative data produced a dizzying array of implementation challenges. Most importantly, the bureau would have to secure administrative records from federal and state agencies to match with census data—a cumbersome task that would have to be accomplished on a relatively tight timeline. And even if this were successful, there would still be problems. In a test conducted with 2010 Census data, about 10 percent of census records did not have a matching record in administrative data. Many of the unmatched were US citizens or legal immigrants who simply lacked adequate personally identifying information.

While both techniques remained "on the table" well into the summer of 2020, the bureau's implementation of Executive Order 13880 began with the assemblage of administrative data from federal and state agencies that could potentially resolve citizenship status.[74] The bureau signed memoranda of understanding with numerous federal agencies to obtain data sources that would help to resolve, or at least partially resolve, citizenship status for various segments of the population. The most complete of these was the Social Security Administration's Numident file, which records all applications for Social Security cards. Because these applications contain the applicant's country of birth and citizenship status for all applicants, they can be used to identify citizens and those born in the United States. Still, the Numident file has limitations. It cannot, for example, be used to resolve the citizenship status of residents who lack Social Security numbers. Further, Numident file data may not capture naturalizations that occur after an application is submitted. Record linkage errors can also lead to errors in citizenship status for any data source.[75]

Because of the Numident file's limitations, the bureau collected a variety of other sources of information from federal agencies, which would help to resolve the status of individuals not captured by Social Security data as well as individuals whose status was recorded incorrectly in the Numident file. For example, the bureau collected Individual Taxpayer Identification Numbers (ITINs), which are issued only to noncitizens, as well as data from the Department of Homeland Security (DHS) on persons who had naturalized or had lawful permanent resident status. With these three sources of administrative data, the bureau's methodologists could establish a "business rule" that would classify persons as a citizen (for example, when they were recorded as a US-born citizen in the Numident file), as a person who did not have an ITIN, and persons who did not appear in the lawful permanent resident/naturalized citizen data.[76]

Naturally, however, federal agencies were not the only source of administrative data the bureau sought to acquire. In the past, the bureau had established data sharing agreements through which state (and, more infrequently) local governments would provide information on participation in federal-state programs such as Temporary Assistance to Needy Families (TANF); Women, Infants, and Children (WIC); and the Supplemental Nutrition Assistance Program (SNAP). As with other programs at the federal level, eligibility rules for these programs might help to partially resolve the legal status of some participants. An even more useful source of state-level data were the databases of driver's license records maintained by state Departments of Motor Vehicles (DMVs). The REAL ID Act of 2005, which implemented a recommendation of the 9/11 Commission, required that citizenship be a minimum criterion for the issuance of a state driver's license. By 2020, all but three states had implemented REAL ID, which meant that state databases would contain all information on state drivers' licenses and ID cards, as well as drivers' histories—making them a potentially valuable source of citizenship data.[77]

By the fall of 2019, the bureau's effort to obtain the necessary federal and state data to implement Executive Order 13880 had begun in earnest. Slide decks from the bureau's performance management meetings show that the target date for completing data collection was December 31, 2019.[78] Meeting this deadline, however, proved more difficult in practice, especially where data from state and local governments were concerned. Even prior to Trump's executive order, the bureau faced numerous obstacles when attempting to persuade state and local officials to share data on participants in programs like SNAP and TANF for purposes such as enhancing the bureau's Master Address File and imputing missing data. Officials in Wyoming, for example, had cut off negotiations over sharing TANF data, citing confidentiality concerns. In other states, the bureau's contacts cited a lack of resources or staff capacity. In 2018, West Virginia officials had requested funding to offset the costs of sharing SNAP and TANF data. Yet even after the Census Bureau made an initial offer, the state's chief information officer stopped responding to bureau requests. In other states, such as Kentucky and Mississippi, the bureau had occasionally been unable to establish contact with the appropriate parties to initiate data sharing agreements. The result was an incomplete patchwork of these agreements. Even after phone calls from Secretary of Commerce Wilbur Ross to governors in key states, this patchwork remained.[79] As figure 5.1 shows, by July 30, 2020, the state of the data sharing agreements varied across the three programs. Twenty-one states agreed to share WIC data. Twenty-nine had agreed to share data from the SNAP program. And twenty-seven had agreed to share TANF data. Yet only thirteen states had signed data sharing agreements across all three programs (SNAP, TANF, and WIC).[80] And an additional fifteen states, including states with large undocumented populations—Texas and California—had no agreement with the bureau to share data in *any* of these three programs.

Attempts to persuade state DMVs to share driver's license records—which unfolded only after the issuance of Executive Order 13880—fared even worse.[81] Officials in Oregon rejected the request as a violation of state laws preventing state agencies from sharing personal information other than names, addresses, and DMV customer numbers. Similarly, officials in New Hampshire and Maine suggested that their respective agencies had no explicit legal authorization to share driver's license information requested by the bureau. As Maine's Secretary of State Matthew Dunlap put it: "We sort of believe that the information that's in our databases belongs to the citizens to whom it refers. So we're the custodians of that information—it's not ours to give away."[82] Even Texas, where top Republican elected officials had contemplated redistricting the state legislature on the basis of citizen voting age population, eventually declined the bureau's request for driver's license data.[83]

Ultimately, the bureau successfully established agreements to share

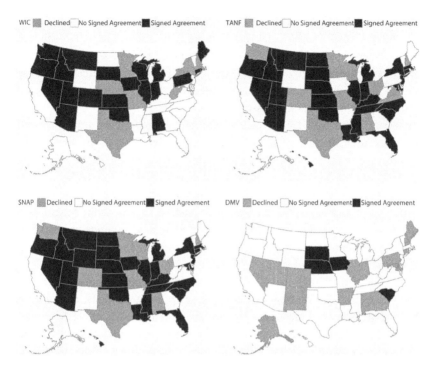

Figure 5.1: State data sharing agreements with Census Bureau, by data source. Source: "Economic Reimbursable Division Spreadsheets," Census Bureau, July 30, 2020. Note: WIC: Women, Infants, and Children Program; TANF: Temporary Assistance to Needy Families; SNAP: Supplemental Nutrition Assistance Program; DMV: Departments of Motor Vehicles (driver's license records). The figures here reflect agreements made as of July 30, 2020.

driver's license data with only four states: Iowa, Nebraska, South Carolina, and South Dakota.[84] When questioned about whether these agreements violated state DMV records laws, officials in these states provided vague citations to "qualifying exemptions" or, in some cases, no justifications at all.[85] Even with access to this data, however, DMV records would prove problematic as a source of data on citizenship. This is in part because DMV records—like those in the Numident file—provide proof of citizenship status or lawful presence only as of the date of application. Should citizens naturalize after a license is obtained, the agency's citizenship record would only be updated when the license expires. For example, when the Texas Secretary of

State David Whitley claimed to have identified ninety-five thousand "non-US citizens" on the state's voter rolls, subsequent evidence revealed—almost immediately—that tens of thousands of voters were on the secretary's list erroneously, since they had naturalized only after the issuance of their license and before they registered to vote. A federal district court soon ordered counties to halt the planned purges of voter rolls.[86]

When compared to the coordination of data sharing across federal agencies, then, the use of state administrative data proved problematic in two regards. First, it was far more difficult to obtain. By the end of July 2020, the bureau only had access to patchwork of WIC, SNAP, and TANF data, as well as driver's license records from a small handful of states. Second, and perhaps more importantly, the state administrative records the bureau *was* able to access proved to be of limited utility. State records often covered limited populations, were out of date or poorly maintained, and proved difficult to link with other sources.[87]

By the time that President Trump issued a memorandum on July 21, 2020, directing the secretary of commerce to "exclude illegal aliens from the apportionment base following the 2020 Census," the effort to implement the executive order he had signed one year earlier had already begun to encounter significant obstacles. In early August, Census Bureau officials suggested to Ross a far more modest option for estimating the undocumented population. Rather than using American Community Survey data or matching administrative records to 2020 Census data, it was suggested that the bureau could tabulate only people enumerated in ICE detention centers as of census day, April 1, 2020. This would be far less likely to invite a legal challenge than using ACS data. Moreover, it would be far simpler than matching highly problematic administrative records to census data for the entire population. Still, this option would mean removing only a small sliver of undocumented individuals from apportionment counts, potentially far less than the number required to swing control of congressional seats to Republicans. Moreover, it was hardly the case that all individuals living in ICE detention centers were in the United States illegally.[88] It is not apparent which direction Ross wished to take. As 2020 drew to a close, the massive gaps in data helped to give the bureau's top career staff, including Chief Scientist John Abowd and Chief Demographer Tori Velkoff, good reason to object to the administration's plans on the grounds that they would cause the bureau to fall short of its standards for data accuracy.[89] At the same time, the sweeping language of Trump's July 21st memorandum had mobilized state and local governments into yet another legal battle to preserve the integrity of the 2020 Census.

From Partners to Litigants: State and Local Governments Safeguard the Census in Court

Arguably the most important role state and local governments played in preserving the integrity of the census during the final months of 2020 was not as the bureau's partners, nor as custodians of administrative records, but as the Trump administration's adversaries in federal court. As plaintiffs and amici, state and local officials helped to bring to light the contours of the Trump administration's plan to exclude undocumented persons from apportionment counts as well as the threats to census accuracy presented by both the exclusion plan itself as well as the August 3rd rush plan aimed at delivering apportionment counts by the statutory deadline of December 31, 2020, weeks before the winner of the presidential election would be inaugurated. While these lawsuits ultimately did not succeed in persuading the Supreme Court, they nevertheless helped to exhaust what was arguably the Trump Administration's most problematic plan for the census.

Litigation on the Apportionment Exclusion Plan

Less than a week after Donald Trump had issued a memorandum ordering the secretary of commerce to exclude undocumented immigrants from census apportionment counts, a coalition of twenty-one states and fifteen units of local governments led by New York's attorney general (AG) was suing to stop the plan from going into effect. *New York v. Trump*—soon consolidated with a case brought by the New York Immigration Coalition—was in fact only one of several challenges to the memorandum, yet it represented the most extensive concerted effort to enjoin the secretary of commerce from carrying out the exclusion plan.[90]

The state and local plaintiffs in *New York v. Trump* made six core legal arguments—supported by dozens of declarations from academic researchers, state and local government demographers, and officials involved with census outreach—which pointed to the deleterious effects of the Trump memorandum on the 2020 Census.[91] First, they claimed that the Trump memorandum had, by declaring that undocumented immigrants are not "persons" for the purposes of apportionment, ignored both Supreme Court precedent and the plain text of the Fourteenth Amendment. Second, by requiring the commerce secretary to tabulate and transmit reports to the president based on data other than the actual enumeration of each state, the memorandum had violated the text of the Census Act itself. Third, they argued that the memorandum had violated the Fifth Amendment's prohibition on discrimination, as it targeted undocumented immigrants for exclusion from apportionment counts and was motivated by a "bare desire to harm immigrant communities of color" by reducing their political influence.[92]

By advancing this scheme, the plaintiffs argued, the Trump administration had violated the separation of powers by usurping powers Congress had delegated to the secretary of commerce. Moreover, because the memorandum made numerous changes to federal policy without analysis and without notice-and-comment rulemaking, it violated the Administrative Procedure Act (APA). Finally, because the Census Bureau had never taken an "actual enumeration" of the undocumented population, it would be forced to conduct some form of statistical sampling in order to produce the congressional apportionment counts requested by Trump, a move that clearly violated the statutory prohibition on statistical sampling for apportionment purposes.[93]

Soon after the plaintiffs were granted a hearing before a three-judge panel in the Southern District of New York, the federal government filed a motion to dismiss the suit.[94] The federal government's argument hung largely on the question of the plaintiffs' standing to sue. Because it was not yet known what numbers the secretary of commerce would provide to the president, "any allegation as to the impact of the President's apportionment decision on matters such as congressional representation or federal funding is wholly theoretical and legally insufficient to meet the ripeness and standing requirements."[95] Similarly, the administration argued that plaintiffs' claims that apportionment exclusion would have a chilling effect on census participation were based on "generalized, second- or third-hand accounts of alleged harm and unsubstantiated conjectures." Finally, the administration claimed, many of the legal arguments made by the plaintiffs were baseless. Because the president was not an "agency" under the APA, and because there had been no "final agency action," the memorandum was not subject to judicial review. Whereas the plaintiffs argued that the president had violated the separation of powers, for example, the government cited *Franklin v. Massachusetts*—a 1992 case surrounding the Census Bureau's residence rules—to support its contention that the executive branch had broad authority over apportionment. Nor had the plaintiffs plausibly alleged "animus" or "discriminatory intent" under the Fifth Amendment.

In an eighty-six-page opinion, a unanimous three-judge panel ruled in favor of the plaintiffs. First, the Court found that the plaintiffs had standing to proceed in federal court, but not because of their claims about the potential harm to their respective states' apportionment counts. Given that the secretary had not yet made clear how he would calculate the number of undocumented persons in each state or whether it was "feasible" to do so, this injury was "too speculative" to allow for standing. Rather, the uncontested expert analyses submitted by the plaintiffs showed that the presidential memorandum had yielded a "chilling effect" on participation in the census in hard-to-count communities, degrading the quality of census data used to allocate federal dollars and forcing some plaintiffs to divert their own resources to "thaw" the chill on participation. On the merits of the case, the Court ruled that Trump's memorandum had violated the Census Act by requiring the secretary of commerce to report numbers other than the tabulation of the total population in each state and by excluding "illegal aliens" from the "whole number of persons in each state" to be used as an apportionment base.[96]

The ruling dealt a significant blow to the Trump administration's exclusion plan. While not preventing the Department of Commerce or the Census Bureau from "from continuing to study whether and how it would be feasible to calculate the number of illegal aliens in each State," the Court permanently enjoined the secretary of commerce from including "any information concerning the number of aliens in each State 'who are not in a lawful immigration status under the Immigration and Nationality Act'" and requiring the secretary's section 141(b) report to include only "the tabulation of total population by States . . . according to the methodology set forth in [the Census Bureau's Residence Rule]."[97]

The plaintiffs' sense of relief did not last long, however. Within a few weeks, the Supreme Court had granted the administration's request for an expedited review of the three-judge panel's findings, setting oral argument for November 30th. In short order, local and state governments, along with NGOs, social scientists, historians, members of Congress, and former Census Bureau directors, submitted amicus briefs, many of which highlighted the potential effects of the exclusion scheme on congressional apportionment and federal funding.

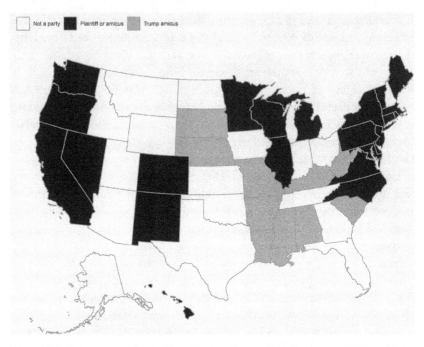

Figure 5.2: States as parties in *New York v. Trump* (2020). Source: US Supreme Court, Docket No. 20–366. Note: Data includes all states serving as plaintiffs, plaintiffs' amici, and Trump administration amici in the southern district of New York and on appeal in the Supreme Court.

At the state level, participants in the litigation were starkly divided along party lines (see figure 5.2). Every state AG participating in the case as a plaintiff or filing an amicus brief in support of the plaintiffs was a Democrat. Every state AG filing an amicus in support of the Trump administration was a Republican.[98] In contrast, all local and tribal governments submitting amicus briefs did so on the side of the government plaintiffs.[99] As their brief noted, the local government amici represented communities with "a significant population of undocumented residents," community members who would be "omitted from the apportionment base under the Memorandum." Cook County, Illinois, for example, was home to more than three hundred thousand undocumented immigrants. The removal of these individuals from the apportionment counts would virtually guarantee that the state of Illinois would lose a congressional seat.[100]

The plaintiffs in the case attracted the majority of amici, including significant figures like former Census Bureau directors. Even so, the context for the Supreme Court's review proved less advantageous for the plaintiffs—now appellees—for two reasons. First, the death of Justice Ruth Bader Ginsburg in September of 2020 had created a rare political opportunity for the Trump administration to nominate a third conservative justice, a seventh circuit appeals court judge named Amy Coney Barrett, to the court. Second, while the three-judge panel had held that the plaintiffs had standing based on the "chilling effect" of the memorandum on census participation—not on the injury that resulted from the "remote and hypothetical" effects of the exclusion plan on congressional apportionment—the end of field operations allowed Trump administration lawyers to claim that the argument about "census-count harms" was now moot. State and local governments would be forced to pivot to arguments about apportionment and federal funding that the three-judge panel had found less persuasive.[101]

The oral arguments in *Trump v. New York*, held through a phone conference due to the pandemic, were defined by conflicting interpretations of what the Trump memorandum's actual effects would be. More than anything else, colloquies between Trump's lawyers and the justices revealed that the possibility of a successfully implemented exclusion plan was dwindling with each passing day. Between the onslaught of litigation and significant gaps in administrative data, the window for the secretary of commerce to report apportionment tabulations to the president by the December 31st deadline was rapidly closing. The first exchange between Chief Justice John Roberts and Solicitor General Jeffrey Wall was illustrative:

> *Chief Justice Roberts:* We expedited this case in light of the December 31 deadline for the Secretary to transmit the census to the President. Is that date still operative? Do you still need a decision by that date?
> *General Wall:* Well, the situation is fairly fluid, Mr. Chief Justice. We—because of the two weeks that we lost to the California injunction and some subsequent issues in processing the data, we are not currently on pace to send the report to the President by the year-end statutory deadline. But just this morning, I confirmed with senior leadership at the Department of Commerce and the Census Bureau that we are hopeful, and it remains possible, that we can get at least some of the [Presidential Memo]-related data to the President in January, so we do still need relief from the Court, yes.

Chief Justice Roberts: Sounds like you had a busy morning.[102]

The president's lawyers sought to turn implementation chaos into an argument that New York's claims were unripe for judicial review. As the solicitor general would put it at oral argument, given remaining uncertainties about the feasibility of any approach to implementing the memorandum, "you could have the Court issuing an opinion on what the President may or may not do, only to discover days or weeks later that it's effectively advisory because the numbers aren't large enough to affect the apportionment and the appellees here and other potential appellees wouldn't be injured, either with respect to apportionment or funding." Because there were simply "too many unknowns," the Court would have to wait for post-apportionment litigation. Not all the justices were sympathetic to Wall's argument. Justice Elena Kagan, for example, reminded Wall that the government was already in possession of the names of seven hundred thousand recipients of the Deferred Action for Childhood Arrivals (DACA) program as well as the names of 3.2 million people in deportation proceedings. "You're 30 days out," Kagan said, "It seems to me you either know whether you can do matching or you don't know whether you can do matching. Why the uncertainty on this?"[103]

Yet the uncertainty was the point of the Trump administration's legal strategy, as New York's Solicitor General Barbara Underwood soon found. Arguing on behalf of the government appellees, Underwood claimed that the government's representations about the uncertainty of the effects of its plan were highly overstated at best. While she could not opine on just how successful the effort to exclude undocumented immigrants from the apportionment account might be, she emphasized the evidence that, by its own admission, the government was working as hard as it could to implement as much as it could, and that even a partial implementation of the memorandum—removing only fifty thousand persons in ICE custody—would likely have an effect on apportionment. Indeed, as Underwood argued, it would be far more speculative to conclude that the plan could *not* be implemented. This argument did not evidently persuade Justice Neil Gorsuch, who insisted that it was nevertheless speculative to draw conclusions about just how far the government would be able to go, which was significant for analyzing whether the state of New York and other governments had a "substantial risk of injury."[104]

Underwood held fast to her claims on the merits of the case, which seemed to receive at least some support from Justice Amy Coney Barrett, who observed that the historical evidence "cut against" the government's position on the president's authority to exclude undocumented immigrants from the apportionment count. Nevertheless, both she and Justice Brett Kavanaugh entertained the possibility that the president may be able to exclude some, though not all, categories of undocumented immigrants, such as noncitizens in ICE detention centers.

If the oral arguments demonstrated that the majority of conservative justices were unwilling to accept Underwood's argument on standing, the Court's seven-page per curiam opinion confirmed it. Issued less than two weeks before the December 31st deadline for apportionment counts, the opinion did not reach the merits of the case. Instead, the majority—composed of the six conservative justices—concluded that the case was "riddled with contingencies and speculation that impede judicial review."[105] It was virtually certain that the government could not "feasibly implement the memorandum by excluding the estimated 10.5 million aliens without lawful status." Yet, in the Court's view, the only evidence proffered in the record concerning the effects of the order—an analysis by political scientist Christopher Warshaw—"unrealistically" assumed that the president would "exclude the entire undocumented population" and did not address the consequences of a "partial implementation of the memorandum." Without this evidence, it was essentially impossible to speculate on how the memorandum would affect interstate apportionment, which was one of the pillars of the plaintiffs' theory of injury. Plaintiffs' arguments about the effects of the memorandum on population-derived federal grants were no more persuasive, the Court suggested, because while federal funding formulas relied on census data, they did not necessarily use the apportionment counts affected by the memorandum. This mean that changes to the secretary's report would not "inexorably" alter "downstream access to funds or other resources." In light of these uncertainties, the Court could not identify any "concrete harm" suffered by the plaintiffs. It was thus "too soon" to tell if the government would act in a manner "substantially likely to harm any of the plaintiffs here."[106]

In a fiery dissent, nearly three times the length of the Court's opinion, Justices Stephen Breyer, Elena Kagan, and Sonia Sotomayor pointed to the history of census litigation, noting that the Court had—in advance of the 2000 Census—"reached and resolved controversies concerning the decennial census based on a substantial risk of an anticipated apportionment harm." While the majority focused on the uncertainties involved in the implementation of Trump's memorandum, the dissenters emphasized that the Court had never held that plaintiffs must demonstrate that it is "literally certain that the harms they identify will come about." Rather, the Court had employed a standard of "substantial risk," which the plaintiffs in the case certainly met. The government had at no point disclaimed its intent to carry out the policy to the greatest extent feasible. As of early December, the government had submitted that it could exclude "aliens without lawful status housed in ICE detention centers on census day," which would exclude approximately fifty thousand ICE detainees. Even this comparatively low number of exclusions from the tabulation would be certain to affect apportionment counts. Added to this, however, the bureau had shown that it was able to "individually identify" at least "several million additional aliens without lawful status," including nearly two hundred thousand persons subject to final orders of removal, seven hundred thousand DACA recipients, and 3.2 million nondetained individuals in removal proceedings. Taken together, the dissenters argued, these figures would certainly be large enough to affect apportionment. Where the argument about federal grants was concerned, the dissent cited an amicus brief by George Washington University social scientist Andrew Reamer, noting that numerous federal statutes required that funding formulas be based on figures "certified" or "reported" on the decennial census, which had historically meant numbers based on apportionment counts like those affected by Trump's memorandum. While the government argued that individuals removed from apportionment tabulations could be "added back in" for funding statutes, the dissenters reasoned that there was no evidence to suggest the secretary "could or would do any such thing—unless of course a court holds that the removal was unlawful." Further, the dissent argued, the memorandum's stated goal of reducing the number of representatives in states that were home to a disproportionate number of undocumented immigrants was itself illegal. As such, they concluded, the Court should not "decline to resolve the case simply because the Government speculates that it might not fully succeed."[107]

The Court's decision notwithstanding, the litigation process and the sheer administrative complexity of the plan itself had made it essentially impossible for the government to meet the December 31st deadline. As the federal government's legal adversaries, state and local officials constituted a powerful support structure for census integrity. To be sure, Trump appointees—including Census Bureau Director Steven Dillingham—continued in vain to advance the apportionment exclusion plan in one way or another.

Yet, thanks to the work of civil servants—whose dedication to scientific integrity was strong enough to withstand pressure for political expediency—these efforts bore no fruit. In early January, an inspector general's report revealed Dillingham's last-ditch effort to offer bureau employees a financial incentive to finish the technical report on noncitizens before Trump left office. Days later, Dillingham resigned.[108]

Litigation on the Rush Plan

A second significant focus of census litigation in 2020 concerned not the exclusion plan but the Trump administration's revised operational schedule for the census. In *National Urban League v. Ross*, a coalition of local and tribal governments joined NGOs like the National Urban League, the League of Women Voters, and the Black Alliance for Just Immigration to argue that the Trump administration's shortening of the operational schedule was an arbitrary and capricious decision under the Administrative Procedure Act.[109] Not only did the bureau fail to explain its decision to adopt the August 3rd rush plan, the plaintiffs argued before a district court judge in San Jose, California, the real reason for the rush plan was to advance the Trump administration's apportionment exclusion scheme. Soon after the National Urban League filed the complaint, a coalition of twenty-one states, eleven counties, fifteen cities, and the US Conference of Mayors filed amicus briefs in support of the plaintiffs.

The plaintiffs' case hinged on three legal arguments. First, they alleged that the bureau violated the Enumeration Clause of the Constitution. By adopting the rush plan, which bureau staff recognized would make it "impossible to produce . . . a full, fair, and accurate count" by the December 31st deadline, the bureau had made a decision that did not "bear a reasonable relationship to the accomplishment of an actual enumeration of the population." Second, the plaintiffs claimed that the bureau's rush plan violated the APA, which requires that agencies provide some explanation for their decisions grounded in a "rational connection" between the "facts found and the choices made." Whereas the bureau's initial operational changes to accommodate the COVID-19 pandemic had been based on consultation with experts and census stakeholders, the bureau's about-face in August was—in the language of the APA—"arbitrary and capricious," lacking any apparent justification or citation to relevant evidence. Third, the plaintiffs claimed, the justification the Census Bureau *did* provide for its plan was mere pretext.

Just as the Trump administration had contrived a rationale for including a citizenship question on the census questionnaire, they now used a similarly false basis for the rush plan. While the Census Bureau justified the August 4th decision by citing the statutory deadline for the delivery of apportionment data to the president, the same officials had for months insisted that they could not deliver a "complete and accurate" count by December 31st, 2020. Their newly found interest in meeting the deadline was, as the plaintiffs' briefs had it, a smokescreen meant to conceal the real reason for the rush: allowing Trump ample time to implement his apportionment exclusion scheme.[110]

Because the new replan schedule adopted by the Census Bureau required data collection to stop on September 30th, 2020, the plaintiffs took an aggressive approach to litigation—asking the district court to immediately enjoin the plan's implementation. The Trump administration did little to assuage the Court's skepticism about the reasons for these operational changes. For example, the administration's lawyers repeatedly claimed that there was no administrative record for the decision aside from the August 3rd press release. At the same time, Trump appointees studiously avoided the district court's order to produce an administrative record. With hours to go before a document production deadline of September 13th, the Census Bureau produced an assortment of heavily redacted emails and suggested that compliance with the court's order would be a "physical impossibility." Illustrating the flimsiness of this argument, the plaintiffs in the case quickly submitted documentation of an inspector general "request for information" memorandum sent to Secretary Ross on August 13th, a document that the administration had failed to disclose to the Court. In the absence of a full administrative record, the government clung to a single declaration provided by Albert E. Fontenot Jr., associate director for the Decennial Census Programs, who asserted that the replan was designed "to meet the statutory deadline without compromising quality to an undue degree" and that he was "confident" in the bureau's ability to succeed.[111]

The district court was not inclined to agree with Fontenot's assessment, and on September 24th, Judge Lucy Koh issued a preliminary injunction in favor of the plaintiffs. Within days of the injunction, Koh received a flood of new evidence that the Census Bureau was violating her order, continuing with a plan to conclude data collection as soon as possible. Emails from at least one regional director maintained that the deadline stood while tweets and a press release published by the Census Bureau announced a new deadline of October 5th—which was soon approved by Secretary Ross. A day after the ninth circuit court of appeals upheld her original preliminary injunction, Koh issued another order clarifying that her injunction reinstated the October 31st data collection deadline that the bureau had adopted in April and requiring the bureau to issue a correction to its earlier messages as well as a new compliance plan.[112]

A week later, on October 7th, a unanimous three-judge panel of the Ninth Circuit Court of Appeals again upheld Koh's injunction against the bureau's ending of data collection, but stayed her injunction on the December 31st deadline for delivering apportionment totals. The same day, the Trump administration petitioned Supreme Court Justice Elena Kagan, who oversees the ninth circuit, to stay Koh's injunction pending appellate review. The administration's application for a stay cited the "sworn testimony in the record . . . of the government's ability to meet the statutory deadline on its proposed schedule." Nevertheless, as the plaintiffs in the case were quick to point out, administration officials had repeatedly stated in their submissions to lower courts that they could not meet the December 31st deadline "under any conditions."[113]

Kagan referred the matter to the full Supreme Court and on October 13th the justices granted the stay in an unsigned opinion and over the vigorous dissent of Justice Sonia Sotomayor who argued that meeting the December 31st deadline "at the expense of the accuracy of the census is not a cost worth paying, especially when the Government has failed to show why it could not bear the lesser cost of expending more resources to meet the deadline or continuing its prior efforts to seek an extension from Congress."[114] Within hours of the ruling, census data collection ceased. Practically speaking, however, the lawsuit at least helped to slow the Trump administration down, pushing back the end of field operations by at least two weeks after the intended stop date. If meeting the December 31st deadline appeared impossible before, it now appeared delusional. Under a stipulated dismissal agreement brokered following the Biden administration's transition to office, the Census Bureau agreed not to release apportionment data before April 26, 2021, to abandon the apportionment exclusion scheme, and to declare any citizenship data products as "statistically unfit for use."[115]

Protecting Census Integrity in a Crisis

To call COVID-19 a "stress test" for census taking would be a severe under-statement. Whereas a patient undergoes a cardiac stress test in a controlled clinical environment, the 2020 Census played out in a climate of radical un-certainty. The pandemic not only caused death and severe disease but also brought on significant limits on in-person interaction and deep economic hardship. These conditions required a significant extension of operational timelines, a thorough reworking of outreach strategies, and an uncommon sensitivity to potential sources of error. Officials at the Census Bureau, as well as in state and local governments, endeavored mightily to adapt to the pandemic emergency. Their efforts collided, however, with President Trump's unprecedented attempt to exclude undocumented immigrants from the census apportionment counts and his administration's gutting of the Census Bureau's COVID-19 operational plan to provide him with the new numbers before leaving office. The US Census did not undergo a stress test in 2020. It was instead the victim of an attempted homicide.

If the pandemic and the Trump administration's power grab constituted rather singular threats to the 2020 Census, they nevertheless exposed how census integrity hinges on several contrasting patterns of intergovernmental relations. First, intergovernmental partnerships remained crucial to sustaining and adapting census outreach during the pandemic. Through-out 2020, state and local governments were critical in coordinating campaigns in which trusted messengers provided up-to-date reminders about the census to hard-to-count populations. To a large extent, the quality of these efforts hinged on the preparations governments had made in prior years, however. States and cities with extensive staff capacity dedicated ex-clusively to the census were well-poised to adapt outreach campaigns to the pandemic. By contrast, some jurisdictions delegated census responsibilities to individuals with broader job descriptions who found themselves pulled away from census outreach and toward emergency response with the onset of the pandemic. Similarly, states and cities where census outreach teams had strong ties to other agencies as well as other units of government stood a better chance of learning from peers in other jurisdictions and identifying alternative conduits for census messaging that did not, for example, require in-person door-to-door canvasses as well as learning about best practices.

The bureau's state and local partners were not limitlessly flexible, however. The publication of the apportionment exclusion memo, the introduction of the August 3rd rush plan, and the cancellation of the Group Quarters Count Review event all presented obstacles to census integrity that could not simply be addressed through the adoption of new approaches to outreach and communication. Indeed, one major conclusion of this chapter is that state and local officials contributed to census integrity through un-cooperative or even adversarial relationships with the federal government. For example, the Census Bureau found it difficult to obtain consistent co-operation of state governments when pursuing the Trump administration's ill-fated plan to use administrative records for excluding undocumented immigrants from state apportionment counts. States provided only patch-work of low-value data from programs like SNAP, TANF, and WIC. Only four state DMVs signed agreements with the bureau to supply driver's license information.

Perhaps more importantly, state and local governments helped to pre-serve census integrity as the Census Bureau's *legal adversaries*. To be sure, the final disposition of *New York v. Trump* and *National Urban League v. Ross* did not favor the state and local government plaintiffs or amici. Yet by filing these lawsuits, governments and NGOs were able to "run down the clock" on the administration's efforts. Both lawsuits contributed to opera-tional delays, making it impossible to deliver apportionment counts—with or without the exclusions requested by the president—prior to the Decem-ber 31st deadline. The preliminary injunction in *National Urban League v. Ross* also ensured that data collection extended nearly two weeks beyond the date envisioned by the August 3rd rush plan. Even after the presidential transition occurred, litigants in the case secured additional orders for addi-tional time for data processing and a commitment to label citizenship data products as unfit for use.

In the end, the efforts of state and local officials—either as the Census Bureau's partners or adversaries—could not fully mitigate threats to census integrity. As the next chapter will show, the pandemic and the Trump ad-ministration's power grab dealt a serious blow to census accuracy that many governments would continue to grapple with for years after the figures were released. Yet in the absence of state and local efforts, the outcomes could have been far more severe.

CHAPTER SIX

Counting the Forgotten

How Governments Respond to Flawed Data

Mike Duggan was fed up. It had been two years since the 2020 Census, and Detroit's sixty-four-year-old mayor was practically begging for someone to help his city deal with the aftermath. Duggan's audience was Senator Gary Peters (D-MI), chairman of the Senate Homeland Security and Governmental Affairs Committee. It was late July 2022 and Peters had come to Detroit for a special field hearing at the downtown campus of Wayne County Community College. The reason for his visit, he said, was obvious: The 2020 Census faced "unprecedented challenges that could impact Michigan communities like Detroit for years."[1] And his constituents needed a platform.

Peters listened as an exasperated Duggan—his voice nearly hoarse—explained that the 2020 Census had failed to count roughly fifty thousand Detroiters. This, the mayor argued, was nothing short of "systemic racism." "In a city that's 84 percent Black and brown," said Duggan, an undercount would hit Detroit harder than any other city in the country. It would result in the loss of "[ten] million [dollars] in state revenue sharing and much more in federal funds," heaping yet more misery on a city that was still dealing with the effects of the COVID-19 pandemic and only beginning to recover from the effects of its 2013 bankruptcy.

The Census Bureau's figures, Duggan suggested, simply did not make sense. While Detroit's annual population estimates had shrunk between 2010 and 2019, they did so incrementally (see figure 6.1). Yet between the 2019 population estimate and the 2020 Census count, the city saw an implausibly steep loss of over thirty thousand people. A team of researchers working for the city found still more anomalies. According to a visual audit of census addresses conducted by University of Michigan researchers, the bureau had ignored thousands of housing units. A look at US Postal Service data further illustrated that the 2020 Census had undercounted the number of occupied housing units in a sample of five neighborhoods by more than 8 percent.[2]

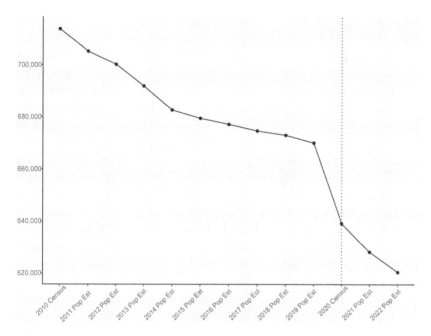

Figure 6.1: Census Bureau population counts and annual population estimates for Detroit, Michigan, 2010–2021. Source: Jeffrey D. Morenoff, *Testimony Before the United States Senate Committee on Homeland Security and Government Affairs*, Hearing on "Reviewing the 2020 Census: Local Perspectives in Michigan" (Jul. 25, 2022), hsgac.senate.gov/wp-content /uploads/imo/media/doc/Testimony-Morenoff-2022-07-25.pdf; "Annual Estimates of the Resident Population for Incorporated Places in the United States: April 1, 2020 to July 1, 2022," US Census Bureau, SUB-IP-EST2022-POP; "Annual Estimates of the Resident Population for Incorporated Places: April 1, 2010 to July 1, 2019," US Census Bureau, SUB-IP-EST2019-POP. Note: Data for 2010 and 2020 are derived from Census population counts. Data for all other years are annual Census Bureau population estimates.

But that was not the end of it. In May, the bureau had released its 2021 population, which said that Detroit had lost over seven thousand additional people. Duggan was incredulous, defying anyone listening to "drive around the city of Detroit today, where there are cranes everywhere, where there's a housing shortage and rents rising . . . and tell me we're 7,000 people less." In fact, the city's electrical utility, DTE Energy, had reported that over the last year, it had seen eight thousand additional housing units with gas and electricity. In his testimony, Duggan wondered aloud who might be occupying those households. "There's two possibilities," he quipped, "We've either been invaded by a group of ghosts, or the Census Bureau data is wrong."[3]

All the mayor wanted, he said, was an appeal process with "objective standards" in which the city could bring forward data that reflected the true size of the city's population. Because the Census Bureau was not willing to accept the kind of data he had presented in his testimony, he hoped that Peters' committee could help apply some pressure. Detroiters, after all, "just wanted to be counted like everybody else."[4] Yet, during a tense midterm election season, Congress was hardly capable of delivering the relief Duggan sought. And so, a little under two months after his testimony, Detroit petitioned a federal court to order the Census Bureau to "promptly accept and fairly evaluate" its challenge to the 2021 population estimates and to use the kind of evidence Duggan has discussed in his congressional testimony.[5] The lawsuit would grind on for the better part of the next year.

Duggan was hardly alone in his frustration at the bureau. Indeed, there is ample evidence that the 2020 Census resulted in a significant undercount of cities across the country, especially those with large populations of racial and ethnic minorities, renters, college students, and low-income residents. For Detroit's mayor, and for local officials like him across the country, the question was how best to respond to flawed census data.

State and local governments, as this chapter shows, can pursue post-census challenges in several distinctive institutional venues. For its part, the Census Bureau provides state and local governments multiple opportunities to review and correct census counts and population estimates. Yet tight administrative rules limit the kinds of challenges local governments can bring and the kinds of data they can use to support their cases. Adjusting these administrative processes to address 2020 anomalies proved a cumbersome process for the Census Bureau, however. For this reason, some governments can be expected to pay well into the millions for a "special census"—a fresh enumeration that updates the bureau's annual population estimates. Where large cities like Detroit are concerned, however, special censuses entail steep costs without a guaranteed return on investment.

When these administrative remedies fail to provide adequate relief, state and local officials might try to shift the debate to another venue. For Detroit, this ultimately meant filing suit in federal court. Even so, the law of the census is particularly ambiguous when it comes to post-census review programs. This has limited the courts' ability to provide the remedies sought by cities like Detroit and, as we shall see, states like Alabama.

If the courts cannot provide a remedy, governors and mayors will have to search for other sources of political leverage to force the bureau to act. For Mayor Duggan, it proved difficult to find that leverage. One reason for this is that Detroit acted largely on its own, without political support from a broad coalition of census stakeholders. Intergovernmental organizations that are frequent participants in census politics did not become involved. Moreover, Detroit was contesting Census Bureau policies that were largely finalized and thus more difficult to reverse. As Washington entered a period of divided government, Congress proved an unreliable ally in the fight to remedy census undercounts. At best, officials like Mayor Duggan could hope for legislative reforms and bureau-based initiatives that might improve the 2030 Census.

Not all battles over Census Bureau procedures turned out this way. As we will see in the story of the 2020 Census's Disclosure Avoidance System (DAS), when state and local officials can coordinate to alter bureau decisions that are in flux, they may stand a better chance of exerting pressure. Census officials treated the adoption of a new approach to preventing the disclosure of confidential census information—based on the concept known as differential privacy—as a fait accompli. Yet state demographers, city planners, and other users of census data nevertheless took action to oppose the initial design parameters of this system, which would have created significant problems for the accuracy and usability of census data. While those efforts did not lead the bureau to abandon differential privacy, they nevertheless led to significant changes in the DAS.

Judging the 2020 Census

The phrase "perfect storm" understates the cyclone of hazards and operational risks the bureau encountered in implementing the 2020 Census. Even before the COVID-19 pandemic, the Census Bureau had to confront a decade of inadequate congressional appropriations and four years of mismanagement and deliberate political sabotage by the Trump administration. Even after the pandemic began, wildfires and extreme weather events plagued enumeration efforts in the summer and fall of 2020. Against this chaotic backdrop, the Census Bureau faced the challenge of implementing numerous technological and operational changes, including the first online census questionnaire.[6]

By the time the bureau's first decennial data products were ready for public consumption in the spring and summer of 2021, census observers had good reasons to be concerned. The answers to some of their most important questions hinged on the results of two key indicators of census quality. The first was the demographic analysis (DA), which used data on births, deaths, and immigration to estimate the size of the total US population. The second was the Post-Enumeration Survey (PES), which measures census accuracy through conducting a sample survey and matching responses to census records. These data help to generate estimates of the net population undercount and overcount as well as the sources of those miscounts. The problem, however, was that the results of the DA and the PES would not be available until the spring of 2022.[7]

Aware of these challenges, leaders at the Census Bureau called for multiple independent reviews of the 2020 count. The bureau asked for the help of JASON, an advisory group composed of elite government scientists, which published an initial assessment of census data quality in February of 2021.[8] Six months later, another independent task force on census quality indicators convened by the American Statistical Association published a preliminary report of its own. The Census Bureau supported this work by granting three of the task force's researchers permission to analyze confidential 2020 Census data.[9] Finally, the bureau commissioned the Committee on National Statistics, part of the National Academies of Sciences, Engineering, and Medicine to convene an expert panel on the quality of the 2020 Census. The bureau's charge to the panel—ultimately chaired by Teresa Sullivan, a demographer and former president of the University of Virginia—was expansive. It was to review a variety of indicators from the Census Bureau and other sources, which would inform not only conclusions about the quality of the 2020 Census but also a set of recommendations for the 2030 count.[10]

If census observers hoped for a simple, easy-to-digest story about the quality of census data, they were sorely mistaken. The work of the bureau and outside reviewers revealed not one but multiple layered narratives. At a surface level, the 2020 Census appeared to be a kind of miracle. Despite repeated sabotage efforts by the Trump administration, multiple independent reviews found no apparent evidence of political interference in the enumeration process itself. If anything, the bureau's staff—both permanent and temporary—appeared to have gone above and beyond the call of duty

to shepherd census operations through pandemic disruptions and procedural chaos. Further, in the face of the pandemic and technological changes
associated with the first online census, the overall self-response rate improved relative to the 2010 benchmark. Whereas 61 percent of households
had self-responded in 2010, 65 percent of census addresses were resolved
by self-response in 2020. Most importantly, the overall population count
closely mirrored the estimates from demographic analysis and the Post-
Enumeration Survey. The PES, for example, estimated that the household
population was undercounted by roughly 0.24 percent (roughly seven hundred and eighty thousand people); this was a slightly higher undercount
than in 2010, but the increase was not statistically significant.[11]

Yet this surface-level analysis hid as much as it revealed. First, more
fine-grained metrics of census errors had worsened relative to 2010. For
example, the number of whole-person imputations—which indicate people who did not self-respond and who could not be identified through
follow-up—doubled from six million in 2010 to just under eleven million
in 2020.[12]

A second relevant indicator of census data quality was the phenomenon
of "age heaping." When respondents do not know the precise age of household members, they typically guess some ages more frequently than others.
In the United States, the "preferred" ages are those that end in zero or five.
As these guesses grow more numerous in census data, they leave a signature
on age distribution charts: sharp peaks (or "heaps") in the number of people
at the preferred ages. Guessing at ages matters not only because it renders
census data less useful for important policy purposes, but also because it
indicates broader problems with coverage and data quality. And there was
indeed evidence of age heaping in the 2020 Census. Age distribution charts
from 2020 show "a sawtooth pattern" with "large spikes in the age distribution starting at age 25 and continuing in 5-year intervals until age 65."[13] As
the Committee on National Statistics (CNSTAT) panel on the 2020 Census
concluded, there was over twice as much age heaping in 2020 as there was
in 2010.[14]

Third, the 2020 Census significantly undercounted or overcounted
members of racial and ethnic groups. On the one hand, the non-Hispanic
white population was overcounted by nearly 2 percent—a significant increase relative to 2010. By contrast, as table 6.1 shows, both the Hispanic
and Black populations experienced a far worse undercount than they had
in 2010. Between 2010 and 2020, the net undercount also increased for

Table 6.1a. Net Coverage Error Rates in the United States by Race and Hispanic Origin (in Percent)

	2010 Estimate	2020 Estimate
Overall	+0.01	−0.24
White	+0.54*	+0.66*
Non-Hispanic White Alone	+0.84*	+1.64*
Black or African American	−2.06*	−3.30*
Asian	−0.08	+2.62*
American Indian or Alaska Native	−0.15	−0.91*
On Reservation	−4.88*	−5.64*
Off Reservation	+3.86	+3.06
Native Hawaiian or Other Pacific Islander	−1.02	+1.28
Some Other Race	−1.63*	−4.34*
Hispanic or Latino	−1.54*	−4.99*

Table 6.1b. Net Coverage Error Rates in the United States by Tenure Status (in Percent)

	2010 Estimate	2020 Estimate
Owner	+0.57	+0.43
Renter	−1.09	−1.48

Table 6.1c. Net Coverage Error Rates in the United States by Age and Sex (in Percent)

	2010 Estimate	2020 Estimate
0 to 17	+0.33	−0.84*
18 to 29 Males	−1.21*	−2.25*
18 to 29 Females	+0.28	−0.98*
30 to 49 Males	−3.57*	−3.05*
30 to 49 Females	+0.42*	−0.10
50+ Males	+0.32*	+0.55*
50+ Females	+2.35*	+2.63*

Source: Shadie Khubba, Krista Heim, and Jinhee Hong, *National Census Coverage Estimates for People in the United States by Demographic Characteristics* (US Census Bureau, 2022), https://www2.census.gov/programs-surveys/decennial /coverage-measurement/pes/national-census-coverage-estimates-by-demographic -characteristics.pdf.
Note: * Denotes a (percent) net coverage error that is significantly different from zero.

American Indian and Alaska Native populations living on reservations, from 5 percent to 6 percent.

Fourth, undercounts also varied by age and housing tenure. Those younger than fifty—especially children aged zero to seventeen—were severely undercounted in the 2020 Census. The fifty-and-older population—which is disproportionately white—was overcounted in 2020. It is also worth noting that the net undercount for young children in the 2020 Census (5.4 percent) is higher than the same figure for this group in the 1950 Census. According to the PES, the 2020 Census produced a 1.48 percent net undercount of renters compared to a 0.43 percent overcount of homeowners.

Fifth, the national results also masked geographic variation in census errors. In the 2020 Census, the populations of eight states were statistically, significantly overcounted. This included Delaware (+5.4 percent), Hawaii (+6.8 percent), Massachusetts (+2.2 percent), Minnesota (+3.8 percent), New York (+3.4 percent), Ohio (+1.5 percent), Rhode Island (+5 percent), and Utah (+2.6 percent). By contrast, six states experienced a statistically significant net undercount. This included Arkansas (–5 percent), Florida (–3.5 percent), Illinois (–2 percent), Mississippi (–4.1 percent), Tennessee (–4.8 percent), and Texas (–1.9 percent). In the 2010 Census, by contrast, none of the fifty states or the District of Columbia had been significantly undercounted or overcounted.[15]

Finally, analyses of the 2020 Census also simply left some questions unanswered. For example, in contrast to 2010, the Census Bureau announced that it would not release Post-Enumeration Survey data for demographic groups at the state level. Nor would it release population coverage estimates below the state level. These and other gaps in data led the American Statistical Association's task force to include that the "indicators released to date by the bureau do not permit a thorough assessment of the 2020 Census data quality." The expert panel assembled by the CNSTAT came to a similar conclusion in its 2022 interim report, noting that it "will not be possible for this panel (or any other evaluator) to understand and characterize the quality of the 2020 Census unless the Census Bureau is forthcoming with informative data quality metrics."[16] This included fine-grained local measures "unperturbed" by the statistical noise infused of the Disclosure Avoidance System. By the time the CNSTAT panel released its final report in 2023, the bureau had honored its commitment to provide this data to the panel, yet there remained "major issues and complications" about what the panel could "actually publish and report" from their analyses, largely because of the bureau's

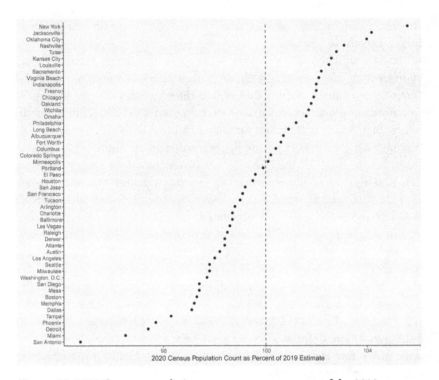

2020 Census Population Count as Percent of 2019 Estimate

Figure 6.2: 2020 Census population counts as a percentage of the 2019 population estimates, fifty largest US cities. Source: Jeffrey D. Morenoff, *Testimony Before the United States Senate Committee on Homeland Security and Government Affairs*, Hearing on "Reviewing the 2020 Census: Local Perspectives in Michigan" (Jul. 25, 2022), http://hsgac.senate.gov/wp-content /uploads/imo/media/doc/Testimony-Morenoff-2022-07-25.pdf; "Annual Estimates of the Resident Population for Incorporated Places in the United States: April 1, 2020 to July 1, 2021," US Census Bureau, SUB-IP-EST2021-POP; "Annual Estimates of the Resident Population for Incorporated Places: April 1, 2010 to July 1, 2019," US Census Bureau, SUB-IP-EST2019-POP.

commitment to the nondisclosure of confidential information.[17] In the end, the CNSTAT panel's evaluations represent as good an assessment as presently exists of the quality of the 2020 Census results. Yet detailed analyses of census data quality take time to produce. As a result, in the immediate aftermath of receiving their 2020 Census figures, state and local officials—as well as nongovernmental census advocates—experienced a high level of uncertainty and registered a growing level of alarm.[18] This included mayors from cities across the country who, like Mike Duggan, were puzzled by the Census population counts. Of the fifty largest cities in the United States, more than half saw their population decrease relative to the Census Bureau's July 2019 population estimates (see figure 6.2). In San Antonio, that decrease was 7.3 percent.

What did elected officials make of these anomalies? And, assuming negative population changes reflected errors in census data, what could be done about it? With billions in federal and state aid potentially on the line, officials disturbed by the new counts surveyed their options.

Setting the Record Straight? The Promise and Limits of Count Question Resolution

On a chilly December day in 2022, Cavalier Johnson stood surrounded by reporters in the lobby of Milwaukee's towering city hall. The city's plucky thirty-five-year-old mayor wanted to "set the record straight," he said. Milwaukee's 2020 Census tally—which found that the city had lost nearly 3 percent of its population over the past decade—had been a severe undercount. According to analyses by the Milwaukee's Departments of City Development and Administration, approximately fifteen thousand eight hundred residents living in the city had not been counted. Whereas the current count placed Milwaukee at its lowest population since 1930, a corrected count would indicate that there had been virtually no population change since 2010. For a city that would soon face an impending structural budget deficit of over $150 million, the consequences of a corrected count were significant. Without a change in census figures, the city alone stood to lose $7 million in federal aid over the next ten years. The city's public schools would lose $14 million.[19]

Milwaukee had lodged its challenge to census figures under the bureau's Count Question Resolution (CQR) program, which provides state and local governments the opportunity to request a review of their housing inventory.[20] Yet however mayors might frame their CQR challenges to the public, the program is *not* an all-purpose tool for responding to undercounts. To understand why, it is worth dwelling a bit on the program's history, which extends back to the heated debate over statistical adjustment in the 1990 Census. In response to a lawsuit filed by the City of New York in 1988,

Secretary of Commerce Robert Mosbacher agreed to reconsider his refusal to follow the Census Bureau's suggestion that he statistically adjust the 1990 Census to correct for differential undercounts. In July of 1991, Mosbacher again refused to perform statistical adjustment. The Census Bureau had prepared for this eventuality by crafting a policy for local officials and other data users to submit questions about their census counts and for the bureau "to correct for underenumeration and overenumeration problems identified by local data users."[21] In dismissing lawsuits challenging 1990 Census procedures, multiple district courts cited the new Count Question Resolution policy as an available alternative to a judicial remedy.[22]

The importance of Count Question Resolution only grew in the decades that followed. One reason for this is that the 1990 Census was the last one in which bureau officials released "preliminary" counts to local officials for review prior to the end of the census year as part of the Postcensus Local Review (PCLR) Program. After receiving their preliminary counts, local review liaisons would have roughly three weeks to provide a response identifying any discrepancies along with supporting documentation, ranging from "tax assessment and utility connection records" to "address lists and locally conducted canvasses." In 1990, the PCLR Program received responses from roughly 25 percent of all government units the bureau contacted, including the country's fifty-one largest cities.[23] Yet while the PCLR Program allowed governments to check for problems prior to the tabulation of state apportionment counts, it also created operational struggles for the bureau. For example, the release of "preliminary count" figures prompted criticism in the media, which forced the bureau to explain that the preliminary counts were, in fact, subject to change. And as bureau officials saw it, the costs outweighed the benefits. Despite revisiting over 20 percent of the country's census blocks, the bureau had only found a small portion of individuals who had been missed.[24]

Census officials did not include the PCLR in their plans for the 2000 count. In their view, the adoption of new census operations, including the Local Update of Census Addresses (LUCA), "obviated the need" for PCLR.[25] By 2000, the bureau had developed the capacity to release daily running tallies of local area response rates down to the level of zip codes. Yet with less than a year to go before field operations, members of Congress attempted to reintroduce the PCLR by force. At the heart of this effort was Rep. Dan Miller (R-FL), the chairman of the House Census Subcommittee. Miller's legislation, the Local Census Quality Check Act, would have required each decennial census to include post-census local review. The Census Bureau's director, Ken Prewitt, loudly protested. As he told *The New York Times*, the legislation would only provide "an incentive for anyone to try to boost their numbers for either economic or political gain."[26] While Miller's bill passed the House on a nearly party line vote, the Senate referred it to committee—effectively killing the proposal.[27]

With the PCLR gone, governments hoping to challenge their census figures had to rely on the Count Question Resolution program. CQR was not a vehicle for solving all identifiable defects in census data, however. For example, the bureau stated that any corrections it made to local population counts could not affect the data products used for congressional apportionment and redistricting. On the positive side, corrections could affect official census figures and inform the population base used in the bureau's annual estimates—which plays a crucial role in the allocation of billions of dollars in federal grants. Still, because the CQR could not be a "continuation of the census," the bureau reasoned that submissions to the program *could not be based on new data.* Nor did the program allow for the correction of errors that occur outside the data processing phase. As Matthew Frates, the chief of the Decennial Census Management Division's CQR Branch, puts it, "Even if a field worker went to a census block . . . and saw an address and listed it in the wrong place, that is not something we can fix in CQR."[28]

Second, governments can only bring forward CQR challenges related to legal boundaries or housing counts. In so-called boundary cases, governments may ask the bureau to correct inaccurate placement of jurisdictional boundaries that were legally in effect as of the year of the census and to reallocate housing counts accordingly. By contrast, in housing count cases, governments may bring a claim that housing units that should have been counted were either missed or geographically mislocated during data processing.

The bar for a successful CQR challenge is thus a high one. New York City's unsuccessful 2010 CQR case provides a useful illustration here. In the boroughs of Brooklyn and Queens, the Census Bureau misclassified many housing units as vacant. This, New York's Department of City Planning suggested, contributed to a significant undercount. New York City's 2010 Census population was 8.175 million, two hundred and twenty-five thousand people short even of the bureau's own population estimate for the city. CQR rules forbade this kind of challenge, however. While the bureau could not accept the challenge, it agreed to examine the anomaly anyway to inform its planning efforts for 2020.[29]

Thus while the CQR program gives governments a critical opportunity to report data errors to the Census Bureau, it is not the remedy for undercounts it might appear to be at first blush. Following the 2010 Census, the bureau reported receiving 238 CQR challenges from the highest elected officials in local governments and one from the state of Massachusetts.[30] The bureau's published case list reports making "changes" to census counts in response to 76 percent of these challenges. This figure overstates the scale of the program's effects on population counts. The bureau lists New York City's response as having resulted in a "change." Yet, the bureau's 2010 errata sheet for the state of New York reveals no changes in the population of any of the city's five boroughs. Overall, the CQR program resulted in a net addition of 527 people to the total US population count.[31]

To be sure, since 1990, the Census Bureau has adopted numerous other quality-improvement operations, such as LUCA, which occur at earlier stages of census implementation. As Frates explained it, the bureau believes that these processes, when combined with a narrowly defined CQR program, were "robust enough and fleshed-out enough" to protect census accuracy.[32] Given the anomalous circumstances of the 2020 Census, however, some state and local officials begged to differ.

After the Census Bureau publicly announced the design of the 2020 CQR program, it received numerous formal requests to expand the scope of the program.[33] One issue that incited complaints was the bureau's increased use of administrative records to determine the vacancy status of households. This, as some local officials reported, increased the risk of false vacancies. In turn, these officials requested that the accuracy of a housing unit's occupancy status be eligible for review under CQR. As noted previously, officials contended that the newly adopted "differential privacy" technique had produced implausible housing occupancy rates at the local level. Why then couldn't the bureau expand CQR to allow local governments to review the accuracy of persons-per-household figures?

The bureau denied all such requests, maintaining that the CQR "cannot be an extension of the decennial enumeration."[34] As a result, even when cities found substantial undercounts, their formal challenges under CQR applied to a far narrower slice of the population they charged that the 2020 Census had missed. Whereas Milwaukee officials cited an undercount of roughly fifteen thousand eight hundred people, for example, its formal challenge focused on 2,394 housing units containing approximately 5,226 people. Milwaukee's evidence on the remaining undercounted population relied primarily on evidence that the bureau had overestimated the city's housing vacancy rate—a subject that falls outside the scope of the CQR. Thus while Mayor Johnson's announcement of the city's undercount may have been dramatic, it did not reflect the content of the formal filing under CQR.[35]

Yet while bureau officials remained averse to altering the CQR program itself, they nevertheless took the concerns submitted by state and local governments seriously. Even if the bureau itself could not legally take actions that might be construed as continuing the 2020 enumeration, it could still collect information that would improve the quality of population data between censuses. So in late November 2021, the bureau announced the creation of the Post-Census Group Quarters Review (PCGQR), a one-time operation that gave state, local, and tribal officials the opportunity to request a review of population counts conducted in group quarters facilities like prisons, military barracks, nursing homes, and college dormitories.[36]

The need for this additional review program was particularly great in college towns like Bloomington, Indiana, home to the main campus of Indiana University (IU).[37] As the census was just getting underway in 2020, the COVID-19 pandemic forced the university to tell its forty-eight thousand students—most of whom were then on spring break—not to return to IU. While the Census Bureau's residence rules require students who reside on campus most of the year to be counted there, the mass exodus of IU students had sewn confusion about this. While IU staff were luckily able to use administrative data to enumerate students who typically resided in dormitories, students residing off campus presented a host of challenges. Due to privacy concerns, universities are often reluctant to give out information about students residing locally off campus. And in some cases, data on off-campus students is simply incomplete. In any event, the confusion augured poorly for Bloomington's census figures. Despite the city's projections of modest population growth between 2010 and 2020, the initial census estimates reflected that the city lost twelve hundred people.[38] As a 2022 Officer of Inspector General report confirmed, problems like these were prevalent in college towns across the country.[39]

The creation of PCGQR at least held out the promise of resolving such problems. Under the program, mayors in cities like Bloomington could submit administrative data as well as other contextual information to address the discrepancies in their group quarters counts.[40] There was one drawback, however. As the bureau noted in its guide to participants, corrections made under the program would *not* lead to revisions in a government's official 2020 Census count. The reason, the bureau explained, was that unlike the Count Question Resolution program, the PCGQR allowed governments to present new data on group quarters populations that were not counted during the 2020 Census. As such, it would not be legal to use these new data to revise an official census count. On the positive side, however, PCGQR data could still be used to update the base the bureau used to revise annual population estimates, which affect federal grant allocations.

Thus post-census review programs like CQR and PCQGR do matter, even if their effects are highly variable. Of 394 government units affected by CQR in 2010, 178 (45 percent) saw population increases no greater than 10 percent. One hundred and sixty-three (41 percent) saw population decreases of no greater than 10 percent.[41] Yet even if these changes may seem insignificant in aggregate, consider that even marginal increases in a municipality's population count can have dramatic effects on its ability to secure aid from state and federal government agencies. While the CQR program for 2020 is not yet complete, preliminary data suggest some illustrative patterns. Consider, for example, the city of Whitewater, Wisconsin, whose initial population count in the 2020 Census was 14,889. The 2020 CQR program resulted in the addition of 1,248 persons to the section of Whitewater located in Jefferson County.[42] This change will result in an increase of over $10,000 per year in supplemental municipal aid from the state of Wisconsin, a program that accounts for nearly 10 percent of the city's entire annual budget.[43]

When population is an important allocation factor in intergovernmental grant programs, the effects for smaller towns that see large increases (or decreases) in aid can be massive. The small town of Whiteville, Tennessee, saw a population increase from 2,606 to 4,564 thanks to the correction of an error that resulted in the misallocation of persons incarcerated in one of the town's two prisons.[44] This 75 percent increase in the town's population netted an additional $167 per person in annual state aid. It is doubtful, of course, that Whiteville's carceral population, which is three times the size of its household population, will benefit from this enhancement of municipal aid payments. In recent years, the town has become emblematic of the phenomenon of "prison gerrymandering," in which small jurisdictions with large carceral populations siphon resources and representation away from urban areas.[45]

The reallocation of incarcerated persons also yielded a population boost for Milwaukee. As a result of a CQR challenge filed by the State of Wisconsin,

811 persons incarcerated at the Milwaukee County Jail who had been erroneously enumerated in the suburban city of Franklin were reallocated to
the city of Milwaukee.[46] Unlike Whiteville, however, the practical effects
of this change in a large metropolitan city were marginal. And what of the
Milwaukee mayor's effort to use the CQR to "set the record straight" on fifteen thousand eight hundred undercounted residents? In July of 2023, the
bureau sent a letter to Milwaukee officials closing its CQR challenge without evaluating evidence related to the claim of a larger undercount. This
was, the mayor's office explained, "not because the city's information was
deemed incorrect, but because federal law prevented its consideration."[47]
Mayoral announcements about 2020 CQR challenges added an element of
political drama to what would otherwise have been a mundane administrative process. Yet it is worth distinguishing between cities' claims about the
full scope of their 2020 undercount from the kinds of claims the bureau will
accept under CQR. As the evidence here suggests, the program has proven
to be a valuable means of correcting census processing errors, yet it is simply not capable of correcting many other kinds of errors that occurred in
2020 and which provided cities like Milwaukee and Detroit with credible
evidence of large undercounts.

Do It Again: Special Censuses

The walls of Diane Marlin's office are lined with pictures of Urbana, Illinois.
Since 1971, the town—which shares the main campus of the University of
Illinois with its twin city Champaign—has been her home. And since 2017,
Marlin—who is now in her seventies—has been Urbana's mayor. Like other
college towns across the country, Urbana was hit with an abrupt and unex-
pected population decline in the spring of 2020—when the COVID-19 pandemic forced large swathes of the town's student population to temporarily
move out of town, just as census enumeration was beginning.[48]

"COVID just slammed us because of the impact on campus," said Marlin, "Plus you had the fear among the immigrant population of participating
in the census." The result was that, whereas the neighboring town of Champaign's population grew substantially between 2010 and 2020, Urbana's
population had shrunk by nearly three thousand people. The mayor was
skeptical that this figure reflected actual demographic trends. "I just can't
believe we lost 7 percent of our population," she said.[49]

Marlin's solution to this problem: Count Urbana again. Since 1903, the Census Bureau has been authorized to conduct "special censuses" at the request of local officials. It conducted the first of these in 1915. By the 1940s, the bureau conducted such counts for some four hundred units of local government. In the decade that followed, that number doubled.[50] One reason for this was rapid change in the landscape of local governments. As new municipalities formed, and as others were annexed or consolidated into larger units of government, their elected leaders needed accurate population data, often well in advance of the next decennial census. Additionally, cities experiencing rapid population growth in the years between decennial censuses wanted to capture the gains that growth would provide, not only in federal and state aid but also in private-sector investment.[51]

In more recent decades, governments requesting a special census have tended to be smaller municipalities, with populations smaller than fifty thousand people. More than half of the special censuses taken since the year 2000 have been "partial" censuses—focused on a designated set of census tracts that officials believe were undercounted.[52] As it happens, this was precisely the sort of count Mayor Marlin was pushing for in Urbana.

While the Census Bureau explicitly advertises the Special Census Program as a means of capturing population growth between censuses, the program may also have benefits for jurisdictions that experienced an undercount. Unlike the CQR program, which does not allow the collection of new data to update census counts, the entire purpose of a special census is to conduct a new enumeration of population, housing units, group quarters, and transitory locations. As with updates made through CQR, changes made by a special census cannot be used in apportionment or redistricting counts. Additionally, as the Census Bureau frequently reminds local officials, special censuses cannot change the results of the 2020 Census. Nevertheless, population changes from special censuses are incorporated into the annual population estimates that are used in determining how intergovernmental aid from the federal and state governments is allocated.[53]

The benefits of a special census, while appreciable, come at a cost. Governments that request a special census must bear the direct financial burdens of carrying out the operation. To be sure, the Census Bureau itself picks up the costs of project management as well as the development of census forms, technologies, and training materials. Yet local governments requesting a special census must set up temporary office space for managing the enumeration and employ new temporary enumerator staff. Local governments must pay for the printing and shipping of any new census materials as well as computer equipment that will be required for the operation. Finally, local governments must subsidize staffing at the Census Bureau's headquarters and regional offices related to the special census, as well as the preparation of new data products.[54]

The cost of conducting a special census varies widely and depends on a range of factors, including on the size of the population and the number of housing units that must be counted as well as the geography to be covered and the rate at which households are expected to self-respond. In the decade following the 2010 Census, the overall costs for local governments requesting a special census ranged from $14,000 to $4 million. For a government requesting enumeration of sixteen hundred housing units, the median cost of a special census was roughly $113,000.[55]

Local officials like Urbana Mayor Diane Marlin must weigh these costs before deciding to pursue a special census. Yet they must also consider the potential benefits of a fresh enumeration. To see why, look no further than the city of Naperville, Illinois, an affluent suburb roughly one hundred miles north of Urbana. Following the 2010 Census, the city's population continued to grow in ways that local officials believed were not captured in the Census Bureau's annual population estimates. As a result, the city was missing out on millions in shared revenue from the state. By 2017, Naperville's city council had unanimously adopted a plan for the Census Bureau to conduct a partial special census, focused on fifty-eight census blocks where housing had recently been built. While some residents initially balked at the price tag for the new count—which came to over $200,000—officials at the city's planning department countered with evidence of their own. Assuming that the special census found 4,650 new residents, Naperville would receive an additional $1.6 million increase in state aid payments— a seven-to-one return on investment. As it happened, the special census found an additional 5,988 Naperville residents, over a thousand more than the city had projected. With the new count, the city expected to receive over $2.38 million in state aid by 2021.[56]

For officials in Naperville, conducting a special census was an easy sell. First, the city's planning department could be reasonably certain—given recent trends in housing construction—that the city's population would increase relative to annual population estimates. Second, given that Naperville typically has census response rates that are significantly higher than the national average, officials could also be confident that the special census would not produce a severe undercount. In areas with higher rates of self-response, the cost of conducting a special census is also typically lower than areas where households must be contacted multiple times before they respond. Third, because population growth had occurred in a few specific areas where new construction had occurred, the city could further reduce its costs by conducting a partial census rather than a full enumeration of the entire city.

Would a special census have the same return on investment for larger cities like Detroit? To answer this question, we must first consider whether a special census might generate a more accurate count of the city's population when compared to the 2020 Census. If the 2020 undercount of Detroit were due exclusively to the publicity of the Trump administration's proposed citizenship question or pandemic-related departures from the city, the answer to this question might be a cautious "yes." Yet the evidence is far more complicated on both counts. For one thing, Detroit has a far smaller foreign-born and noncitizen resident population than other cities like Phoenix and Miami, which saw comparable population decreases between 2019 and 2020. Additionally, while most large cities in the Northeast and the Midwest saw at least some pandemic-related population decline, Detroit's population decrease was an order of magnitude larger.[57]

In short, simply "rerunning" the 2020 Census in 2024 might not produce gains in population-driven federal and state aid. Rather, a special census would have to address other problems that contributed to the city's 2020 undercount. This includes the role of the "digital divide" in shaping census participation. While the 2020 Census was the first to use internet-based self-response, households in wide swaths of Detroit—which has been called one of the "least connected" metropolitan cities in the United States report limited internet access.[58] Ideally, a special census would take this into consideration when designing a self-response option. Yet the 2020 Special Census Program employs a self-response methodology that intentionally parallels the one used in the 2020 Census. An internet self-response period is followed by a series of four mailings followed by field enumeration. If connectivity was a significant barrier to census participation in Detroit, a new count with the same outreach techniques might simply replicate the problem.

Another reason for Detroit's 2020 undercount has to do with the completeness of the bureau's Master Address File. Residential housing counts produced by the Census Bureau between 2010 and 2020 reveal a startling anomaly. Between 2010 and 2019, the American Community Survey's estimates of residential housing units in Detroit hover around three hundred and sixty thousand, with little change. Then, in 2020, there is an abrupt change. The 2020 Census counted only 309,913 housing units, an impossibly sharp 13.8 percent drop in residential housing stock from 2019. As part of Detroit's research for its CQR submission, researchers at the University of Michigan investigated this anomaly. According to their visual audit, the 2020 Census undercounted the number of housing units on nearly 70 percent of the census blocks they surveyed. The researchers concluded that the Census Bureau missed 11.8 percent of the residential housing units located on these blocks. Thus, to remedy Detroit's undercount, a special census would need an address listing operation that represents a significant improvement over the 2020 operation.[59]

Assuming these problems could be remedied, a special census for a city like Detroit would still be expensive. Even if the city opted for a partial special census limited to an eighth of the city's hardest-to-count households, a conservative estimate suggests that the costs could exceed $3.5 million.[60] That figure could also be far higher, given that self-response rates in Detroit are lower than the national average.[61] In Detroit, which declared bankruptcy just over a decade ago, finding the resources to support a special census—regardless of its benefits—might be difficult. According to one independent analysis of the city's finances, following the resumption of pension payments to city employees, Detroit is likely to face an $11 million baseline budget gap, starting in fiscal year 2027.[62] As of 2024, Detroit had not formally declared an intention to pursue a special census. Indeed, the combination of unlikely outcomes and high costs led local officials to pursue other means of responding to the city's undercount.

Challenging Population Estimates

A third administrative venue states and local governments can use to respond to flawed census data is the Population Estimates Challenge Program (PECP). Since the 1940s, the Census Bureau has produced annual population estimates for every state. With the growth of federal grants-in-aid to state and local governments—which made population a central factor in funding formulas—the demand for up-to-date population data only grew. Perhaps most importantly, the State and Local Fiscal Assistance Act of 1972—which created general revenue sharing payments to over thirty-six thousand units of local government—required updated population estimates for over thirty-six thousand units of local government. Thus, when Congress revised the Census Act in 1976, it required the publication of annual estimates of population for all states, counties, and local units of general-purpose government with populations over fifty thousand. As the other post-census programs, these estimates cannot affect apportionment or redistricting yet nevertheless become official population figures used in the allocation of federal (and often state) funds.[63]

To produce annual population estimates, Census Bureau demographers use what is known as the "cohort-component" method. Starting with population base, they use vital statistics to add in births and subtract deaths from the population.[64] Then, employing a mix of administrative data from federal agencies, they estimate both net migration to the United States as well as domestic migration within the country. The result is an updated population estimate for the current year or what the Census Bureau refers to as the "vintage year."

The process is far harder than it sounds, and the Census Bureau relies on the assistance of state-level officials to make it happen. Following a 1966 meeting hosted by the National Governor's Conference (now the National Governors Association) and the Council of State Governments to draw attention to the need for updated population figures, Census Bureau employees and state officials began hammering out a formal agreement to coordinate the preparation of population estimates for state and local governments. Through the arrangement—dubbed the Federal-State Cooperative for Population Estimates (FSCPE)—state agencies provide vital statistics and information about the population living in group quarters like nursing homes and college dormitories. The Census Bureau then combines these statistics with data from federal sources, like tax records and Social Security files, to produce population estimates. State agencies can then review and comment on preliminary estimates before they are published.

The bureau has historically allowed governments to challenge estimates produced through this program if they possessed evidence that their populations deviated from those produced by the bureau.[65] Government officials interested in filing a challenge first request a document known as a derivation sheet, which contains the components the Census Bureau uses to prepare population estimates for their jurisdiction. Officials who find problems with these estimates then submit a formal challenge letter along with data to support their claims.[66] The bureau's Population Estimates Challenge Team then reviews these data for usability, completeness, and consistency before forwarding them on to the Estimates and Projections Area "input teams" for further review. After collecting reviews and recommendations from these teams, the Challenge Team presents them to the Estimates and Projections Area Change Control Board, whose members recommend approval or rejection of the challenge to the Population Division chief and associate director for Demographic Programs.

Until 2013, the bureau accepted a wide range of data to support these challenges. For example, between 2001 and 2008, cities and towns could submit property tax records and data on public utility connections as evidence of population growth. But that changed. When the bureau revised the program following a temporary suspension for the 2010 Census, some senior bureau officials expressed concerns about the reliability of the data governments had been submitting. For example, as one official reported, evaluations of data submitted to the bureau suggested that public utility records were of highly variable quality when it came to measuring population growth. By contrast, these officials came to believe that administrative data on births, deaths, and migration were, broadly speaking, far more accurate.[67]

In 2012, the Census Bureau proposed a tighter set of regulations governing population estimates challenges. Under the new rules, the bureau would only consider challenges where "evidence provided identifies the use of incorrect data, processes, or calculations in these estimates."[68] This meant that officials could only support their challenges with administrative records of the same kind used by the bureau when preparing their estimates. For example, under the new rule, subcounty governments could only submit data on public utility connections and property taxes as "corroborating evidence." Similarly, counties were prohibited from using permitting data and encouraged instead to rely on statistics covering births, deaths, and immigration.

Perhaps unsurprisingly, state and local officials expressed serious concerns with the proposed changes.[69] Jack Baker, New Mexico's FSCPE representative at the time, insisted that "the policy flies in the face of all available scientific evidence as well as good judgment." While Baker agreed that the pre-2010 rules were "overly-accepting of challenges," the new methodology was far too restrictive. Suppose, Baker suggested, that officials in Bernalillo County saw the bureau's estimate and, based on housing-unit data they knew to be more accurate, believed it was too low. In 2009, for example, housing-unit data suggested that the county's population was 664,000, "well above the bureau's Vintage 2009 estimate of 642,527 persons." Under the new challenge process, Baker contended, the county would "find no recourse for discussing an estimate that existing information and research clearly suggests is in need of reconsideration."[70]

In its response to critics like Baker, bureau officials maintained that internal research and evaluation revealed that accepting challenges that relied on housing-unit data of the sort he suggested would lead to population estimates that were more biased than those based on administrative records alone. Moreover, it was not possible—the bureau argued—to "identify a clear-cut means" for deciding when the housing-unit method for population estimation would "yield a more accurate estimate."[71] In the absence of such a decision rule, the bureau was compelled to push forward with its changes.

Tightening the rules had two major consequences. First, the number of successful challenges to population estimates dropped. For vintage years 2001 to 2008, the bureau had accepted three hundred challenges. Following the adoption of the changes—for vintage years 2012 through 2018—it accepted only eighteen. Second, the effects of the program on population estimates shrank. For challenges submitted in vintage years 2001 to 2008, the average accepted population estimates challenge resulted in an adjustment of 9 percent. As table 6.2a shows, the largest changes occurred in small communities of under one hundred thousand, which saw a population increase of nearly 13 percent. By contrast, in the years following the change, the average accepted challenge resulted in a population increase of less than 2 percent (see table 6.2b).

By 2021, cities like Detroit had fewer opportunities to use alternate data sources to challenge the bureau's annual population estimates. Yet the uniquely problematic character of the 2020 Census complicated matters even further. For one thing, population estimates staff experienced problems simply getting the challenge program off the ground. Typically, the bureau suspends the challenge program during the period of census data collection and processing. During the suspension, the program's staff are occupied conducting the demographic analysis of census results.[72] In its 2020 suspension rule, the bureau announced that it expected to resume the challenge program in 2022. Yet this did not happen. Due to the operational delays caused by the COVID-19 pandemic, program staff did not

Table 6.2a. Population Changes Resulting from Population Estimates
Challenge Program, Before 2013 Rules Change (Vintage Years 2001–2008)

Population	Avg. Pop. Change	Avg. % Change
<100,000	2,130	12.90%
≥100,000 and <500,000	8,755	3.64%
≥500,000 and <1 million	19,852	2.85%
≥1 million	29,140	1.49%
All Communities	7,507	9.14%

Table 6.2b. Population Changes Resulting from Population Estimates
Challenge Program, After 2013 Rules Change (Vintage Years 2012–2018)

Population	Avg. Pop. Change	Avg. % Change
<100,000	630	2.10%
≥100,000 and <500,000	2,854	1.40%
≥500,000 and <1 million	4,394	0.67%
≥1 million	29,140	1.33%
All Communities	1,209	1.89%

Source: Author's analysis of US Census Bureau, "Population Estimates Challenge
Program, Challenge Results," accessed March 24, 2023, https://www.census.gov
/programs-surveys/popest/about/challenge-program/results.html.
Note: For all communities and for each subgroup, the difference in average percent
change between the two periods is statistically significant at the $p < 0.05$ level.

have access to the data on the 2020 population base until June 24, 2021, six months after they typically receive it. Whereas program staff intended to complete local population estimates by the fall of 2021, they would now be delayed until the spring of 2022.[73] At roughly the same time, the bureau began to experience vacancies in the Local Government Estimates and Migration Processing Branch, whose staff oversee challenges to population estimates.[74] By February 2022, the bureau announced that it would not resume the program until 2023.[75] This made it impossible for governments to challenge the population estimates issued for vintage year 2021.

Beyond the delay, officials in cities like Detroit saw another problem on the horizon: the results of the 2020 Census.[76] When making population estimates for the current year, demographers must begin with data from the prior year in the time series as a population base. Thus, if a decennial census undercounts a city by a significant margin, that undercount is "baked in" to every subsequent year's population estimates. This was especially problematic for regions that experienced significant migration and displacement during the pandemic. Even so, the challenge program's rules do not allow governments to contest the base itself, only the "year-over-year" components of population change.[77]

Census officials were aware of the ramifications of a flawed census count for population estimates. In response to numerous operational challenges in enumeration and data processing, staff at the Population Estimates Program developed what they called a "blended" population base, which integrated three separate sources of data. This included 2020 population counts from the 2020 Census Redistricting File, age and sex estimates from the 2020 Demographic Analysis, and race and ethnicity data for the entire country, as well as states and counties, from 2010-based population estimates, updated through 2020. For example, using demographic analysis estimates for age and sex helped to alleviate the undercount of young children. As demographers Susana Quiros and William O'Hare note, there are 379,183 more young Hispanic children (ages zero to four) in the blended base than there are in the 2020 Census count—a difference of 7.6 percent.[78]

Population Estimates Program staff argued that changes to the population base should not be made in haste but should instead rely on careful research. To carry out this research, census officials formed the Base Evaluation and Research Team (BERT). Led by Christine Hartley, assistant division chief for Estimates and Projections, BERT began meeting in March 2022. At the same time, nongovernmental organizations like the Coalition on Human Needs and the Partnership for America's Children—both of which target their advocacy toward improving the undercount of young children and communities of color—expressed dismay with the pace of the research, insisting that BERT release a timeline for how their research would inform decisions in the program.[79]

The anomalies contained in the 2020 Census also called into question the rules governing the challenge program. As officials in cities like Detroit pointed out, the narrow restrictions adopted in 2013 would prevent them from bringing forward data that would clearly confirm the city had been undercounted. This included data from the US Postal Service's Delivery Sequence File and a canvass of residential housing units that showed undercounts in some tracts that were as high as 22 percent.[80] At the same time, other census stakeholders urged the bureau to proceed with caution. The most prominent of these was the Committee on Population Statistics, a prestigious group of scientists from the Population Association of America. As the members of the committee saw it, allowing challenges based on a wide variety of data might improve accuracy in some cases but created new threats to data integrity and would stretch the bureau's administrative capacity. Given the cost of collecting and preparing this data, it might also unfairly disadvantage jurisdictions without the resources to file a successful challenge.

Additionally, the committee pointed out, even if all challenges led to greater estimation accuracy in a local jurisdiction, this could cause problems for estimates elsewhere. For example, if a county's population estimate were revised upward by ten thousand, the state population estimate could only be maintained by reducing other counties' population estimates by the same amount, potentially introducing new county-level estimation errors. The alternative to this approach—allowing state population totals to drift upward—would introduce new errors at the state level.[81]

In the face of these competing concerns, census officials proceeded cautiously. In its amended regulations for the PECP, published in March 2023, the bureau announced that it was "open to expanding the scope of the Challenge Program where science indicates that such changes support more accurate estimates and ensure equity for all general-purpose governmental units and the public." It would also consider "alternative data sources, including administrative records, and methodologies for estimates production."[82] By that point, however, Detroit had already launched a fight against its population estimates in federal court.

Population Estimates and the Allure of Post-Census Litigation

Despite the range of administrative options for challenging census counts and population estimates, state and local officials may nevertheless find a reason to engage in "venue shifting"—strategically moving the debate out of the Census Bureau and into another arena of conflict. After all, administrative programs like CQR and PECP are governed by rules that sharply limit the kinds of challenges governments can bring and the data they can use to support these challenges. And while special censuses offer governments a chance for a do-over, they may be prohibitively costly for fiscally constrained jurisdictions. Since special censuses must use the same procedures as the prior decennial census, they may also be ineffective at correcting errors that were the product of those procedures. Perhaps most importantly, these programs may not offer the kind of relief governments seek. Neither corrected census counts nor special census data can be used to reapportion Congress or redraw legislative maps. Similarly, if the bureau suspends one of these programs and governments lose the ability to file a challenge, there is no obvious way to recover federal or state funding that may have been lost as a result.

In the face of these barriers, can governments successfully pursue their post-census claims in court? On the surface, post-census litigation may appear to be a "lighter lift" when compared to pre-census challenges. Whereas pre-census litigants must establish standing by alleging a harm that is likely to occur in the future, post-census litigants can point to concrete evidence of undercounts and their effects on congressional apportionment and the allocation of federal aid. Moreover, as the Supreme Court held in *Utah v. Evans* (2002), there is no clear statutory or constitutional prohibition on remedying harms caused by census undercounts. Nor, the Court reasoned, is there a legal barrier on relief simply because it may be difficult for the Census Bureau to provide.[83]

Yet just because courts *can* provide relief does not guarantee a successful outcome. As in the lawsuits we saw in chapters 2 and 5, post-census challengers must establish that the Census Bureau's actions have caused a "concrete and particularized injury" that is redressable by the court.[84] The bar is high. For example, when the Census Bureau announced that it would not be able to release redistricting data to state legislatures until September 2021—well into redistricting season—the state of Ohio sued for a writ of mandamus, "ordering the United States Secretary of Commerce to provide the State with redistricting data by March 31, 2021." Yet the District Court soon dismissed the case because the relief Ohio sought was not available—since the bureau was still processing the data and would not be finished by any new deadline a court was likely to impose. Further, because the state constitution allowed the state legislature to use other data sources to carry out redistricting if census data was not available, the state could not claim "injury in fact."[85]

Even when plaintiffs are successful on their standing claim, post-census litigation can fail in other ways. Courts can also dismiss cases that are not

subject to judicial review. Under the Administrative Procedure Act (APA)—
a common vehicle for post-census challenges—courts can only review
agency actions if a separate statute, like the Census Act, authorizes it to do
so or if the agency's action is final—marking the end of a decision-making
process—and "there is no other adequate remedy in a court."[86] Additionally, only "discrete" agency actions are reviewable. In other words, plaintiffs
cannot bring lawsuits in order to make "generalized grievances" or broad
requests that requires courts force the agency to improve its performance.[87]
For example, plaintiffs in the citizenship question case from 2019 could not
file suit until Secretary of Commerce Wilbur Ross issued a final decision
memo instating the citizenship item on the 2020 Census questionnaire. Nor
could they file suit to force Ross to alter his approach to managing the census in general.[88]

Not all discrete and final agency actions can be challenged, however.
For example, courts cannot review agency actions that Congress has committed to the agency's discretion.[89] Over the last few decades, the Supreme
Court has identified numerous circumstances in which this rule applies,
either because statutes provide insufficient guidance on how to adjudicate
agency actions or because agency actions require a "complex balancing of
multiple factors" that only an agency's experts could perform. Additionally, courts can only review agency actions if they have a "sufficiently direct
and immediate impact on the aggrieved party and a direct effect on [its]
day-to-day business."[90] If the government's actions harm a plaintiff only indirectly, through affecting the behavior of a third party, APA review may be
precluded.

Finally, plaintiffs must challenge agency actions at the right time. The
APA bars plaintiffs from suing agencies over decisions that are more than
six years old. Similarly, plaintiffs cannot challenge agency decisions before
their effects are clear. As the Supreme Court held in *Trump v. New York*
(2020), it had no jurisdiction to review a presidential memorandum where
the effects on funding for local governments were highly certain—a fact
that required "contingencies and speculation that impede judicial review."[91]

Only if plaintiffs can prove standing and clear these "justiciability" hur-
dles do courts even need to reach the legal merits of a case. Here, too, the
path to victory is a narrow one. Except for the Constitution's requirement
that the census be an "actual enumeration," courts have generally given
Congress broad discretion over the content and operations of the count.
And aside from Title 13's explicit prohibition on statistical sampling in the

production of decennial census data, courts have accorded the same deference to the executive branch's interpretation of the Census Act. Practically speaking, this means that plaintiffs must lean heavily on the APA's restrictions on actions that are "arbitrary and capricious" and "contrary to law." As we saw in chapter 2, however, a recent string of precedents has significantly narrowed its interpretation of these provisions.

There is perhaps no better example of the challenges of post-census litigation than the lawsuit filed by the city of Detroit in 2022. The origins of the lawsuit stretch back to May of that year, when the Census Bureau released its 2021 population estimates. Mayor Duggan, already furious about the 2020 undercount, now discovered to his surprise that the new estimate reflected an additional decrease of over seven thousand people relative to the 2020 count. In August, Duggan emailed the bureau's Christine Hartley to formally launch a challenge to the estimates. The day after Duggan's email, however, Hartley responded by noting that the Challenge Program had been suspended and that she could not accept challenges to the 2021 estimates. The next month, Detroit filed suit in the eastern district of Michigan. By December, the city had requested a preliminary injunction directing the Census Bureau to consider its challenge to the 2021 population estimates immediately.[92]

The city made several major allegations in its filings. First, it charged that by extending its suspension of the Challenge Program, the bureau had violated the Administrative Procedure Act. On the one hand, the decision was "contrary to law" because it contradicted both the federal regulations outlining the Challenge Program and the statute that required the creation of population estimates. The decision to suspend the program also constituted an "arbitrary and capricious" abuse of the bureau's discretion as well as an "unreasonable delay" of action that violated Congress's command that the bureau produce annual population estimates for units of general local government with a population of fifty thousand or more "for every year between each decennial census."[93]

Second, Detroit alleged that several other decisions about the Challenge Program were arbitrary and capricious too. This included the bureau's decision not to consider evidence about flaws in the 2020 population base and its refusal to consider alternative sources of "clear and convincing" data, such as data from utility companies. Further, echoing claims made by state and local officials elsewhere, Detroit found fault with the bureau's "county cap" rule. Under this rule, the total population of subcounty areas like cities and towns cannot—when summed up—exceed the population estimate for the county in which they are located. Thus if a challenge submitted by one municipality results in a population increase, there must be a corresponding decrease in the population of other municipalities in the county so that the population "cap" is not exceeded. In Detroit's view, this arbitrarily hindered an accurate count of the city's population.

Finally, Detroit alleged that the bureau's failure to correct the city's undercount in the 2021 population estimates was a violation of the Fifth Amendment's guarantee of equal protection under the law. At the heart of this claim was the racially disparate nature of the undercount. As the Post-Enumeration Survey had shown, the 2020 Census substantially undercounted the Black and Hispanic populations while overcounting the white population (see table 6.1). The bureau's refusal to revise these figures, which deprived the city of federal funds, thus had a "disparate impact" on the city's predominantly Black and Hispanic population.

In January of 2023, the Commerce Department moved to dismiss the suit as well as Detroit's request for a preliminary injunction.[94] The department argued that each one of the city's claims was deficient. First, Detroit did not have standing to bring the suit. Among other things, it had not demonstrated exactly how the bureau's 2021 population estimates had deprived the city of federal funds and how much a change in population would be necessary before those funds were restored. Detroit's lawyers replied that they did not need to go into great detail to demonstrate what was obviously true: "The amount of federal funds that Detroit receives is tied directly to the Census Bureau's population estimates. An estimate that is too low results in too little funding."[95]

Second, the Commerce Department argued that the city's claims were not justiciable because they were not challenges to a "discrete and final" agency rule. In one instance, Detroit had challenged a filing that was not a rule at all but an announcement on the bureau's website that the Challenge Program would be delayed until 2023. The city disagreed, claiming that even though the bureau had not *called* the announcement a "rule," it nevertheless satisfied the APA's definition of one. It was, after all, an "agency statement" describing the agency's "procedures" and "practice requirements." In another case, Detroit contested a notice in the *Federal Register* announcing that the bureau was restarting the Challenge Program but that it would not accept challenges to data for vintage year 2021. As the Commerce Department saw it, this was not a final agency action with binding legal consequences because it simply described the "*existing* state of the Population Estimates Challenge Program." Detroit pushed back, arguing that the announcement did nothing less than "preclude the City's legal right to request review of its 2021 population estimate."[96]

A third key point of contention was whether the Census Bureau's decision to suspend the Challenge Program was "committed to agency discretion by law" and thus immune to judicial review. Detroit's filings told a relatively simple story here. Congress had given the Census Bureau broad discretion on whether to create the Challenge Program. Yet when the bureau codified that program into Title 15 of the Code of Federal Regulations, it empowered courts to review whether the agency was acting in accordance with its own regulations. The Commerce Department countered that nothing in these regulations guaranteed a "clear right of relief" for the city. Nor did the rules establish an "unequivocal command" for the bureau to maintain the Challenge Program in the years between censuses; indeed, the bureau routinely suspended during the years surrounding the census.

Finally, there was the issue of timing. As the Commerce Department argued, several of Detroit's claims came about four years too late. The APA's six-year window for raising a challenge to the bureau's 2013 rules governing the Challenge Program—including the kinds of data cities could bring forward—had closed in 2019. At the same time, the department argued that Detroit had filed its suit too *early* since the Census Bureau was currently considering comments from the public about how to improve the Challenge Program. Yet as Detroit pointed out, it was not challenging any *proposed* rules, only the existing Challenge Program. It had not missed the window, however, because the clock only started ticking once the city had been aggrieved. It could not have brought the suit prior to being injured by what it claimed were erroneous 2021 population estimates.

The Commerce Department was no less skeptical when it came to the merits of Detroit's suit, and the city was no less ready to defend itself. Yet the department's most forceful arguments could arguably be found in its motion to dismiss Detroit's preliminary injunction. Even if the city had "carried its burden on all of the other factors," the department argued, a preliminary injunction would be "contrary to the public interest."[97] Its reasoning was grounded in the current state of play at the bureau. Honoring Detroit's request would require "the immediate processing of challenges to the Vintage 2021 estimates," which would in turn "disrupt or derail a variety of important Census Bureau functions," including both the production of the vintage

2022 estimates as well as the reestablishment of the Population Estimates Challenge Program.[98] Handing Detroit a legal victory would thus have the practical effect of causing more delay and chaos in producing population estimates, which would harm both Detroit and other units of government that depended on them. But as the city's lawyers saw it, the bureau's own decisions on staffing and program management were no excuse for failing to follow the law.[99]

By late March of 2023, the writing was on the wall for Detroit. In a brief opinion, Judge Robert Cleland dismissed the city's motion for a preliminary injunction against the Census Bureau.[100] As Cleland saw it, bureau officials had no clear duty to respond to Detroit's challenge. Most importantly, after carefully reviewing Bureau regulations Detroit had cited, he could find no "unambiguous right" for the city to have its 2021 population estimates challenged immediately. Because the bureau had created the PCEP under a wide delegation of authority from Congress, Detroit's search for relief for the courts would be in vain. Several days after Cleland issued his order, Detroit stipulated to the dismissal of the case.[101]

From Litigation to Legislation?

The fate of Detroit's post-census litigation contained an important lesson for local governments seeking to contest their 2020 Census figures in federal court. As long as the Census Bureau retains broad discretion over its post-census review processes, and as long as Congress does not intervene to change this, the likelihood of obtaining effective judicial relief is slim. Even in these circumstances, however, adversarial litigation can still be useful. As we saw in chapter 2, even before a single opinion is issued, a lawsuit can alter the dynamics of census politics. Through public hearings and document discovery, census lawsuits can—among other things to their credit—draw greater attention to threats to data quality that might otherwise be overlooked. Lawsuits' ability to influence policy outside of the courtroom, however, hinges on whether they elicit decisive action from other key decision-makers. In the case of the census, that means bureau officials and the members of Congress who oversee them.

One significant barrier Detroit faced in pressing its case was that the relief it sought would have had significant ramifications for rules that the Census Bureau had already finalized. Bureau officials, as we have seen, were aware of the problems with the census data raised in Detroit's complaint. They were also conscious of how programs like CQR and PECP limited their ability to respond to anomalies that cities like Detroit had identified. On the one hand, the bureau had long interpreted Title 13 to prohibit altering census counts based on data gathered after enumeration and data processing had concluded. Even in cases where Congress had given the bureau broader discretion to act, the organization's culture, reinforced by external data integrity standards, emphasized that programmatic changes should happen slowly, and only after extensive research and analysis. Thus, rather than quickly altering the PECP's rules in response to 2020 Census anomalies, the bureau formed a research team to evaluate potential changes to its methodology for preparing population estimates. Census officials maintained they were open to altering this methodology but only after scientific review and analysis and not at the pace Detroit demanded.[102]

Thus, short of a court order, a lawsuit alone was unlikely to compel the Census Bureau to swiftly respond to Detroit's demands, whatever their merits. If they wanted relief, Detroit's leaders would have to turn their attention to Congress, which created the Census Bureau, controls its budget, and conducts legislative oversight.

The Census Bureau is no stranger to congressional oversight. Much of what we know about the organizational turmoil the Census Bureau experienced under the Trump administration comes from extensive reports prepared by the Government Accountability Office, the congressional agency responsible for auditing, evaluating, and investigating executive agencies, which complement the work of the Commerce Department's Office of Inspector General.[103] These reports signaled to Congress, journalists, and the public the numerous risks threats to the integrity of the count brought on by the Trump administration's mismanagement of census operations.[104]

Congressional committees are routinely briefed on Census Bureau activities, but to what extent can they translate this information into action? As the dotted line in figure 6.3 shows, congressional oversight hearings on the census peaked in the infamously troubled 1980 cycle. Yet even as the raw number of oversight hearings has waned even in recent years, Congress has still managed to respond when audits or investigations reveal major problems in decennial census operations, as they did prior to the 2020 Census. It helps, of course, if congressional committees are controlled by a political party with the incentive to fulfill legislative oversight responsibilities.

Congress has been far less likely, however, to enact legislation that alters

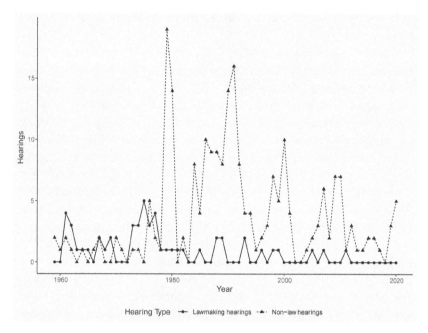

Figure 6.3: Congressional hearings on the census and statistics, 1959–2020. Source: Author's analysis of Comparative Agendas Project at the University of Texas at Austin, 2023, accessed March 24, 2023, www.comparativeagendas .net.

Census Bureau rules once they have been made. As one indicator of this, consider the solid line in figure 6.3, which represents the number of *lawmaking* hearings related to the census. In recent years, this number has dropped to zero. It would be tempting to explain the relative absence of census reforms by pointing to Title 13 itself, which gives the Commerce Department wide discretion over the census. Even so, the last thirty years have been defined by clashes between the legislative and executive branches over census content and procedures. Nevertheless, comprehensive legislative changes to the decennial census have grown exceedingly rare. One reason for this is that proposed changes to census procedures have been caught in the yawning chasm of partisan polarization in Congress. Between 1950 and 1980, the average margin of victory on census-related roll-call votes was over 40 percent. In the last decade, that average has fallen to just over 6 percent.[105] Even proposals to alter census procedures that do not die in committee or on the floor of the House are often "dead on arrival" in the Senate.

Another important resource Duggan lacked was the support of a broad, cross-cutting coalition in favor of the changes he sought. And in the absence of sustained pressure from a broad, cross-cutting coalition, it is unlikely that Congress will take action to remediate that undercount's effects. Major intergovernmental organizations such as the National League of Cities did not immediately pursue advocacy efforts along these lines. Thus while Duggan's advocacy had helped to convince Senator Gary Peters to host Census Bureau Director Robert Santos for a visit in Detroit, it did not result in effective congressional pressure to modify the PECP.[106] In September of 2022, Democrats in the House of Representatives shepherded through the Ensuring a Fair and Accurate Census Act, which aimed to insulate the decennial census from legislative interference.[107] If passed, the legislation would have required that the Census Bureau director could only be fired in cases of "neglect of duty" or "malfeasance in office." It would also have vested the director with control over "all technical, operational, and statistical decisions" at the bureau and set tighter limits on the kinds of individuals a president could appoint to be a deputy director. Finally, the legislation would have given Congress greater oversight over census operations by explicitly prohibiting changes to the census that were not formally reported to Congress well in advance and requiring presidential budgets to include costs for a census over a five-year life cycle. Yet the bill, which passed on a party-line vote in the House, received no subsequent action in the Senate during Congress's lame-duck session. When Republicans again took control of the House in 2023, the bill was effectively dead.[108]

Where structural changes to the Census Bureau failed, however, more robust financing for the 2030 Census succeeded. In their 2022 year-end budget package, Democrats succeeded in appropriating an impressive $1.4 billion for the Census Bureau.[109] This included funds designated specifically for "promotion, outreach, and marketing activities" that census advocates like Senator Peters would help to reduce the likelihood of a 2030 undercount in cities like Detroit. This was by no means the relief mayors like Mike Duggan had asked for. Yet it nevertheless illustrated that Congress, even if divided, was capable of learning at least one lesson from 2020: In the absence of adequate resources, larger undercounts are guaranteed.

Confronting the Trade-Offs: The Battle
over Differential Privacy

Despite new congressional investments for 2030, Detroit's attempt to alter its census counts ended in a resounding defeat thanks to at least two formidable obstacles. First, in preparing the challenge, the city's officials had acted on their *own*, without the resources, legal expertise, or political leverage of the intergovernmental coalitions we saw in chapter 2. Second, Detroit could not win the game under the existing rules. Rather, to prevail, the city had to compel the bureau to make changes to program rules it had already laid down.

By contrast,state and local officials appeared to have more success when they were capable of acting collectively and challenging bureau decisions that had not yet been finalized. There is no better example of this than how state and local users of census data influenced the tug of war between accuracy and privacy in the 2020 Census.

Among all the controversies that emerged during the 2020 cycle, the battle over the bureau's adoption of what is called "differential privacy" may be the most technically complex. Yet it has its roots in the Census Bureau's bedrock commitment to protecting confidential information. As one 2020 flyer puts it: "Your responses to the 2020 Census are safe, secure, and protected by federal law. Your answers can only be used to produce statistics—they cannot be used against you in any way. By law, all responses to U.S. Census Bureau household and business surveys are kept completely confidential."[110]

While such messaging might have felt especially significant in light of the Trump administration's crackdown on undocumented immigrants, the Census Bureau's commitment to confidentiality has deep roots. To encourage participation in the 1910 census—the first decennial count taken after the creation of the US Census Bureau—President William Howard Taft assured the public that there was "no fear that any disclosure will be made regarding any individual person or his affairs."[111] At the time, however, legal protections against the disclosure of individual census information were minimal; legislation enacted by Congress in 1909 required confidentiality for economic data, not population data. Thus, during the First World War, the bureau released individual census records to aid in military conscription. And while Congress enacted additional protections on the confidentiality of individual census responses in the 1929 Census Act, these were effectively overridden during the Second World War. In the 1942 War Powers Act, Congress gave the secretary of commerce the authority to release census records to aid in the war effort, authority that was swiftly used to assist in the internment of Japanese Americans under Executive Order 9066. Yet in 1954, seven years after the War Powers Act expired, Congress codified and clarified earlier privacy protections in Title 13 of the US code, which prohibited census officials from making "any publication whereby the data furnished by any particular establishment or individual under this title can be identified" or permitting "anyone other than the sworn officers and employees of the Department or bureau or agency thereof to examine the individual reports."[112]

Making good on these commitments has required the Census Bureau to adapt to evolving threats to privacy and confidentiality. The 1954 legislation was arguably a response to the possibility that census officials would be strong-armed into providing other government agencies with data from census records. Yet in the decades that followed the creation of Title 13, new threats emerged. As the bureau began to produce an array of new data products featuring census results for smaller and smaller geographical areas, new computing technologies made it possible to disclose individual information *indirectly*. Briefly, this could occur by matching fine-grained demographic data at the census block level with personal information contained in commercially available data sets. As new threats emerged, the census officials responded by updating what is known as the Disclosure Avoidance System (DAS). For decades the Bureau had adopted a policy of suppressing data in cells or entire tables in census geographies containing small numbers of persons or housing units. Yet innovations to bolster confidentiality often came at the cost of data usability. Suppressing cells, after all, meant missing data. With each passing decade, the bureau performed a delicate balancing act. By the 1990s, census officials had abandoned suppression in favor of new techniques that would enhance data usability while effectively "blurring" household data that might allow for disclosure. This included, among a number of techniques, both "data swapping"—exchanging data between households in different locations that have similar characteristics—as well as the "blank and impute" technique, which identifies census records that have "outlier" data that might make them easy to identify, erases the outlier values, and replaces them with a response based on a statistical imputation.[113]

While the balancing act between confidentiality and usability has continued unabated, the bureau's approach to disclosure avoidance made a significant shift in the 2020 cycle.[114] The impetus for this shift was a simulation exercise, conducted by the bureau in 2018, which took the form of a "reconstruction attack" in which census tabulations were combined with commercially available data to identify specific individuals. The results of the exercise revealed that 17 percent of the US population could be correctly identified.[115] Census officials reasoned that maintaining the current iteration of the DAS was thus a violation of Title 13.[116] By year's end, the bureau had announced that it would update the DAS using a technique known as differential privacy.

Developed by a team of computer scientists in 2006—and strongly advocated by the Census Bureau's Chief Scientist John Abowd, who had first read about the research while on the economics faculty at Cornell—the differential privacy approach differs in some important respects from earlier approaches to disclosure avoidance.[117] Specifically, it aims to protect confidentiality not by suppressing cells or swapping data but by injecting random statistical noise—that is, error—into census tabulations. This, as one bureau guide explains, "[obscures] the presence or absence of any individual (in a database), or small groups of individuals, while at the same time preserving statistical utility."[118] For example, imagine that the actual enumerated count of a single census block (see Block 1 in Panel A of table 6.3) contains one hundred people, seventy-five voting-age persons (aged eighteen and over) and twenty-five nonvoting-age persons.[119] The bureau's differential privacy algorithm would then add noise to obscure the total number of persons in that block as well as their demographics. In this case, the algorithm adds two persons to the block's population and subtracts four persons of voting age. Thus in the block's preliminary "noisy" count, there are 102 people total, seventy-one voting-age persons and twenty-five nonvoting-age persons. In a second step, called "post-processing," a series of constraints are applied to these noisy counts, such as eliminating negative cell entries (see Block 4 in Panels C and D of table 6.3).

As this simple example shows, there are obvious trade-offs between data privacy and data accuracy. As the amount of noise injected into the data increases, data privacy improves, but accuracy is sacrificed. Implementing the DAS thus meant deciding the maximum acceptable level of privacy loss for a given data file. The term the bureau used to describe this maximum is the *privacy-loss budget*. In mathematical terms, this budget is represented as the Greek letter epsilon (ε). Choosing a value of $\varepsilon = 0$ would produce

Tables 6.3a–d. Noise Infusion for a Group of Five Hypothetical Census Blocks

	Block 1	Block 2	Block 3	Block 4	Block 5
6.3a. Enumerated Count					
Population Under Age 18	25	20	10	1	1
Population Aged 18+	75	70	40	9	2
Total Population	100	90	50	10	3
6.3b. Noise					
Population Under Age 18	0	-3	2	-2	0
Population Aged 18 +	-4	2	-3	1	2
Total Population	2	3	-2	1	0
6.3c. Preliminary Noisy Counts					
Population Under Age 18	25	17	12	-1	1
Population Aged 18 +	71	72	37	10	4
Total Population	102	93	48	11	3
6.3d. Post-Processed Counts					
Population Under Age 18	27	19	12	0	1
Population Aged 18 +	71	72	37	11	4
Total Population	98	91	49	11	5

Source: Adapted by the author from US Census Bureau, *Disclosure Avoidance for the 2020 Census: An Introduction* (US Census Bureau, 2021), https://www2.census.gov /library/publications/decennial/2020/2020-census-disclosure-avoidance-handbook .pdf.

data that protects privacy perfectly but is entirely inaccurate, and therefore useless. By contrast, an infinite value of ε would produce perfectly accurate data with no privacy protections whatsoever. Finding an appropriate trade-off between privacy and usability was especially consequential because differential privacy would be applied to virtually *all* census geographies. Exact counts for the 2020 Census would ultimately be published only for "states, the number and type of group quarters facilities at the block level, and the number of housing units, whether occupied or not, at the block level."[120] Every other census geography would be published with some level of statistical noise.

The stark nature of the trade-offs between privacy and data usability came into full view—to census insiders—during a two-day workshop commissioned by the Census Bureau in December of 2019.[121] Hosted by the Committee on National Statistics (CNSTAT) at the National Academy of Sciences in Washington, DC, the workshop brought together two communities that often found themselves in tension—the DAS development team and the community of data users—to examine the effects of differential privacy on the utility of a wide variety of census tabulations. It also served as a deliberate response to sharp criticisms of differential privacy that had emerged in the community of census data users following the bureau's initial announcement of the policy change.[122] Among those leading the charge—which included an open letter signed by hundreds of scholars—was University of Minnesota population historian Steven Ruggles. He argued that differential privacy constituted a set of "arbitrary and [had] burdensome new rules, with no basis in law or precedent."[123] Differential privacy, as Ruggles saw it, was nothing more than Abowd's "science project." Abowd had, all things considered, "gotten a whole lot of people worked up about this dire threat that doesn't exist," Ruggles said.[124] Abowd responded with a kind of public relations campaign targeted at data users and oriented around a "demonstration data product," which applied the new differential privacy method to 2010 census records. Researchers presenting at the December workshop could use this data to test-drive the new disclosure avoidance system for themselves.[125] Indeed, if there was any doubt that the workshop was an attempt to assuage the concerns of data users, one only needed to look at the program for the event. Whereas concerns about data accuracy occupied fifteen hours of discussion, only ninety minutes were explicitly devoted to discussions of how the new technology would address the policy goals of privacy or confidentiality.[126]

Yet if the workshop was intended to build trust in differential privacy, it also gave a platform to a growing list of concerns about the implementation of differential privacy, which by December of 2019 was beginning to seem like a fait accompli. Data users were also frustrated with the fact that the results from the bureau's reidentification experiment that had been used to justify differential privacy were presented only on a few slides with little detail. Some would later argue, for example, that the experiment was flawed because it did not consider whether the matches between census records and outside sources could have occurred simply by chance. In other words, if the reidentification experiment had been a clinical trial, it would have been difficult to distinguish the effects of the treatment from that of a placebo.[127]

And what of the effects of differential privacy on the quality of census data? By mid-morning on the workshop's first day, some of census data users' worst fears already appeared to be confirmed. First, the new system appeared to yield significant errors in the allocation of government aid. Nicholas Nagle, a geographer at the University of Tennessee, presented an analysis demonstrating that differential privacy would significantly skew Tennessee's allocation of sales and use tax revenue to municipal governments. "Every place is supposed to get $115 per capita," Nagle suggested, "but the difference between winners and losers is just over $80 for the biggest 'loser' to $180 for the biggest 'winner.'"[128] This was especially concerning, Nagle suggested, for small municipalities—where even minor discrepancies in revenue shape "whether or not [these towns] can afford to repave their roads each year, or whether or not they can afford to hire a full-time or part-time police chief."[129]

Differential privacy also appeared to create significant problems for redistricting data. Justin Levitt, a law professor at Loyola Marymount University, reported that adding too much statistical noise would, among other things, lead to a "systematic shift in political power allocated to rural populations."[130] University of Florida political scientist Michael McDonald found that differential privacy had produced imbalances in the population of Georgia legislative districts in ways that may violate the constitutional requirement of "one person, one vote" as well as the Voting Rights Act's protections for minority voters' ability to elect their preferred representatives. These results, McDonald predicted, would open the door to new census litigation that would ultimately wend its way to the US Supreme Court, which could order, under seal, the delivery of confidential data contained in the Census Edited File—including the original counts, untainted by differential privacy.[131] Not everyone agreed, however. Simson Garfinkel—the bureau's chief computer scientist for confidentiality and data access—called McDonald's worries a "fantasy," particularly given that Title 13 made confidential census data "immune from legal process." McDonald shot back that the Constitution's requirements for an "actual enumeration" overrode any statutory command.[132]

The controversy over differential privacy did not stop there. City planners attending the workshop cited several instances in which infusing noise into census data had led to errors that would misrepresent the needs of households and neighborhoods. Clifford Cook, an urban planner in Cambridge, Massachusetts, presented maps illustrating how differential privacy had incorrectly lowered the ratio of children per household from 1.73 to 1.22, a change that could have significant effects on the planning for the city's schools. In one cluster of eighteen census block groups, Cook also found that more than half of elder households had been redistributed around the city. If census taking makes it possible for the city to "see" its residents, and hence plan for their needs, differential privacy seemed to officials like Cook to be the equivalent of an eye gouge.

The problems were not restricted to urban settings. Noise-infused data also appeared to threaten census tabulations of American Indian and Alaska Native (AIAN) populations. Norman DeWeaver, an independent statistical consultant, presented evidence that in small reservations throughout the country differential privacy yielded severe undercounts. On reservations with fewer than five hundred people, the infusion of statistical noise resulted in a median population decrease of 52 percent. This sort of result, DeWeaver suggested, would constitute a "breach of faith" with tribal governments with whom the bureau was attempting to build greater trust. The bureau had, he argued, three options for resolving the problem. First, it could allocate a larger share of its privacy loss budget to smaller communities like those in his analysis, where the risk of large undercounts was highest. If this were not possible, the bureau could attempt to secure funding for tribal governments to prepare their *own* tabulations for local planning and service allocation. To mitigate the threat of undercounts for the allocation of federal grants, however, Congress would still have to pass legislation revising funding formulas in programs targeted at AIAN populations.

Most significant, however, is what DeWeaver *did not* propose: abandoning differential privacy. Indeed, despite numerous bleak projections about the effect of differential privacy on the quality of census data, participants at the workshop continued to emphasize that in the absence of differential privacy, the threat of disclosure remained. As Microsoft researcher danah boyd put it in one of the last sessions of the workshop, the bureau's estimate that as many as 17 percent of the US population could be reidentified was arguably too low, especially given that the analysis had been based on 2010 data. Thanks to the emergence of new sources of commercial data on individuals, the reidentification rate could be as high as 60 percent, boyd suggested. Failing to address this sort of risk would not only heighten the fears that inhibited census participation—especially in immigrant communities—it would leave open real opportunities for the misuse and abuse of census data.

Thus rather than scuttling differential privacy, census officials now focused their efforts on communicating with census stakeholders about their efforts to improve the algorithm and releasing public metrics of data quality. But information about these improvements seeped out slowly and, in the judgment of some census watchers, quite ineffectively. With the onset of the COVID-19 pandemic and the Trump administration's renewed political interference in the 2020 count, census officials had few opportunities to communicate or rebuild trust with data users, whose concerns about differential privacy only grew.

This was perhaps especially true of state officials responsible for legislative redistricting. In theory, the states had a means for cooperating with the bureau to secure adjustments to differential privacy. For four decades, the bureau had collaborated with state officials in the production of redistricting datasets. As we saw in chapter 1, a series of landmark Supreme Court cases in the 1960s required state and local governments to draw new legislative districts following each decennial census. This ramped up the demand for accurate and timely delivery of census data to officials charged with redistricting. To smooth the process for creating this data, Congress passed Public Law 94–171 in 1975 to require the secretary of commerce to create a process through which the bureau would consult with the states to define the geographies for which census data would be tabulated. By the 2020 Census cycle, the bureau's Redistricting Data Program had become a well-institutionalized federal-state partnership. The program commenced in 2014, long before census enumeration began. During the first phase of the program, state officials worked with the bureau to ensure that features of local geography are captured in census tabulation blocks. In the second phase, which began several years before enumeration, state officials submitted information that helps the bureau define the boundaries of voting precincts or wards.

Yet while the PL 94–171 program had proven a viable mechanism for intergovernmental collaboration in the 2020 Census cycle, it did not offer states a means of confronting the issue of differential privacy. Despite demands from redistricting officials, census officials did not reopen PL 94–171 program as a venue for consultation.[133] Nevertheless, throughout 2020 and 2021, state and local officials continued to express their concerns in other ways. Leaders from major intergovernmental organizations like the National Conference of State Legislators, the National Governors Association, the National Congress of American Indians convened meetings to explain to their members the stakes of the issue and to describe the state of play.[134] State officials furnished the bureau's director, Steven Dillingham, with analyses that illustrated the consequences of the unacceptable levels of error that would result from noise-infused data and repeatedly requested that the bureau increase the size of the privacy loss budget to mitigate these negative impacts.[135] "The current implementation of [differential privacy]," wrote Maine's state data center lead and its state economist, "creates a group of regions and people, predominantly rural and already marginalized, that . . . will be left behind for the remainder of the decade unless action is taken to improve the algorithm."[136] Leaders from the National Conference of State Legislatures bluntly informed Dillingham that the noise-infused data had produced errors that were simply "too large to be of use for redistricting."[137]

The bureau, as we will soon see, ultimately took this feedback quite seriously. Yet in the heat of the moment, census officials could not convincingly reassure data users that the errors they identified would ultimately be remedied. One reason for this is that the beta version of the DAS—released in October of 2019—maintained a very conservative privacy loss budget, with an epsilon value set at $\varepsilon = 6$.[138] To allow users to isolate the impacts of small tweaks to the bureau's algorithm, the bureau maintained a similarly conservative privacy loss budget ($\varepsilon = 4.5$) in three subsequent updates of the DAS, all of which were released in 2020. The upshot of this choice was that, even as the bureau made important improvements to the algorithm, the DAS data still contained errors so significant as to make critical census tabulations unfit for use.

Accentuating these fears, the COVID-19 pandemic had led to significant delays in the processing of census data. PL 94–171 requires the delivery of redistricting data no later than April 1st—one year after the census date. The bureau announced in February of 2021 that this was simply not operationally possible. It would instead deliver redistricting data by September 30th.[139] This created a cascading series of problems for redistricting officials in the states. New Jersey and Virginia had legislative elections slated for November of that year. Twenty-five additional states had legal redistricting deadlines that fell within 2021.[140] For many state officials, the new schedule meant that in addition to receiving erroneous redistricting data—which could invite an onslaught of lawsuits from voters and interest groups—they would now have little time to meet their own legal deadlines let alone confront the bureau over the errors they found.

By early March, officials in Alabama were ready to litigate. Along with

Congressman Robert Aderholt and two residents of the state, Alabama asked a panel of three federal judges to both require the bureau to release redistricting data by the statutory deadline and to prohibit the implementation of differential privacy. The delayed data release, the lawsuit alleged, would cause Alabama to miss its redistricting deadlines. Perhaps more importantly, the bureau's decision to implement differential privacy would result in data unfit for redistricting purposes, causing an unconstitutional dilution of minority voting power. Because the bureau did not adequately consider the effects of differential privacy on data quality, its decision to adopt this technique represented an "arbitrary and capricious" use of authority. Because these violations would irreparably harm the state's right to receive timely and lawful census tabulations, Alabama asked the court for legal relief immediately.

Yet after receiving several expert reports and amici briefs, one of which was filed by officials from no fewer than sixteen states, and following extensive oral arguments, the panel of judges remained unpersuaded. In a unanimous opinion filed on June 29th, the court ruled that Alabama's claims about the negative effects of differential privacy on the accuracy of their redistricting data were unripe for adjudication. The court could not say whether "differential privacy will inflict the harm alleged by the Individual Plaintiffs until the bureau releases a final set of redistricting data."[141] Moreover, because the harms were essentially speculative, the judges reasoned that Alabama was not entitled to injunctive relief.

To the surprise of some observers, Alabama neither returned to court following the delivery of its redistricting data nor did it appeal the panel's decision to the US Supreme Court. One potential reason for this is that even as a cloud of uncertainty lingered over the redistricting process, census officials—no doubt acutely aware of the practical and legal ramifications of data quality—*had* made substantial improvements to the DAS to accommodate the concerns of data users.[142] On April 28, 2021, the bureau published a DAS update with a global private loss budget of *twice* the original size ($\varepsilon = 12.2$).[143] A little over a month later, that budget grew further still. On June 8th, the Data Stewardship Executive Policy Committee—a fourteen-member body within the bureau that manages compliance with Title 13—issued its final DAS settings, announcing a global private loss budget of $\varepsilon = 19.61$.[144]

How did these changes to the DAS affect the accuracy of census data? To answer this question, we can employ several measures that help us evaluate the extent to which noise-infused census data contained in the Microdata

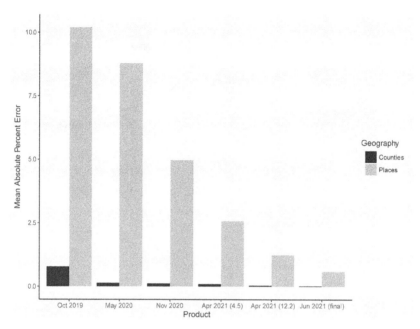

Figure 6.4: Mean absolute percent error in total population for counties and incorporated places, by DAS demonstration product. Source: Adapted by author from Jan Vink, "Differential Privacy and Accuracy," presentation at the 2021 New York State Data Center Meeting, September 29, 2021, https:// pad.human.cornell.edu/presentations/index.cfm#PADtop. Note: In April of 2021, the Census Bureau released two DAS demonstration datasets, one with a global privacy loss budget of ε = 4.5 and another with a global privacy loss budget of ε = s12.2. Accuracy metrics for both datasets are included here with the epsilon values in parentheses.

Detail File (MDF) differ from the publicly available 2010 Census Hundred-Percent Detail File (HDF).[145] One important measure here is mean absolute percent error, which captures the average percentage difference in population counts between the two data sets for a given census geography. In the bureau's initial October 2019 demonstration data product—which employed a conservative global privacy loss budget (ε = 6)—the mean absolute percent error for the total population of all counties was 0.78 percent persons (see figure 6.4). By the time that the bureau finalized the 2020 DAS in June of 2021, employing a far more generous privacy-loss budget (ε = 19.6), the mean absolute error for county population had fallen to 0.02 percent. A

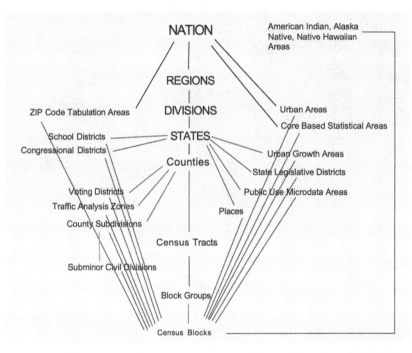

Figure 6.5: Standard hierarchy of census geographic entries. Source: "Standard Hierarchy of Census Geographic Entities," US Census Bureau, accessed March 3, 2024, https://www2.census.gov/geo/pdfs/reference/geodiagram.pdf.

similar decrease in error could be observed for incorporated places. In the October 2019 product, the mean absolute percent error in total population for incorporated places was 10.2 percent. By June of 2021, that figure had fallen to 0.6 percent.

Yet changes to the privacy loss budget did not address all the concerns that data users identified during and after the December 2019 CNSTAT workshop. One important lingering issue had to do with the challenges of applying differential privacy to some kinds of important geographical units. While some important geographical units are nested within one another as part of the so-called spine—census tracts composed of block groups, which are composed of census blocks—others are not (see figure 6.5). These "off-spine" geographies include incorporated places, school districts, and minor civil divisions (see figure 6.5). Especially when the populations of these off-spine geographies are small, the application of differential privacy resulted

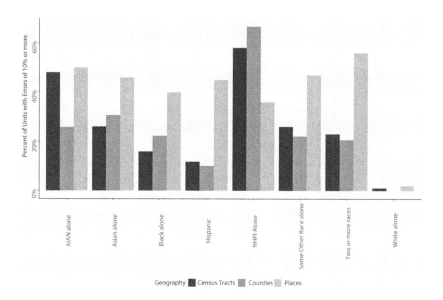

Figure 6.6: Percentage of census tracts, counties, and places with errors of 10 percent or more in June 2021 DAS production settings product in estimates of population by race and Hispanic origin. Source: National Academies of Sciences, Engineering, and Medicine, *Assessing the 2020 Census: Final Report* (National Academies Press, 2023), 274.

in a larger number of errors. Though the bureau evidently attempted to "optimize" the spine to ensure greater accuracy, some errors remained in the June 2021 DAS product. While incorporated places with large populations saw only very small errors, 16 percent of places with populations under five hundred had a mean absolute percent difference exceeding 5 percent.[146] It is also worth noting that the application of differential privacy resulted in numerous "impossible" situations. Data users investigating the Census Bureau's DAS updates found, for example, that there were more than one hundred and sixty thousand census blocks where the total population was age zero to seventeen, with no adults. Before the application of differential privacy, there were fewer than one hundred such blocks.[147]

These problems were magnified for some racial and ethnic groups. To illustrate this, figure 6.6 considers the extent to which the total population size by race and Hispanic origin in the June 2021 DAS product differed by more than 10 percent from the original 2010 file after data swapping had been applied. Forty-five percent of incorporated places in the United States saw a mean absolute percentage error in the size of the Hispanic population exceeding 10 percent. Forty percent of incorporated places saw a mean absolute percentage error in the size of the Black population above that same threshold.

Similar problems can be found in the data on young children. An analysis prepared by the demographer William O'Hare, which examines demonstration data released in August of 2022, found that 18 percent of unified school districts—another off-spine census geography—saw absolute percent errors in the population of young children (ages zero to four) of 5 percent or more. Error rates for the population of young children in minority groups were far higher, O'Hare found. For example, in 38 percent of unified school districts, the absolute percent error in the population of young Black children was 25 percent or more.[148]

The June 2021 version of the DAS also left significant biases at the level of voting districts—a tabulation geography used extensively in legislative redistricting. As the political scientist Christopher Kenny and his colleagues found in 2021, the final DAS had eliminated many of the most egregious problems found in previous iterations of the data, including blatant violations of the long-standing legal requirement that legislative districts have roughly equal populations, the so-called One Person, One Vote rule. The errors that remained, the researchers concluded, were likely the product of the bureau's choice to preserve accuracy at the level of census tracts as opposed to voting precincts.[149]

Data users' emphasis on the trade-offs of differential privacy techniques has produced results. In December 2022, the bureau announced that "given its current assessment of the science," it would not use differential privacy methodology in the annual American Community Survey, which provides detailed data on a wide range of important topics.[150] Census data users have continued to raise important questions and to probe the usability of 2020 data for policy purposes ranging from city planning to allocating aid to municipalities and school districts. In a 2022 letter, the FSCPE leadership alerted top census officials to a range of concerns related to differential privacy. These included persistent inaccuracies in data for off-spine geographies. The letter also cited concerns about "not well understood interactions between the characteristics of an area and the bias and accuracy loss in the data for that area in the 2020 demonstration files."[151] State demographers, state data center staff, and other users also voiced frustration with a lack of guidance from the bureau over how to use noise-infused data, including a lack of guidance on how to construct statistical confidence intervals for noise-infused population estimates. The solution, FSCPE leaders suggested, was to commission an independent review of the bureau's procedures for adopting differential privacy, its interactions with users, and evidence on the "timeliness, accuracy, and relevance (or lack thereof) of the privatized data." At the time of this writing, the Census Bureau is reportedly "seriously considering" these and other recommendations. Yet, if anything, it seems evident that the conflict over differential privacy is far from over.

What Becomes of the Uncounted?

Along with war mobilization and tax collection, the US Census is among the most large-scale and complex tasks the federal government undertakes. Even under the best of circumstances, a successful census cannot be taken for granted. Yet the 2020 count unfolded at the confluence of a pandemic, an unprecedented attempt at political sabotage, and an effort to make substantial operational changes in the absence of adequate funding. As the members of the National Academies expert panel on the 2020 count has written, "The basic fact that the 2020 Census was completed, as close to schedule as it was, is itself a major accomplishment."[152]

The heroic work of public officials to produce the 2020 Census not withstanding, important concerns about the quality of the count remain. While evaluations of census quality are ongoing, there is sufficient evidence to suggest that the 2020 Census resulted in the most sizable net undercounts of the Black, Hispanic, and American Indian and Alaska Native populations living on reservations in thirty years. The net undercount of young children (5.4 percent) was the highest in seventy years, since the Census Bureau started systematically tracking the net undercount. The geographic effects of that undercount were not evenly experienced. Cities like Detroit, where tens of thousands of residents were allegedly not counted, stood to lose millions in federal and state aid. In the 2010 Census no state had a net coverage rate that was statically significantly different from zero based on the PES. In the 2020 Census, several states had statistically significant net undercounts and several had statistically significant net overcounts. In short, differential coverage rates in the 2020 Census were far more pronounced than they were in the 2010 Census.

Local officials around the country had several options for responding to evidence of an undercount. First, the bureau provided states, cities, and tribes with opportunities for challenging both census counts as well as annual population estimates. Yet due to both legal constraints on the bureau as well as the bureau's own internal scientific culture, these challenge programs impose sharp limits on the kinds of data local governments can use to support their cases. In practice, that means that even in the face of substantial, credible evidence of an undercount, the bureau's hands may be tied unless Congress acts to unbind them.

The bureau also allows governments—at their own expense—to request a "special census," a new enumeration that alters the baseline for future population counts. Following the 2020 Census, for example, many small college towns across the country whose student populations had to leave town during the COVID-19 pandemic appeared poised to follow this path. For larger cities like Detroit, however, the costs of a special census were much higher. Moreover, because the circumstances that produced the undercount went far beyond the pandemic, it was unclear that a repeat enumeration would guarantee revenue gains that outweighed the expense.

Local officials who found themselves at a disadvantage in these bureaucratic venues could of course opt to shift the arena of contention. For Detroit, this meant filing suit in federal court to force the bureau to widen the scope of its Population Estimates Challenge Program. Yet as the outcome of that case suggests, courts cannot easily intervene here. Because the bureau created this program using its discretionary authority, there is no clear statutory duty to act to respond to Detroit's demands.

Given the limits of adversarial legalism, local officials like Mike Duggan have also engaged in some amount of ordinary legislative politics—lobbying Congress to apply pressure to the Census Bureau, which they believed was moving at too slow a pace in response to their demands. This effort has been the victim of poor timing in two senses. First, with 2022 midterm campaigns in full swing, Congress could not respond rapidly to demands for relief, especially given that those demands did not seem to attract a coordinated effort from major intergovernmental lobbying organizations. Second, over the last thirty years, the census has attracted an increasing level of partisan conflict, which narrows the bargaining space for legislative reforms. Democrats did manage to push through a significant increase to Census Bureau funding in the 2022 lame-duck session. Yet by 2023, the shift in the partisan control of the House of Representatives from Democrats to Republicans pushed Detroit's entreaties off the agenda almost entirely. Detroit's officials also lacked coalition partners in their fight. The fact that a widespread adjustment to the 2020 Census data might produce new losers as well as new winners may have made large intergovernmental organizations reticent to join this effort.

Not only did the city act alone, its challenge—premised on a relatively weak legal foundation—hinged on compelling the bureau to alter a rule it had already laid down. As we saw in the battle over differential privacy, state and local data users had far greater success by exerting collective pressure on decisions that were not yet finalized, most importantly the size of the privacy-loss budget in the 2020 Disclosure Avoidance System. These efforts hardly resolved all the problems that data users identified. Yet they helped to shift the way census officials confronted the trade-offs between privacy and accuracy. When compared to the 2019 beta version, the final DAS yielded far fewer errors and far more usable data.

Where does this leave the tens of thousands of Detroiters, or the hundreds of thousands around the country, who went uncounted in 2020? On the one hand, the evidence in this chapter suggests that fixing the undercount will hinge on the work of state and local officials, either in making formal administrative challenges, financing special censuses, filing lawsuits, or petitioning their members of Congress. At the same time, while these officials may be highly motivated to make such appeals, their success will be limited by legal constraints on the Census Bureau, the bureau's need to preserve its scientific integrity, the limited jurisdiction of the federal courts, and partisan polarization that impedes effective action by Congress. In short, for the time being, many of those who were uncounted will *stay* uncounted.

CONCLUSION

Census taking is a perennial subject for American editorial cartoonists, and the 2020 cycle was no exception. In newspapers across the country, editorial pages were littered with sendups of the chaos and controversy that surrounded the troubled decennial count.

If these cartoons had one common theme, it was that of anxiety—often personified in the familiar encounter between enumerator and enumerated. In one panel, an Immigration and Customs Enforcement officer, dressed in black tactical gear and armed with a census form, stands before the cracked-open door of an apartment building. "Are you a citizen?," he asks the man behind the door, who is nervously peering out at the fortified passenger van waiting for him on the street below.[1]

Nameless street-level workers were not the only sources of census anxiety. Cartoonists also trained their sights on high-ranking members of the Trump administration, and often Trump himself. In one *Buffalo News* panel, George Washington solemnly proposes to his fellow founding fathers that "slaves count as three fifths of a person." Behind him, Trump—dressed in period garb—adds, "And immigrants shall be zero fifths." Another, published in the *Minneapolis Star–Tribune*, depicts a pint-sized Wilbur Ross gazing up with a rictus grin at a chalkboard full of tally marks that spell out the word *WHITES*. "Our official census count," he says, "rounded off to the nearest Caucasian."[2]

Other cartoons focused on anxieties at the bureau and in the states. In the *Austin American-Statesman*, one panel depicts a worried man wearing a black Census Bureau T-shirt, lying awake in his bed at night. "I can't sleep," he says. From the other side of the bed, his wife replies: "Have you tried undercounting minorities?" A cartoonist at *The Capital-Star*—an online publication in Pennsylvania—displays a car labeled with the Keystone State's two-letter abbreviation, which has crashed into a ditch after driving off an unfinished bridge labeled "2020 Census." On the other side, a green highway sign reads "FEDERAL HIGHWAY $$$$."[3]

The anxiety in these cartoons stems from a sharp division of labor in census taking. On one side is the figure of government—the federal government, to be specific. Whether in the form of the White House, the

Commerce Department, the Census Bureau, or Immigrations and Customs Enforcement, the federal government is depicted as the primary mover. The Census Bureau's enumerators appear at doorsteps to collect information. The president and his minions cook up schemes to skew census figures. Census Bureau officials fret about data quality.

On the other side of the line is the figure of society, typically represented as the individual or the household. The counted may cower behind their doors, express dismay at the content of census forms, or threaten Bureau employees to get off their lawns. State and local governments are also personified as being primarily on the receiving end of the federal government's decisions. Undercounted states, deprived of resources, might well not make needed investments in crumbling roads and rusting bridges. In any case, states and cities—like individuals and families—are depicted as little more than passive subjects of the federal government's power.

This "state-centered" view of census taking is hardly exclusive to editorial cartoonists. It has also been a long-running feature of academic writing on official statistics. The writings of philosopher and historian Michel Foucault characterize censuses as a tool of *power-knowledge*, used by governments to control society by shaping the everyday categories and concepts individuals use to understand the world. At first glance, census counts also appear to be the sort of large-scale top-down government project dissected by the political scientist James C. Scott. In his 1998 classic *Seeing Like a State*, Scott shows numerous examples of how governments officials exercise power through counting and classifying the world, often with tragic unintended consequences.[4]

In the last several decades, however, a growing number of scholars have recognized the limitations of this view, emphasizing that census counts are not necessarily a top-down projection of state power. Rather, censuses are a vibrant terrain of political conflict among cross-cutting interests in society. To understand how the US Census is made, these scholars argue, we must consider how political parties, interest groups, professional associations, and bureaucrats interact with one another. For it is in these interactions that critical features of each decennial count—from racial categories to residency rules—are constructed.[5]

Yet it is not simply the case that parties and organized interests affect the census by shaping the decisions of "the state." The state is never a unitary actor but an assemblage of multiple institutions whose cooperation and conflict can leave an indelible mark on who is counted and how.[6] In the US federal system, "counting like a state" inevitably requires interactions not only between legislators, presidents, courts, and judges but also between federal, state, and local officials. Even so, as I argue in this final chapter, the emergence of a "census federalism" over the past half century has resulted in a network of programs and intergovernmental relationships that are frequently porous, underinstitutionalized, and enmeshed in broader political and legal struggles. While the knowledge and capacities of state and local governments are vital to census taking, there are also opportunities for policy reforms that would strengthen this patchwork of intergovernmental relationships in future censuses, beginning with the 2030 count.

Census Federalism: An Unfinished Project

Why should the contours of American federalism matter at all for census taking, a task the Constitution assigns to Congress and then Congress has delegated to the Commerce Department and the Census Bureau? The answer can be found, as I have suggested in this book, in three historical developments that have taken place since the middle of the twentieth century, which together have made census taking in the United States an increasingly intergovernmental affair, one that is undertaken not by one federal agency but by the "many hands" of the American state.

First, over the last fifty years, state and local governments have become increasingly invested in the accuracy of census data. The growth of the intergovernmental grant system—which employs population data to allocate trillions in federal aid—has made the census a critical determinant of the revenue that states, counties, municipalities, townships, and tribes receive. The "reapportionment revolution" of the 1960s, which required the redrawing of federal, state, and local legislative maps each decade, only reinforced the role of these governments as users of census data. Congress recognized this in 1974 when it passed legislation requiring the Census Bureau to transmit population data to state and local governments for use in redistricting. The Census Bureau, in collaboration with the governors of the fifty states, also created the Federal-State Cooperative for Population Estimates, through which the bureau and state agencies work together to prepare updated annual population figures. By the late 1970s, the bureau had also begun convening a national network of state data centers to better facilitate the use of census data products.

Second, as state and local governments became increasingly dependent on census data to carry out core governance tasks, operational changes to the census made the bureau increasingly reliant on local knowledge and collective action. The advent of the mail census and "self-enumeration" demanded an accurate, up-to-date portrait of household addresses. In a country whose population was both rapidly growing and increasingly mobile, the Census Bureau needed information on addresses that only state and local governments could provide. By 1994, Congress had passed formal legislation requiring intergovernmental cooperation in the production of the census address list. Nearly three decades later, as chapter 3 shows, the Local Update of Census Addresses (LUCA) has become an essential part of decennial census operations.

If households were expected to self-respond to the census, they also needed to be mobilized to do so. As chapter 4 shows, the Census Bureau could not do this on its own. Even with the emergence of a robust national advertising campaign for the 2000 count, the bureau relied on outreach efforts by state and local governments as well as community-based organizations. In a context of declining public trust in the federal government, state and local campaigns could create an ecosystem of "trusted messengers" in a way that a remote federal bureaucracy that enjoys little routine contact with the population could not.

All these changes occurred in the shadow of a third development: the Census Bureau's discovery of differential undercounts and the subsequent battle over whether the census could be statistically adjusted to correct for errors. With state and local governments increasingly reliant on accurate census data, and with the federal government struggling to modernize census operations, the revelation that the 1980 Census had neglected thousands of residents in cities like Detroit and New York set off two decades of conflict in the courts and Congress over what the Census Bureau should do to respond to large undercounts of the American population.

That these undercounts were concentrated in large urban areas that had historically been strongholds for the Democratic Party—and not in the growing Republican-dominated Sunbelt states—gave census politics an undeniable partisan hue. The 1990s were dominated by conflicts between Republican congressional leaders and a Democratic White House over what to do about undercounts. By 2000, the Supreme Court had declared that the Census Act prohibited the bureau from statistically adjusting the counts used to apportion the House of Representatives and the Electoral College.

While this decision left the door open for future congresses to revise the Census Act to permit adjustment, it left the bureau, as well as state and local governments, with a limited set of options for correcting errors. Still, as chapter 2 shows, decades of adversarial litigation had also created a body of census law that shaped the relationship between state and local governments and the Census Bureau. When the Trump administration launched its plan to include a citizenship question, states, cities, and counties drew on this body of law to launch a successful legal challenge—based on credible claims that the question would result in a significant undercount of their populations.

These institutional developments may have increasingly drawn state and local officials into the arena of census taking, but that hardly guaranteed that the "many hands of the state" worked together effectively. There are several reasons for this. First, because the formal-legal authority for census taking still rests with the federal government, state and local governments' institutional capacity to support census operations has developed rather unevenly. At one end of the spectrum, states like California and major metros like New York have developed extensive capacities to support census operations. Yet in many states, institutional investments in operations like LUCA have been more modest. Over the last few decades, local officials have routinely raised concerns about the inadequacy of resources to support operations like LUCA, count review, and Count Question Resolution. And while state and local governments collectively made unprecedented investments in census outreach prior to the 2020 count, as we saw in chapter 4, the level and adequacy of those resources varied widely across the country in ways that reflected governments' overall levels of fiscal capacity.

One reason why these resource disparities persist is that the Census Bureau is not, strictly speaking, a grantmaking agency. Legislative appropriations for the bureau have never been significant enough to sustain a program of grantmaking to support operations like LUCA or census outreach, and there appears to be little appetite at the bureau for transforming into such an agency. Instead, the bureau's partnerships with state and local governments hinge on a combination of exhortation, technical assistance, and limited contractual arrangements to facilitate data agreements or operations like count review. Yet in the estimation of major intergovernmental organizations and census advocacy organizations, these residual forms of aid are insufficient to support critical operations.

Even where the Census Bureau itself is concerned, inadequate legislative appropriations have brought with them organizational changes that tend to frustrate effective intergovernmental relationships. The downsizing of area census offices in recent years has, for example, contributed to significant problems with communications between the bureau and state and local officials in the run-up to the 2020 Census.

Yet the difficulties of intergovernmental collaboration cannot be charged to the absence of resources alone. The chapters of this book are littered with examples of how the intensely partisan nature of recent census controversies has threatened the sort of collaboration that is necessary for effective census implementation. During the Trump administration, census management has been defined by "executive-centered partisanship," a style of governance in which core governance tasks—including the design of the census questionnaire—are instrumentalized to advance the goals of the president's party. Fending off these attacks on census integrity required state and local officials to engage in venue shifting, filing federal lawsuits to stop the introduction of the citizenship question. This effort, while successful, did not stop the Trump administration from advancing another plan to remove noncitizens from census apportionment accounts. What ultimately thwarted this second scheme was a combination of subtle resistance from federal civil servants as well as state and local governments, additional litigation on the part of state and local governments, and Trump's loss in the 2020 election.

As the evidence in chapter 4 suggests, Trump's scheme also forced state and local governments—along with their partners in the nonprofit and philanthropic sectors—to redouble their efforts at census outreach and mobilization. Here, too, partisanship made a dent. States with Republican governors and state legislatures were, all else equal, far less likely than their Democratic peers to invest in census outreach campaigns.

Not all the intergovernmental conflicts that emerged during the 2020 Census were the result of partisan politics, however. Others have resulted from a tension between the demands of local governments and the legal obligations and internal culture of the Census Bureau, which limit how it can respond to those demands. For example, while state and local governments increasingly depend on accurate census data, Title 13 leaves many important decisions fully out of state and local control. This includes decisions about the rules for contesting census counts or population estimates local officials believe are erroneous. Officials in Detroit demanded immediate changes to that program to correct for what they reasonably suspect was a massive undercount in 2020, one that is costing the city millions in federal and state aid. Yet while bureau officials are keenly aware of the problems with the 2020 Census data, they have no clear legal obligation to respond to Detroit's claims straightaway. Moreover, they have emphasized that any changes to the Population Estimates Challenge Program will be based on thorough analyses conducted by a bureau research team rather than the demands of local units of government. Especially in the aftermath of the Trump administration's sabotage attempt, bureau staff are faced with the challenge of balancing their response to obvious data errors with a commitment to their own internal guidelines for the maintenance of data quality.

The case of Detroit reveals one other point of intergovernmental friction. After an unsuccessful attempt to persuade the bureau to change its policies, the city has appealed to both the courts and Congress for relief. Yet neither venue is ideally suited to address challenges like this one. Where Title 13 gives the Department of Commerce or the Census Bureau broad discretion over the management of decennial census programs, courts have little ability to offer meaningful relief, as Detroit's failed challenge to its 2022 population estimates shows. Congress, too, has been of little avail to cities seeking redress for flawed census figures. Without a broad coalition of intergovernmental organizations to support it, and in the face of a Congress sharply divided along partisan lines, the city's claims would not receive legislative action. And unlike smaller, more affluent cities, Detroit could not easily finance a special census to solve the problem on its own.

Strengthening Partnerships with Resources and Technical Assistance

If the evidence in this book suggests anything at all, it is that state and local governments have unique characteristics that make them pivotal to the production of an accurate census. State and local officials have access to important sources of information such as property and tax records that are essential for building the Master Address File and carrying out postcensus review. Where outreach is concerned, these officials typically garner far higher levels of public trust when compared to the Census Bureau or the federal government as a whole—trust that enables them to be far more effective at mobilizing census participation than the bureau could on its own. Relatedly, governors, mayors, county executives, and tribal officials may possess channels of information and points of brokerage with key community leaders that would otherwise be out of reach for the bureau's partnership specialists. If properly harnessed, these tools can produce census outreach strategies tailored to local populations.

One obvious policy recommendation that follows from my evidence is that state and local governments—especially those at risk of undercounts—should carefully evaluate the adequacy of their existing census investments, including but not limited to their investments in census outreach and LUCA operations. Thanks to the work of scholars and census advocates, it is now easier than it has ever been to see the potential losses in federal dollars that might result from a state census undercount. The same type of analysis can be done for state intergovernmental aid—which in many states constitutes a sizable chunk of municipal and county budgets. Even if it is difficult to precisely measure the effectiveness of any single outreach strategy on the mitigation of the undercount, these data should in theory allow elected officials to do a crude cost-benefit analysis of census investments.

Still, despite the obvious advantages of developing state and local institutions to support an accurate census, a near-constant refrain when I spoke with anyone involved with the census at the state and local level is that their work often suffers from a lack of dedicated institutional support. In states where the 2020 count fell into the maw of partisan conflict, census investments proved difficult to make. Small, fiscally constrained units of local government routinely report lacking adequate staff time or resources to participate in programs like LUCA. Especially given that census taking is often seen by state and local officials as a primary responsibility of the federal government, investments in census outreach programs can easily fall toward the bottom in terms of funding priorities. This was certainly true in many fiscally constrained states, cities, and counties I examined. In cities that underinvested in census outreach, responsibilities for coordinating Complete Count Committees often fell into the lap of employees already managing a diverse mix of projects and initiatives. Given the chaotic environment of the 2020 Census, this strained their capacity in the best of times. Yet with the onset of the COVID-19 pandemic, these staff were often tasked with immediate crisis-response work, eclipsing census outreach entirely. As chapter 5 shows, states and cities that created dedicated census-year positions, such as California and Philadelphia, could more easily pivot their outreach work when the pandemic arrived. State and local outreach work was further inhibited by policy changes at the federal level, including limited funding for the bureau's partnership programs, the downsizing of area census offices, and labor-market conditions that impeded the hiring of partnership specialists.

There are some obvious steps that the bureau—with sufficient appropriations from Congress—could take to strengthen the intergovernmental programs described in this book. Where the Community Partnership and Engagement Program (CPEP) is concerned, the bureau could hire an adequate number of permanent partnership specialists with strong ties to the local communities for which they are responsible. Ensuring that these partnership specialists are hired far enough in advance would allow them adequate time to identify and mobilize local governmental agencies and nongovernmental organizations that would be ideally suited to create an ecosystem of trusted partners to advance census outreach campaigns. If anything, the 2020 CPEP operation illustrated the problems that can arise when partnership specialists are incentivized to maximize the quantity, rather than the quality, of the community ties they build. Changing those incentives means conceiving of CPEP as an ongoing, permanent program through which the bureau builds and maintains ties with partners in government as well as in the nonprofit and business sectors.

Furthermore, it is imperative that the bureau continue to develop strategies and tools for incentivizing state and local governments to take part in census outreach. Currently, the bureau's approach to stimulating intergovernmental cooperation in census outreach is largely informational. State and local officials are advised of the benefits of census outreach campaigns and are given informational tools, including messaging strategies and marketing collateral to assist in these campaigns. Yet the evidence in this book suggests that these strategies are not enough. Clearly, units of government with large historically undercounted populations could benefit from targeted federal support for census outreach programs. This could either be structured as a categorical grant from the Department of Commerce or as a subcomponent of the bureau's Integrated Communications Contract. In either case, implementing these changes would require Congress to adequately support decennial operations. If the last decade is any indication, partisan polarization will remain an impediment here.

Assuming Congress is unwilling to extend resources to support state and local census outreach, it will be incumbent on bureau leadership to rethink the strategies CPEP uses to encourage state and local census investments. This will mean building on the work it has already done to illustrate the return on investment from census outreach investments. As the bureau prepares for future censuses, it should conduct evaluations that help to illustrate how state and local governments benefitted from census outreach programs in the past, in terms of representation and resources. This may well include expanding on the work of scholars like Andrew Reamer, whose research illustrates the relationship between census population counts and federal grant funding.[7] Beyond developing a stronger pitch for census investments, the bureau should consider creating tools to assist governments in planning their outreach strategies to maximize their effect. In other words, if the bureau cannot directly subsidize census outreach, it can still take steps to reduce the costs state and local governments bear when planning outreach campaigns. A low-cost example of this would be compiling best practices from 2020 Census outreach campaigns that governments can adapt and implement in 2030. Yet the bureau could also go further, by building a database tool similar to California's Statewide Outreach and Rapid Deployment database (SwORD), which allowed state officials to map hard-to-count populations, identify organizational assets, and monitor outreach efforts and activities.

When it comes to LUCA, some similar lessons apply. As chapter 3 shows, over the last few decades, the bureau has made significant improvements with its outreach to governments on LUCA participation. By developing a more user-friendly platform for LUCA submissions, enhanced training opportunities, and opportunities for states to submit address data on behalf of low-resource local governments, the bureau has made local participation far easier than it has been in the past. Yet there is clearly room for improvement. As much as the bureau has done to ease LUCA participation in recent years, resource gaps continue to impede some governments from preparing adequate submissions. This undermines the statutory purpose of the program as it was envisioned in 1994. Hence the Department of Commerce should propose to Congress a program to assist state, local, and tribal governments in supporting LUCA participation. As much as the bureau has done to ease LUCA participation in recent years, resource gaps continue to impede some governments from preparing adequate submissions.

Whether or not Congress decides to provide these funds, the Census Bureau can take additional steps to support LUCA participation. Perhaps most importantly, LUCA should begin earlier in the decade, allowing for enhanced testing prior to implementation. It goes without saying that Congress must provide adequate funding throughout the decade to support

LUCA testing, especially when new operations are introduced, in a way that includes all relevant stakeholders and provides opportunities for feedback and quality control. Finally, the bureau can ensure that LUCA participants have access to tools, such as address count lists and geocoding tools, that will help them prepare their own address list prior to the beginning of LUCA.

Improving Intergovernmental Coordination by Building on Existing Networks

The challenges that state and local officials face in their relationships with the Census Bureau are in no way unique to the production of official statistics. Rather, they are emblematic of more widespread trends identified by scholars of intergovernmental relations. As David Hamilton and Carl Stenberg note, an important policy shift over the last thirty years has been the "deinstitutionalization" of relationships between federal, state, and local officials.[8] Since Congress terminated the Advisory Commission on Intergovernmental Relations in 1996, state and local officials have lacked a venue for high-level communication and policy negotiations with top federal officials. Thus in addition to relying on intergovernmental lobbying to advance their collective interests, state and local officials must navigate a patchwork of advisory structures that exist within individual federal agencies. What to do?

Within the Census Bureau, there are several structures that have the potential to facilitate better intergovernmental coordination. First, the bureau maintains two permanent advisory bodies. The Census Scientific Advisory Committee (CSAC), composed of leading statisticians, demographers, and economists, advises the director on technical matters, including "developments in statistical data collection, survey methodology, geospatial and statistical analysis, econometrics, cognitive psychology, business operations, and computer science" as they relate to Bureau activities.[9] The National Advisory Committee on Racial, Ethnic, and Other Populations (NAC) is composed of a wide range of census stakeholders, ranging from academic researchers to data users to advocates for historically undercounted groups. It advises the bureau on, among other things, "the identification of new strategies for improved census operations, and survey and data collection methods, including identifying cost-efficient ways to increase census participation."[10] Both committees meet at least twice a year, with opportunities for public comments. These meetings result in recommendations to the bureau on how to improve census operations. The committees also regularly convene working groups to study and suggest recommendations on emergent issues such as the undercount of young children and concerns about the effects of "differential privacy" on census data quality.

While neither CSAC nor the NAC is oriented exclusively toward intergovernmental issues, they frequently make recommendations of interest to state and local officials. Hence these organizations have the capacity to serve as useful conduits of information from state and local stakeholders to top Census Bureau officials interested in strengthening the intergovernmental partnerships that play a pivotal role in decennial operations.

Second, the bureau can also create temporary advisory bodies and panels devoted to decennial operations as well as more specific emergent concerns. In 2023, for example, the bureau announced the creation of a 2030 Census Advisory Committee. As in earlier census cycles, this temporary body has been charged with providing feedback on plans for the 2030 count and, in particular "devis[ing] strategies to increase census awareness and participation, reduce barriers to response, and enhance the public's trust and willingness to respond."[11] As of this writing, the members of this committee have not yet been named. Yet the committee's charter explicitly notes that the members of this committee will have experience in, among other things, "historically undercounted populations," "state, local, and tribal areas," and "state officials and redistricting experts." In the past, committees like these have served as valuable sites of policy learning and deliberation as the decennial operational plans are developed.[12]

Third, the bureau also organizes national networks of state-based organizations that are explicitly designed to promote intergovernmental communication and coordination. The oldest of these is the Federal-State Cooperative for Population Estimates (FSCPE), whose member agencies in the states and US territories supply the bureau with vital statistics and administrative data for use in the development of annual population updates.[13] Among other things, FSCPE agencies also review and comment on annual estimates prior to their official release. Still, as the evidence in this book suggests, FSCPE agencies often lack adequate fiscal and institutional resources to perform the critical roles they play in decennial operations. Because the bureau is not a grantmaking agency, it cannot easily step in to support FSCPE agencies states have neglected. Nevertheless, were Congress to provide sufficient appropriations, it would be possible for the Department of Commerce—the bureau's parent agency—to use its authority to support these state agencies in future census cycles, either through categorical grants or cooperative agreements.[14]

Like the FSCPE, the state data center (SDC) network draws its members from state and territorial "lead" agencies across the country who regularly work with census data.[15] In over half of the states and territories, the lead agencies in these two networks are the same. Unlike the FSCPE, however, the SDC network does not play a formal role in coordinating the submission or review of census data. Rather, its work is often focused on disseminating knowledge about the bureau's data products and programs "horizontally" among its network of over eighteen hundred state data centers and affiliates throughout the country. SDC officials possess deep reservoirs of expertise about a range of census operations. And, as the evidence in chapter 4 suggests, their relationships to a variety of census users means that SDCs are often vital to the development of statewide Get Out the Count campaigns. Still, the fiscal and institutional resources available to these agencies varies widely across the states—a problem that the Census Bureau has, in the absence of grantmaking power, been unable to solve. Still, as with the FSCPE, Congress could allocate funds to the Commerce Department, which could use its authority to provide enhanced fiscal support to the activities of SDCs, which demonstrate a lack of state resources.

The most residual of the bureau's intergovernmental structures is the Governors' Liaison Network (GLN).[16] Unlike the FSCPE and the SDC network, its members do not meet on a regular basis to share information. Rather these census liaisons exist mainly as a single point of contact when the bureau and its regional offices need to communicate important operational information. Because these liaisons often serve in the governor's office rather than permanent agencies, the GLN is also subject to frequent staff turnover. At the time of this writing, sixteen states and all five US territories lacked a governors' census liaison. Given the important role of state governments in coordinating critical census programs, it is worth considering whether the roles of governors' census liaisons can be consolidated into state FSCPE agencies or state data centers.

The success of all these efforts might benefit from investments in the Census Bureau's Office of Congressional and Intergovernmental Affairs, which advises the bureau director on both federal legislative issues and serves as a point of contact for state, local, and tribal governments. In the years to come, intergovernmental coordination will remain a major challenge throughout the federal government.[17] Yet even if Congress does not resuscitate formal institutions like the Advisory Commission on Intergovernmental Relations, the Census Bureau has numerous opportunities to leverage institutions that already exist to improve relationships with state, local, and tribal governments. Strengthening intergovernmental partnerships will involve more than coordination, however. It will also require rethinking important policies and fiscal capacities that affect those partnerships.

Correcting the Count

A central theme running through this book is that the quality of the census hinges on investments that occur in the middle of the decade—investments that affect, among other things, the design and testing of census questionnaires, the preparation of address lists, and the formation of outreach plans. As chapter 6 shows, once census data are collected and processed, state and local governments have a far more limited range of options to correct the count. The bureau's existing administrative programs for challenging and correcting census undercounts are narrowly focused on data-processing problems and do not allow for the collection of new data. In a limited range of circumstances, special censuses provide a potential solution to these problems, but they can also impose significant costs on local governments. The utility of litigation in areas where the Census Bureau and the Commerce Department have been granted broad discretion is doubtful. And Congress is far less likely to respond to undercounts in the most recent census than it is to make reforms that affect future counts. The upshot of this conjunction of circumstances is that cities like Detroit, which were obviously undercounted in the 2020 Census, have access to few available remedies.

Officials at the Census Bureau have been sensitive to these issues but have been understandably cautious about making swift changes that could have unanticipated effects on efforts to correct undercounts. Nevertheless, there are clear opportunities for remediating undercounts that emerged in 2020. The most obvious of these is reforming the appeals process within the Census Population Estimates Challenge Program (PECP). As chapter 6 noted, the PECP once accepted a broader range of evidence from localities to evaluate the validity of its population estimates. Yet following the 2010 Census, the bureau sharply limited the kinds of administrative records that local governments could submit as part of this challenge process. It is encouraging news that census officials have introduced a "blended base" for population estimates, which makes a number of improvements on the 2020 count. It is equally encouraging that the bureau has recently convened the Base Evaluation and Research Team (BERT), which is now seriously evaluating the PECP's rules. BERT's research has already shown promising avenues for improving the base, which will ideally inform future population estimates.[18] In the meantime, however, undercounts will continue to deprive cities like Detroit of vital federal and state population-based aid. Absent changes to PECP, local officials in undercounted cities should request, and Congress should fund, a federally subsidized special census, citing—where appropriate—evidence of how both the pandemic and the bureau's incomplete address list contributed to problems for which current review programs were not designed.[19]

Confronting Political Threats to Census Integrity

The barriers to an accurate census count in the United States are not merely technical, they are political. As the evidence in chapter 2 shows, the rise of executive-centered partisanship constitutes a significant threat to census integrity, perhaps especially during a decennial year that coincides with a closely contested presidential election. Donald Trump represented, if nothing else, the apotheosis of executive-centered partisanship. Evidence given at trial clearly demonstrates that the Trump administration deliberately aimed to include the citizenship question as a means of engineering a structural electoral advantage for the Republican Party. When the Supreme Court narrowly thwarted the effort to include the citizenship question, the administration bluntly directed the secretary of commerce to remove undocumented immigrants from census apportionment counts. While the Supreme Court was more solicitous of this plan, as chapter 5 shows, a combination of litigation and administrative frustrations sank it.

Efforts to reintroduce the citizenship question, and to politicize the Census Bureau, endure. In advance of the 2024 election, the Heritage Foundation—a think tank that has long been a cornerstone of the conservative movement—released *Mandate for Leadership: The Conservative Promise*, a nearly one-thousand-page volume of policy proposals intended to guide a future Trump administration's reorganization of the federal government.[20] The book, the result of the Foundation's "Project 2025," included the reintroduction of the citizenship question on the 2030 census. As Thomas F.

Gilman, a former Trump Commerce Department appointee, noted in his chapter for the volume, the Supreme Court had rejected the Trump administration's citizenship question on procedural grounds but nevertheless held that "the Secretary of Commerce does have broad authority to add a citizenship question to the decennial census."[21] If the Commerce Department got the process right, Gilman argued, the Supreme Court would have to allow introduce the question on the 2030 questionnaire.

But the citizenship question was just the tip of the iceberg. Gilman also recommended major changes that would enhance the power of political appointees at the bureau, including the allocation of "additional political appointee positions to the Census Bureau."[22] The bureau was hardly the only target of plans to enhance the president's control of the bureaucracy. Rather, *Mandate for Leadership* developed a top-to-bottom reorganization plan that would politicize agencies throughout the federal government. This included, among other things, the conversion of over fifty thousand career civil servants throughout government into so-called Schedule F political appointees, an idea that Trump initially attempted to enact via executive order in late 2020.[23]

Trump's new political appointees, Gilman suggested, should undertake a thoroughgoing reevaluation of all Census Bureau operations. That meant, among other things, reevaluating all of the bureau's advisory committees and immediately abolishing the bureau's National Advisory Committee, which Gilman argued had become a "hotbed for left-wing activists intent upon injecting racial and social-justice theory into the governing philosophy of the Census Bureau."[24]

In the wake of the Trump administration's sabotage attempts, there have been a number of legislative proposals to insulate future censuses from the same sort of political meddling. In 2022, the House of Representatives passed the Ensuring a Fair and Accurate Census Act (H.R. 8326), which would have added a number of procedural checks on the secretary of commerce's power, such as explicitly prohibiting the bureau from including in the census "any subject, type of information, or question that was not submitted to Congress."[25] Other legislative proposals—none of which has seen floor action in Congress—explicitly bar the introduction of a citizenship question on the census and prohibit the communication of census information known to be materially false.[26]

Were any of these proposals enacted, they would add to important policy and legal protections already in place that aim to protect official statistics from political interference. These include statutes, directives issued by the Office of Management and Budget, and statistical guidelines issued by the Committee on National Statistics. As Constance Citro notes, these protections have been crucial to the formation of "a culture of objectivity, independence, and professionalism" at the bureau.[27] Yet in the current context of partisan polarization, legislation to further insulate the bureau from political interference has been stalled. The Ensuring a Fair and Accurate Census Act—the only census integrity legislation to receive a vote on the House floor in 2022—passed on along strict party lines before dying in the Senate.[28]

Assuming assaults on census integrity will continue over the next decade, the evidence in this book shows that state and local governments can play an important, if imperfect, role in safeguarding the count. First, state and local officials can protect census integrity through coordinated *legal mobilization*. As chapters 2 and 5 suggest, cooperation among states, cities, counties, and nonprofit organizations was pivotal to thwarting the Trump efforts to introduce the citizenship question. This coalition's work during the legal discovery process and the bench trial helped to expose the administration's explicit motives for creating the question. This significantly undermined the arguments made by Trump's lawyers and exposed what would otherwise have been a secret plan to intense public scrutiny. Even though the Supreme Court appeared to be more favorable to Trump's second sabotage plan, litigation filed by the same coalition of state and local officials helped to stall the administration's actions until the inauguration of President Biden.

Second, state and local officials can safeguard the census by *refusing to cooperate* with schemes to undermine data integrity. As chapter 5 shows, officials from across the political spectrum played a key supporting role in stalling Trump's attempt to remove undocumented immigrants from census apportionment counts. In many states, including states with large undocumented populations, officials refused to furnish the bureau with administrative data that it requested to advance this plan. This strengthened the efforts of career civil servants to pump the brakes on the president's plan, by emphasizing that even if the president had the authority to make his request, fulfilling it would violate legal standards for data quality.

Third, state and local officials—in partnership with nonprofit organizations and businesses—can safeguard census integrity by making investments in census operations, such as the preparation of LUCA submissions, the formation of state and local Complete Count Committees, and the financing of census outreach campaigns populated by trusted community-based messengers. To be sure, the impact of these investments can be difficult to estimate with precision, and outreach campaigns could hardly be expected to fully cancel out the effects of a pandemic and a deliberate attempt to sabotage census operations. Still, it is easy to see that, in the absence of state and local campaigns, the Census Bureau would have had a far more difficult time in generating the same level of knowledge, trust, and motivation to respond to the census that we saw on the ground in 2020.

Building support for these outreach campaigns can be a political struggle in its own right. As chapter 4 shows, this was especially true at the state level—as proposals to finance census outreach campaigns were swept up into national partisan controversies over the 2020 count as well as budget battles between governors and legislatures. Yet partisanship did not always foreclose census investments. At the local level, partisan opposition to census investments simply did not have the traction that it did in state legislatures. In cities and counties, the most significant barrier to census investments was a lack of resources rather than a surplus of rancor. All of this suggests that, for state and local governments to play a positive role in the development of census outreach campaigns, it may be necessary to develop advocacy coalitions that include a broad range of "strange bedfellows" that straddle state partisan divides. Allowing these leaders, rather than the most visible state-level elected officials, to lead the charge for census outreach may help to diffuse partisan skirmishes before they begin. It may also be advantageous to begin developing these coalitions funding earlier in the decade, before census preparations become the hot-button issue they often become in the two years prior to the count.

Of course, even the best efforts of state and local officials are no cure for partisan assaults on census integrity. On their own, the actions of state and local governments cannot reverse the trend of executive-centered partisanship, which has reduced the census into nothing more than a tool for entrenching the power of one party. In the face of this trend, however, investments in outreach campaigns, LUCA submissions, and lawsuits play a dual role. On a functional level, these actions can clearly improve the quality and accuracy of census data. Yet because they occur in the public sphere, these actions also shape the popular understanding of the census in ways that challenge partisan narratives. They do so by calling attention to why the census exists and how the manipulation of census data has negative material consequences for communities, businesses, and the fairness of elections.

Official Statistics in a Compound Republic

My main objective when I began writing this book was a simple one. I wanted merely to illustrate that census taking in the United States should not be thought of as an exclusively top-down project of the federal government. Nor should it be seen as merely the product of interactions between the federal government, interest groups, and partisan actors. Rather, it should be seen as a thoroughly intergovernmental undertaking, whose outcomes depend on interactions between federal, state, and local governments. If I have persuaded the reader of this, I will be satisfied. As my conversations with dozens of interviewees have taught me, the idea that the census is the federal government's business alone is among the greatest barriers to encouraging state and local governments to invest resources in improving the quality of census data. Those investments matter. State and local governments have access to institutional knowledge about where their residents should be counted, the languages they speak, and their most significant barriers to census. They are also far better situated to communicate directly with their residents about the importance of completing the census. Public trust in local and state governments far outpaces trust in the federal government. When compared to the Census Bureau, state and local government agencies also have far more routine contact with their residents as well as "trusted messengers" in the community. Finally, given the effects of the census on the allocation of federal resources and redistricting processes, state and local governments have a unique ability to defend census integrity using tools of litigation and legislative advocacy.

The tendency of the public   and even of elected officials—to miss these connections parallels an important intellectual gap within federalism scholarship that I also hope this book will begin to remedy. When examining interactions among levels of government, federalism scholars tend to focus their attention on relationships that emerge from the transfer of resources (grants), the imposition of regulatory authority (mandates), or the friction generated by these relationships as it enters the courts or Congress. Yet all such relationships depend in one way or another on the production of official statistics. While this subject has attracted very little attention from scholars of federalism, statistics have important lateral effects on the substance of intergovernmental relations.

First, official statistics produced by federal agencies set the parameters of state and local politics. The delivery of redistricting data files plays a key role in structuring state political cycles in the years that follow a census. Similarly, the long-term population trends that census data reveal can shape policy debates in state legislatures and city councils about how to plan for growth or stem outflow.[29] Beyond population data, comparative health statistics on issues like maternal mortality can both focalize attention to crises in poor performing states and present the opportunity for investigating policies that are associated with the reduction in poor health outcomes.[30]

Second, official statistics also shape politics in the traditional domains of fiscal and regulatory federalism. Hundreds of billions of federal dollars are allocated with formulas that rely on economic and population data collected by the Census Bureau. In turn, state and local governments transmit data back to Washington about how they invested federal dollars. Similarly, data sharing can be a critical component of "regulatory federalism." For example, the Secure Communities program, initiated by US Immigration and Customs Enforcement (ICE) in 2008, aimed to encourage states to forward the biometric data of arrestees who may be deportable under US immigration law. At the outset, data sharing in this program initially occurred through voluntary agreements between the federal government and the states. Yet in 2011, when some states exercised their right to terminate agreements, ICE rescinded all memoranda of understanding and announced that the program was now mandatory.[31]

A federal agency inventing a data-sharing mandate is hardly surprising. Yet what is far more remarkable—and extraordinarily understudied—is the extent to which data sharing in the United States is designed to occur on a purely *voluntary* basis. Indeed, while some legal scholars have suggested that there may be a data-sharing exception to the Supreme Court's "anti-commandeering" doctrine, the federal government has rarely tested the legal limits of that exception. Instead, federal agencies frequently rely on states, cities, and counties to transmit data to Washington of their own volition and sometimes with modest compensation. As the evidence in this book suggests, census federalism is emblematic of this voluntary approach. In the absence of any regulatory or fiscal inducements, state and local governments are expected to take actions that will improve the quality of census population data through the preparation of address lists and the planning of outreach campaigns. The main resource the federal government provides to support this work is technical assistance.

Understanding how this voluntary cooperation occurs—even in an era of extreme partisan polarization—may have something to teach us about how to strengthen intergovernmental relations in other policy domains. As the evidence in this book suggests, relying on voluntary cooperation does not consistently yield intergovernmental cooperation, and there are good reasons to believe that the creation of dedicated grant programs would greatly support census investments, especially in fiscally constrained states. Even so, the extent state and local investments in census accuracy, even in the absence of fiscal support or intergovernmental mandates, is nothing short of astonishing. And if nothing else, the evidence here suggests that some of the most important "raw materials" of census taking—including local knowledge of address lists and the capacity for mobilizing civic participation—exist not in Washington but in communities scattered across the country.

Cooperation aside, one of the most important lessons in this book is that state and local governments can also preserve census integrity through adversarial actions, ranging from multistate litigation to the refusal to sign data-sharing agreements when individual privacy and census integrity are on the line. The success of efforts to thwart census sabotage raises important questions about the conditions under which "uncooperative federalism" can help to *protect* federal programs or objectives that are under assault.

What we can learn from the US Census, of course, depends on whether we are paying attention. One of the most defining attributes of the census, especially though not exclusively of its political dynamics, is the time horizon on which it plays out. Unlike election cycles, budget battles, and debates over reauthorizing major federal programs, census taking happens once every ten years. In practice, this can mean that—except for a small world of federal officials, state demographers, city planners, statisticians, and advocacy groups—the census is mired in obscurity, pushed to the recesses of the public sphere, where it is often deprived of needed oxygen. And to the extent that the count is thought of at all, it is hardly associated with the legions of anonymous state and local officials who take active part in its production. Yet the work of those officials—however obscure or underappreciated—is nonetheless essential to ensuring that everyone is counted once, only once, and in the right place.

APPENDIX

To disentangle the facilitators of and barriers to state and local governments' investments in census operations, I conducted interviews with actors at the state and local level who are primarily engaged in census-related work. I recruited interviewees from a sample of thirty-three states representing a cross-section of the areas served by the Census Bureau's six regional offices (Atlanta, Chicago, Denver, Los Angeles, New York City, and Philadelphia). As table A1 shows, at least 50 percent of the states in each region were included in the sample. There was no statistically significant difference in the projected undercount between in-sample and out-of-sample states (see table A2).

Within the sampled states, I developed lists for potential interviewees from publicly available documents furnished by the Census Bureau as well as state and local government websites. In the first round, I interviewed seventy-six individuals between December 2019 and April 2020 by telephone and in person. At the state level, I contacted 102 individuals and completed thirty-six interviews (a response rate of 35 percent). Interviewees included governors' census liaisons, members of State Complete Count Commissions, and directors of state data centers. At the local level, I contacted eighty-one individuals and completed thirty-three interviews (a response rate of 41 percent). These interviewees included members of Complete Count Committees as well as key census staff in the offices of

Table A1: States Sampled for Qualitative Interviews by Census Bureau Region

Bureau Region	N (%) States in Sample
ATL (N=8)	3 (38%)
CHI (N=9)	6 (67%)
DEN (N=11)	4 (36%)
LAX (N=7)	5 (71%)
NYC (N=9)	5 (56%)
PHL (N=6)	4 (67%)

Table A2: Projected State 2020 Census Undercount for In-Sample and Out-of-Sample States

Is State in Sample?	Mean (SE) Undercount Projection	T=	P<0.05?
Yes (N=27)	−0.92 (0.10)	0.27	No
No (N=23)	−0.88 (0.11)		

Source: Author's analysis, based on data from Diane Elliott, Rob Santos, Steven Martin, and Charmaine Runes, *Assessing Miscounts in the 2020 Census* (Urban Institute, 2019).

mayors and county executives. Finally, I contacted eighteen representatives of national and regional nonprofit organizations with census-related portfolios and completed seven interviews of these individuals (a response rate of 39 percent). Table A3 presents summary statistics on first-round interviewees by sector and region.

I invited all state and local interviewees to have a follow-up conversation. These interviews were conducted between fall of 2020 and ended in the winter of 2021. Of thirty-six state interviewees contacted, fifteen responded and agreed to a second interview (a response rate of 42 percent). As in the first round, these interviewees included governors' census liaisons, members of State Complete Count Commissions, and directors of state data centers. Of thirty-three local interviewees, fifteen responded and agreed to a second interview (a response rate of 39 percent). These interviewees included members of Complete Count Committees as well as key census staff in the offices of mayors and county executives. Table A4 presents summary statistics on follow-up interviewees by sector and region.

To ensure that interviewees felt comfortable giving candid responses to my questions, I anonymized all interview transcripts and assigned each transcript to a numerical code. When quoting from interviews, I do not reference interviewees by name and do not discuss features of their state or organizational context that would allow for interviewees to be identified. Each interview lasted between thirty and sixty minutes.

During the first round of interviews, I used a semi-structured interview protocol. The follow-up interviews were unstructured, with questions tailored to subjects interviewees and I had discussed in their initial interview, as well as developments that had occurred since the onset of the COVID-19 pandemic. In both sets of interviews, I inquired about the circumstances surrounding the initiation of state and local census investments, including

Table A3: Interviewees by Region and Primary Organizational Affiliation

A. State Interviewees

Census Bureau Region	State Data Center	State Complete Count Commission	State Agency or Governor's Office	Total
ATL	3 (27%)	1 (7%)	0 (0%)	4 (11%)
CHI	2 (18%)	2 (13%)	0 (0%)	4 (11%)
DEN	2 (18%)	3 (20%)	4 (40%)	9 (25%)
LAX	1 (9%)	6 (40%)	1 (10%)	8 (22%)
NYC	1 (9%)	1 (7%)	4 (40%)	6 (17%)
PHL	2 (18%)	2 (13%)	1 (10%)	5 (14%)
Total	11 (100%)	15 (100%)	10 (100%)	36 (100%)

B. Local Interviewees

Census Bureau Region	City	County	Regional Agency	Other CCC Member	Total
ATL	2 (11%)	0 (0%)	1 (33%)	0 (0%)	3 (9%)
CHI	2 (11%)	1 (17%)	1 (33%)	2 (40%)	6 (18%)
DEN	5 (26%)	3 (50%)	0 (0%)	1 (20%)	9 (27%)
LAX	1 (5%)	1 (17%)	1 (33%)	0 (0%)	3 (9%)
NYC	4 (21%)	0 (0%)	0 (0%)	0 (0%)	4 (12%)
PHL	5 (26%)	1 (17%)	0 (0%)	2 (40%)	8 (24%)
Total	19 (100%)	6 (100%)	3 (100%)	5 (100%)	33 (100%)

C. Nonprofit Interviewees

Scope of Work	N (%)
National Focus	3 (43%)
State/Local Focus	4 (57%)
Total	7 (100%)

their organization, administrative support, and financing. I asked about each organization's objectives, work to date to accomplish these objectives, and planned work up to and beyond the beginning of the census self-response period. Based on interviewees' answers to these questions, I inquired about factors that were important in facilitating their work related to the census as well as barriers to accomplishing the organization's goals. I also

Table A4: Follow-Up Interviewees by Region and Primary Organizational Affiliation

A. State Interviewees

Census Bureau Region	State Data Center	State Complete Count Commission	State Agency or Governor's Office	Total
ATL	0 (0%)	0 (0%)	0 (0%)	1(7%)
CHI	1 (33%)	1 (10%)	0 (0%)	2(13%)
DEN	1 (33%)	0 (0%)	1 (50%)	2(23%)
LAX	0 (0%)	6 (60%)	0 (0%)	6(40%)
NYC	1 (33%)	1 (10%)	1 (50%)	3(20%)
PHL	0 (0%)	2 (20%)	0 (0%)	2(13%)
Total	3 (100%)	10 (100%)	(100%)	15(100%)

B. Local Interviewees

Census Bureau Region	City	County	Regional Agency	Other CCC Member	Total
ATL	1 (13%)	0 (0%)	1 (50%)	0 (0%)	2 (15%)
CHI	1 (13%)	0 (0%)	0 (0%)	1 (50%)	2 (15%)
DEN	2 (25%)	1 (100%)	0 (0%)	1 (50%)	4 (31%)
LAX	1 (13%)	0 (0%)	1 (50%)	0 (0%)	2 (15%)
NYC	0 (0%)	0 (0%)	0 (0%)	0 (0%)	0 (0%)
PHL	3 (38%)	0 (0%)	0 (0%)	0 (0%)	3 (23%)
Total	8 (100%)	1 (100%)	2 (100%)	2 (100%)	13 (100%)

Source: Author's analysis.

asked interviewees to describe how participants in local or state efforts attempted to resolve challenges that arose in engaging with the census. I took detailed notes on all interviews and collected audio recordings of all interviews. With the assistance of both transcription software and a research assistant, I transcribed all interview recordings and notes. With the help of a research assistant, I coded all transcript quotations by topic.

NOTES

INTRODUCTION

1. For a flavor of the media coverage of Remote Alaska enumeration, see Hansi Lo Wang, "Along The Rim of Alaska, The Once-A-Decade U.S. Census Began In Toksook Bay," National Public Radio, January 21, 2020, https://www.npr.org/2020/01/21/796703843 /along-the-rim-of-alaska-the-once-a-decade-u-s-census-begins-in-toksook-bay.

2. Tripp J. Crouse, "Alaska Native Language Groups Convene to Translate Census Materials," KNBA, December 18, 2019, https://www.knba.org/news/2019-12-18/alaska -native-language-groups-convene-to-translate-census-materials?fbclid=IwAR3m-zn QFkfiRn-5CtDLv8SOXcu7aV8SfpuYubZfhVPBC6dHzfAL-uP9AfA.

3. James C. Scott, *Seeing like a State: How Certain Schemes to Improve the Human Condition Have Failed* (Yale University Press, 1998); Rebecca Jean Emigh, Dylan Riley, and Patricia Ahmed, *Antecedents of Censuses from Medieval to Nation States: How States and Societies Count* (Palgrave Macmillan, 2015); Rebecca Jean Emigh, Dylan Riley, and Patricia Ahmed, *Changes in Censuses from Imperialist to Welfare States* (Palgrave Macmillan, 2016).

4. "Reapportionment Studies," Election Data Services, accessed October 22, 2024, https://www.electiondataservices.com/reapportionment-studies/.

5. Andrew Reamer, *Estimating the Costs of a Fiscal Undercount to States* (George Washington University Institute of Public Policy, 2018).

6. Miriam Jordan, "New Findings Detail Trump Plan to Use Census for Partisan Gain," *New York Times*, July 20, 2022.

7. Michael Wines and Jose A. Del Real, "In 2020 Census, Big Efforts in Some States. In Others, Not So Much," *New York Times*, December 15, 2019, https://www.nytimes .com/2019/12/15/us/census-california-texas-undercount.html.

8. On the role of nonprofits in census mobilization, see Deborah A. Gona, "Not-for-Profit Organizations," in *Encyclopedia of the US Census*, ed. Constance F. Citro, Margo J. Anderson, Joseph J. Salvo (CQ Press, 2011), 323–324.

9. Peter Gourevitch, *Politics in Hard Times* (Cornell University Press, 1986), 221.

10. Margo Anderson, *The American Census: A Social History*, 2nd ed. (Yale University Press, 2015), 2.

11. The first major work on the politics of official statistics in the United States can be found in William Alonso and Paul Starr, eds., *The Politics of Numbers* (Russell Sage Foundation, 1987). The definitive historical account of the US census is that of Anderson, *The American Census*. More recent works on the politics of official statistics include Cosmo Howard, *Government Statistical Agencies and the Politics of Credibility* (Cambridge University Press, 2021); Deborah Stone, *Counting: How We Use Numbers to Decide What Matters* (Liveright, 2021); Jerry Z. Muller, *The Tyranny of Metrics* (Princeton

University Press, 2019); Robert Saldin, *When Bad Policy Makes Good Politics: Running the Numbers on Health Reform* (Oxford University Press, 2017).

12. Quoted in Diane Coyle, *GDP: A Brief but Affectionate History* (Princeton University Press, 2015), xi.

13. "Eight Years of Government Persecution of Greek Statistician," American Statistical Association News Update, October 8, 2021, https://www.amstat.org/news-list ing/2021/10/08/eight-years-of-government-persecution-of-greek-statistician.

14. Emily Klancher Merchant, *Building the Population Bomb* (Oxford University Press, 2021).

15. Emigh, Riley, and Ahmed, *Antecedents of Censuses from Medieval to Nation States.* Studies undertaken over the last decade or so have born this out claim, documenting partisan, geographic, and group-based conflict over census undercounts, the collection of data on racial and ethnic identities, and the confidentiality of census data. See Anderson, *The American Census*; Cristina Mora, "Cross-Field Effects and Ethnic Classification: The Institutionalization of Hispanic Panethnicity, 1965 to 1990," *American Sociological Review* 79, no. 2 (2014): 183–210; Paul Schor, *Counting Americans* (Oxford University Press, 2017); Joel Perlmann, *America Classifies the Immigrants* (Harvard University Press, 2018); Victoria Hattam, "Ethnicity and the Boundaries of Race: Rereading Directive 15," *Daedalus* 134, no. 1 (2005): 61–69; Dan Bouk, *Democracy's Data: The Hidden Stories in the U.S. Census and How to Read Them* (Macmillan, 2022); Emily Klancher Merchant, *Building the Population Bomb* (Oxford University Press, 2021); Cristina Mora, *Making Hispanics: How Activists, Bureaucrats, and Media Constructed a New American* (University of Chicago Press, 2014).

16. Anderson, *The American Census.*

17. Debra Thompson, *The Schematic State: Race, Transnationalism, and the Politics of the Census* (Cambridge University Press, 2016), 15.

18. US Office of Management and Budget, *Analytical Perspectives: Budget of the U.S. Government, Fiscal Year 2023* (Office of Management and Budget, 2022), 225–232.

19. Philip Rocco, Jessica A. J. Rich, Katarzyna Klasa, Kenneth A. Dubin, and Daniel Béland, "Who Counts Where? COVID-19 Surveillance in Federal Countries," *Journal of Health Politics, Policy and Law* 46, no. 6 (2021): 959–987.

20. "Unemployment Insurance Data," US Department of Labor, Employment and Training Administration, accessed September 1, 2022, https://oui.doleta.gov/unemploy /data_summary/DataSum.asp.

21. "How States Join," National Center for Education Statistics, National Assessment of Educational Progress, accessed September 1, 2022, https://nces.ed.gov/nationsreport card/about/statejoin.aspx. On the intergovernmental politics of producing educational statistics, see Janet A. Weiss and Judith E. Gruber, "The Managed Irrelevance of Federal Education Statistics," in *The Politics of Numbers*, ed. William Alonso and Paul Starr (Russell Sage Foundation, 1987), 363–391.

22. "List of All Surveys and Programs," US Census Bureau, accessed September 1, 2022, https://www.census.gov/programs-surveys/surveys-programs.html; "Historical Overview of U.S. Census Bureau Data Collection Activities About Governments, 1880 to 2005," US Census Bureau, accessed September 1, 2022, https://www.census.gov/his tory/pdf/1984278.pdf.

23. National Research Council, *State and Local Government Statistics at a Crossroads* (National Academies Press, 2007).

24. See, e.g., Contreras. v. Illinois State Board of Elections, No. 1:21-cv-03139 (N.D. Ill.), Amended Complaint for Declaratory and Injunctive Relief (July 28, 2021).

25. Vera Bergengruen, "'We Continue to Spin in Circles.' Inside the Decades-Long Effort to Create a National Police Use-of-Force Database," *Time*, June 30, 2020, https://time.com/5861953/police-reform-use-of-force-database/; "National Use of Force Data Collection," Federal Bureau of Investigation, accessed September 1, 2022, https://www.fbi.gov/services/cjis/ucr/use-of-force.

26. Philip Rocco, Walid F. Gellad, and Julie M. Donohue, "Modernizing Medicaid Managed Care: Can States Meet the Data Challenges?," *JAMA* 314, no. 15 (2015): 1559–1560.

27. "Count Question Resolution Program," US Census Bureau, May 13, 2021, https://www.census.gov/newsroom/press-kits/2021/2020-census-count-question-resolution.html.

28. See, e.g., Baldrige v. Shapiro, 455 U.S. 345 (1982); Wisconsin v. City of New York, 517 U.S. 1 (1996); Franklin v. Massachusetts, 505 U.S. 788 (1992); Utah v. Evans, 536 U.S. 452 (2002); U.S. Department of Commerce v. New York, 588 U.S. ___ (2019).

29. Joseph Salvo, "Local Involvement in Census Taking," in *Encyclopedia of the US Census*, 302–305; Margo J. Anderson, "State and Local Censuses," in *Encyclopedia of the US Census*, 369; Nancy Krieger, "A Century of Census Tracts: Health and the Body Politic (1906–2006)," *Journal of Urban Health* 83, no. 3 (2006): 355–361.

30. See, e.g., Walter Laidlaw, *A Sketchy History of the Census Tract System of New York City, and an Account of the (1935) Expansion of Its Census Tract Maps into Census Tract Block Maps* (Mayor's Committee on City Planning, 1935); Krieger, "A Century of Census Tracts," 355–361. At the same time, census tract data were also used to exclude noncitizens from state-level redistricting, which was then required by the New York Constitution. See N.Y. Const. of 1894, art. III, §1, § 4.

31. Bouk, *Democracy's Data*, 78; Edward Dana Durand, *Report of the Director to the Secretary of Commerce and Labor Concerning the Operations of the Bureau for the Year 1909–10* (Government Printing Office, 1911), 26.

32. Anderson, *The American Census*; Robert Scardamalia, "State Data Centers," in *Encyclopedia of the US Census*, 371–372.

33. Robert Scardamalia, "State Data Centers," in *Encyclopedia of the US Census*, 371–372.

34. "2020 Census: Bureau Needs to Take Additional Actions to Address Key Risks to a Successful Enumeration," Government Accountability Office, July 24, 2019, https://www.gao.gov/products/gao-19-685t.

35. "2000 Census: Review of Partnership Program Highlights Best Practices for Future Operations," US General Accounting Office, August 2001, https://www.gao.gov/assets/gao-01-579.pdf.

36. "State Complete Count Commissions," US Census Bureau, July 2018, https://www.census.gov/content/dam/Census/newsroom/press-kits/2018/sccc.pdf.

37. US Census Bureau, *2020 Census Complete Count Committee Guide* (US Census Bureau), 4.

38. Albert E. Fontenot Jr., *2020 Census Program Memorandum Series: 2021.22* (US Department of Commerce, 2019), https://www2.census.gov/programs-surveys/decennial/2020/program-management/planning-docs/CRO-detailed-operational-plan.pdf.

39. Tim Henderson, "Detroit Challenges 2020 Census Count," Pew Stateline, April 6, 2022, https://www.pewtrusts.org/en/research-and-analysis/blogs/stateline/2022/04/06/detroit-challenges-2020-census-count; US Census Bureau, *2020 Census Count Question Resolution Operation (CQR) Cases Received as of 9/6/2022* (US Census Bureau, 2024), https://www2.census.gov/programs-surveys/decennial/2020/program-management/cqr/cqr-cases-received.pdf.

40. On intergovernmental cooperation and information gathering, see Robert Agranoff, *Crossing Boundaries for Intergovernmental Management* (Georgetown University Press, 2017), 64–66.

41. Analysis of annual reports of state data centers, obtained by author via Freedom of Information Act Request DOC-CEN-2020–000547.

42. Mike Maciag, "6 Innovative Ways States and Localities Are Preparing for the 2020 Census," Governing, December 17, 2018, https://www.governing.com/archive/gov-2020-census-count.html.

43. On instrument-based accounts of intergovernmental cooperation and conflict, see William T. Gormley, "Money and Mandates: The Politics of Intergovernmental Conflict," *Publius: The Journal of Federalism* 36, no. 4 (2006): 523–540.

44. Government Accountability Office, *Update on the Bureau's Implementation of Partnership and Outreach Activities* (US Government Accountability Office, 2020), https://www.gao.gov/assets/gao-20-496.pdf.

45. On the role of partisanship in relatively low-salience, bureaucratic policy domains, see Philip Rocco, Andrew S. Kelly, and Ann C. Keller, "Politics at the Cutting Edge: Intergovernmental Policy Innovation in the Affordable Care Act," *Publius: The Journal of Federalism* 48, no. 3 (2018): 425–453.

46. Miriam Jordan, "New Findings Detail Trump Plan to Use Census for Partisan Gain."

47. One way of understanding this conflict is that state partisan politics is highly nationalized. Whereas Democrats' coalition and party brand hinges on support both for federal programs allocated using census population data and policies that support historically undercounted minority groups, state-level Republican parties are agents of an ideological movement that favors federal social policy retrenchment and espouses negative views of groups typically undercounted in the census. Matt Grossmann and David A. Hopkins, *Asymmetric Politics: Ideological Republicans and Group Interest Democrats* (Oxford University Press, 2016); Daniel Hopkins, *The Increasingly United States* (University of Chicago Press, 2018).

48. See Carol S. Weissert, "Beyond Marble Cakes and Picket Fences: What US Federalism Scholars Can Learn from Comparative Work," *Journal of Politics* 73, no. 4 (2011): 965–979; Carol S. Weissert, *Rethinking Federalism Studies* (Edward Elgar, 2023).

49. Richard P. Nathan, "The Politics of Printouts: The Use of Official Numbers to Allocate Federal Grants-in-Aid," in *The Politics of Numbers*, ed. William Alonso and Paul Starr (Russell Sage Foundation, 1987), 331–342; Judith Innes de Neufville, "Federal Statistics in Local Governments," in *The Politics of Numbers*, 343–362.

50. For more on lateral effects, see Suzanne Mettler, "The Policyscape and the Challenges of Contemporary Politics to Policy Maintenance," *Perspectives on Politics* 14, no. 2 (2016): 369–390.

51. As I have argued elsewhere, state governments are better thought of as an infrastructure rather than relatively insulated laboratories because they constitute the national polity through the administration of elections, the drawing of legislative districts, and the operation of formative institutions—such as schools, prisons, and labor-market policies—which can affect the culture of democratic participation. See Philip Rocco, "Laboratories of What? American Federalism and the Politics of Democratic Subversion," in *Democratic Resilience: Can the United States Withstand Rising Polarization*, ed. Robert C. Lieberman, Suzanne Mettler, and Kenneth M. Roberts (Cambridge University Press, 2021), 297–319.

52. On the challenge of managing interdependency, see Robert Agranoff, *Crossing Boundaries for Intergovernmental Management* (Georgetown University Press, 2017).

53. My interviews focused largely on partnerships created under the auspices of the Community Partnership and Engagement Program (CPEP), the Local Update of Census Addresses (LUCA), Count Review, and Count Question Resolution. I did not conduct extensive interviews on state and federal officials' collaboration to produce redistricting data under Public Law 94–171.

1. CENSUS POLITICS AND THE FEDERAL SYSTEM

1. "Minnesota Councilman Dons Cape as 'Census Man' to Promote Upcoming Count," Fox 9 Minneapolis–St. Paul, May 9, 2019, https://www.fox9.com/news/minnesota-councilman-dons-cape-as-census-man-to-promote-upcoming-count.

2. *Last Week Tonight with John Oliver*, season 6, episode 30, "Census," YouTube, November 17, 2019, https://www.youtube.com/watch?v=1aheRpmurAo.

3. John Croman, "Census 'Nerds' Spread Word on 2020 Head Count," KARE News, August 27, 2019, https://www.kare11.com/article/news/local/census-nerds-spread-word-on-head-count/89-eb27cb1c-b8eb-47c3-9eb4-4b370a5e6805.

4. "Efforts of Census Man Pay Dividends for City of Circle Pines," NorthMetroTV, August 19, 2021, https://www.youtube.com/watch?v=5dWiB0AicOI.

5. Phone interview with Ditas Katague, January 5, 2023.

6. California Complete Count—Census 2020 Office, *California Census 2020 Outreach and Communication Campaign Final Report* (California Census, 2021), https://census.ca.gov/wp-content/uploads/sites/4/2021/05/California-Census-2020-Outreach-and-Communications-Campaign-Final-Report-5.11.2021.pdf?emrc=cc0448.

7. A sample of ten bestselling introductory textbooks in American politics is illustrative here. In six of the ten, the word *census* does not appear in the index. Of the four texts that do mention the census, three mention it in passing. Only one provides at least a paragraph-length description of the Census Bureau's role. See David Canon and William Bianco, *American Politics Today*, 8th ed. (W. W. Norton, 2022); James Morone and Rogan Kersh, *By the People: Debating American Government*, 5th ed. (Oxford University Press, 2020); Samuel Kernell, Gary Jacobson, Thad Kousser, Lynn Vavreck, and Timothy

R. Johnson, *The Logic of American Politics*, 10th ed. (CQ Press, 2021); Benjamin Gins-berg, Theodore J. Lowi, Margaret Weir, Caroline J. Tolbert, and Andrea L. Campbell, *We the People*, 13th ed. (W. W. Norton, 2021); Theodore Lowi, Benjamin Ginsberg, Ken-neth Shepsle, and Stephen Ansolabehere, *American Government: Power and Purpose*, 16th ed. (W. W. Norton, 2021); Edward S. Greenberg, Benjamin I. Page, David Doherty, Scott L. Minkoff, and John M. Ryan, *The Struggle for Democracy: 2020 Presidential Elec-tion Edition* (Pearson, 2022); James Q. Wilson, John DiIulio, Meena Bose, Matthew S. Levendusky, *American Government: Institutions and Policies*, 17th ed. (Engage, 2021); Cal Jillson, *American Government: Political Development and Institutional Change*, 11th ed. (Routledge, 2021); Christine Barbour and Gerald C. Wright, *Keeping the Republic: Power and Citizenship in American Politics*, 9th ed. (CQ Press, 2021); Ken Kollman, *The American Political System*, 3rd ed. (W. W. Norton, 2017).

8. David Brian Robertson, *The Original Compromise: What the Constitution's Framers Were Really Thinking* (Oxford University Press, 2012), 57–78.

9. Robertson, *The Original Compromise*, 246.

10. Margo Anderson, *The American Census: A Social History*, 2nd ed. (Yale University Press, 2015), 8–9.

11. Robertson, *The Original Compromise*, 179.

12. The delicate wording of this provision has been called a "masterpiece of circumlo-cution." See William Lee Miller, *The Business of May Next: James Madison and the Found-ing* (University of Virginia Press, 1992), 120.

13. This paragraph draws on Anderson, *The American Census*, 16–18.

14. See, in general, Charles W. Eagles, *Democracy Delayed: Congressional Reapportion-ment and Urban–Rural Conflict in the 1920s* (University of Georgia Press, 1990), 21–31.

15. David M. Potter, *The Impending Crisis, 1848—1861* (Harper & Row, 1976).

16. Anderson, *The American Census*, 140.

17. Potter, *The Impending Crisis*. Because a congressional majority has never voted to reverse this decision, the size of Congress has remained constant at 435 members, even though the US population has more than tripled in size since 1910. Today, while most countries' parliaments grow in proportion to their populations, the United States remains an outlier, with a House of Representatives that is significantly undersized. See Jeffrey W. Ladewig and Mathew P. Jasinski, "On the Causes and Consequences of and Remedies for Interstate Malapportionment of the US House of Representatives," *Perspec-tives on Politics* 6, no. 1 (2008): 89–107.

18. Eagles, *Democracy Delayed*, 32–84; Jeffery A. Jenkins and Nicholas G. Napolio, "Conflict over Congressional Reapportionment: The Deadlock of the 1920s," *Journal of Policy History* 35, no. 1 (2023): 91–117; Dan Bouk, *House Arrest: How an Automated Algorithm Has Constrained Congress for a Century* (Data and Society, 2021), https://da tasociety.net/wp-content/uploads/2021/04/House-Arrest-Dan-Bouk.pdf.

19. Margo Anderson, "The Ghosts of Census Past and Their Relevance for 2020," *Proceedings of the American Philosophical Society* 163, no. 3 (2019): 227–238; Margo Anderson, "*Baker v. Carr*, the Census, and the Political and Statistical Geography of the United States: The Origin and Impact of Public Law 94–171," *Case Western Reserve Law Review* 62, no. 4 (2012): 1153–1178.

20. Anderson, "*Baker v. Carr*," 1162.

21. Advisory Commission on Intergovernmental Relations, *Apportionment of State Legislatures* (Government Printing Office, 1962), A-7.

22. Gordon E. Baker, *The Reapportionment Revolution: Representation, Political Power, and the Supreme Court* (Random House, 1966), 6.

23. Colegrove v. Green 328 U.S. 549 (1946).

24. Gordon E. Baker, *The Reapportionment Revolution*.

25. "2020 Census Tallies of Census Tracts, Block Groups & Blocks," US Census Bureau, accessed February 16, 2024, https://www.census.gov/geographies/reference-files/time-series/geo/tallies.html#tract_bg_block; "Geography Program Glossary," US Census Bureau, accessed February 16, 2024, https://www.census.gov/programs-surveys/geography/about/glossary.html#:~:text=Census%20tracts%20generally%20have%20a,on%20the%20density%20of%20settlement.

26. See Anderson, *"Baker v. Carr."*

27. Anderson.

28. Shelby County v. Holder, 570 U.S. 529 (2013), https://supreme.justia.com/cases/federal/us/570/529/.

29. Stephen B. Billings, Noah Braun, Daniel B. Jones, and Ying Shi, "Disparate Racial Impacts of Shelby County v. Holder on Voter Turnout," *Journal of Public Economics* 230 (2024): 105047.

30. Brnovich v. Democratic National Committee, 594 U.S. ___ (2021).

31. Allen v. Milligan, 599 U.S. ___ (2023).

32. Anderson, *The American Census*, 209–223.

33. See, e.g., Richard P. Nathan, "The Politics of Printouts: The Use of Official Numbers to Allocate Federal Grants-in-Aid," in *The Politics of Numbers*, ed. William Alonso and Paul Starr (Russell Sage Foundation, 1987), 331–342.

34. Young and Rubicam, "Emergency Services," advertisement for the 2000 Census, accessed January 25, 2023, https://www.youtube.com/watch?v=JojQTag_J2o.

35. "State and Local Finance Data: Exploring the Census of Governments," Urban Institute, accessed January 23, 2023, https://state-local-finance-data.taxpolicycenter.org.

36. This section draws on Andrew Reamer, *Estimating the Costs of a Fiscal Undercount to States* (George Washington University Institute of Public Policy, 2018).

37. Reamer, *Estimating the Costs of a Fiscal Undercount to States*, 3.

38. Dan Bouk, *Democracy's Data: The Hidden Stories in the U.S. Census and How to Read Them* (Macmillan, 2022), 131–134.

39. See Kenneth Prewitt, "The US Decennial Census: Political Questions, Scientific Answers," *Population and Development Review* 26, no. 1 (2000): 7.

40. US Commission on Civil Rights, *Counting the Forgotten: The 1970 Census Count of Persons of Spanish Speaking Background in the United* States (US Commission on Civil Rights, 1974), 50.

41. David Heer, ed., *Social Statistics and the City* (Joint Center for Urban Studies, 1968), 11.

42. Managing intergovernmental interdependencies, as public administration scholar Robert Agranoff suggests, is an "eminently political as well as managerial process." See Robert Agranoff, *Crossing Boundaries for Intergovernmental Management* (Georgetown University Press, 2017), 117.

43. Matt Grossman and David A. Hopkins, *Asymmetric Politics: Ideological Republicans and Group-Interest Democrats* (Oxford University Press, 2016).

44. Mark Tushnet, "Constitutional Hardball," *John Marshall Law Review* 37 (2004): 523–544.

45. Jacob S. Hacker and Paul Pierson, "Confronting Asymmetric Polarization," in *Solutions to Political Polarization in America*, ed. Nathaniel Persily (Cambridge University Press, 2015), 66.

46. "About APDU," Association of Public Data Users, accessed January 25, 2023, https://www.apdu.org/about-apdu/; "State Data Center (SDC) Program," US Census Bureau, accessed January 25, 2023, https://www.census.gov/about/partners/sdc.html.

47. US Census Bureau, *2020 Census Tribal Consultations with Federally Recognized Tribes: Final Report* (US Census Bureau, 2020), https://www.census.gov/content/dam/Census/library/publications/2020/dec/census-federal-tc-final-report-2020-508.pdf.

48. US Census Bureau, "Final 2020 Census Residence Criteria and Residence Situations," *Federal Register* 83, no. 27 (February 8, 2018): 5526.

49. See Constance Citro, "Advisory Committees," in *Encyclopedia of the US Census*, 32–35.

50. Albert Fontenot Jr., *2020 Census Update: Presentation to the National Advisory Committee* (US Census Bureau, 2017), https://www2.census.gov/cac/nac/meetings/2017-11/fontenot-2020-census.pdf.

51. See, e.g., Betty Yee, Nancy Kopp, Thomas DiNapoli, Tobias Read, Joe Torsella, Seth Magaziner, David Damschen, Mark J. F. Schroeder, Ron Galperin, Alan Butkovitz, Michael Lamb, and Scott M. Stringer, "Letter Re: Ensuring the Success of the 2020 United States Census," Census Monitoring Board, June 20, 2017, https://censusproject.files.wordpress.com/2015/12/census-letter-062017.pdf.

52. For a cross-national comparative perspective of the position of statistical agencies within the executive branch, see Cosmo Howard, *Government Statistical Agencies and the Politics of Credibility* (Cambridge University Press, 2021).

53. Phung Nguyen, "The Census Bureau and Its Accountability," *The American Review of Public Administration* 37, no. 2 (2007): 226–243.

54. Presidential Appointment Efficiency and Streamlining Act of 2011, Pub. L. No. 112–166.

2. BATTLE ROYALE: HOW STATE AND LOCAL OFFICIALS STOPPED THE CITIZENSHIP QUESTION

1. Lori Robertson and Robert Farley, "Fact Check: The Controversy over Trump's Inauguration Crowd Size," *USA Today*, January 24, 2017, https://www.usatoday.com/story/news/politics/2017/01/24/fact-check-inauguration-crowd-size/96984496/; Sarah Frostenson, "A Crowd Scientist Says Trump's Inauguration Attendance Was Pretty Average," Vox, January 24, 2017.

2. Philip Rocco, "The Policy State and the Post-Truth Presidency," in *American Political Development and the Trump Presidency*, ed. Zac Callen and Philip Rocco (University of Pennsylvania Press, 2020), 114–129.

3. US Congress, *Select Committee to Investigate the January 6th Attack on the United States Capitol*, Final Report, 117th Cong., 2d Sess., H.R. Rep. No. 117–663 (2022), https://www.govinfo.gov/content/pkg/GPO-J6-REPORT/html-submitted/index.html.

4. Gary C. Jacobson, "The Dimensions, Origins, and Consequences of Belief in Donald Trump's Big Lie," *Political Science Quarterly* 138, no. 2 (2023): 133–166.

5. See, e.g., Sophia Jordán Wallace and Chris Zepeda-Millán. *Walls, Cages, and Family Separation: Race and Immigration Policy in the Trump Era* (Cambridge University Press, 2020).

6. The battle over the citizenship question was highly documented in the media even prior to the filing of the first lawsuit in the case. See "Census Media Tracking on Requested Citizenship Question January 29, 2017 to March 23, 2018," New York v. Department of Commerce, Ad. Rec., 666–733.

7. Thomas Wolf and Brianna Cea, "A Critical History of the United States Census and the Citizenship Question," *Georgetown Law Journal Online* 108 (2019): 1–37.

8. Diana Elliott, Rob Santos, Steven Martin, and Charmaine Runes, *Assessing Miscounts in the 2020 Census* (Urban Institute Report, 2019), https://www.urban.org/sites/default/files/publication/100324/assessing_miscounts_in_the_2020_census_1.pdf.

9. There were, in fact, seven lawsuits filed in federal courts related to Ross's decision to include a citizenship item on the 2020 questionnaire. In Washington, DC, the Electronic Privacy Information Center (EPIC) filed a challenge to the citizenship question: EPIC v. U.S. Department of Commerce, No. 1:18-cv-02711 (D.D.C. 2018). Lawsuits filed by the State of California and the city of San Jose were consolidated into a single case, California v. Ross, No. 3:18-cv-01865 (N.D. Cal 2018). A district court in Maryland consolidated a lawsuit filed by residents of Arizona and Maryland was consolidated with another filed by a coalition of twenty-five organizations representing Asian Americans, African Americans, Latinos, Native Americans, and immigrants into Kravitz v. U.S. Department of Commerce, 8:18-cv-01041 (D. Md. 2019). Finally, a federal court in New York consolidated a lawsuit filed by a coalition of state attorneys general with another filed by the New York Immigration Coalition into New York v. Department of Commerce, No. 1:18-cv-2921 (S.D.N.Y. 2018). This chapter is focused on this final case, which became the central site of the battle over the citizenship question.

10. Shane Goldmacher, "New York Loses House Seat After Coming Up 89 People Short on Census," *New York Times*, April 26, 2021, https://www.nytimes.com/2021/04/26/nyregion/new-york-census-congress.html.

11. Andrew Reamer, *Estimating the Fiscal Costs of a Census Undercount to States* (George Washington University Institute of Public Policy Report, 2019), https://gwipp.gwu.edu/sites/g/files/zaxdzs2181/f/downloads/GWIPP%20Reamer%20Fiscal%20Impacts%20of%20Census%20Undercount%20on%20FMAP-based%20Programs%2003-19-18.pdf.

12. Robert Kagan, *Adversarial Legalism: The American Way of Law* (Harvard University Press, 2001).

13. Wisconsin v. City of New York, 517 U.S. 1 (1996).

14. This process began with the creation of the Census Office in 1902, which effectively ended the ad hoc approach to census taking that defined the nineteenth century. In 1954, Congress codified census statutes when it passed the Census Act. See An Act to

Revise, Codify, and Enact into Law, Title 13 of the United States Code, entitled "Census,"
Pub. L. No. 740, Stat. 68 (1954).

15. See Margo Anderson, *The American Census: A Social History*, 2nd ed. (Yale University Press, 2015), 117, 224–250.

16. An Act to Amend Title 13, United States Code, to Provide for a Mid-Decade Census of Population, and for Other Purposes, Pub. L. 521, Stat. 90 (1976).

17. Pub. L. 521, § 4(a).

18. Pub. L. 521, § 10.

19. See Anderson, *The American Census,* 239–250.

20. See, e.g., Franklin v. Massachusetts, 505 U.S. 788 (1992).

21. Nicholas F. Jacobs, Desmond King, and Sidney M. Milkis, "State Building in Crisis Governance: Donald Trump and COVID-19," *Political Science Quarterly* 137, no. (2022): 225–261.

22. Rogers M. Smith and Desmond King, "White Protectionism in America," *Perspectives on Politics* 19, no. 2 (2021): 460–478.

23. Philip Rocco, "The Policy State and the Post-Truth Presidency," in *American Political Development and the Trump Presidency*, ed. Zachary Callen and Philip Rocco (University of Pennsylvania Press, 2020), 114–129.

24. New York Immigration Coalition v. Department of Commerce, No. 1:18-cv-05025 55 (Aug. 30, 2018) (Deposition of Earl Comstock).

25. Wolf and Cea, "A Critical History of the United States Census and the Citizenship Question."

26. US Bureau of the Census, *1960 Censuses of Population and Housing: Procedural History* (Government Printing Office, 1966), 194.

27. See New York v. Department of Commerce, 345 F.Supp.3d 444 (S.D.N.Y. 2018).

28. Justin Levitt, "Citizenship and the Census," *Columbia Law Review* 119 (2019): 1388.

29. Sean Trende, "The Most Important Redistricting Case in 50 Years," RealClearPolitics, June 3, 2015, http://www.realclearpolitics.com/articles/2015/06/03/the_most_important_redistricting_case_in_50_years_126831.html.

30. Levitt, "Citizenship and the Census," 1390. On the role of state legislatures in shaping democracy at the national level, see Philip Rocco, "Laboratories of What? American Federalism and the Politics of Democratic Subversion," in *Democratic Resilience*, ed. Robert Lieberman, Suzanne Mettler, and Kenneth M. Roberts (Cambridge University Press), 297–319.

31. Hans von Spakovsky and Elizabeth Slattery, *One Person, One Vote: Advancing Electoral Equality, Not Equality of Representation* (Heritage Foundation Legal Memorandum, 2015), http://thf_media.s3.amazonaws.com/2015/pdf/LM161.pdf.

32. Evenwel v. Abbott, 578 U.S. ____ (2016).

33. Thomas Hofeller, "The Use of Citizen Voting Age Population in Redistricting," ACLU Foundation, 2015, https://www.supremecourt.gov/DocketPDF/18/18-966/101439/20190530142417722_2019.05.30%20NYIC%20Respondents%20Notice%20of%20Filing%20--%20Final.pdf.

34. Hofeller, "The Use of Citizen Voting Age Population in Redistricting," 9.

35. Michael Wines, "Deceased G.O.P. Strategist's Hard Drives Reveal New Details on

the Census Citizenship Question," *New York Times*, May 30, 2019, https://www.nytimes .com/2019/05/30/us/census-citizenship-question-hofeller.html.

36. Kris Kobach email to Wilbur Ross, *New York*, 764.

37. Commerce Second Supplemental Response to Interrogatory at 1, *New York*, Commerce Second Supplemental Response to Interrogatory 1 (Plaintiffs' Ex.), 2–3.

38. Wilbur Ross email to Earl Comstock, *New York*, Wilbur Ross, E-mail to Earl Comstock, 3710.

39. Trial Transcript, *New York*, 1378–1379.

40. Paperwork Reduction Act, 44 U.S.C., § 3501 et seq.; Office of Management and Budget, "Statistical Policy Directive No. 1: Fundamental Responsibilities of Federal Statistical Agencies and Recognized Statistical Units," *Federal Register* 79, no. 231 (2014): 71610; Office of Management and Budget, "Statistical Policy Directive No. 2: Standards and Guidelines for Statistical Surveys; Addendum: Standards and Guidelines for Cognitive Interviews," *Federal Register* 81, no. 197 (2016): 70586.

41. *New York Immigration Coalition* (Deposition of Earl Comstock), 153–154, 181.

42. Comstock email to Ross, *New York*, 3710. As Comstock put in an email to Ross: "We need to work with Justice to get them to request that citizenship be added back as a census question, and we have the court cases to illustrate that DOJ has a legitimate need for the question to be included."

43. *New York*, 345 F. Supp. 3d 444, 67.

44. Comstock email to Ross, *New York*, 12476.

45. *New York*, 345 F. Supp. 3d 444, 72–73.

46. Arthur E. Gary Letter to Ron S. Jarmin, *New York*, 663.

47. Gary Letter to Jarmin, *New York*, 663.

48. *New York*, 345 F. Supp. 3d 444, 77–79.

49. The results of these analyses are summarized in *New York*, "Technical Review of the Department of Justice Request to Add Citizenship Question to the 2020 Census," 1277–1305.

50. Technical Review, *New York*.

51. Preliminary Analysis of Alternative D (Combined Alternatives B and C), *New York*, 1312.

52. Correspondence can be found in *New York*, 767–1276.

53. *New York*, 1206, 8325.

54. See, e.g., Steven Camarota, "Testimony Prepared for the House Subcommittee on Federalism and the Census," Center for Immigration Studies, December 6, 2005, https:// cis.org/Testimony/Impact-NonCitizens-Congressional-Apportionment; Hans von Spakovsky, "How Noncitizens Can Swing Elections (Without Even Voting Illegally)," *Daily Signal*, October 6, 2015, https://www.dailysignal.com/2015/10/06/how-noncitizens -can-swing-elections-without-even-voting-illegally/.

55. Memorandum Re: *Reinstatement of a Citizenship Question on the 2020 Decennial Census Questionnaire*, *New York*, Wilbur Ross, Memorandum, 1313–1320.

56. Memorandum, *New York*, 1319.

57. Memorandum, 1316.

58. Eric T. Schneiderman, Maura Healey, Xavier Becerra, John W. Hickenlooper, George Jepsen, Matthew Denn, Karl A. Racine, Russell Suzuki, Lisa Madigan, Thomas J.

Miller, Janet T. Mills, Brian Frosh, Jim Hood, Gurbir Grewal, Hector H. Balderas, Ellen F. Rosenblum, Josh Shapiro, Peter Kilmartin, Thomas J. Donovan Jr., and Bob Furguson, "Letter to Wilbur Ross," NY.gov, February 12, 2018, https://ag.ny.gov/sites/default/files /multi-state_letter_2020_census.pdf.

59. Major cases involving the 1970 Census include Borough of Bethel Park v. Stans, 449 F.2d 575 (3d 1971); Confederacion de la RazaUnida v. Brown, 345 F. Supp. 909 (N.D. Cal. 1972); United States v. Little, 321 F. Supp. 388 (D. Del. 1971); Prieto v. Stans, 321 F. Supp. 420 (N.D. Cal. 1970); West End Neighborhood Corp. v. Stans, 312 F. Supp. 1066 (D.D.C. 1970); Quon v. Stans, 309 F. Supp. 604 (N.D. Cal. 1970); City of East Chicago v. Stans, No. 70H156 (N.D. Ind. Oct. 21, 1970).

60. Of the fifty-two federal lawsuits related to the 1980 Census, state or local governments filed twenty. None of these cases made it as far as the Supreme Court and half were dismissed by district courts. See US Bureau of the Census, *1990 Census of Population and Housing: History* (Government Printing Office, 1995), app. 12B.

61. See, e.g., Ridge v. Verity, 715 F. Supp. 1308 (W.D. Pa. 1989); Lindsey v. Prewitt, Civil No. 00–6091-TC (D.Or. Aug. 8, 2000).

62. Federation for American Immigration Reform v. Klutznick, 486 F. Supp. 564 (D.D.C. 1980).

63. *New York*, 345 F. Supp. 3d 444, 139–145.

64. Paul Nolette and Colin Provost, "Change and Continuity in the Role of State Attorneys General in the Obama and Trump Administrations," *Publius: The Journal of Federalism* 48, no. 3 (2018): 469–494; see also Paul Nolette, *Federalism on Trial: State Attorneys General and National Policymaking in Contemporary America* (University Press of Kansas, 2015).

65. Cornell W. Clayton and Jack McGuire, "State Litigation Strategies and Policymaking in the US Supreme Court," *Kansas Journal of Law and Public Policy* 11 (2001): 17–34.

66. Nolette and Provost, "Change and Continuity in the Role of State Attorneys General in the Obama and Trump Administrations."

67. The difference is greater if we eliminate parties in consolidated cases.

68. Nolette and Provost, "Change and Continuity in the Role of State Attorneys General in the Obama and Trump Administrations."

69. State attorneys general do not always act alone, and sometimes their actions conflict with those of the state's governor. Four examples from the citizenship-question cases are illustrative. While Colorado was one of the government plaintiffs, Colorado's Republican attorney general filed an amicus brief supporting the Trump administration during the motion-to-dismiss (MTD) phase of the case in federal district court. Maine was not a party to the case yet its Republican governor also signed on to an amicus brief at the MTD stage. Mississippi's attorney general joined the Schneiderman letter; the state's governor, however, later joined an amicus brief in support of the Trump administration before the Supreme Court. While Kentucky's Democratic AG did not join as an amicus in the case, its Republican governor joined an amicus supporting the Trump administration in the Supreme Court. See States of New York, Connecticut, Delaware Illinois, Iowa, et al. v. United States Department of Commerce and Wilbur L. Ross Jr., Complaint for Declaratory and Injunctive Relief, April 3, 2018, https://www .brennancenter.org/sites/default/files/legal-work/New-York-et-al_v_Department_of

_Commerce_Complaint.pdf; States of Oklahoma, Louisiana, Alabama, Arkansas, Florida, et al., Motion for Leave to File a Brief as *Amici Curiae* in Support of Defendants' Motion to Dismiss, June 1, 2018, https://www.brennancenter.org/sites/default/files /legal-work/NewYork_v_Dept-of-Commerce_Motion-for-Leave-to-File-Amicus-Brief -OK-etal.pdf; States of Oklahoma, Alabama, Arkansas, Florida, Georgia, et al., Brief as *Amici Curiae* in Support of Petitioners, March 6, 2019, https://www.supremecourt.gov /DocketPDF/18/18-966/90944/20190306152155269_Amicus%20Brief%20of%20Okla homa%20et%20al.pdf.

70. Author's analysis of Department of Commerce v. New York, Supreme Court Docket 18–966, https://www.supremecourt.gov/docket/docketfiles/html/public/18-966.html.

71. On APA claims, see, e.g., Franklin v. Massachusetts; Citizens to Preserve Overton Park, Inc. v. Volpe, 401 U.S. 402; Motor Vehicle Manufacturers. Association v. State Farm Mutual Automobile Insurance Company, 463 U.S. 29, 52 (1983); Michigan v. Environmental Protection Agency, 135 S. Ct. 2699, 2710 (2015).

72. On the traditional three-part standing test, see Gill v. Whitford, 138 S. Ct. 1916 (2018), 1929.

73. In May 2018, amid accusations of physical abuse, New York attorney general Eric Schneiderman resigned and was replaced by solicitor general Barbara Underwood.

74. On the procedural history of the case, see *New York*, 345 F. Supp. 3d 444 (S.D.N.Y. 2018), 28–30.

75. *New York*, 345 F. Supp. 3d 444, 28–30.

76. Hansi Lo Wang, "Multi-State Lawsuit Against Census Citizenship Question to Move Ahead," National Public Radio, July 26, 2018, https://www.npr.org/2018/07 /26/629773825/multi-state-lawsuit-against-census-citizenship-question-to-move -ahead.

77. Memorandum of Law in Support of Defendants' Motion to Dismiss, May 25, 2018, https://www.brennancenter.org/sites/default/files/legal-work/New-York-et-al_v _Department_of_Commerce_Memorandum-of-Law-in-Support-of-Motion-to-Dis miss.pdf.

78. Memorandum of Law in Support of Defendants' Motion to Dismiss.

79. *New York*, 345 F. Supp. 3d 444, 29.

80. *New York*, 345 F. Supp. 3d 444, 101.

81. *New York*, 345 F. Supp. 3d 444, 62n19.

82. *New York*, 345 F. Supp. 3d 444, 263.

83. Hansi Lo Wang, "Judge Says Administration Can't Change Lawyers in Census Citizenship Question Case," National Public Radio, July 7, 2019, https://www.npr .org/2019/07/07/739369416/justice-department-changes-legal-team-behind-census -citizenship-question-case.

84. Trial Transcript, *New York*, 24–172.

85. Trial Transcript, 173–196.

86. Trial Transcript, 198–203.

87. Trial Transcript, 857–874.

88. *New York*, 345 F. Supp. 3d 444, 142.

89. Trial Transcript, *New York*, 24–172.

90. Trial Transcript, 288–453.

91. Trial Transcript, 876–1394.

92. *New York*, 345 F. Supp. 3d 444, 94.

93. Trial Transcript, *New York*, 1303.

94. Trial Transcript, 1312.

95. Trial Transcript, 1326.

96. The NGO plaintiffs also argued that Ross's decision violated the Fifth Amendment Due Process Clause because it was based on "animus towards people whose origin is not in the United States." Judge Furman eventually ruled that they had not shown a preponderance of evidence to support this claim but "could have carried their burden on that score had they had access to sworn testimony from Secretary Ross himself." See *New York*, 345 F. Supp. 3d 444, 263.

97. Trial Transcript, *New York*, 1448–1463.

98. Trial Transcript, 1463.

99. *New York*, 345 F. Supp. 3d 444, 8.

100. *New York*, 207–224.

101. *New York*, 225–244.

102. *New York*, 245–252.

103. *New York*, 276.

104. US Department of Commerce et al., Petition for a Writ of Certiorari Before Judgment to the United States Court of Appeals for the Second Circuit, January 25, 2019, https://www.supremecourt.gov/DocketPDF/18/18-966/81777/20190125163140500_2019-01-25%20Commerce%20CBJ%20petn.pdf.

105. 28 U.S.C. § 2101.

106. *Department of Commerce*, S.C. Docket No. 18–966.

107. This section is indebted to Gillian E. Metzger, "The Roberts Court and Administrative Law," *Supreme Court Review* 2019, no. 1 (2020): 1–71.

108. Jen Kirby, "7 Legal Experts on How Kavanaugh Views Executive Power—and What It Could Mean for Mueller," Vox, July 11, 2018, https://www.vox.com/policy-and-politics/2018/7/11/17551648/kavanaugh-mueller-trump-executive-power-legal; Elliott Ash and Daniel Chen, "Kavanaugh Is Radically Conservative. Here's the Data to Prove It," *Washington Post*, July 10, 2018, https://www.washingtonpost.com/news/posteverything/wp/2018/07/10/kavanaugh-is-radically-conservative-heres-the-data-to-prove-it/.

109. Metzger, "The Roberts Court and Administrative Law."

110. Trump v. Hawaii, 138 S. Ct. 2392 (2018), 34.

111. *Department of Commerce*, Brief for the Petitioners, March 6, 2019, 41–42.

112. States of Oklahoma, Alabama, Arkansas, Florida, Georgia, et al., Brief as *Amici Curiae* in Support of Petitioners, March 6, 2019, 3.

113. Brief as *Amici Curiae* in Support of Petitioners, March 6, 2019, 3.

114. Joan Biskupic, *The Chief: The Life and Turbulent Times of Chief Justice John Roberts* (New York: Basic Books, 2019), 221–248; Alex Badas, "The Chief Justice and Judicial Legitimacy Evidence from the Influence of Public Opinion," *Justice System Journal* 42, no. 2 (2021): 150–163; Logan Stroger and Colin Glennon, "An Experimental Investigation of the Effect of Supreme Court Justices' Public Rhetoric on Perceptions of Judicial Legitimacy," *Law & Social Inquiry* 46, no. 2 (2021): 435–454.

115. Based on author's analysis of dockets in Franklin v. Massachusetts, 505 U.S. 788

(1992); Department of Commerce v. Montana, 503 U.S. 442 (1992); Wisconsin v. City of New York, 517 U.S. 1 (1996); Department of Commerce v. United States House of Representatives, 525 U.S. 316 (1999); Utah v. Evans, 536 U.S. 452 (2002).

116. Trial testimony suggested that the bureau *could* extend the deadline to October 31, 2019, if it received additional resources from Congress. Trial Transcript, *New York*, 1023.

117. Oral Argument Transcript, *Department of Commerce* (Apr. 23, 2019), 4.

118. Oral Argument Transcript, 22.

119. Oral Argument Transcript, 42.

120. Oral Argument Transcript, 44–45.

121. Oral Argument Transcript, 56.

122. See *Department of Commerce*, 139 S. Ct. 2551, 11–23.

123. Joan Biskupic, "Exclusive: How John Roberts Killed the Census Citizenship Question," CNN, September 12, 2019, https://www.cnn.com/2019/09/12/politics/john-roberts-census-citizenship-supreme-court/index.html.

124. As Thomas would later put it in a partial dissent: "I do not deny that a judge predisposed to distrust the Secretary or the administration could arrange those facts [from the record] on a corkboard and—with a jar of pins and a spool of string—create an eye-catching conspiracy web." *Department of Commerce*, 139 S. Ct. 2551 (Thomas, J., concurring in part and dissenting in part), 13.

125. Letter of respondents New York Immigration Coalition et al. notifying Court of new proceedings in the district court (proposed redacted motion attached) filed, May 30, 2019.

126. Letter of petitioners updating Court on District Court Proceedings, June 3, 2019.

127. *Department of Commerce*, 139 S. Ct. 2551.

128. *Department of Commerce*, 1–11.

129. *Department of Commerce*, 16–20.

130. *Department of Commerce*, 20–23.

131. *Department of Commerce*, 26.

132. *Department of Commerce*, 28.

133. *Department of Commerce* (Breyer, J., concurring in part and dissenting in part).

134. *Department of Commerce*.

135. Amy Howe, "2020 Census Questionnaires Go to Printer Without Citizenship Question—but Government Says It Will Continue to Look for 'Path Forward' (UPDATED)," *SCOTUSBlog*, July 3, 2019, https://www.scotusblog.com/2019/07/2020-census-questionnaires-go-to-printer-without-citizenship-question/.

136. Donald J. Trump (@realDonaldTrump), "United States Supreme Court is given additional information from which it can make a final and decisive decision on this very critical matter. Can anyone really believe that as a great Country, we are not able the ask whether or not someone is a Citizen. Only in America!," Twitter (now X), June 27, 2019, https://twitter.com/realdonaldtrump/status/1144298734311878657?lang=en.

137. Hansi Lo Wang, "Trump Backs Off Census Citizenship Question Fight," National Public Radio, July 11, 2019, https://www.npr.org/2019/07/11/739858115/trump-expected-to-renew-push-for-census-citizenship-question-with-executive-acti; Ex. Or.

13880, "Collecting Information About Citizenship Status in Connection with the Decennial Census," *Federal Register* 84, no. 136 (July 16, 2019): 33821–33825.

138. Memorandum Opinion, *Alabama v. Department of Commerce*, No. 2:18-cv-
00772 (N.D. Ala. Jun. 5, 2019), https://www.brennancenter.org/sites/default/files/legal
-work/Opinion_%202019-06-05.pdf.

139. Complaint for Declaratory Relief, Alabama v. Department of Commerce, No.
2:18-cv-00772 (N.D. Ala. May 21, 2018)), https://www.brennancenter.org/sites/default
/files/legal-work/Alabama_v_Dept-of-Commerce_Complaint.pdf.

140. Tara Bahrampour, "The Census Citizenship Question Failed. But Alabama Is
Seeking to Exclude Undocumented Immigrants in Apportioning Congressional Seats,"
Washington Post, August 15, 2019, https://www.washingtonpost.com/local/social-issues
/the-census-citizenship-question-failed-but-an-alabama-lawsuit-seeks-to-exclude-un
documented-immigrants-in-apportioning-congressional-seatsopponents-decry-the
-effort-as-unconstitutional-and-an-attempt-by-republicans-to-normalize-the-concept
-with-the-public/2019/08/14/1887f190-b777-11e9-b3b4-2bb69e8c4e39_story.html.

141. Bahrampour, "The Census Citizenship Question Failed."

142. Bahrampour.

143. Local Government Inventors' Supplemental Memorandum, *Alabama*, No. 2:18-
cv-00772 (N.D. Ala. Jan. 4, 2019), https://www.brennancenter.org/sites/default/files
/legal-work/LocalGovtIntervenors_suppmem_%202019-01-04.pdf.

144. Proposed Defendant-Intervenors' Memorandum of Law in Support of Their
Motion for Leave to Intervene, *Alabama*, No. 2:18-cv-00772 (N.D. Ala. Aug. 12, 2019),
https://www.brennancenter.org/sites/default/files/legal-work/N.D.%20Ala.%2018-cv
-00772%20dckt%20000097_000%20filed%202019-08-12.pdf; Arlington County and
Atlanta's Reply Memorandum in Support of Motion to Intervene, *Alabama*, No. 2:18-
cv-00772 (N.D. Ala. Aug. 23, 2019), https://www.brennancenter.org/sites/default/files
/legal-work/ArlingtonCountyandAtlanta_ReplyMeminSupport_MTI_ 2019-08-23.pdf.

145. Elizabeth A. Poehler, Dorothy A. Barth, Lindsay Longsine, Sarah K. Heimel,
and Gregory J. Mills, *2019 Census Test Report* (US Census Bureau, 2020), https://
www2.census.gov/programs-surveys/decennial/2020/program-management/census
-tests/2019/2019-census-test-report.pdf.

146. Hansi Lo Wang, "Census Bureau Finds Latinos, Asians Sensitive to Now-Blocked
Citizenship Question," National Public Radio, December 30, 2019, https://www.npr
.org/2019/10/31/774481039/blocked-citizenship-question-not-likely-to-lower-census
-response-test-finds.

3. A SENSE OF WHERE YOU ARE: LOCAL KNOWLEDGE
AND THE MASTER ADDRESS FILE

1. In 2020, 66.3 percent of households responded to the census via self-enumeration.
See Earl Letourneau, Lydia Shia, and Brett Moran, *2020 Census Self-Response and Return
Rates Assessment* (US Census Bureau, 2024), https://www2.census.gov/programs-sur
veys/decennial/2020/program-management/evaluate-docs/EAE-2020-self-response
-return-rates-assessment.pdf.

2. For the 2020 Census, there were four primary types of enumeration area. Self-enumeration is the largest, accounting for 95 percent of the households in the United States. Almost 5 percent of the population—located in predominantly rural locations—were in the "Update Leave" area, receiving invitations when census-takers dropped it off at their homes. The remaining less than a percent of households were counted in person, either as part of the "Update Enumerate" or "Remote Alaska" operations. US Census Bureau, "2020 Census: Type of Enumeration Area Viewer," accessed October 12, 2022, https://mtgis-portal.geo.census.gov/arcgis/apps/webappviewer/index.html?id=66cb1f187d4e4 5fd984a1a96fcee505e.

3. The cost of the 2010 Census per housing unit was 38 percent higher than the 2000 Census, which was in turn 76 percent higher than the 1990 Census. Government Accountability Office, *2020 Census: Census Bureau Can Improve Use of Leading Practices When Choosing Address and Mapping Sources* (GAO, 2014), https://www.gao.gov/assets /gao-15-21.pdf.

4. On the history of addresses as a state-building project, see Deirdre Mask, *The Address Book: What Street Addresses Reveal About Identity, Race, Wealth, and Power* (St. Martin's Griffin, 2020).

5. National Academies of Sciences, Engineering, and Medicine, *Assessing the 2020 Census: Final Report* (National Academies Press, 2023), 146.

6. National Research Council, *Change and the 2020 Census: Not Whether but How. Panel to Review the 2010 Census* (National Academies Press, 2011), 20–21.

7. National Research Council, *Modernizing the US Census. Panel on Census Requirements in the Year 2000 and Beyond* (National Academy Press, 1995), 37.

8. US Census Bureau, *Report to the Congress—The Plan for Census 2000*, rev. ver. (Bureau of Census, 1997), 41.

9. Decennial Census Management Division, *2020 Census Detailed Operational Plan for: 7. Local Update of Census Addresses Operation (LUCA)—Including New Construction Program* (US Census Bureau, 2018), https://www2.census.gov/programs-surveys /decennial/2020/program-management/planning-docs/LUCA-detailed-operational -plan-v2.pdf.

10. On the politics of responding to policy drift, see Daniel J. Galvin and Jacob S. Hacker, "The Political Effects of Policy Drift: Policy Stalemate and American Political Development," *Studies in American Political Development* 34, no. 2 (2020): 216–238.

11. National Research Council, *The 2000 Census: Counting Under Adversity. Panel to Review the 2000 Census* (National Academies Press, 2004).

12. Anderson, *The American Census*, 274.

13. Anderson, 216.

14. Earlier censuses had used self-enumeration on a more limited scale, but 1960 was the first time the technique was used as a significant means of data collection. See Robert A. Lamacchia, "Address List Development," in *Encyclopedia of the US Census: From the Constitution to the American Community Survey*, ed. Margo J. Anderson, Constance F. Citro, and Joseph J. Salvo (CQ Press, 2011), 26–30.

15. National Academies of Sciences, Engineering, and Medicine, *Reengineering the 2010 Census: Risks and Challenges* (National Academies Press), 59.

16. Geography Division, *Census 2020 Address Canvassing Recommendation* (US Cen-

sus Bureau, 2014), https://www2.census.gov/geo/pdfs/gssi/Address_Canvassing_Rec
ommendation.pdf.

17. Comptroller General of the United States, *Problems in Developing the 1980 Census Mail List, Report to the Subcommittee on Census and Population Committee of Committee on Post Office and Civil Service* (US House of Representatives, 1980), https://www.gao
.gov/assets/ggd-80-50.pdf.

18. US Census Bureau, *1980 Census of Population and Housing: Procedural History* (GPO, 1986), 5–36.

19. US Census Bureau, *1980 Census of Population and Housing*, 5–37.

20. Robert Reinhold, "Census Bureau Alters Its Plans to Allow Review by Cities," *New York Times*, February 28, 1980, B19.

21. Cuomo v. Baldridge, 674 F. Supp. 1089 (S.D.N.Y. 1987).

22. Baldridge v. Shapiro, 455 U.S. 345 (1982).

23. Margo J. Anderson and Stephen E. Fienberg, *Who Counts? The Politics of Census Taking in Contemporary America* (Russell Sage Foundation, 1999), 35–53.

24. Shoreh Elhami and Robert A. Lamacchia, "Geographic Information Systems," in *Encyclopedia of the U.S. Census*, 247–253.

25. Kristen O'Grady and Leslie Godwin, "The Positional Accuracy of MAF/TIGER," Working Paper (US Census Bureau, 2000), https://citeseerx.ist.psu.edu/document?repi
d=rep1&type=pdf&doi=3398ed1b4527b58d29ba384a63ebd3067ef6e3fc.

26. Barbara Everitt Bryant, "Decennial Censuses: 1990 Census," in *Encyclopedia of the U.S. Census*, 163–166.

27. US General Accounting Office, *Expanding the Role of Local Governments: An Important Element of Census Reform* (GAO, 1991), http://archive.gao.gov/d38t12/144153
.pdf.

28. Steven A. Holmes, "Census Chief Accuses Panel of Meddling with Details," *New York Times*, February 11, 1999, A23.

29. US General Accounting Office, *Decennial Census: 1990 Results Show Need for Fundamental Reform* (GAO, 1990), https://www.gao.gov/assets/ggd-92-94.pdf.

30. Anderson, *The American Census*, 245.

31. US General Accounting Office, *Decennial Census*.

32. Felicity Barringer, "2 Million Blacks Not Counted, Head of Census Panel Asserts," *New York Times*, March 12, 1991, A19; Felicity Barringer, "US Won't Revise 1990 Census, Says Chief of Commerce," *New York Times*, July 16, 1991, A1.

33. 103rd Cong., 2nd Sess., Cong. Rec. 140 (Rep. Sawyer, speaking on H.R. 5084, 1994), 27362.

34. Steve Pierson, "Remembering Federal Statistics Champion Tom Sawyer," Amstat News July 1, 2023, https://magazine.amstat.org/blog/2023/07/01/sawyer/.

35. Jorge Hernandez Caballero, "Planner's Work Helps with Economic Development, Policy Making," *(Utica) Observer-Dispatch*, August 22, 2011, https://www.uticaod.com
/story/news/2011/08/22/planner-s-work-helps-with/44843893007/.

36. Peggy Sweeney, Matthew Simmont, Stephan Matheis, and Brian Timko, *2010 Census: Local Update of Census Addresses Participant Survey* (US Census Bureau, 2012), 2012; Rebecca Swartz, Peter Virgile, and Brian Timko, *2010 Census: Local Update of Census Addresses Assessment* (US Department of Commerce), August 30, 2012, https://

www2.census.gov/programs-surveys/decennial/2010/program-management/5-review
/cpex/2010-cpex-199.pdf.

37. *Subcommittee on Information Policy, Census, and the National Archives of the Committee on Oversight and Government Reform*, 110th Cong., 1st Sess. (2007) (statement of Charles Louis Kincannon), 10.

38. *Subcommittee on Information Policy*, 10, 64.

39. Population Division, *Laying the Foundation for an Accurate 2020 Census in NYC: How City Planning Added Over a Quarter Million Missing Housing Units to the Census Bureau's Master Address File* (NYC Department of City Planning, 2021), https://story maps.arcgis.com/stories/47d5aee928374e1aa23d85ca34ac3d78.

40. Katie Kuba, "County Turns Down Census Request," *Record Delta*, December 18, 2017.

41. Sweeney, Simmont, Matheis, and Timko, *Participant Survey* (US Census Bureau, 2012), 95.

42. Sweeney, Simmont, Matheis, and Timko.

43. Office of Inspector General, *MAF/TIGER Redesign Project Needs Management Improvements to Meet Its Decennial Goals and Cost Objective* (US Department of Commerce, 2003), https://www.oig.doc.gov/OIGPublications/OSE-15725.pdf.

44. Dale Miller, Preparing for Local Update of Census Addresses, Webinar Presentation, State Data Center Network, November 29, 2017, author's files.

45. Daniel L. Cork, "Census Testing," in *Encyclopedia of the US Census*, 79–82.

46. US Census Bureau, Census 2000 Dress Rehearsal Evaluation Summary, August 1999, https://www2.census.gov/programs-surveys/decennial/2000/program-manage ment/5-review/escap/finalrep.pdf.

47. Government Accountability Office, *2010 Census: Census Bureau Is Making Progress on the Local Update of Census Addresses Program, but Improvements Are Needed* (GAO, 2007), https://www.gao.gov/assets/gao-07-1063t.pdf.

48. Government Accountability Office, *2010 Census*, 9.

49. Alfred Pfeiffer, "State LUCA Pilot in Indiana and Wisconsin," US Census Bureau, May 8, 2006; Christine Gibson Tomaszewski, "2008 Census Dress Rehearsal Local Update of Census Addresses (LUCA) Assessment Report," US Census Bureau, December 4, 2007.

50. To be sure, as part of a broader effort to develop the 2020 address frame, the bureau did test out its operations for address canvassing in 2015. Decennial Management Division, *2020 Census Research and Testing 2015 Address Validation Test: A New Design for the 21st Century* (US Census Bureau, 2016), https://www2.census.gov/programs -surveys/decennial/2020/program-management/final-analysis-reports/2020-report -2015-address-validation.pdf.

51. Brian Timko, "Local Update of Census Addresses (LUCA) Program Improvement," presentation at Census State Data Center Network Steering Committee, US Census Bureau, Suitland, Maryland, April 16, 2013, https://www2.census.gov/about/part ners/sdc/events/steering-committee/2013-04/2013-timko.pdf.

52. Rebecca Swartz, "Local Update of Census Addresses (LUCA) Program Improvement," presentation at Census State Data Center Network Steering Committee, Virtual Conference, October 23, 2014, https://www2.census.gov/about/partners/sdc/events /steering-committee/2014-10/2014-swartz.pdf.

53. Timko, "Local Update of Census Addresses."

54. Sweeney, Simmont, Matheis, Timko, *Participant Survey*; Rebecca Swartz, Peter Virgile, and Brian Timko, 2010 Census Local Update of Census Addresses Assessment (US Census Bureau, 2012), https://www.census.gov/content/dam/Census/library/publi cations/2012/dec/2010_cpex_199.pdf.

55. Office of Inspector General, *The US Census Bureau's Efforts to Ensure an Accurate Address List Raise Concerns over Design and Lack of Cost-Benefit Analysis* (US Department of Commerce, 2015), https://www.oig.doc.gov/OIGPublications/OIG-16-018-A .pdf.

56. Dale Miller, "Preparing for Local Update of Census Addresses," webinar presentation, State Data Center Network, November 29, 2017, author's files.

57. Population Division, *Laying the Foundation for an Accurate 2020 Census in NYC.*

58. See Cal. Assemb. B. 97, 2017–2018 Reg. Sess. (Cal. 2017), https://leginfo.legisla ture.ca.gov/faces/billTextClient.xhtml?bill_id=201720180AB97.

59. "Geography Division Address Canvassing Recommendation," US Census Bureau, November 15, 2014, https://www2.census.gov/geo/pdfs/gssi/Address_Canvassing_Rec ommendation.pdf.

60. Geography Division, "Census Address Summit 2011," meeting notes, US Census Bureau, 2012, https://www2.census.gov/geo/pdfs/gssi/CAS_Meeting_Notes.pdf.

61. Geography Division, "Census Address Summit 2011."

62. "United States Thoroughfare, Landmark, and Postal Address Data Standard 2011," Federal Geographic Data Committee, accessed October 12, 2022, https://www.fgdc.gov /standards/projects/address-data.

63. Geography Division, "Address Summit Pilot Update," Community Addressing Conference, Leesburg, Virginia, April 18, 2013, https://www2.census.gov/geo/pdfs/gssi /Address_Summit_Pilot_Update.pdf.

64. Geography Division, "Census 2020 Address Canvassing Recommendation."

65. "Geographic Support System," US Census Bureau, accessed November 12, 2022, https://www.census.gov/programs-surveys/geography/about/gss.html.

66. Office of Inspector General, "2020 Census: Issues Observed During the 2018 End-to-End Census Test's Address Canvassing Operation Indicate Risk to Address List Quality," US Department of Commerce, February 6, 2019, https://www.oig.doc.gov/OIGPub lications/OIG-19-008-A.pdf.

67. US Government Accountability Office, *2020 Census: Actions Needed to Improve Census Bureau's Process for Working with Governments to Build Address List* (GAO, 2019), https://www.gao.gov/assets/gao-20-17.pdf.

68. This figure includes Alaska Native Regional Corporations (ANRCs).

69. These states include Iowa, Kansas, Kentucky, Maine, New Hampshire, Pennsylvania, South Dakota, Texas, and Wisconsin.

70. The model uses 2017 county population estimates. "Population, Population Change, and Estimated Components of Population Change: April 1, 2010 to July 1, 2019," US Census Bureau, accessed November 8, 2024, https://www.census.gov/data /tables/time-series/demo/popest/2020s-counties-total.html#par_textimage.

71. Here, the model employs the five-year estimates of the 2020 American Community Survey. "S1903: Median Income in the Past 12 Months," US Census Bureau,

https://data.census.gov/cedsci/table?q=median%20household%20income%20by%20county&tid=ACSST5Y2020.S1903.

72. The model uses 2010 final self-response rates. "Decennial Census Self-Response Rates," US Census Bureau, 2000, 2010, https://www.census.gov/data/developers/data-sets/decennial-response-rates.html.

73. The tribal figure includes Alaska Native Regional Corporations (ANRCs).

74. Lyndsey Richmond and Shawn Hanks, *2020 Census In-Office Address Canvassing Operational Assessment Report* (US Census Bureau, 2022), 75.

75. National Academies of Sciences, Engineering, and Medicine, *Assessing the 2020 Census: Final Report* (National Academies Press, 2023), 111.

76. National Academies of Sciences, Engineering, and Medicine, *Assessing the 2020 Census: Final Report*, 113.

77. James C. Scott, *Seeing Like a State: How Certain Schemes to Improve the Human Condition Have Failed* (Yale University Press, 1998).

78. Thomas M. Cook, Janet L. Norwood, and Daniel L. Cork, eds., *Change and the 2020 Census: Not Whether but How* (National Academies Press, 2011).

79. Indeed, the programs discussed here are only part of a broader suite of "geographic partnerships" maintained by the bureau. This includes the Participant Statistical Areas Program (PSAP), which allows governments to review and modify the boundaries of statistical geographies like tracts and block groups to suit their needs. It also includes the Boundary and Annexation Survey, through which governments provide updated information about changes to local governments' legal boundaries.

80. Thomas A. DeGise, letter to Steven Fulop, August 13, 2018, https://cdn5-hosted.civiclive.com/UserFiles/Servers/Server_6189660/File/Homepage/Census/Results FromJerseyCityLUCAsubmission.pdf.

81. US Government Accountability Office, *2020 Census*.

4. GETTING OUT THE COUNT: PARTNERSHIPS, POLITICS, AND CENSUS PROMOTION

1. Less than half of CBAMs respondents knew that census data is used to determine "how much money communities will get from the federal government." See Kyley McGeeney, Brian Kriz, Shawnna Mullenax, Laura Kail, Gina Walejko, Monica Vines, Nancy Bates, and Yazmín García Trejo, *2020 Census Barriers, Attitudes, and Motivators Study Survey Report: A New Design for the 21st Century* (US Census Bureau, 2019), https://www2.census.gov/programs-surveys/decennial/2020/program-management/final-analysis-reports/2020-report-cbams-study-survey.pdf.

2. McGeeney et al., *2020 Census Barriers*.

3. D'Vera Cohn, Anna Brown, and Scott Keeter, "Most Adults Aware of 2020 Census and Ready to Respond, but Don't Know Key Details," Pew Research Center, February 20, 2020, https://www.pewresearch.org/social-trends/2020/02/20/most-adults-aware-of-2020-census-and-ready-to-respond-but-dont-know-key-details/.

4. "Public Trust in Government, 1958–2022," Pew Research Center, https://www.pewresearch.org/politics/2022/06/06/public-trust-in-government-1958-2022/.

5. William Howard Taft, "A Proclamation," Bureau of the Census, July 2, 1909, https://www.census.gov/history/img/proclamation1910-artifact.jpg.

6. Margo Anderson, "Advertising the Census," in *Encyclopedia of the US Census: From the Constitution to the American Community Survey*, ed. Margo J. Anderson, Constance F. Citro, and Joseph J. Salvo (CQ Press, 2011), 31.

7. D. Sunshine Hillygus, Norman H. Nie, Kenneth Prewitt, and Heili Pals, *The Hard Count: The Political and Social Challenges of Census Mobilization* (Russell Sage Foundation, 2006), 46–47.

8. On the growth of outsourced and privatized Census Bureau operations, see Steven Ruggles and Diana L. Magnuson, "Census Technology, Politics, and Institutional Change, 1790–2020," *Journal of American History* 107, no. 1 (2020): 19–51. For more on these trends in general, see Donald F. Kettl, "From Intergovernmental to Intersectoral," in *Public Administration Evolving: From Foundations to the Future*, ed. Mary E. Guy and Marilyn M. Rubin (Routledge, 2015), 18–37; Paul L. Posner, "Scarcity and the Federal System," in *Intergovernmental Relations in Transition: Reflections and Directions*, ed. Carl W. Stenberg and David K. Hamilton (Routledge, 2018), 77–91.

9. Robert Agranoff, *Crossing Boundaries for Intergovernmental Management* (Georgetown University Press, 2017), 168.

10. Richard P. Nathan, "The Politics of Printouts," in *The Politics of Numbers*, ed. William Alonso and Paul Starr (Russell Sage Foundation, 1987), 331–342.

11. US Census Bureau, *1990 Census of Population and Housing—History* (US Census Bureau, 1993), 1–12.

12. US Census Bureau, *2000 Census of Population and Housing—History*, vol. 1 (US Census Bureau, 2009: 173–212.

13. US Census Bureau, *2000 Census of Population and Housing*, 207.

14. Jim Poyer, *Census 2000 Evaluation D.3, Report of Survey of Partners* (US Census Bureau, 2000, https://www2.census.gov/programs-surveys/decennial/2000/program-management/5-review/txe-program/D_3.pdf.

15. Hillygus, Nie, Prewitt, and Pals, *The Hard Count*, 69–71.

16. Kirk Wolter, Bob Calder, Ed Malthouse, Sally Murphy, Steven Pedlow, and Javier Porras, *Census 2000 Evaluation D.1, Partnership and Marketing Program Evaluation* (US Census Bureau, 2002), https://www2.census.gov/programs-surveys/decennial/2000/program-management/5-review/txe-program/D_1.pdf.

17. Chandra Erdman and Nancy Bates, *The US Census Bureau Mail Return Rate Challenge: Crowdsourcing to Develop a Hard-to-Count Score* (US Census Bureau, 2013), https://www.census.gov/content/dam/Census/library/working-papers/2014/adrm/rrs2014-08.pdf; US Census Bureau, *Planning Database with 2010 Census and 2014–2018 American Community Survey Data* (US Census Bureau, 2020), https://www.census.gov/content/dam/Census/topics/research/pdb-2020/2020_Block_Group_PDB_Documentation.pdf; Antonio Bruce, J Gregory Robinson, and Jason E. Devine, *A Planning Database to Identify Areas that Are Hard-to-Enumerate and Hard-to-Survey in the United States* (American Statistical Association, 2012), http://www.asasrms.org/Proceedings/H2R2012/A_Planning_Database_to_Identify_Areas_That_Are_Hard-to-Enumerate_and_Hard-to-Survey_in_the_United_St.pdf.

18. Arnold Jackson, *Memorandum Re: 2010 Census Evaluation of National Partner-*

ship Research Report (US Census Bureau, 2012), https://www2.census.gov/programs-surveys/decennial/2010/program-management/5-review/cpex/2010-cpex-196.pdf.

19. "Nation Achieves 74 Percent Final Mail Participation in 2010 Census," press release, US Census Bureau, October 21, 2010, https://www.census.gov/newsroom/releases/archives/2010_census/cb10-cn81.html.

20. "Response Outreach Area Mapper," US Census Bureau, June 2019, https://www.census.gov/library/visualizations/2017/geo/roam.html.

21. "Decennial Census Management Division, 2020 Census Detailed Operational Plan for: 11. Integrated Partnership and Communications Operation (IPC)," US Census Bureau, 2020, https://www2.census.gov/programs-surveys/decennial/2020/program-management/planning-docs/IPC_detailed_operational_plan.pdf.

22. Robert Groves, "A Restructuring of Census Bureau Regional Offices," US Census Bureau, June 29, 2011, https://www.census.gov/newsroom/blogs/director/2011/06/a-restructuring-of-census-bureau-regional-offices.html.

23. Government Accountability Office, *2020 Census: Office Managers' Perspectives on Recent Operations Would Strengthen Planning for 2030* (GAO, 2021), https://www.gao.gov/assets/gao-21-104071.pdf.

24. Government Accountability Office, *Actions Needed to Address Challenges to Enumerating Hard-to-Count Groups* (GAO, 2018), https://www.gao.gov/assets/gao-18-599.pdf.

25. Government Accountability Office, *2020 Census: Status Update on Early Operations* (GAO, 2019), https://www.gao.gov/assets/files.gao.gov/assets/gao-20-111r.pdf.

26. Filed in late 2019, the suit's chief complaint was that the Census Bureau's 2020 Operational Plan "drastically and arbitrarily reduces the necessary resources for key activities" for outreach, constituting a violation of both the Administrative Procedure Act and the US Constitution's Enumeration Clause. In March 2020, US District Judge Alvin Hellerstein granted the bureau's motion to dismiss the suit on procedural grounds. See Center for Popular Democracy Action and City of Newburgh v. Bureau of the Census, Steven Dillingham, and Wilbur Ross, Complaint, No. 1:19-cv-10917 (Nov. 26, 2019), https://www.brennancenter.org/sites/default/files/2019-12/Complaint_2019-11-26.pdf; Memorandum of Law in Support of Defendants' Motion to Dismiss, No. 1:19-cv-10917-AKH (Jan. 31, 2020), https://www.brennancenter.org/sites/default/files/2020-02/DefendantsMTD_%202020-01-31.pdf; Order Granting Defendants' Motion to Dismiss and Denying Plaintiffs' Motion for a Preliminary Injunction, No. 1:19-cv-10917-AKH (Mar. 18, 2020), https://www.brennancenter.org/sites/default/files/2020-03/Order_2020-03-18.pdf.

27. For example, in the region covered by the Chicago RCC, which included eight states with a total population of 53.6 million people, there were thirty-two ACOs. By contrast, in the New York region—which included eight states and Puerto Rico, a total population of 47.9 million people—there were forty-five ACOs.

28. Government Accountability Office, *2020 Census: Update on the Census Bureau's Implementation of Partnership and Outreach Activities* (GAO, 2020), https://www.gao.gov/assets/710/706984.pdf.

29. Albert Fontenot Jr., "Informational Memorandum (Week of 2018.10.01)," Department of Commerce, accessed December 30, 2024, https://docs.google.com/document

/d/1Sq6JakziaDtrMq9qVjFitNkS1zpn7T1g/edit?usp=sharing&ouid=108185370996117
813275&rtpof=true&sd=true.

30. State interviewees 8 and 21; local interviewees 13 and 23.

31. State interviewee 21.

32. In Mississippi, which created its SCCC on August 7, 2019, a public records request revealed only three meetings held between its creation and the beginning of the decennial year. State of Mississippi, "Census 2020 Complete Count Committee," meeting minutes, August 14, 2019, September 27, 2019, and October 18, 2019, author's files.

33. Governor of South Dakota, "Executive Order 2020–32," South Dakota Department of Health, August 31, 2020, https://covid.sd.gov/docs/EO2020–32_CompleteCensusCommittee.pdf.

34. State Interviewee 2; Nonprofit Interviewee 2.

35. State Interviewee 3.

36. State Interviewee 32.

37. State Interviewee 29.

38. State Interviewee 21.

39. On sensemaking, see Karl E. Weick, "Enacted Sensemaking in Crisis Situations," *Journal of Management Studies* 25, no. 4 (1988): 305–317.

40. State Interviewees 3, 4, 8, 16, and 22; Local Interviewees 4, 19, and 21.

41. State Interviewee 4.

42. State Interviewees 8 and 19.

43. State Interviewee 16.

44. State Interviewee 22.

45. State Interviewee 23.

46. State Interviewee 9.

47. State Interviewee 16.

48. See, for example, Andrew Reamer, *Counting for Dollars Report #2: Estimating Fiscal Costs of a Census Undercount to States* (George Washington University, 2018).

49. State Interviewees 3, 5, 7, 9, 10, 13, 14, 15, and 17.

50. State Interviewee 1.

51. State Interviewee 17.

52. State Interviewee 16.

53. State Interviewee 18.

54. Local Interviewee 19.

55. Local Interviewee 6.

56. State Interviewee 22.

57. State Interviewees 18 and 22.

58. State Interviewees 23 and 24.

59. State Interviewees 31 and 35.

60. State Interviewee 35.

61. State Interviewees 1 and 6.

62. State Interviewee 7.

63. State Interviewee 36.

64. Local Interviewee 9; State Interviewee 31.

65. State Interviewees 21 and 36.

66. State Interviewees 11 and 12.

67. State Interviewee 12.

68. State Interviewee 12.

69. State Interviewee 22.

70. US Census Bureau, *Weekly Field Division Reports*, June 28, 2018–August 21, 2019, author's files.

71. Local Interviewees 1 and 4.

72. State Interviewee 25.

73. State Interviewee 33.

74. State Interviewee 28.

75. State Interviewee 10.

76. State Interviewee 30.

77. State Interviewees 15, 23, and 24; Local Interviewees 1, 10, 13, 14, 15, 18, 19, and 27. Nonprofit interviewees 1, 3, 4, 6, and 7.

78. State Interviewee 6.

79. State Interviewees 16 and 17.

80. State Interviewee 22.

81. State Interviewees 18 and 23; Local Interviewees 14, 15, 18, 19, and 26.

82. State Interviewee 24.

83. State Interviewee 32.

84. State Interviewee 32.

85. In addition to the full multivariate models, I analyzed the results of fourteen reduced multivariate models, each of which eliminated a single variable from the full multivariate analysis, for the purposes of assessing the robustness of the main findings. For a full description of those results, see Philip Rocco, "Counting like a State: The Politics of Intergovernmental Partnerships in the 2020 Census," *Political Science Quarterly* 138, no. 2 (2023): 189–216.

86. Rocco, "Counting Like a State." These patterns are broadly consistent with the results of reduced models.

87. Rocco. The results of reduced models are consistent with those presented here.

88. National League of Cities, *City Fiscal Conditions—2019* (National League of Cities, 2019), https://www.nlc.org/wp-content/uploads/2019/10/CS_Fiscal-Conditions-20 19Web-final.pdf.

89. Joel Griffith, Jonathan Harris, Emilia Istrate, *Doing More With Less: State Revenue Limitations and Mandates on County Finances* (National Association of Counties, 2016), https://www.naco.org/sites/default/files/documents/Doing%20More%20with%20Less _Full%20Report.pdf.

90. US Bureau of Labor Statistics, "All Employees, Local Government," Federal Reserve Bank of St. Louis, https://fred.stlouisfed.org/series/CES9093000001.

91. Restricting our attention only to contacts made with general units of local government or tribal governments reveals a substantially similar pattern.

92. Unfortunately, the bureau's data on the number of "commitments" made by each of these partners is not publicly available.

93. Local Interviewee 1.

94. See Rocco, "Counting Like a State," 189–216.

95. See National League of Cities, *Side by Side: Lessons Learned from 2020 Census + Voting Initiative* (Institute for Youth, Education, and Families, 2020), https://www.nlc.org/wp-content/uploads/2020/11/Census_Voting_Survery_Issue_Brief.pdf.

96. Local Interviewee 19.

97. Local Interviewee 4.

98. While local governments are not immune to the trend of polarized partisan politics, there is good reason to believe that partisan patterns are less prevalent on issues that affect external resources or political representation available to the city. See Christopher Warshaw, "Local Elections and Representation in the United States," *Annual Review of Political Science* 22 (2019): 461–479; Elisabeth R. Gerber and Daniel J. Hopkins. "When Mayors Matter: Estimating the Impact of Mayoral Partisanship on City Policy," *American Journal of Political Science* 55, no. 2 (2011): 326–339.

99. Local Interviewee 14.

100. Local Interviewees 1, 23, and 26.

101. Local Interviewee 19.

102. Local Interviewee 23.

103. Local Interviewee 2.

104. Local Interviewee 2.

105. Local interviewee 4

106. Local interviewee 12

107. Local interviewee 22.

108. Local interviewee 9.

109. National League of Cities, *Side by Side*.

110. Local Interviewee 7.

111. Local Interviewee 20.

112. National League of Cities, *Side by Side*.

113. State of California, "California Complete Count—2020," Administrative Community-Based Organizations, accessed November 1, 2024, https://census.ca.gov/wp-content/uploads/sites/4/2019/07/CA-CENSUS-Admin-Community-Based-Organizations-Contacts.pdf.

114. Local Interviewee 29.

115. State Interviewees 11 and 12.

116. State Interviewee 6.

117. State Interviewee 28.

118. Local interviewee 21.

119. Local interviewee 3.

120. Local Interviewee 30; follow-up Interview with Local Interviewee 30.

121. National League of Cities, *Side by Side*.

122. Nonprofit Interviewee 6.

123. Barsoum Policy Consulting, *Together We Count: Assessing Efforts to Support a Fair and Accurate Census* (Funders' Committee for Civic Participation, 2021), https://funderscommittee.org/wp-content/uploads/2021/07/Together-We-Count-Assessing-Efforts-to-Support-a-Fair-and-Accurate-2020-Census-7.17.21.pdf.

124. William H. Woodwell Jr., *Philanthropy and the 2020 Census: Stories and Lessons from an Unprecedented Funder Collaborative to Protect a Pillar of American Democracy*

(Funders' Committee for Civic Participation, 2021), https://funderscommittee.org/wp-content/uploads/2021/10/Philanthropy-and-the-2020-Census-final.pdf.

125. Barsoum Policy Consulting, *Together We Count*.

126. Local Interviewee 12.

127. Local Interviewees 1, 10, 14, and 16.

128. Nonprofit interviewees 1, 4.

129. Nonprofit interviewee 1.

130. Nonprofit interviewee 1.

131. Local interviewee 1.

132. National League of Cities, *Side by Side*.

133. Nonprofit interviewee 4.

134. Nonprofit interviewee 4.

135. Local interviewee 1.

136. Local interviewee 2.

137. Author's field notes, December 10, 2019.

138. Local interviewee 16; Local interviewee 14.

5. BETWEEN A PANDEMIC AND A POWER GRAB: FEDERALISM AND THE POLITICS OF CENSUS INTEGRITY

1. Hansi Lo Wang, "Census Field Operations Further Delayed Until April 15 by COVID-19 Pandemic," NPR, March 28, 2020, https://www.npr.org/sections/coronavirus-live-updates/2020/03/28/823295346/census-field-operations-further-delayed-until-april-15-by-covid-19-pandemic.

2. Local Interviewee 33, follow-up interview.

3. Hansi Lo Wang, "Coronavirus Is Making It Even Harder for the Census to Count Every US Resident," NPR, March 11, 2020, https://www.npr.org/2020/03/11/814603337/how-the-coronavirus-outbreak-may-impact-the-2020-census.

4. Suhail Bhat, "NYC's Population Plummeted During Peak COVID—And It's Still Likely Shrinking," The City, May 31, 2022, https://www.thecity.nyc/2022/5/31/23145072/nycs-population-plummeted-during-peak-covid-and-its-still-likely-shrinking; Mark H. Zabarsky, "2020 Census Alert: The Census Bureau May Not Accurately Count College and University Students Living Off-Campus During the 2020 Census," US Department of Commerce, Final Memorandum No. OIG-20–044-M, https://www.oig.doc.gov/OIGPublications/OIG-20-044-M.pdf.

5. See "U.S. Census Bureau Director Steven Dillingham on Operational Updates," US Census Bureau, March 18, 2020, https://www.census.gov/newsroom/press-releases/2020/operational-update.html; "2020 Census Operational Adjustments Due to COVID-19 Fact Sheet," US Census Bureau, April 27, 2020, https://omb.report/icr/202111-0607-003/doc/original/116310700.pdf.

6. "The 2020 Census Could Be the Least Accurate Ever—and It's Ending a Month Early," NPR, August 14, 2020, https://www.npr.org/transcripts/901833534.

7. "Statement by Former U.S. Census Bureau Directors," US Census Bureau, April 14, 2020, https://www.documentcloud.org/documents/6838166-Statement-by-Former

-CensusBureau-Directors-04.html; see also Tamika Turner, "Census Timeline Must Protect Health, Ensure Fair Count," Leadership Conference Education Fund, April 13, 2020, https://civilrights.org/edfund/2020/04/13/census-timeline-must-protect-health -ensure-fair-count/.

8. "User Clip: President Trump On Census Bureau's Request For 120-Day Deadline Extension For 2020 Census Apportionment Count," C-SPAN, April 13, 2020, https:// www.c-span.org/video/?c4868473/user-clip-president-trump-census-bureaus-request -120-day-deadline-extension-2020-census-results.

9. Hansi Lo Wang, "'Not Enough Time': Census Workers Fear Rushing Count Could Botch Results," NPR, August 11, 2020, https://www.npr.org/2020/08/11/901202892/not -enough-time-census-workers-fear-rushingcount-could-botch-results.

10. Lo Wang, "Not Enough Time."

11. This is consistent with the Office of the Inspector General's findings on the August 3rd replan. Office of the Inspector General, *The Acceleration of the Census Schedule Increases the Risks to a Complete and Accurate 2020 Census* (US Department of Commerce, 2020), https://www.oig.doc.gov/OIGPublications/OIG-20-050-M.pdf.

12. The funding was intended to support supplemental hiring, pay incentives, additional advertising, and replenished contingency funding for NRFU. Yet it is not entirely clear how the aid, which even in the best-case scenario would not reach the bureau until the fall, would allow the bureau to meet a revised deadline for apportionment counts.

13. President Donald Trump, "Memorandum of July 21, 2020, Excluding Illegal Aliens from the Apportionment Base Following the 2020 Census," *Federal Register* 85 (142): 44679–44681; Exec. Order No. 13880, "Collecting Information About Citizenship Status in Connection with the Decennial Census," *Federal Register* 84 (136): 33821–33825.

14. Common Cause v. Donald Trump, No. 1:20-cv-02023 (D.D.C. Aug. 19, 2020) (Expert Declaration of Dr. Christopher Warhsaw).

15. Mark H. Zabarsky, "2020 Census Alert: The Census Bureau Faces Challenges in Accelerating Hiring and Minimizing Attrition Rates for Abbreviated 2020 Census Field Operations," US Department of Commerce, Final Memorandum No. OIG-20–041-M, August 18, 2020, https://www.oig.doc.gov/OIGPublications/OIG-20-041-M. pdf; "Operational Press Briefing—2020 Census Update," US Census Bureau, July 8, 2020, https://www.census.gov/content/dam/Census/newsroom/press-kits/2020/news -briefing-program-transcript-july8.pdf; "Census Bureau Drop-Outs Complicate Door-Knocking Efforts," Associated Press, August 8, 2020, https://www.usnews.com/news/us /articles/2020-08-08/census-bureau-drop-outs-complicate-door-knocking-efforts; Lo Wang, "Not Enough Time."

16. National Urban League et al. v. Wilbur J. Ross, et al., No. 5:20-cv-05799-LHK (Sept. 22, 2020) (Supplemental Brief in Support of Motion for Stay and for Preliminary Injunction), https://www.brennancenter.org/sites/default/files/2020-09/Supplemental brief_020-09-22_final.pdf.

17. "Letter from US Philanthropy Leaders to Wilbur Ross and Steven Dillingham, Re: Completion Date of the 2020 Decennial Census," Funders' Committee for Civic Participation, August 5, 2020, https://funderscommittee.org/wp-content/uploads/2020/08 /Letter-Philanthropic-Leaders-on-Census-Being-Cut-Short-8-5.pdf.

18. "Statement by Former US Census Bureau Directors."

19. Office of the Inspector General, *The Acceleration of the Census Schedule Increases the Risks to a Complete and Accurate 2020 Census.*

20. Albert E. Fontenot Jr., "2020 Census Update," US Census 2020, September 17, 2020, https://www2.census.gov/cac/sac/meetings/2020–09/presentation-2020-census-update.pdf.

21. "Operational and Processing Options to Meet Statutory Date of December 31, 2020 for Apportionment," US Census Bureau, August 3, 2020, https://oversight.house.gov/sites/democrats.oversight.house.gov/files/documents/Census%20Slide%20Deck%20Aug%203%202020.pdf.

22. Office of the Inspector General, *The Acceleration of the Census Schedule Increases the Risks to a Complete and Accurate 2020 Census.*

23. Local Interviewees 12, 14, and 15, follow-up interviews.

24. Christopher Adolph, Kenya Amano, Bree Bang-Jensen, Nancy Fullman, and John Wilkerson, "Pandemic Politics: Timing State-Level Social Distancing Responses to COVID-19," *Journal of Health Politics, Policy and Law* 46, no. 2 (2021): 211–233.

25. Christopher Adolph, Kenya Amano, Bree Bang-Jensen, Nancy Fullman, Beatrice Magistro, Grace Reinke, Rachel Castellano, Megan Erickson, and John Wilkerson, "The Pandemic Policy U-Turn: Partisanship, Public Health, and Race in Decisions to Ease COVID-19 Social Distancing Policies in the United States," *Perspectives on Politics* 20, no. 2 (2022): 595–617.

26. Raymond Foxworth, Laura E. Evans, Gabriel R. Sanchez, Cheryl Ellenwood, and Carmela M. Roybal, "'I Hope to Hell Nothing Goes Back to the Way It Was Before': COVID-19, Marginalization, and Native Nations," *Perspectives on Politics* 20, no. 2 (2022): 439–456.

27. This section draws on Alice Cooper, Daniel Warner, Gabriela Raczka, Mark Rooney, Nicole Cousounis, Pedro Rodriguez, Stephanie Reid, and Vanessa Caracoza, *Philly Counts 2020: Final Report* (Philly Counts, 2021), https://www.phila.gov/media/20210128210854/Philly-Counts-Final-Report-1.28.2021.pdf.

28. Cooper, Warner, Raczka, Rooney, Cousounis, Rodriguez, Reid, and Caracoza, *Philly Counts 2020*, 48.

29. State Interviewee 19, follow-up interview.

30. Local Interviewee 11.

31. Local Interviewee 16, follow-up interview; State Interviewee 5, follow-up interview.

32. Local Interviewee 16, follow-up interview.

33. Local Interviewee 33, follow-up interview.

34. State Interviewee 29, follow-up interview.

35. State Interviewee 25, follow-up interview.

36. Local Interviewee 15, follow-up interview.

37. State Interviewee 27, follow-up interview.

38. The section on California draws extensively on LPC Consulting Associates, Inc., *Evaluating the California Complete Count Census 2020 Campaign: A Narrative Report* (California Census, 2021), https://census.ca.gov/wp-content/uploads/sites/4/2021/04/EvaluatingTheCACompleteCountCensus2020Campaign_ANarrativeReport.pdf; California Complete Count—Census 2020 Office, *California Census 2020 Outreach and*

Communication Campaign Final Report (California Census, 2021), https://census.ca
.gov/wp-content/uploads/sites/4/2021/05/California-Census-2020-Outreach-and
-Communications-Campaign-Final-Report-5.11.2021.pdf?emrc=cc0448.

39. LPC Consulting Associates, Inc., "Evaluating the California Complete Count Census 2020 Campaign."

40. LPC Consulting Associates, Inc.

41. LPC Consulting Associates, Inc., 39.

42. State Interviewee 28, follow-up interview.

43. State Interviewee 18, follow-up interview.

44. State Interviewee 25, follow-up interview.

45. Government Accountability Office, "Supplemental Material For GAO-21-104071: 2020 Census Survey of Area Census Office Managers," GAO, July 27, 2021, https://www
.gao.gov/products/gao-21-105237.

46. State Interviewee 30, follow-up interview.

47. Local Interviewee 16, follow-up interview.

48. State Interviewee 27, follow-up interview.

49. Mike Schneider, "College Towns Plan to Challenge Results of 2020 Census," Associated Press, October 18, 2021, https://apnews.com/article/coronavirus-pandemic
-lifestyle-education-pennsylvania-alabama-bddf3c13c35f2cd309f2ff636173415b; Alice Cooper, Warner, Raczka, Rooney, Cousounis, Rodriguez, Reid, and Caracoza, *Philly Counts 2020.*

50. "2020 Census Self-Response Rate Map Data and Technical Documentation," US Census Bureau, February 1, 2021, https://www2.census.gov/programs-surveys/decen
nial/2020/data/tracking-response-rates/response-rate-map-technical-documentation
.pdf.

51. Trump v. New York, Joint Appendix, Ex. 34 (Declaration of Bitta Mostofi), https://www.supremecourt.gov/DocketPDF/20/20-366/159468/20201103115400744
_Trump%20v.%20New%20York%2020-366%20J.A.pdf.

52. *Trump*, Joint Appendix, Ex. 44 (Declaration of Vatsady Sivongxay), https://www
.supremecourt.gov/DocketPDF/20/20-366/159468/20201103115400744_Trump%20
v.%20New%20York%2020-366%20J.A.pdf.

53. State Interviewee 10, follow-up interview.

54. Edwin R. Byerly, "2010 Census Count Review Program Assessment Report," US Census Bureau, June 26, 2012, https://www.census.gov/content/dam/Census/library
/publications/2012/dec/2010_cpex_203.pdf.

55. Byerly, "2010 Census Count Review Program Assessment Report," 21.

56. Tim Henderson, "Census Recounts Fail to Account for COVID Chaos, Cities Say," Pew Research Center, January 5, 2022, https://www.pewtrusts.org/en/research
-and-analysis/blogs/stateline/2022/01/05/census-recounts-fail-to-account-for-covid
-chaos-cities-say.

57. All but ten of these entities provided data on both housing units and group quarters. Sonia Collazo, "2020 Census Count Review," presentation, US Census 2020, October 8, 2020, https://www2.census.gov/about/policies/foia/records/Census-Integration
-Group-Presentations/Count-Review/Count-Review-Readiness_CIG-Brief_10082020
_clean.pdf.

58. State Interviewee 16, follow-up interview.

59. Hansi Lo Wang, "Leak Reveals Warnings Inside Census that Shortened Schedule Risks 'Serious Errors,'" NPR, September 2, 2022, https://www.npr.org/2020/09/02/908852878/leak-reveals-warnings-inside-census-that-shortened-schedule-risks-serious-errors.

60. Jeffrey Mervis, "Will the 2020 Census Numbers be Good Enough, and How Soon Will We Know?," Science, August 24, 2020, https://www.science.org/content/article/will-2020-census-numbers-be-good-enough-and-how-soon-will-we-know.

61. "Operational and Processing Options to Meet Statutory Date of December 31, 2020 for Apportionment," US Census Bureau, August 3, 2020. https://www2.census.gov/about/policies/foia/records/Census-Integration-Group-Presentations/Misc-Presentations/Operational-and-Processing-Options-to-meet-September-30-Final-v2.pdf.

62. Hansi Lo Wang, "Running Out of Time, Census Scales Back a Critical Step: Checking Its Own Work," NPR, August 29, 2020, https://www.npr.org/2020/08/29/905846761/the-census-scales-back-a-critical-step-checking-its-own-work.

63. "2020 Census: Innovations Helped with Implementation, but Bureau Can Do More to Realize Future Benefits," Government Accountability Office, June 2021, https://www.gao.gov/assets/gao-21-478.pdf.

64. Collazo, "2020 Census Count Review."

65. The Federal State Cooperative for Population Estimates Steering Committee, "Letter to Nancy Potok and Denice Ross," National Conference of State Legislatures, November 24, 2020, https://www.ncsl.org/Portals/1/Documents/Redistricting/FSCPE_Nov2020_Letter_re_census_and_differentialprivacy.pdf.

66. See, e.g., Fair and Accurate Census Act, H.R. 7974, 116th Cong., 2nd Sess.; Fair and Accurate Census Act, S. 4048, 116th Cong., 2nd Sess.; 2020 Census Deadline Extension Act, S. 4571, 116th Cong., 2nd Sess.

67. First Amended Complaint, National Urban League v. Ross (N.D. Cal. Sept. 1, 2020).

68. "2020 Post-Census Group Quarters Review, Frequently Asked Questions," US Census Bureau, June 28, 2022, https://www2.census.gov/programs-surveys/decennial/2020/program-management/pcgqr/2020-pcgqr-frequently-asked-questions.pdf; Tim Henderson, "Census Bureau to Review Potential Miscounts of Institutions," Pew Research Center, June 1, 2022, https://www.pewtrusts.org/en/research-and-analysis/blogs/stateline/2022/06/01/census-bureau-to-review-potential-miscounts-of-institutions.

69. Jessica Bulman-Pozen, and Heather K. Gerken, "Uncooperative Federalism," Yale Law Journal 118 (2009): 1256–1310.

70. Exec. Order No. 13880, 33821–33825.

71. Donald Trump, "Remarks by President Trump on Citizenship and the Census," The White House, July 11, 2019, https://trumpwhitehouse.archives.gov/briefings-statements/remarks-president-trump-citizenship-census/#:~:text=There%20used%20to%20be%20a%20time%20when%20you%20could%20proudly,proud%20to%20be%20a%20citizen.

72. John Abowd, email to Enrique Lamas, September 1, 2020, FOIA Release B.C.-DOC-CEN-2020–001602–005214.

73. Utah v. Evans, 536 U.S. 452 (2002).

74. Office of Management and Budget, *Supporting Statement: A Department of Commerce U.S. Census Bureau Paperwork Reduction Act Program Information Collection Request* (US Census Bureau, n.d.), https://omb.report/icr/201912-0607-003/doc/97407600
.pdf.

75. Alternative Sources of Citizenship Data for the 2020 Census, Department of Commerce v. New York, Joint Appendix (Dec. 22, 2017) (Plaintiff's Ex. 102), https://www
.supremecourt.gov/DocketPDF/18/18-966/94964/20190401161123490_18-966%20
US%20Dept%20of%20Commerce%20v%20State%20of%20New%20York%20et%20
al%20Joint%20Appendix%20Vol%202.pdf.

76. Victoria Velkoff and John Abowd, "Memorandum Re: Estimating the Undocumented Population by State for Use in Apportionment," US Census Bureau, March 27, 2020,https://www2.census.gov/about/policies/foia/records/2020-census-and-acs/20200
327-memo-on-undocumented.pdf.

77. Alternative Sources of Citizenship Data for the 2020 Census, *Department of Commerce*, 588 U.S. ___ 2019, No. 18-966, Joint Appendix, Vol. 2 (Dec. 22, 2017), https://www
.supremecourt.gov/DocketPDF/18/18–966/94964/20190401161123490_18-966%20
US%20Dept%20of%20Commerce%20v%20State%20of%20New%20York%20et%20
al%20Joint%20Appendix%20Vol%202.pdf.

78. Exec. Order No. 13880, "US Census Bureau, Status Reporting: 2020 Decennial Census," March 23, 2020, https://www.brennancenter.org/sites/default/files/2022-02
/may_21_2021_reassess.pdf.

79. Anthony Foti, "Briefing Memorandum for Secretary Ross Re: Sharing Records with the Census Bureau," Brennan Center, August 16, 2019, https://www.brennancenter
.org/sites/default/files/2022-02/may_11_2021_reassess.pdf.

80. Not all the states that had signed agreements were providing the bureau with data. This is true for three out of twenty-one states with WIC agreements, three out of thirty states with SNAP agreements, and four out of twenty-eight states with TANF agreements.

81. Tara Bahrampour, "Census Bureau's Request for Citizenship Data from DMVs Raises Privacy, Accuracy Concerns," *Washington Post*, October 17, 2019, https://www
.washingtonpost.com/local/social-issues/census-bureaus-request-for-citizenship-data
-from-dmvs-raises-privacy-accuracy-concerns/2019/10/17/aa8771f2-f114-11e9-89eb
-ec56cd414732_story.html.

82. Nora Flaherty, "Dunlap: Maine Will Not Hand Over Driver's License Info on Citizenship and Race," Maine Public, October 15, 2019, https://www.mainepublic.org
/politics/2019-10-15/dunlap-maine-will-not-hand-over-drivers-license-info-on-citi
zenship-and-race.

83. Alexa Aura, "Texas Considering Whether to Hand Driver's License, Citizenship Information to Census Bureau," *Texas Tribune*, October 18, 2019, https://www.texastri
bune.org/2019/10/18/census-bureau-driver-license-citizenship/.

84. As of July 30, 2020, however, South Carolina was still not sharing DMV data with the bureau.

85. Hansi Lo Wang, "Nebraska Is 1st State to Share Driver's License Records with Census Bureau," NPR, November 20, 2019, https://www.npr.org/2019/11/20/781373128

/nebraska-1st-to-say-it-will-share-drivers-license-records-with-census-bureau; Kim Norvell, "Iowa to Share Driver's License Data to Help Feds Determine Citizenship," *Des Moines Register*, July 15, 2020, https://www.desmoinesregister.com/story /news/2020/07/15/iowa-shares-drivers-license-data-census-bureau-find-citizenship -status/5445010002/.

86. Order, Texas League of United Latin American Citizens v. David Whitley (W.D.- Tex.), No. 5:19-cv-00074-FB (Feb. 27, 2019), https://campaignlegal.org/sites/default /files/2019-02/61-main.pdf.

87. Ron Jarmin, "Memorandum Re: Topics to Discuss with Secretary Ross through December 31, 2020," FOIA release, Brennan Center, https://www.brennancenter.org /sites/default/files/2022-01/BC-DOC-CEN-2020-1602-1445-1447.pdf.

88. "The Status of Data Acquisition and Options for Estimating the Illegal Population Enumerated in the 2020 Census," Briefing Materials for Secretary Ross, Brennan Center, August 10, 2020, https://www.brennancenter.org/sites/default/files/2022 -02/6._2021-05-17_reproduction.pdf.

89. Emily Bazelon and Michael Wines, "How the Census Bureau Stood Up to Donald Trump's Meddling," *New York Times*, August 12, 2021, https://www.nytimes .com/2021/08/12/sunday-review/census-redistricting-trump-immigrants.html.

90. See also City of San Jose v. Trump (N.D. Cal. 2020); Common Cause v. Trump (D.D.C. 2020); California v. Trump (N.D. Cal. 2020).

91. *Trump*, No. 1:20-cv-05770-JMF, Joint Appendix, https://www.supremecourt. gov/DocketPDF/20/20-366/159468/20201103115400744_Trump%20v.%20New%20 York%2020–366%20J.A.pdf.

92. First Amended Complaint, *New York*, No. 1:20-cv-05770-JMF (Aug. 5, 2020), https://www.brennancenter.org/sites/default/files/2020–08/FirstAmendedCom plaint_2020-08-05.pdf.

93. First Amended Complaint, *New York*, No. 1:20-cv-05770-JMF.

94. Memorandum of Law In Support of Defendants' Motion to Dismiss and in Op- position to Plaintiffs' Motion for Partial Summary Judgment or Preliminary Injunction, *New York*, No. 1:20-cv-05770-JMF (Aug. 19, 2020), https://www.brennancenter.org /sites/default/files/2020-08/MTD_2020-08-19.pdf.

95. *New York*, No. 1:20-cv-05770-JMF.

96. Opinion and Order, *New York*, No. 1:20-cv-05770-JMF (Sept. 10, 2020), https:// www.brennancenter.org/sites/default/files/2020-09/OpinionandOrder_2020-09-10_0 .pdf.

97. Opinion and Order, *New York*, No. 1:20-cv-05770-JMF.

98. Sixteen Republican AGs did not participate in the litigation. In six of these non- participating states (Arizona, Florida, Georgia, Kansas, Texas, and Utah), the share of undocumented residents was larger than the fifty-state average.

99. Brief of Local Governments as *Amici Curiae* In Support of Appellees, *Trump*, No. 20-366, https://www.brennancenter.org/sites/default/files/2020-11/AmicusBrief _LocalGovts.pdf; Brief for City of San Jose, California, King County, Washington, Arlington County, Virginia, Harris County, Texas, Black Alliance for Just Immigra- tion, Sam Liccardo, Rodney Ellis, Zerihoun Yilma, Lovette Kargbo-Thompson, and Santcha Etienne as *Amici Curiae* in Support of Appellees, *Trump*, No. 20-366, https://

www.brennancenter.org/sites/default/files/2020-11/AmicusBrief_SanJose.pdf; Brief of *Amicus Curiae* National Congress of American Indians, *Trump*, No. 20-366, https://www.brennancenter.org/sites/default/files/2020-11/AmicusBrief_NationalCongressofAmericanIndians.pdf.

100. Brief of Local Governments as *Amici Curiae* In Support of Appellees, *Trump*, No. 20-366, https://www.brennancenter.org/sites/default/files/2020-11/AmicusBrief_Local Govts.pdf; Brief for City of San Jose, California, King County, Washington, Arlington County, Virginia, Harris County, Texas, Black Alliance for Just Immigration, Sam Liccardo, Rodney Ellis, Zerihoun Yilma, Lovette Kargbo-Thompson, and Santcha Etienne as *Amici Curiae* in Support of Appellees, *Trump*, No. 20-366, https://www.brennancenter.org/sites/default/files/2020-11/AmicusBrief_SanJose.pdf.

101. Brief for New York and Other Government Appellees, *Trump*, No. 20-366, https://www.supremecourt.gov/DocketPDF/20/20-366/160902/20201116192141784_20-366%20Br%20for%20Government%20Appellees.pdf.

102. Oral Argument Transcript, *Trump*, 7.

103. Oral Argument Transcript, *Trump*, 29.

104. Oral Argument Transcript, *Trump*, 65–66.

105. *Trump*, 592 U.S. ___ (2020).

106. *Trump*.

107. *Trump*.

108. Peggy Gustafson, "Request for Information Pursuant to the Inspector General Act of 1978," as Amended, US Department of Commerce, January 12, 2021, https://www.oig.doc.gov/OIGPublications/OIG-21-019-M.pdf; Tara Bahrampour, "Embattled Census Bureau Director Steven Dillingham Resigns," *Washington Post*, January 18, 2021, https://www.washingtonpost.com/local/social-issues/embattled-census-bureau-director-steven-dillingham-resigns/2021/01/18/63c8d1aa-59bb-11eb-a976-bad6431e03e2_story.html.

109. *National Urban League v. Ross* (N.D. Cal. Sept. 1, 2020), https://www.brennancenter.org/sites/default/files/2020-09/First%20Amended%20Complaint_%202020-09-01.pdf.

110. *National Urban League*.

111. *National Urban League v. Ross* (N.D. Cal. Sept. 20, 2020) (Declaration of Albert E. Fontenot Jr.), https://www.brennancenter.org/sites/default/files/2020-09/Declaration_AlbertEFontenot_%202020-09-22.pdf.

112. *National Urban League* (N.D. Cal. Oct. 1, 2020), https://www.brennancenter.org/sites/default/files/2020-10/Order_10.1.2020.pdf.

113. *Ross v. National Urban League*, No. 20A62 (Oct. 10, 2022), https://www.brennancenter.org/sites/default/files/2020-10/20201010094824719_2020-10-10%20Response%20to%20Application%20with%20app.pdf.

114. *Ross*, 592 U.S. ___ (2020).

115. National Urban League v. Gina Raimondo, No. 3:20-cv-08697 (N.D. Cal. Apr. 22, 2021), https://www.brennancenter.org/sites/default/files/2021-04/order_granting_stipulated_dismissal.pdf.

6. COUNTING THE FORGOTTEN: HOW GOVERNMENTS RESPOND TO FLAWED DATA

1. "Reviewing the 2020 Census: Local Perspectives in Michigan," Committee on Homeland Security and Governmental Affairs, July 25, 2022, https://www.hsgac.senate .gov/hearings/reviewing-the-2020-census-local-perspectives-in-michigan/.

2. Jeffrey D. Morenoff, *Testimony Before the United States Senate Committee on Homeland Security and Government Affairs, Hearing on "Reviewing the 2020 Census: Local Perspectives in Michigan* (US Government Printing Office, 2022), hsgac.senate.gov/wp -content/uploads/imo/media/doc/Testimony-Morenoff-2022–07–25.pdf.

3. "Reviewing the 2020 Census," Committee on Homeland Security and Governmental Affairs.

4. "Reviewing the 2020 Census."

5. Corey Williams and Mike Schneider, "Detroit Sues Census in 2nd Fight over Population Counts," Associated Press, September 20, 2022, https://apnews.com/article /lawsuits-detroit-census-2020-us-bureau-government-and-politics-f02a419f415d12bfff 3e6796f2b91133.

6. For a review of these conditions, see National Academies of Sciences, Engineering, and Medicine, *Understanding the Quality of the 2020 Census: Interim Report* (National Academies Press, 2022).

7. "2020 Demographic Analysis," US Census Bureau, accessed November 10, 2024, https://www.census.gov/programs-surveys/decennial-census/about/coverage-measure ment/da.2020_Demographic_Analysis.html#list-tab-45290861; "2020 Post-Enumeration Survey," US Census Bureau, accessed November 10, 2024, https://www.census.gov /programs-surveys/decennial-census/about/coverage-measurement/pes.2020 .html#list-tab-400924250.

8. JASON, *Consistency of Data Products and Formal Privacy Methods for the 2020 Census* (MITRE Corporation, 2022).

9. 2020 Census Quality Indicators Task Force, *2020 Census Quality Indicators: A Report from the American Statistical Association* (American Statistical Association, 2020), https://www.amstat.org/asa/files/pdfs/POL-2020CensusQualityIndicators.pdf.

10. National Academies of Sciences, Engineering, and Medicine, *Understanding the Quality of the 2020 Census*, 15–20.

11. For a plain-language summary, see D'Vera Cohn and Jeffrey Passel, "Key Facts about the 2020 Census," Pew Research Center, June 8, 2022, https://www.pewresearch .org/fact-tank/2022/06/08/key-facts-about-the-quality-of-the-2020-census/.

12. Cohn and Passel, "Key Facts about the 2020 Census."

13. Eric Jensen, Andrew Roberts, and Luke Rogers, "Age Heaping in the 2020 Census Demographic and Housing Characteristics File (DHC)," US Census Bureau, May 25, 2023, https://www.census.gov/newsroom/blogs/random-samplings/2023/05/age-heap ing-2020-census-dhc.html.

14. National Academies of Sciences, Engineering, and Medicine, *Assessing the 2020 Census: Final Report* (National Academies Press, 2023), 54.

15. Courtney Hill, Krista Heim, Jinhee Hong, and Nam Phan, *Census Coverage Estimates for People in the United States by State and Census Operations: 2020 Post-Enumer-*

ation Survey Estimation Report (US Census Bureau, 2022); Peter Davis and James Mulligan, *Census Coverage Measurement Estimation Report: Net Coverage for the Household Population in the United States* (US Department of Commerce, 2012), https://www2.census.gov/programs-surveys/decennial/2010/technical-documentation/methodology/g-series/g03.pdf.

16. National Academies of Sciences, Engineering, and Medicine, *Understanding the Quality of the 2020 Census*, 60.

17. National Academies of Sciences, Engineering, and Medicine, *Assessing the 2020 Census*, 26–27. While this is the most complete evaluation of the 2020 Census available at the time of publication, there are also additional evaluations yet to be published.

18. See the National League of Cities, "2020 Census City Undercounts: Risks, Consequences, and Solutions," webinar, National League of Cities, January 14, 2021, https://www.nlc.org/resource/from-the-event-2020-census-city-undercounts-risks-conse quences-and-solutions/.

19. Alison Dirr and Vanessa Swales, "Milwaukee Mayor Johnson Files Challenge to 2020 US Census Tally, Says the City Was Undercounted by Thousands," *Milwaukee Journal Sentinel*, December 20, 2022, https://www.jsonline.com/story/news/local/milwaukee/2022/12/20/milwaukee-challenges-2020-u-s-census-population-drop/69742133007/; Jeramey Jannene, "Milwaukee Believes Census Didn't Count 15,800 Residents," *Urban Milwaukee*, December 20, 2022, https://urbanmilwaukee.com/2022/12/20/city-hall-milwaukee-believes-census-didnt-count-15800-residents/.

20. "2020 Count Question Resolution Operation," US Census Bureau, December 1, 2021, https://www.census.gov/programs-surveys/decennial-census/decade/2020/planning-management/evaluate/cqr.html.

21. See James L. Dinwiddie, Memorandum Re: Policy for Correcting Geographic/Coverage Errors Through the Count Question Resolution and 1990 Census Errata Process (Sept. 4, 1991); Susan M. Miskura, Memorandum Re: Policy for Count Question Resolution and 1990 Census Errata (Feb. 22, 1991). See, in general, Subcommittee on Census and Population, *Hearing to Review Major Alternatives for the Census in the Year 2000*, 102nd Cong., 1st Sess., 1991.

22. US Census Bureau, *1990 Census of Population and Housing: History* (US Census Bureau, 1996), 12–10–12–11.

23. US Census Bureau, *1990 Census of Population and Housing*, 6–45.

24. Steven A. Holmes, "Census Chief Accuses Panel of Meddling with Details," *New York Times*, February 11, 1999, https://www.nytimes.com/1999/02/11/us/census-chief-accuses-panel-of-meddling-with-details.html.

25. US Census Bureau, *History: 2000 Census of Population and Housing*, vol. 2 (US Census Bureau, 2009), 525.

26. Holmes, "Census Chief Accuses Panel of Meddling with Details."

27. *Local Census Quality Act*, H.R. 472, 106th Cong., 1st Sess., https://www.congress.gov/bill/106th-congress/house-bill/472; "Measures Referred," *Congressional Record*, 106th Cong., 1st Sess., vol. 145, no. 52 (1999): S3775.

28. Matthew Frates, "Census Count Question Resolution (CQR) Workshop," presen-

tation at the Maryland Department of Planning, YouTube, March 24, 2022, https://www
.youtube.com/watch?v=w-6jATg7wGw.

29. Joseph J. Salvo and Arun Peter Lobo, "Misclassifying New York's Hidden Units as
Vacant in 2010: Lessons Gleaned for the 2020 Census," *Population Research and Policy
Review* 32, no. 5 (2013): 729–751.

30. "2010 Census Count Question Resolution Challenging Jurisdictions," US Census
Bureau, January 31, 2014, https://www2.census.gov/programs-surveys/decennial/2010
/program-management/5-review/cqr/cqr-gu-status-rpt-01-31-14.pdf.

31. "Corrected 2010 Census Total Population, Household Population, Group Quarters Population, Total Housing Unit, Occupied Housing Units and Vacant Housing Unit
Counts for Governmental Units, Census Tracts, and Census Blocks," US Census Bureau, accessed November 8, 2024, https://www2.census.gov/programs-surveys/decen
nial/2010/program-management/5-review/cqr/notes/cqr-NY-tb.pdf; "Notes and Errata:
2010 Census of Population and Housing," US Census Bureau, accessed November 8,
2024, https://www2.census.gov/programs-surveys/decennial/2010/technical-document
ation/errata-notes/errata.pdf.

32. Frates, "Census Count Question Resolution (CQR) Workshop."

33. US Census Bureau, "Count Question Resolution Federal Register Notice," Regula
tions.gov, August 17, 2020, https://www.regulations.gov/document/USBC-2020-0005
-0002/comment.

34. US Census Bureau, "Agency Information Collection Activities; Submission to the
Office of Management and Budget (OMB) for Review and Approval; Comment Request;
2020 Post-Census Group Quarters Review," *Federal Register* 86, no. 221 (2021): 64897.

35. John D. Johnson, "Assessing the City of Milwaukee's 2020 Census Challenge,"
Marquette University Law School, January 5, 2023, https://law.marquette.edu/faculty
blog/2023/01/assessing-the-city-of-milwaukees-2020-census-challenge/#:~:text
=The%202020%20census%20measured%20257%2C723%20housing%20units%20
in%20Milwaukee.

36. US Census Bureau, "Agency Information Collection Activities."

37. Mike Schneider, "College Towns Plan to Challenge Results of 2020 Census," Associated Press, October 18, 2021, https://apnews.com/article/coronavirus-pandemic
-lifestyle-education-pennsylvania-alabama-bddf3c13c35f2cd309f2ff636173415b.

38. Bureau of the Census, "Comment on FR Doc # 2021-25283," Regulations.gov,
March 22, 2022, https://www.regulations.gov/comment/USBC-2021-0025-0013.

39. Office of Inspector General, *Lessons Learned from the 2020 Decennial Census*,
Final Report No. OIG-22–030 (US Department of Commerce, 2022), https://www.oig
.doc.gov/OIGPublications/OIG-22-030.pdf.

40. US Census Bureau, "Agency Information Collection Activities."

41. Author's analysis of US Census Bureau, "Corrected 2010 Census Counts," US
Census Bureau, accessed November 8, 2024, https://www2.census.gov/programs-sur
veys/decennial/2010/program-management/5-review/cqr/notes/.

42. City of Whitewater, *Wisconsin, 2023–2025 Strategic Planning Issues* (University
of Wisconsin-Madison, n.d.), accessed March 2, 2024, https://whitewater-wi.gov/Docu
mentCenter/View/3513/Whitewater-Strategic-Plan?bidId=.

43. Municipal aid boost based on author's calculation, using formulas for Act 12 supplemental aid payments provided by Wisconsin Department of Revenue, "Shared Revenue Estimates," State of Wisconsin Department of Revenue, accessed March 2, 2024, https://www.revenue.wi.gov/Pages/Report/Shared-Revenue-Estimates.aspx; Capital Improvement Program, "2024–2025 Municipal Budget," City of Whitewater, accessed March 2, 2024, https://www.whitewater-wi.gov/ArchiveCenter/ViewFile/Item/1614.

44. See "Corrected Census 2020 Total Population, Household Population, Group Quarters Population, Total Housing Units, Occupied Housing Units, and Vacant Housing Unit Counts for Governmental Units, Tennessee," US Census Bureau, accessed March 2, 2024, https://www2.census.gov/programs-surveys/decennial/2020/program-management/cqr/errata-notes/cqr_TN_gu.xlsx.

45. Tim Henderson, "Some Towns Get Funding Boost from Census Corrections," Stateline, February 10, 2024, https://stateline.org/2023/02/10/some-towns-get-funding-boost-from-census-corrections/; "Fixing Prison-Based Gerrymandering After the 2010 Census: Tennessee," Prison Policy Initiative, March 2010, https://www.prisonersofthe census.org/50states/TN.html.

46. See "Corrected Census 2020 Total Population."

47. Jeramey Janene, "Milwaukee Census Challenge Denied," Urban Milwaukee, October 19, 2023, https://urbanmilwaukee.com/2023/10/19/milwaukee-census-challenge-denied/.

48. Christine Walsh, "Making a Difference," At Home in Central Illinois, Spring 2019, https://athomeillinois.com/content/2019-april-may-june/featured/making-a-difference/.

49. Tom Kacich, "Illinois, Urbana Have Legit Complaints About the Census," The (Illinois) News-Gazette, May 24, 2022, https://www.news-gazette.com/opinion/columns/tom-kacich-illinois-urbana-have-legit-complaints-about-the-census/article_3aa6f000-1a3c-5093-9897-47741a672023.html.

50. Henry D. Sheldon, "Special Census Program of the bureau of the Census," American Statistician 11, no. 2 (1957): 7. For historical information on special censuses, see US Bureau of the Census, Current Population Reports, Series P–28: Special Censuses (US Department of Commerce, 2018).

51. For an example of a special census conducted to capture rapid population growth, see US Bureau of the Census, "Special Census of Manhattan Beach, California," Current Population Reports, no. 1301. For an example of a special census conducted following annexation, see US Bureau of the Census, "Special Census of South Bend, Indiana," Current Population Reports, no. 1143.

52. See US Census Bureau, "Official Census Statistics Released to Government Units," US Census Bureau, accessed November 8, 2024, https://www.census.gov/programs-surveys/specialcensus/data_products/official_counts.html.

53. Ross Davis, Christian Garcia, and Heather Polo, Sponsor Guide: 2020 Special Census (US Census Bureau, 2022), https://www2.census.gov/programs-surveys/special-census/2020-special-census-program-sponsor-guide.pdf.

54. Davis, Garcia, and Polo, Sponsor Guide, 11.

55. Davis, Garcia, and Polo, 12.

56. Marie Wilson, "Special Census Boosts Naperville's Population by 5,988," Daily (Naperville) Herald, August 3, 2018; City of Naperville, City Council Meeting, August

15, 2017, https://naperville.granicus.com/player/clip/1100?view_id=4&meta_id=15682
8&redirect=true&h=a8a029b524b57f08624c256bd3fd313f.

57. Morenoff, *Testimony Before the United States Senate Committee on Homeland Security and Government Affairs*; Patrick Cooney, Ren Farley, Samiul Jubaed, Kurt Metzger, Jeffrey Morenoff, Lisa Neidert, and Ramona Rodriguez-Washington, "Analysis of the Census 2020 Count in Detroit," University of Michigan, Ford School of Public Policy, December 2021, https://sites.fordschool.umich.edu/poverty2021/files/2021/12/PovertySolutions-Census-Undercount-in-Detroit-PolicyBrief-December2021.pdf.

58. Zach Brown, "The Digital Divide and Census 2020," Data-Driven Detroit, October 1, 2018, https://datadrivendetroit.org/blog/2018/10/01/internet-access-and-the-census/#:~:text=This%20means%20that%20on%20average,72.2%25%20without%20these%2053%20tracts.

59. Morenoff, *Testimony Before the United States Senate Committee on Homeland Security and Government Affairs*; Cooney, Farley, Jubaed, Metzger, Morenoff, Neidert, and Rodriguez-Washington, "Analysis of the Census 2020 Count in Detroit."

60. My estimate here employs the median cost of a special census of sixteen hundred housing units.

61. Center for Urban Research, "2020 Hard to Count Maps: Detroit," CUNY Graduate Center, accessed November 8, 2024, https://www.censushardtocountmaps2020.us/?latlng=42.35279%2C-83.03363&z=11&query=coordinates%3A%3A42.33215%2C-83.04085&promotedfeaturetype=cities&arp=arpRaceEthnicity&baselayerstate=5&rtrYear=sR2010&infotab=info-rtrselfresponse&filterQuery=false.

62. Citizens Research Council of Michigan, "Analysis of FY2023 City of Detroit Budget," Detroit Bureau, May 2022, http://crcmich.org/PUBLICAT/2020s/2022/Detroit_FY2023_Budget_Analysis-May2022.pdf.

63. On the use of population estimates in federal programs, see 13 US Code § 183. On the role of population in state shared-revenue formulas, see, e.g., Noga Ardon, *Informational Paper #22: Shared Revenue Program County and Municipal Aid and Utility Aid* (Wisconsin Legislative Fiscal Bureau, 2023), https://docs.legis.wisconsin.gov/misc/lfb/informational_papers/january_2023/0022_shared_revenue_program_county_and_municipal_aid_and_utility_aid_informational_paper_22.pdf.

64. "Methodology for United States Population Estimates: Vintage 2021," US Census Bureau, December 2021, https://www2.census.gov/programs-surveys/popest/technical-documentation/methodology/2020–2021/methods-statement-v2021.pdf.

65. Procedure for Challenging Population Estimates, 15 C.F.R. § 90 (2013).

66. "Review Guide for the Population Estimates Challenge Program," US Census Bureau, April 30, 2023, https://www2.census.gov/programs-surveys/popest/about/challenge-program/challenge-review-guide.pdf.

67. US Government Accountability Office, *2020 Census: Local Administrative Records and Their Use in the Challenge Program and Decennial* (GAO, 2013), https://www.gao.gov/assets/gao-13-269.pdf.

68. Procedure for Challenging Population Estimates.

69. Bureau of the Census, "Resumption of the Population Estimates Challenge Program and Proposed Changes to the Program," Regulations.gov, accessed November 8, 2024, https://www.regulations.gov/docket/USBC-2012-0001/comments.

70. Bureau of the Census, "Comment on FR Doc # 2012-19672," Regulations.gov, September 18, 2012, https://www.regulations.gov/comment/USBC-2012-0001-0008.

71. US Census Bureau, "Resumption of the Population Estimates Challenge Program," *Federal Register* 78, no. 2 (January 3, 2013): 255–260.

72. US Census Bureau, "Temporary Suspension of the Population Estimates Challenge Program," *Federal Register* 85, no. 6 (January 9, 2020): 1100–1102.

73. US Census Bureau, "Resumption of the Population Estimates Challenge Program," 71241.

74. Declaration of Christine Hartley, City of Detroit v. Department of Commerce, et al., No. 3:22-cv-12205 (E.D. Mich.), 6.

75. US Census Bureau, "2020 Population Estimates Challenge Program," screenshot, US Census Bureau, accessed on October 25, 2022, https://perma.cc/55QF-2QA5.

76. Michael Duggan, "Comment on FR Doc # 2022-25415," Regulations.gov, December 16, 2022, https://www.regulations.gov/comment/USBC_FRDOC_0001-0035.

77. "Review Guide for the Population Estimates Challenge Program."

78. Susana Quiros and William P. O'Hare, "The Number of Young Hispanic Children in the Census Bureau's Population Estimates Program Blended Base Compared to the 2020 Census Count," Count All Kids Campaign, June 2023, https://countallkids.org/wp-content/uploads/2023/06/Number-of-Young-Hispanic-Children-in-the-Census-Bureaus-Population-Estimates.pdf.

79. Deborah Weinstein and Michelle Hughes, "RE: November 22, 2022 *Federal Register* Notice of Proposed Rulemaking and Request for Comments in Regard to the Population Estimates Challenge Program," Regulations.gov, https://downloads.regulations.gov/USBC_FRDOC_0001-0043/attachment_1.pdf.

80. Morenoff, *Testimony Before the United States Senate Committee on Homeland Security and Government Affairs.*

81. Kenneth Hodges, Jeffrey Hardcastle, and Narayan Sastry, "FRN-PopEstCommentsPAA-COPS," Regulations.gov, December 22, 2022, https://www.regulations.gov/comment/USBC_FRDOC_0001-0041.

82. US Census Bureau, "Population Estimates Challenge Program," *Federal Register* 88, no. 57 (March 24, 2023): 17696–17706.

83. Utah v. Evans, 536 U.S. 452 (2002).

84. TransUnion LLC v. Ramirez, 594 U.S. ____ (2021), 2203.

85. Ohio v. Raimondo, No. 3:21-cv-064 (S.D. Ohio, W. Div.).

86. Bennett v. Spear, 520 U.S. 154 (1997).

87. City of New York v. Department of Defense, 913 F.3d 423, 431 (4th Cir. 2019).

88. Department of Commerce v. New York, 588 U.S. ____ (2019).

89. Heckler v. Chaney, 470 U.S. 821 (1985).

90. *Bennett*, 520 U.S. 154, 17.

91. *Trump v. New York*, 592 U.S. ____ (2020).

92. Complaint, *City of Detroit v. Department of Commerce, et al.*, No. 3:22-cv-12205 (E.D. Mich.); Mot. for Preliminary Injunction, *City of Detroit*, No. 3:22-cv-12205.

93. Mot. for Preliminary Injunction, *City of Detroit*.

94. Motion to Dismiss, *City of Detroit*; Repl. to Mot. for Preliminary Injunction, *City of Detroit*.

95. Reply to Motion to Dismiss, *City of Detroit*, 7fn4.

96. Reply to Motion to Dismiss, *City of Detroit*, 12.

97. Motion to Dismiss, *City of Detroit*, 34.

98. Motion to Dismiss, 45.

99. Reply to Motion to Dismiss, *City of Detroit*.

100. Opinion and Order Dismissing Count I of the Amended Coplaint and Termining as Moot Plaintiff's Motion for Preliminary Injunction, *City of Detroit*.

101. Joint Stipulation of Dismissal Without Prejudice, *City of Detroit*.

102. Christine Hartley, "Status Update on the Population Estimates," presentation to the Committee on National Statistics 2020 Census Data Products: Workshop on the Demographic and Housing Characteristics Files, June 21, 2022, https://www.nation alacademies.org/documents/embed/link/LF2255DA3DD1C41C0A42D3BEF0989A CAECE3053A6A9B/file/D2A33D990292D28C74CBA76154EEB5BAFC227241A081?n oSaveAs=1.

103. See, e.g., US Government Accountability Office, "2020 Census: Census Bureau Needs to Assess Data Quality Concerns Stemming from Recent Design Changes," GAO, December 3, 2020, https://www.gao.gov/products/gao-21-142; US Government Accountability Office, "2020 Census: Innovations Helped with Implementation, but Bureau Can Do More to Realize Future Benefits," GAO, June 14, 2021, https://www.gao .gov/products/gao-21-478; Office of Inspector General, *Lessons Learned from the 2020 Decennial Census*.

104. See, e.g., Government Accountability Office, "High Risk Area: Decennial Census," GAO, accessed November 10, 2024, https://www.gao.gov/highrisk/decennial-census.

105. Calculation based on author's analysis of data from "New US Media Data," Comparative Agendas Project, accessed March 24, 2023, www.comparativeagendas.net.

106. Hassan Abbas, "Senator Peters Hosts Census Director Robert Santos in Dearborn, Detroit," Arab American News, September 30, 2022, https://www.peters.senate .gov/newsroom/in-the-news/senator-peters-hosts-census-director-robert-santos-in -dearborn-detroit.

107. Committee on Oversight and Reform, Report Together with Minority Views (to Accompany H.R. 8326), 117th Cong., 2nd Sess. (2022), 117–456.

108. Mike Schneider and Kevin Freking, "House OKs Bill to Curb Political Interference with Census," Associated Press, September 15, 2022, https://apnews.com/article /health-covid-race-and-ethnicity-census-2020-us-bureau-6d2fbf0c8fd4953e3dbac70b 6b6ab84b.

109. Consolidated Appropriations Act of 2022, Pub. Law No. 117–103.

110. "The 2020 Census and Confidentiality," US Census Bureau, 2019, https://www .census.gov/content/dam/Census/library/factsheets/2019/comm/2020-confidentiality -factsheet.pdf.

111. William Howard Taft, "Proclamation," US Census Bureau, July 2, 1909, https:// www.census.gov/history/img/proclamation1910-artifact.jpg.

112. 13 U.S.C. § 9.

113. Simon Garfinkel, "Differential Privacy and the 2020 US Census," *MIT Case Studies in Social and Ethical Responsibilities of Computing* (Winter 2022), https://doi .org/10.21428/2c646de5.7ec6ab93.

114. Ron Jarmin, "The Balancing Act of Producing Accurate and Confidential Statistics," US Census Bureau, December 14, 2018, https://www.census.gov/newsroom/blogs/director/2018/12/the_balancing_actof.html.

115. Steven Ruggles, Catherine Fitch, Diana Magnuson, and Jonathan Schroeder, "Differential Privacy and Census Data: Implications for Social and Economic Research," *AEA Papers and Proceedings* 109 (2019): 403–408.

116. V. Joseph Hotz and Joseph Salvo, "A Chronicle of the Application of Differential Privacy to the 2020 Census," special issue, *Harvard Data Science Review* 2 (2022): https://doi.org/10.1162/99608f92.ff891fe5.

117. Garfinkel, "Differential Privacy and the 2020 US Census."

118. Cynthia Dwork, "Differential Privacy: A Cryptographic Approach to Private Data Analysis," in *Privacy, Big Data, and the Public Good* (Cambridge University Press, 2014), 302.

119. "Disclosure Avoidance for the 2020 Census: An Introduction," US Census Bureau, November 2021, https://www2.census.gov/library/publications/decennial/2020/2020-census-disclosure-avoidance-handbook.pdf.

120. "Comparing Differential Privacy with Older Disclosure Avoidance Methods," US Census Bureau, August 12, 2021, https://www.census.gov/library/fact-sheets/2021/comparing-differential-privacy-with-older-disclosure-avoidance-methods.html.

121. National Academies of Sciences, Engineering, and Medicine, *2020 Census Data Products: Data Needs and Privacy Considerations: Proceedings of a Workshop* (National Academies Press, 2020).

122. Dan Bouk and danah boyd, "Democracy's Data Infrastructure," Knight First Amendment Institute, March 18, 2021, https://knightcolumbia.org/content/democracys-data-infrastructure.

123. Ruggles, Fitch, Magnuson, and Schroeder, "Differential Privacy and Census Data," 407.

124. Kriston Capps, "Data Scientists Square Off over Trust and Privacy in 2020 Census," Bloomberg, August 12, 2021, https://www.bloomberg.com/news/articles/2021-08-12/data-scientists-ask-can-we-trust-the-2020-census.

125. Bouk and boyd, "Democracy's Data Infrastructure."

126. Garfinkel, "Differential Privacy and the 2020 US Census."

127. Steven Ruggles and David Van Riper, "The Role of Chance in the Census Bureau Database Reconstruction Experiment," *Population Research and Policy Review* 481 (2022): 781–788. For a critique of Ruggles and Van Riper's analysis, see Ron S. Jarmin, John M. Abowd, Robert Ashmead, Ryan Cumings-Menon, Nathan Goldschlag, Michael B. Hawes, Sallie Ann Keller, Daniel Kifer, Philip Leclerc, Jerome P. Reiter, Rolando A. Rodriguez, Ian Schmutte, Victoria Velkoff, and Pavel Zhuravlev, "An In-Depth Examination of Requirements for Disclosure Risk Assessment," *Proceedings of the National Academy of Sciences* 120, no. 43 (2023): e2220558120.

128. Quoted in National Academies of Sciences, Engineering, and Medicine, *2020 Census Data Products*, 37.

129. National Academies of Sciences, Engineering, and Medicine, 38.

130. National Academies of Sciences, Engineering, and Medicine, 47.

131. National Academies of Sciences, Engineering, and Medicine, 53–55.

132. National Academies of Sciences, Engineering, and Medicine, 58.

133. Margo Anderson, Motion for Leave to File Amicus Brief in Support of Plaintiffs, *Alabama v. Department of Commerce*, No. 3:21-cv-00211 (M.D. Ala.), 19.

134. See, e.g., Tim Storey, "Letter to Sens. Ron Johnson and Gary Peters," National Conference of State Legislators, June 1, 2020, https://documents.ncsl.org/wwwncsl /State-Federal/Senate-Census-Letter-FINAL0620.pdf, accessed March 3, 2024; Kevin Allis, "Letter to Steven Dillingham," Brennan Center, April 23, 2020, https://www.bren nancenter.org/sites/default/files/2022-02/census_bureau_part39.pdf; Ross Hollister email to Sabrina McNeal, Brennan Center, February 25, 2020, https://www.brennancenter .org/sites/default/files/2022-02/census_bureau_part39.pdf.

135. See, e.g., Steering Committees of Census Information Centers, Federal-State Co-operative for Population Estimates, Joint Letter to Steven Dillingham, State Data Centers, November 27, 2019, https://sdcclearinghouse.files.wordpress.com/2019/11/2019_11_27 -jointletter_dp_2020.pdf; John Abowd, Letter to Jeff Hardcastle, June 24, 2020, https:// sdcclearinghouse.files.wordpress.com/2020/06/cqas-09930-signed-002.pdf.

136. Angela Hallowell and Amanda Rector, Letter to Steven Dillingham, February 20, 2020, https://www.brennancenter.org/sites/default/files/2022-02/census_bureau _part39.pdf.

137. Storey, Letter to Sens. Ron Johnson and Gary Peters.

138. Nearly two-thirds of that budget was allocated to the microdata detail file that deals with population ($\varepsilon=4$), with the remainder devoted to the microdata detail file that deals with housing units ($\varepsilon=2$). See Albert Fontenot, "Memorandum Re: 2010 Dem-onstration Data Products—Design Parameters and Global Privacy-Loss Budget," US Census Bureau, October 31, 2019, https://www2.census.gov/programs-surveys/decen nial/2020/program-management/memo-series/2020-memo-2019_25.pdf.

139. "Census Bureau Statement on Redistricting Data Timeline," US Census Bureau, February 12, 2021, https://www.census.gov/newsroom/press-releases/2021/statement -redistricting-data-timeline.html.

140. "2020 Census Delays and the Impact on Redistricting," National Conference of State Legislatures, September 23, 2021, https://www.ncsl.org/redistricting-and-census /2020-census-delays-and-the-impact-on-redistricting.

141. Memorandum Opinion and Order, *Alabama v. Department of Commerce*, No. 3:21-cv-211 (M.D. Ala.), June 29, 2021.

142. See "Developing the DAS: Demonstration Data and Progress Metrics," US Cen-sus Bureau, accessed November 10, 2024, https://www.census.gov/programs-surveys /decennial-census/decade/2020/planning-management/process/disclosure-avoidance /2020-das-development.html.

143. Most of the increase here can be accounted for by person-level data ($\varepsilon = 10.3$) rather than housing units, whose privacy loss budget remained low ($\varepsilon = 1.9$). See "2010 Demonstration Privacy-Protected Microdata Files 2021–04–28," US Census Bureau, accessed November 10, 2024, https://www2.census.gov/programs-surveys/decennial /2020/program-management/data-product-planning/2010-demonstration-data -products/01-Redistricting_File—PL_94-171/2021-04-28_ppmf/2021-04-28-ppmf -factsheet.pdf.

144. The largest share of this increase ($\varepsilon = 17.14$) was allocated to the person's file.

"Census Bureau Sets Key Parameters to Protect Privacy in 2020 Census Results," US Census Bureau, June 9, 2021, https://www.census.gov/programs-surveys/decennial -census/decade/2020/planning-management/process/disclosure-avoidance/2020-das -updates/2021-06-09.html.

145. Note that to truly evaluate accuracy of these products, we would ideally want to consider the extent to which the noise-infused census data contained in the MDF differs not from published HDF data but from the Census Edited File (CEF), which are untainted by any disclosure avoidance system. The problem, however, is that the CEF data are confidential. Thus in order to communicate with data users about the accuracy of its demonstration data products, the bureau had to opt for the HDF instead. Yet the HDF differed from the CEF in one important way: It has already been protected using the bureau's 2010 DAS, which relies on data swapping rather than differential privacy. This, as census researchers danah boyd and Jayshree Sarathy have pointed out, means the public cannot compare noise-infused MDF data to the untainted CEF. The "ground truth" against which we are evaluating differential privacy is also "polluted" by earlier disclosure avoidance techniques. See danah boyd and Jayshree Sarathy, "Differential Perspectives: Epistemic Disconnects Surrounding the U.S. Census Bureau's Use of Differential Privacy," special issue, *Harvard Data Science Review* 2 (2022), https:// doi.org/10.1162/99608f92.66882f0e; Christopher T. Kenny, Shiro Kuriwaki, Cory McCartan, Evan TR Rosenman, Tyler Simko, and Kosuke Imai, "Comment: The Essential Role of Policy Evaluation for the 2020 Census Disclosure Avoidance System," special issue, *Harvard Data Science Review* 2 (2023), https://doi.org/10.1162/99608f92.abc2c765.

146. "Disclosure Avoidance System (DAS) Production Settings," detailed summary metrics tables, US Census Bureau, June 8, 2021, https://www2.census.gov/programs -surveys/decennial/2020/program-management/data-product-planning/2010-demon stration-data-products/01-Redistricting_File—PL_94-171/2021-06-08_ppmf_Produc tion_Settings/2021-06-08-data-metrics-tables_production-settings.xlsx.

147. Email from William P. O'Hare, March 13, 2024.

148. William P. O'Hare, "Analysis of Census Bureau's August 2022 Differential Privacy Demonstration Product: Implications for Data on Young Children," Count All Kids Campaign, September 23, 2022, https://countallkids.org/wp-content/uploads/2022/09 /Implications-of-Differential-Privacy-for-kids-9-23-2022-FINAL.pdf.

149. See, e.g., Christopher T. Kenny, Shiro Kuriwaki, Cory McCartan, Evan T.R. Rosenman, Tyler Simko, and Kosuke Imai, "The Use of Differential Privacy for Census Data and Its Impact on Redistricting: The Case of the 2020 US Census," *Science Advances* 7, no. 41 (2021): eabk3283.

150. Donna Daily, "Disclosure Avoidance Protections for the American Community Survey," US Census Bureau, December 14, 2022, https://www.census.gov/newsroom /blogs/random-samplings/2022/12/disclosure-avoidance-protections-acs.html.

151. Federal-State Cooperative on Population Estimates (FSCPE) Steering Committee, Letter to Rob Santos, August 1, 2022, https://drive.google.com/file/d/1Zk-PG6Da vWFPBD9v9y69pSuYwMych6Iu/view.

152. National Academies of Sciences, Engineering, and Medicine, *Understanding the Quality of the 2020 Census*, 53.

CONCLUSION

1. Dave Granlund, "Census Takers," *Northwest Florida Daily News*, April 6, 2018, https://www.nwfdailynews.com/story/lifestyle/things-to-do/destin/2018/04/06/gran lund-cartoon-census-takers/12803826007/.

2. Adam Zyglis, "Trump Census Policy," *Buffalo News*, March 30, 2018, https://buf falonews.com/opinion/adam-zyglis-trump-census-policy/article_29aa355d-ee68-5aff -8899-770d881b403c.html; Steve Sack, "Who Counts in the 2020 Census?" *Minnesota Star Tribune*, June 7, 2019, https://www.startribune.com/sack-cartoon-who-counts-in -the-2020-census/510992242/.

3. Bill Bramhall, "Census Undercount," *Austin American-Statesman*, March 16, 2022, https://www.statesman.com/story/opinion/cartoons/2022/03/16/editorial-cartoon -march-16-2022-census-undercount/7036064001/; John Cole, "Bridge Out: Pa.'s Census Shortfall, Explained," *Pennsylvania Capital-Star*, May 1, 2021, https://www.penncapital -star.com/blog/bridge-out-pa-s-census-shortfall-explained-editorial-cartoon/.

4. Michel Foucault, *Power/Knowledge: Selected Interviews and Other Writings, 1972– 1977* (Vintage, 1980); James C. Scott, *Seeing Like a State: How Certain Schemes to Improve the Human Condition Have Failed* (Yale University Press, 1998).

5. See, e.g., Rebecca Jean Emigh, Dylan Riley, and Patricia Ahmed, *Antecedents of Censuses from Medieval to Nation States: How States and Societies Count* (Palgrave Macmillan, 2015); Rebecca Jean Emigh, Dylan Riley, and Patricia Ahmed, *Changes in Censuses from Imperialist to Welfare States* (Palgrave Macmillan, 2016); Dan Bouk, *Democracy's Data: The Hidden Stories in the U.S. Census and How to Read Them* (Macmillan, 2022); Emily Klancher Merchant, *Building the Population Bomb* (Oxford University Press, 2021); Cristina Mora, *Making Hispanics: How Activists, Bureaucrats, and Media Constructed a New American* (University of Chicago Press, 2014).

6. Kimberly J. Morgan and Ann Shola Orloff, eds., *The Many Hands of the State: Theorizing Political Authority and Social Control* (Cambridge University Press, 2017).

7. See, e.g., Andrew Reamer, "Counting for Dollars 2020: The Role of the Decennial Census in the Geographic Distribution of Federal Funds," GW Institute of Public Policy, April 29, 2020, https://gwipp.gwu.edu/counting-dollars-2020-role-decennial-census -geographic-distribution-federal-funds.

8. David Hamilton and Carl Stenberg, "Introduction: Intergovernmental Relations in Transition," in *Intergovernmental Relations in Transition: Reflections and Directions*, ed. David Hamilton and Carl Stenberg (Routledge, 2018), 1–12.

9. US Department of Commerce, *Census Scientific Advisory Committee Charter* (Bureau of the Census, 2022), https://www2.census.gov/about/partners/cac/sac/sac-charter .pdf.

10. US Department of Commerce, *Census Bureau National Advisory Committee on Racial, Ethnic, and Other Populations* (Bureau of the Census, 2022), https://www2.cen sus.gov/cac/nac/nac-charter.pdf.

11. US Census Bureau, *2030 Census Advisory Committee Charter* (Bureau of the Census, 2023), https://www2.census.gov/about/partners/cac/2030-cac-charter.pdf.

12. Constance F. Citro, "Advisory Committees," in *Encyclopedia of the US Census:*

From the Constitution to the American Community Survey, ed. Constance F. Citro, Margo J. Anderson, and Joseph J. Salvo (CQ Press, 2011), 32–25.

13. "Federal–State Cooperative for Population Estimates," US Census Bureau, September 3, 2024, https://www.census.gov/programs-surveys/popest/about/fscpe.html.

14. "Grants and Contract Opportunities," US Census Bureau, accessed November 1, 2024, https://www.commerce.gov/work-with-us/grants-and-contract-opportunities.

15. "State Data Center (SDC) Network," US Census Bureau, August 15, 2023, https://www.census.gov/about/partners/sdc.html.

16. "Governors' Liaison Network," US Census Bureau, November 18, 2021, https://www.census.gov/about/partners/gln.html.

17. "Office of Congressional & Intergovernmental Affairs," US Census Bureau, December 27, 2023, https://www.census.gov/about/cong-gov-affairs.html.

18. Christine Hartley and Luke Rogers, "COVID-19 Pandemic Leads to Innovative Census Bureau Methods of Estimating US Population," *America Counts: Stories* blog, June 22, 2023, https://www.census.gov/library/stories/2023/06/blended-base-methodology.html.

19. While never enacted into law, there have been proposals for the federal subsidy of special censuses in disaster areas. See, e.g., *To Provide that a Special Census Shall Be Conducted, Without Charge to a Requesting State, County, or Other Unit Of Government, if Necessary to Correct a Significant Undercount in a Decennial Census Which Is Due, in Whole or in Part, to a Natural Disaster or Similar Situation*, H.R. 534, 103rd Cong., 1st Sess., Cong. Rec. 139, 423–485.

20. Paul Dans and Steven Groves, eds., *Mandate for Leadership: The Conservative Promise* (Heritage Foundation, 2023).

21. Thomas Gilman, "Department of Commerce," in *Mandate for Leadership: The Conservative Promise*, ed. Paul Dans and Steven Groves (Heritage Foundation, 2023), 680.

22. Gilman, "Department of Commerce," 679.

23. Donald Devine, Dennis Dean Kirk, and Paul Dans, "Central Personnel Agencies: Managing the Bureaucracy," in *Mandate for Leadership: The Conservative Promise*, ed. Paul Dans and Steven Groves (Heritage Foundation, 2023), 80.

24. Gilman, "Department of Commerce," 682.

25. *Ensuring a Fair and Accurate Census Act*, H.R. 8326, 117th Cong., 2nd Sess., Cong. Rec. (Sep. 15, 2022), H 7858.

26. *Honest Census Communications Act*, H.R. 5815, 117th Cong., 2nd Sess., Cong. Rec. (Jun. 15, 2022), D 664.

27. Constance Citro, "Are We Up to the Challenge of Protecting Federal Statistics?," *Harvard Data Science Review* 2, no. 1 (2020), https://doi.org/10.1162/99608f92.1a3cd97f.

28. *Ensuring a Fair and Accurate Census Act*.

29. See Burdett Loomis, *Time, Politics, and Policies: A Legislative Year* (University Press of Kansas, 1994), 18–23.

30. Marian F. MacDorman, Eugene Declercq, and Marie E. Thoma, "Making Vital Statistics Count: Preventing US Maternal Deaths Requires Better Data," *Obstetrics and Gynecology* 131, no. 5 (2018): 759–761.

31. Bridget A. Fahey, "Data Federalism," *Harvard Law Review* 135, no. 4 (2022): 1007–1080.

INDEX

Abowd, John, 49–50, 62, 166, 217, 219
address data, 77–82, 99, 235. *See also* Master
 Address File (MAF)
Aderholt, Robert, 224
administrative community-based
 organizations (ABCOs), 134
Administrative Procedure Act (APA), 43, 56,
 63, 168, 175, 207, 208
adversarial legalism, 42–43
advertising campaigns
 communication limitations of, 140
 by Complete Count Committees (CCCs),
  151
 costs of, 102
 origin of, 102
 resources for, 139
 trusted messengers in place of, 102
 in 2020 Census, 151
 See also outreach/promotional campaigns
Advertising Council, 102
Advisory Commission on Intergovernmental
 Relations, 242, 245
Affordable Care Act, 39
African Americans
 partnership campaign impact on, 105
 population counts of, 228
 undercounting of, 31–32, 42, 79, 81, 105,
  180, 185–187, 209, 229
age heaping, 185, 186
aggregate residual method, 161–162
Agranoff, Robert, 103
Alabama, 71–72, 115, 223–224
Alabama v. Department of Commerce, 71–72
Alaska, 1–2, 115
Alaska Native Corporations, 36
Alaska Native Heritage Center, 1, 3
Alaska Native populations, 185–187, 221, 229
Albuquerque, New Mexico, 188
Alito, Samuel, 46, 68, 70
American Civil Liberties Union (ACLU), 52, 69

American Community Survey (ACS)
 aggregate residual method and, 161–162
 citizenship question and, 60, 66
 data from, 106
 differential privacy method and, 228
 function of, 8, 45, 92
 limitations of, 48
 origin of, 76
American Enterprise Institute, 51
American Indians, 25, 185–187, 221, 229
American Recovery and Reinvestment Act, 108
American Statistical Association, 50, 66, 184,
 187
Anderson, Margo, 5, 27
Annual Survey of State and Local Government
 Finances, 7
Anon, Ada, 60
anti-commandeering doctrine, 251
anxiety, in census taking, 232
apportionment exclusion memorandum, 157–
 158, 161–175
apportionment/reapportionment
 changes to, 15–16
 conflict regarding, 25–26
 outcomes of, for House of Representatives,
  22 (*see also* House of Representatives)
 overview of, 234
 population data for, 8, 10
 regional changes in, 26
area census offices (ACOs), 14, 108, 109,
 110–111
Arizona, 27, 115. *See also specific locations*
Arkansas, 22, 115, 187
Arlington County, Virginia, 73
Articles of Confederation, 24, 25
Association of Public Data Users, 35
Atlanta, Georgia, 73, 188, 253, 255, 256
attorneys general (AGs), 40, 41, 54, 55, 170
Austin, Texas, 188
Austin American-Statesman (newspaper), 232

National Academy of Sciences Panel on
  Census Modernization, 80
National Advisory Committee (Census
  Bureau), 247
National Advisory Committee on Racial,
  Ethnic, and Other Populations (NAC),
  242–243
National Assessment of Educational Progress
  (NAEP), 7
National Association of Latino Elected and
  Appointed Officials, 140
National Association of Latino Elected
  Officials, 107
National Center for Education Statistics, 7
National Center for Health Statistics, 7
National Conference of State Legislatures, 28,
  221–222
National Congress of American Indians, 36,
  221–222
National Governors Association, 200, 221–222
National League of Cities, 135, 139, 214
National Park Service, 39
National Partnership Program (NPP), 107
National Processing Center, 144
National Urban League, 175
National Urban League v. Ross, 175, 179
National Vital Statistics System, 7
Nebraska, 115, 165. *See also specific locations*
Nenguryarr, Lizzie Chimiugak, 1
Neuman, A. Mark, 69
Nevada, 115. *See also specific locations*
Newburgh, New York, 109
New Deal, 10, 29–30
New Hampshire, 115, 164
New Jersey, 25, 61, 115, 223
New Mexico, 27, 115
New York
  apportionment outcomes of, 22
  census infrastructure in, 236
  census investment of, 115
  citizenship question and, 45, 61
  lawsuit by, 189–190
  overcounting in 2020 Census, 187
  partnership program dissatisfaction in, 111
  reapportionment in, 27
  2020 Census and, 3
  See also specific locations

New York City
  address list in, 84
  census outreach in, 128
  census tract in, 10
  Count Question Resolution (CQR) and,
    191, 192
  Department of Health, 10
  interviews in, 255, 256
  outreach campaign structure of, 142
  population counts of, 188, 191
  undercounting in, 32, 79, 235
New York Immigration Coalition, 52, 60, 167
New York State Street Address Maintenance
  Data, 87
New York v. Trump, 167, 170, 171, 179, 207
NFIB v. Sebelius, 66–67, 69
1910 Census, 27
1920 Census, 27
1950 Census, 77–78
1960 Census, 75, 78
1970 Census, 52, 103–104
1980 Census, 53, 75, 78–79, 103, 104, 235
1990 Census, 53, 75, 80, 81, 104, 105, 189, 190
Ninth Circuit Court of Appeals, 177
noise infusion, 217–218, 220–221, 223, 224–
  225
Nolette, Paul, 55
nongovernmental organizations (NGOs),
  40, 103, 124, 175. *See also specific
  organizations*
non-Hispanic white population, overcounting
  of, 188
nonprofit organizations, 4, 123, 135–138. *See
  also specific organizations*
Non-response Follow-up (NRFU), 61–62, 150
North Carolina, 22, 115
North Dakota, 115
Numident file (Social Security
  Administration), 162–163, 165

Oakland, California, 188
Office of Congressional and Intergovernmental
  Affairs (Census Bureau), 244–245
Office of the Census (California), 122
Office of Information and Regulatory Affairs,
  82
Office of Inspector General, 212

SHARE Food Program (Philadelphia), 153
Shaw, Amaya, 3
Shelby County v. Holder, 29
Shumate, Brett, 63
Sivongxay, Vatsady, 157
Small Business Administration, 31
Social Security Administration, 162–163
Sotomayor, Sonia, 67, 173, 177
South Carolina, 115, 165
South Dakota, 11, 114, 115, 165
special census/Special Census Program, 182,
    195–199, 230
State Complete Count Commissions (SCCCs)
    confusion regarding, 115–116
    creation process of, 112–113
    function of, 108, 122, 124
    funding for, 114–115, 142–143
    origin of, 112
    partnerships with Census Bureau and, 12
    politicizing of, 120
    prioritizing, 120
    state trends regarding, 118, 126
    statistics regarding, 113, 114
    timing for, 113–114, 127
State Data Center Program, 10, 35
state data centers (SDCs), 8, 90, 104, 122, 244
State and Local Fiscal Assistance Act of 1972,
    103, 199–200
states
    adequacy evaluation by, 239
    census integrity and, 252
    census litigation and, 52–56, 170, 179
    as census partners, 111–116
    census salience and, 116–117
    Complete Count Committees (CCCs)
        statistics of, 129
    correcting undercounts and, 9–10
    Count Question Resolution (CQR) and, 9
    data integrity and, 248
    as disseminators of data, 8
    employment statistics of, 13
    enumerator hiring in, 10
    federal government conflicts with, 145
    gaps in data sharing by, 8–9
    gathering process by, 11–12
    investment in census operations by, 117,
        125–128, 248–249

knowledge of, 11, 18, 238
lack of institutional support structure in,
    13
local census committees in, 10
local investment policies in, 128
in *New York v. Trump*, 170
outreach by, 238, 239–240
outreach funding by, 133–134
participation increase and, 36
partisan identities and, 118–121
post-census challenges of, 182
as producers of data, 7
safeguarding census by, 167–177
as trusted messengers, 18
as trusted partners, 11
as users of data, 8
voluntary cooperation by, 251–252
warehousing and dissemination of data by,
    10
See also specific states
Statewide Outreach and Rapid Deployment
    Database (SwORD) (California), 155,
    241
Statistical Policy Directives and Quality
    Standards, 64
Statistical Quality Standards (Census Bureau),
    64
statistics/statistical system, 5–9, 35, 39
Stenberg, Carl, 242
stress test, COVID-19 pandemic as, 178
students (college/university), 157, 193, 195
subnational government agencies, conflict
    with, 8
substantial risk argument, 56, 174
Sullivan, Teresa, 184
Supplemental Nutrition Assistance Program
    (SNAP), 163, 164, 165, 166, 179
suppressing cells, 216
Supreme Court. *See* US Supreme Court
Swartz, Becky, 90–91

Tacoma, Washington, 10
Taft, William Howard, 102, 215
Tampa, Florida, 188
Temporary Assistance to Needy Families
    (TANF), 163, 164, 165, 166, 179
Tennessee, 115, 187, 220